Singaporean Creatures

Singaporean Creatures

Histories of Humans and Other Animals in the Garden City

EDITED BY
TIMOTHY P. BARNARD

NUS PRESS
SINGAPORE

© 2024 Timothy P. Barnard

NUS Press
National University of Singapore
AS3-01-02, 3 Arts Link
Singapore 117569
Fax: (65) 6774-0652
E-mail: nusbooks@nus.edu.sg
Website: http://nuspress.nus.edu.sg

ISBN 978-981-325-238-7 (paper)
ePDF ISBN 978-981-325-239-4
ePub ISBN 978-981-325-260-8

All rights reserved. This book, or parts thereof, may not be reproduced in any form or by any means, electronic or mechanical, including photocopying, recording or any information storage and retrieval system now known or to be invented, without written permission from the Publisher.

National Library Board, Singapore Cataloguing in Publication Data

Name(s): Barnard, Timothy P., 1963- editor.
Title: Singaporean creatures : histories of humans and other animals in the Garden City / edited by Timothy P. Barnard.
Description: Singapore : NUS Press, [2024] | Includes bibliographical references and index.
Identifier(s): ISBN 978-981-325-238-7 (paper) | 978-981-325-239-4 (ePDF) | 978-981-325-260-8 (ePub)
Subject(s): LCSH: Human ecology--Singapore--History. | Singapore--History--Environmental aspects.
Classification: DDC 304.2095957--dc23

Cover image: Man carrying crocodile, late 1980s. Singapore Tourism Board Collection, courtesy of National Archives of Singapore.

Printed by Integrated Books International

Contents

List of Images · vii

INTRODUCTION **Humans and Other Animals in a Singaporean Anthropocene** · 1
Timothy P. Barnard

CHAPTER ONE **Tilapia, Travel and the Making of a Singaporean Creature** · 19
Anthony D. Medrano

CHAPTER TWO **One Drawback of Tropical Living** · 41
Nicole Tarulevicz

CHAPTER THREE **Mosquitoes, Public Health and the Construction of a Modern Society** · 67
Timothy P. Barnard

CHAPTER FOUR **A Cultural History of Fear, Fascination, Fantasy and Crocodiles in Singapore** · 100
Esmond Chuah Meng Soh

CHAPTER FIVE **Too Much Monkey Business** · 126
Timothy P. Barnard and Jennifer Yip

CHAPTER SIX **Songbirds in a Garden City** · 156
Faizah Zakaria

CHAPTER SEVEN **Marine Life in Service of the State at Public Aquariums and Oceanariums in Singapore** · 186
Miles Alexander Powell

CHAPTER EIGHT **Nation, Nature and the Singapore Zoological Gardens, 1973–2018** · 215
Choo Ruizhi

List of Contributors · 249
Bibliography · 251
Index · 274

List of Images

0.1	A Singaporean otter feeding on fish.	3
1.1	"Mudjair."	25
1.2	Carp pond in Singapore, 1949.	29
1.3	Brackish water pond along West Coast Road, 1949.	32
1.4	*Oreochomis mossambicus*.	39
2.1	Make Your Choice! poster.	45
2.2	Anti-Polio Vaccination at Lim Ah Pin Road Clinic, 21 October 1958, MITA.	56
2.3	Flies Spread Disease poster, Ministry of Culture, 1961.	59
2.4	Flit canister, ca. 1954–55.	61
3.1	Before and after photographs illustrating the role of drains and subsoil pipes in anti-mosquito measures.	74
3.2	Public Health Services' residual spraying of DDT inside a house, 1955.	80

List of Images

3.3	Combat Infectious Diseases poster, 1976.	90
3.4	Keep Singapore Clean and Prevent Mosquito Breeding poster, in Chinese, 1979.	93
3.5	Just Tip It poster, 2005.	97
4.1	Bathing Pagar at Katong Park.	106
4.2	Malay boy sitting on crocodile, 1920s.	110
4.3	Wives of Commonwealth heads visiting crocodile farm, 1971.	117
4.4	Man carrying crocodile, late 1980s.	120
5.1	Feeding monkeys at Singapore Botanic Gardens, 1920s.	131
5.2	A macaque at the Singapore Botanic Gardens.	135
5.3	Protestors at the gates of the Singapore Botanic Gardens on 23 February 1971.	141
5.4	No Feeding of Monkeys sign.	151
6.1	Minister for the Interior and Defence Lim Kim San attending at a bird-singing contest at Cairnhill Community Centre, 17 Dec. 1967.	163
6.2	Exotic non-native birds showcased at an exhibition organized by the Singapore Cage-Bird Society at Happy World Amusement Park, 1950s.	172
7.1	Pink dolphin with skin cancer at Underwater World, Singapore.	187
7.2	The Van Kleef Aquarium at River Valley Road.	194

List of Images

7.3	Noor Aishah Mohammad Salim, the first lady of Singapore, and Norodom Thavet Norleak, the primary spouse of King Norodom Sihanouk of Cambodia, admire the displays at the Van Kleef Aquarium, 1962.	199
7.4	Guppy exhibition at the Van Kleef Aquarium, 20 August 1967.	203
7.5	Young visitor observing fish at Underwater World at Sentosa, 1990.	209
8.1	Goh Keng Swee exchanging pleasantries with an orangutan at the opening of the Singapore Zoological Gardens, June 1973.	216
8.2	Entrance of the Singapore Miniature Zoo in Pasir Panjang.	221
8.3	A worker feeding penguins at the Singapore Miniature Zoo.	222
8.4	Tourists posing with Ah Meng during "Breakfast at the Zoo," 1988.	233
8.5	A seemingly bored Inuka, c. 2006.	243

INTRODUCTION

Humans and Other Animals in a Singaporean Anthropocene

Timothy P. Barnard

In April 2020, as most humans in Singapore stayed home in an attempt to avoid a viral disease, other animals roamed the city. Among these creatures was a romp of smooth-coated otters (*Lutrogale perspicillata*) that had broken off from a bevy that made its home in the Marina Barrage area near Gardens by the Bay.[1] There were simply too many otters at this site; the splintered raft began searching for a new feeding ground. They roamed the city-state, mainly shifting between the Singapore Botanic Gardens and the Singapore River. During a lockdown for the COVID-19 pandemic—which the technocratic government called a "circuit breaker"—the Zouk family, named after a nightclub along the Singapore River, became an obsession for many homebound Singaporeans. The Zouk otters were seemingly everywhere. The raft was spotted wandering the streets of Little India in early May, passing through the Balestier area, they then visited

---

[1] A group of otters can be called a romp, bevy, family or raft.

Tan Tock Seng Hospital before ambling back to the Singapore River. During their journey, to sustain themselves, these wild animals sought out fresh food and new feeding grounds. One of the most convenient locations to find protein were ponds and fountains containing schools of koi (*Cyprinus rubrofuscus*), a valuable and valued fish often kept in bodies of water at condominiums, spas and even church courtyards throughout the manicured nation-state.[2] The otters added to their renown and rebel status through raids on such koi-filled pools. These Singaporean creatures were roaming and eating as they pleased, mocking a human society that stayed behind doors, following government orders. Nature was pushing the limits of its containment in the Garden City.

Otters are both natives and migrants to Singapore, reflecting the complex interaction of history and biology on an island in Southeast Asia. The creature is one of hundreds, if not thousands, of animals that once roamed the land, swam in the streams and relaxed on its shores, until humans began a process of deforestation, pollution and urbanization that made their presence untenable. Smooth-coated otters had disappeared, at least from the island, by the 1960s.[3] There are an estimated 150 otters in Singapore, at least, in 2022. This is almost a doubling of their numbers in five years. The ones found in Singapore in the 21st century are the descendants of a bevy that arrived in the 1990s, swimming over from Malaysia to the Sungei Buloh Nature Reserve; their migration was most likely due to urban development in Johor Baru. A second, more influential raft appeared around 2007, swimming to the northeastern

---

[2] Rachel Tan, "Singapore's Adorable Otters Explained," *Kopi*. https://thekopi.co/2021/04/30/from-love-stories-to-war-singapores-otters-are-surprisingly-human/ (accessed 21 Oct. 2021); Vanessa Liu, "Family of Otters Frolicking Outside Mustafa Centre Is Looking for a New Home," *The Straits Times* [hereafter, *ST*], https://www.straitstimes.com/singapore/family-of-otters-frolicking-outside-mustafa-centre-is-looking-for-a-permanent-home

[3] There is another species of otter, *Aonyx cinerus* (small-clawed otter), that is occasionally found in Singapore, but it is extremely rare. The most recently observed one was most likely an escaped pet. Small-clawed otters were more common than smooth-coated otters prior to the 1960s, but also suffered from the modernization of the island, resulting in a vast reduction in their numbers. Meryl Theng and N. Sivasothi, "The Smooth-Coated Otter *Lutrogale perspicillata* (Mammalia: Mustelidae) in Singapore: Establishment and Expansion in Natural and Semi-Urban Environments," *IUCN Otter Specialist Group Bulletin* 33, 1 (2016): 38.

Image 0.1: A Singaporean otter feeding on fish. Photo by Mark Stoop on Unsplash.

shore of Singapore via Pulau Ubin. This second group multiplied and spread over the island, ultimately forming at least 10 distinct families.[4]

The otters of Singapore have become a phenomenon in the 21st century, featured in news stories, blogs and social media sites. Observers locate, follow and provide detailed notes on their movements, and have named the various troops and their members, making them modern celebrities. This even reaches the official institutions of the state. The Ministry of Sustainability and the Environment highlights their presence as a symbol of the biodiversity found on an urbanized, developed island in Southeast Asia, as well as the success of the efforts of the modern government to maintain a clean and green cityscape, while a caricature often becomes the mascot for various official programs and campaigns.[5]

---

[4] M.D.Y. Khoo and B.P.Y.-H. Lee, "The Urban Smooth-Coated Otters *Lutrogale perspicillata* of Singapore: A Review of the Reasons for Success," *International Zoo Yearbook* 54 (2020): 60–71; Theng and Sivasothi, "The Smooth-Coated Otter *Lutrogale perspicillata*," pp. 37–49; N. Sivosathi and Burhanuddin Hj. Md. Nor, "A Review of Otters (Carnivora: Mustalidae: Lutrinae) in Malaysia and Singapore, *Ecology and Conservation of Southeast Asian Marine and Freshwater Environments including Wetland. Developments in Hydrobiology*, ed. A. Sasekumar, N. Marshall and D.J. Macintosh (Dordrecht: Springer, 1994), pp. 151–70; Ang Qing and Kolette Lim, "Otter Overpopulation in Singapore: Fact or Fiction?," *ST*, 17 Apr. 2022.

[5] This includes promotions for unrelated issues, such as vaccination status during the COVID-19 pandemic. Lena Chan, "Nature in the City," in *Planning Singapore: The Experimental City*, ed. Stephen Hamnett and Belinda Yuen (London: Routledge,

The combination of wildness and fame has made otters a symbol of the ambiguous relationship the humans of Singapore have with the natural environment.

Smooth-coated otters are just one of many Singaporean creatures, consisting of an unimaginable number of species ranging in size from elephants in the Singapore Zoo to the smallest microbes found throughout the island. Each of them has a complex role and position in Singaporean society and history, although much of it is filtered through the perceptions and relationships that these various animals have with the apex species on the island, humans. This book focuses on the human–animal relationship in Singapore and how it has shaped the society—socially, economically, politically—particularly in the past half century. It is a work of historical analysis in which various institutions, perspectives and events involving animals provide insight into how the larger society has been formed and developed in Southeast Asia. The interaction of various Singaporean creatures, thus, provides a lens through which we can understand the creation of a modern, urban nation-state, reflecting the outcomes of the Anthropocene in local history.

A Singaporean Anthropocene

Laying only 137 kilometers north of the equator, Singapore is an island in Southeast Asia. While it is distinguished by its proximity—a close, swimmable kilometer away—to a peninsula jutting out from mainland of the Asian continent, its ecosystems are similar to its archipelagic neighbors. Mangrove forests ring the perimeter, while dipterocarp forest trees grow on rolling hills covering a variety of silt, sand and clay soils. The landscape and surrounding seas support a variety of tropical ecosystems, ranging from marine to forest, in which numerous species of flora and fauna often prosper, reflecting an amazingly high rate of biodiversity.

This idealized picture of Singapore was particularly true several millennia ago, prior to the appearance of a new species, *Homo sapiens*, on the island. Using their cognitive skills, opposable thumbs and tools, humans began to shape the environment to fit their needs. Forests were felled, specific plants cultivated, and animals reared for food and labor, all

---

2019), pp. 118–19; Otter Watch, https://www.facebook.com/OtterWatch/ (accessed 21 Oct. 2021); Otter City, https://www.facebook.com/ottercity/ (accessed 21 Oct. 2021).

of which attracted more humans. While they may not be classified as a typical apex predator, due to an omnivorous diet, humans definitely became the apex species, or hyperkeystone species, shaping the environment to their will. This process went through several cycles under communities with labels such as Temasek, Ujong Tanah and even Singapura before the island became an afterthought in the region as larger communities united, divided and clashed. Humans were present, but their overall impact on the ecosystem was relatively insignificant due to their small population size and limited technology. In the late 18th century the course of societal development and environmental utilization began again. This time, however, it took place on an unprecedented scale, greatly accelerated through the use of the tools of the Scientific Revolution, the Enlightenment and imperialism. This process is still ongoing and reflects a new era in Singaporean history, the Anthropocene.[6]

A geological epoch dating from the commencement of significant human impact on global geography and ecosystems, the Anthropocene is a concept that scientists traditionally utilized to discuss change that took place over many millennia. The term took on new significance and meaning in the early 21st century as social science and humanities scholars debated its applicability in discussions of the significant transformations they were observing in the recent past. Some scholars offered alternative terms to capture the permutations and implications of this change, such as "Homogenocene" for a brief period to describe human-inspired transformations in biogeography that have mainly resulted in diminishing biodiversity as well as the introduction of non-native, or "invasive," species into various ecosystems, or even the "Plantationocene" as a descriptor for the vast spread of large-scale agricultural projects that have transformed regional landscapes. Ultimately, however, the term "Anthropocene" quickly became the most commonly used term to describe recent historical eras in which the human ability to alter ecosystems around the globe—through either completely destroying them or introducing new species or even

---

[6] Boris Worm and Robert T. Paine, "Humans as a Hyperkeystone Species," *Trends in Ecology and Evolution* 31, 8 (2016): 600–7; M.W.F. Tweedie, "The Stone Age in Malaya," *Journal of the Malayan Branch of the Royal Asiatic Society* 26, 2 (1953): 69–70; Timothy P. Barnard, *Imperial Creatures: Humans and Other Animals in Colonial Singapore, 1819–1942* (Singapore: NUS Press, 2019); Kwa Chong Guan and Peter Borschberg (eds.), *Studying Singapore Before 1800* (Singapore: NUS Press, 2018).

climate change—has transformed the relationship of all organisms within them.[7]

It is in the context of human-generated change of ecosystems that these larger global theories are relevant to Singaporean history. The Anthropocene began in Singapore in the 1790s, when Malay nobles from the Johor-Riau Sultanate oversaw the development of plantations on the island using mainly Chinese labor.[8] While this was limited initially to a small area near the mouth of the Singapore River, and supported a community of around 1,000 humans, this metaphorical seed bloomed over the next two and half centuries. When British imperialism arrived in 1819 under the guise of East India Company merchants and administrators, these new humans expanded this plantation system exponentially, developed the port, and created a city that became a hub within imperial networks of power and influence. Various historical forces of the modern era—ranging from imperialism to globalization—literally reshaped the island to meet the needs of humans for over 200 years.[9]

---

[7] Michael Samways, "Translocating Fauna to Foreign Lands: Here Comes the Homogenocene," *Journal of Insect Conservation* 3, 2 (1999): 65–6; Simon L. Lewis, "Defining the Anthropocene," *Nature* 519 (2015): 171–80; Will Steffen, et al., "The Anthropocene: Conceptual and Historical Perspectives," *Philosophical Transactions of the Royal Society* 369, 1938 (2011): 842–67; Yadvinder Malhi, "The Concept of the Anthropocene," *Annual Review of Environment and Resources* 42 (2017): 77–104; Donna Haraway, "Anthropocene, Capitalocene, Plantationocene, Chthulucene: Making Kin," *Environmental Humanities* 6, 1 (2015): 159–65; Wendy Wolford, "The Plantationocene: A Lusotropical Contribution to Theory," *Annals of the American Association of Geographers* 111, 6 (2021): 1622–39; Matthew Schneider-Mayerson, "Introduction: Seeing Singapore with New Eyes," in *Eating Chilli Crab in the Anthropocene: Environmental Perspectives on Life in Singapore*, ed. Matthew Schneider-Mayerson (Singapore: Ethos Books, 2019).

[8] One of the most common debates within Anthropocene studies has been affixing a date to when it began. The most commonly cited one is 1945, marking the beginning of the Atomic Age. Other proposed dates include the beginning of the Agricultural Revolution over 10,000 years ago or the mid-18th-century origins of the Industrial Revolution. Kyle Nichols and Bina Gogineni, "The Anthropocene's Dating Problem: Insights with Geosciences and the Humanities," *The Anthropocene Review* 5, 2 (2018): 107–19; Barnard, *Imperial Creatures*; Koh Keng We, "Familiar Strangers and Stranger-Kings: Mobility, Diasporas, and the Foreign in the Eighteenth-Century Malay World," *Journal of Southeast Asian Studies* 48, 3 (2017): 390–413.

[9] Richard T. Corlett, "The Ecological Transformation of Singapore, 1819–1990," *Journal of Biogeography* 19, 4 (1992): 411–20; Tony O'Dempsey, "Singapore's Changing Landscape since c. 1800," in *Nature Contained: Environmental Histories*

The arrival of imperialism signaled not only a new form of rule over Singapore, but also the complete alteration of its environment. Humans expanded agricultural production of cash crops, mainly non-native species, ranging from nutmeg to coffee, in only a few decades in the early 19th century until it consumed ecosystems throughout the island. This simplification of the landscape—reducing the biodiversity of the tropical environment to a handful of cultivated plants—was rapid, and corresponded with massive deforestation. By the 1880s, only 6 percent of the original forest of Singapore remained; pepper and gambier plantations, or their abandoned, *lalang*-covered remnants, dominated most of the countryside. This deforestation was on an unprecedented scale. It not only transformed ecosystems but also created corresponding challenges for the human society, including changes in rainfall patterns and water shortages. In an attempt to reverse these developments, the colonial government began replanting the devastated interior through the creation of forest reserves that soon came to protect water reservoirs and provide a green lung for the society that surrounds it. Today, this region is known as the Central Catchment Area, a legacy of environmental change from over a century ago.[10]

While colonial authorities addressed the environmental crisis that deforestation produced in the late 19th century, they also were creating altered ecosystems. Introduced species of plants and animals reflected the power of *Homo sapiens* to shape the island to their needs, much of it to cater to a human population that expanded from an estimated 1,000 total residents in 1819 to over 500,000 by the 1930s. Land beyond forest reserves was used for food and cash crop production, while infrastructure—including roads and buildings—spread into rural areas. Modification of the Singaporean environment has quickened further since the Second World War—and the Anthropocene as a distinct era became much clearer in what can be known as the "Great Acceleration"—as humans

---

of Singapore, ed. Timothy P. Barnard (Singapore: NUS Press, 2014), pp. 17–48; Barnard, *Imperial Creatures*.

[10] Corlett, "The Ecological Transformation of Singapore, 1819–1990," pp. 411–20; Barry W. Brook, Navjot S. Sodhi and Peter K.L. Ng, "Catastrophic Extinctions Follow Deforestation in Singapore," *Nature* 424 (24 Jul. 2003): 420–3; Nathaniel Cantley, *Report on the Forests of the Straits Settlements* (Singapore: Singapore and Straits Printing Office, 1883), pp. 2–3; Timothy P. Barnard, *Nature's Colony: Empire, Nation and Environment in the Singapore Botanic Gardens* (Singapore: NUS Press, 2016).

created a modern nation-state in the middle of Southeast Asia with an expanding population, often through migration. Beyond the forests, the land has been built upon as well as reclaimed. Structures were built to house a population and its commerce, land area increased by 40 percent, and nature became a curated activity that blended the native and non-native. In the two centuries of its Anthropocene, and particularly the last six decades, humans have massively deforested, replanted and reclaimed Singapore, transforming it into a home for over 5 million representatives of their own species.[11]

The changes that the Singaporean Anthropocene wrought are apparent in the biodiversity found on the island. The most glaring illustration of this transformation comes from the deforestation of the 19th century. Scientists have theorized—as it is difficult to be exact when there is little data from the period—that it led to an extinction rate as high as 73 percent of all species in Singapore. An illustration of this ecological collapse can be found in the work of Christopher Hails and Frank Jarvis, who estimated that of 383 species of birds recorded in early Singapore as many as 106 were considered extinct on the island during the 1980s, with the vast majority being forest dwellers.[12] These changes to Singaporean biodiversity were clear to those witnessing it. In 1919, for example, when writing a celebratory chapter on the first century of British rule of Singapore, G.P. Owen recounted that "before the introduction of cultivation there were many miles of virgin forest, providing shelter, food, and quiet places for bird and beast to breed. All the forest, original and secondary, has given

---

[11] Miles Alexander Powell, "Harnessing the Great Acceleration: Connecting Local and Global Environmental History at the Port of Singapore," *Environmental History* 27, 3 (2022): 441–66; J.R. McNeill and Peter Engelke, *The Great Acceleration: An Environmental History of the Anthropocene since 1945* (Cambridge, MA: Harvard University Press, 2016); Saw Swee-Hock, "Population Trends in Singapore, 1819–1967," *Journal of Southeast Asian History* 10, 1 (1969): 39; Miles Alexander Powell, "Singapore's Lost Coast: Land Reclamation, National Development and the Erasure of Human and Ecological Communities, 1822–Present," *Environment and History* 27, 4 (2021): 635–63; O'Dempsey, "Singapore's Changing Landscape since c. 1800."

[12] Corlett, "The Ecological Transformation of Singapore, 1819–1990," p. 416; Barry W. Brook, Navjot S. Sodhi and Peter K.L. Ng, "Catastrophic Extinctions Follow Deforestation in Singapore," *Nature* 424 (24 Jul. 2003): 420–3; Christopher Hails and Frank Jarvis, *Birds of Singapore* (Singapore: Times Editions, 1987).

place to ... plantation, mostly clean weeded, alike destitute of edible seeds and fruit, and of insects."[13]

The arrival of humans not only changed the floral and faunal landscape, but also the particular species found within it, making it one of the hallmarks of the Singaporean Anthropocene. Human residents slowly began restocking the island, determining the species that would flourish within its boundaries. Introduced creatures included a mix of native and non-native, ranging from horses and pigs to domesticated pets and displayed exotic animals, which I have labeled "imperial creatures" in another work. These species filled eco-niches throughout the island, often developing their own imprint on the society, such as the tigers (*Panthera tigris*) that searched for prey at the edges of the transforming forest in the first six decades of colonial rule, the American rain trees (*Samanea saman*) that provide shade along city streets, or even the Javan mynas (*Acridotheres javanicus*) that pester visitors to hawker centers in the 21st century. Ultimately, all of these various species—whether introduced, tolerated, eliminated or nurtured—created the Singapore with which residents and visitors are familiar today. The main determinant in this consideration was their relationship with humans, as creatures were utilized for labor, sustenance, entertainment or education.[14]

The re-establishment of forests on the island also reflected the role of utilitarianism in the human relationship with nature. The colonial government replanted the Central Catchment Area and a few scattered forest reserves, ultimately providing about 10 percent forest cover on the island in total, but the primary motivation was to ensure that the imperial society and economy could function. After this success, however, many colonial officials considered the natural environment a disappointment due to the limited land space and reduced utilitarian value of timber within it. This led W. Langham-Carter, the Acting Collector of Land Revenue, to describe most of the Singaporean reserves as "scrub" or "poor jungle" that only merited being "periodically visited both by the Collector of Land Revenue and the Forest Rangers" in the early 20th century. The

---

[13] G.P. Owen, "Shikar," in *One Hundred Years of Singapore, Being an Account of the Capital of the Straits Settlements from its Foundation by Sir Stamford Raffles on the 6th February 1819 to the 6th February 1919*, vol. II, ed. Walter Makepeace, Gilbert E. Brooke and Roland St. J. Braddell (London: John Murray, 1921), pp. 367–8.

[14] Barnard, *Imperial Creatures*; Timothy P. Barnard and Mark Emmanuel, "Tigers of Colonial Singapore," in *Nature Contained: Environmental Histories of Singapore*, ed. Timothy P. Barnard (Singapore: NUS Press, 2014), pp. 55–80.

environment of Singapore was largely a bother, an obstacle to further development of the colonial economy and society that became centered around the port. Increasing biodiversity on the island, and changing attitudes toward nature, would take time.[15]

The role of humans in re-establishing, promoting and understanding the effects of a richer biodiversity in Singapore began in the late 1930s when the government developed "botanical reserves," an important step in the environmental history of the island. Mainly located next to forest reserves, these zones contained "representative areas of natural vegetation" and a rich variety of "mammalian fauna." More importantly, these zones played a role in formulating an increasing appreciation of the ability of humans to maintain diverse tropical ecosystems and inculcating their importance into the mindset of the society. As botanist E.J.H. Corner described these newly designated areas, they were "more valuable still for the civic life of Singapore," as they were "a retreat wherein one can teach the rising generation to have a care for the wild things of wood and water."[16]

This increased attention to biodiversity in Singapore took place against the backdrop of an expanding, urbanizing society in the second half of the 20th century in which human alteration of the landscape achieved levels of total control. Following the Japanese Occupation of 1942 to 1945, the newly established botanical reserves quickly transitioned into nature reserves, and scientists began to conduct research documenting their revival. While British colonialism returned in different capacities over the 20 years that followed, Singaporean society and politics went through various upheavals and transitions from colonial rule to independent nation-state. During this period, humans continued to alter the physical landscape and ecosystems as buildings grew higher, the population boomed, and the economy modernized. Constant change and alteration of the environment became normalized. These developments did not alter the

---

[15] W. Langham-Carter, *Report on the Forest Reserves of the Straits Settlements during the Year 1901* (Singapore: Government Printing Office, 1902), pp. 1–2; Timothy P. Barnard, "Forêts Impériales et Réserves Naturelles à Singapour, 1883–1959," in *Protéger et Détruire: Gouverner la Nature sous les Tropiques (XX-XXIE siècle)*, ed. Guillaume Blanc, Mathieu Guérin and Grégory Quenet (Paris: CNRS, 2022), pp. 83–108.

[16] E.J.H. Corner, *Annual Report of the Director of the Gardens for the Year 1937* (Singapore: Government Printing Office, 1938), p. 8; Barnard, "Forêts Impériales et Réserves Naturelles à Singapour, 1883–1959."

environmental trajectory, and the human factor in it; if anything, the process accelerated. Humans shaped Singapore into a curated natural landscape, a cornerstone of an Anthropocene or, more specifically, the Great Acceleration. Much of this was related to how the island was governed, and how these developments were perceived.[17]

Governed Creatures

The People's Action Party (PAP) became the majority party in the Singaporean Parliament on 30 May 1959. Their rule over the island since that time has been so complete that the government and the party have become synonymous, and its ability to shape Singaporean society has been unparalleled. Much of the literature on the history of PAP rule emphasizes the role it has played in managing economic growth and social programs that have, in the words of its most dominant individual, taken Singapore from "Third World to First." The development of a modern, industrialized nation-state was done through policies that exacted control over almost all aspects of society.[18] This was true even down to the level of nature.

Environmental policies in modern Singapore have taken place under a variety of institutions and programs, although they are usually amalgamated into a concept known as the "Garden City." Originating out of urban planning projects from English stenographer Ebenezer Howard, the primary ambition was to create new urbanized landscapes that accommodated humans in a comforting manner, a concept that gained momentum in Britain after the Second World War. The Garden City consisted of creating a "permanent girdle of open and agricultural land" that would encircle a town, and bring people closer to nature through the designation of greenbelts in smaller self-contained towns. It combined the benefits of urban living with green spaces, and originated

---

[17] Timothy P. Barnard and Corinne Heng, "A City in a Garden," in *Nature Contained: Environmental Histories of Singapore*, ed. Timothy P. Barnard (Singapore: NUS Press, 2014), pp. 281–306; Peter Newman, "Biophilic Urbanism: A Case Study on Singapore," *Australian Planner* 51, 1 (2014): 47–65; Powell, "Harnessing the Great Acceleration."

[18] Lee Kuan Yew, *From Third World to First: The Singapore Story: 1965–2000* (Singapore: Singapore Press Holdings, 2000); Diane K. Mauzy and R.S. Milne, *Singapore Politics under the People's Action Party* (London: Routledge, 2002); Carl A. Trocki, *Singapore: Wealth, Power and the Culture of Control* (London: Routledge, 2006); Powell, "Harnessing the Great Acceleration."

out of long-standing colonial, and influentially British, understandings of the proper constitution of a modern, liveable environment. Alongside the work of Lewis Mumford, and his efforts to create an "organic city," the energetic, young Singaporean government embraced these principles as a road map to transform and mold the society to fit their material goals. Over the next 50 years, the government sanctioned various tree planting and nature programs that enhanced biodiversity, but were also the result of a combination of administrative exercise and disciplining of the space.[19]

The Garden City is manifested in Singapore through well-planted green corridors in which nature is presented as a fundamental part of national identity. The government quantifies these efforts in numerous ways, all of which reinforce the bureaucratic success of these programs. Initially, agencies would report the number of trees and bushes planted annually or heavily promote activities such as "Tree Planting Day." In recent decades, this desire to promote a green image resulted in numerous surveys and presentations of data, which are then used to place the city-state in comparison to its global counterparts. The National Environmental Agency of Singapore, for example, proclaimed in 2007 that 47 percent of the island was covered in greenery, while ecologists at the National University of Singapore raised the estimate to 56 percent four years later.[20] This is also supported by external surveys, such as the "Green View Index of Cities," a comparative database that determines the percentage of urban space that falls under a tree canopy, which lists the "green view index" for Singapore at 29.3 percent, among the highest of 30 global cities surveyed on the site.[21] While the percentage of green cover may vary due

---

[19] Ebenezer Howard, *Garden Cities of To-morrow* (London: Faber and Faber, 1947); Lewis Mumford, *The City in History* (New York, NY: Harcourt, Brace and World, 1961); Belinda Yuen, "Creating the Garden City: The Singaporean Experience," *Urban Studies* 33, 6 (1996): 955–70; Barnard and Heng, "A City in a Garden."
[20] Alex Thiam Koon Yee, et al., "The Vegetation of Singapore: An Updated Map," *Gardens' Bulletin (Singapore)* 63, 1/2 (2011): 205–12; Barnard and Heng, "A City in a Garden," p. 281.
[21] Singapore tied with Breda in this survey. Other cities featured in this database include Vancouver, Tampa and Oslo. As the database focuses on urban areas, the extensive nature reserves and Central Catchment Area in Singapore are not included in their analysis. http://senseable.mit.edu/treepedia (accessed 8 May 2020); Chan, "Nature in the City," pp. 109–29; Barnard and Heng, "A City in a Garden," pp. 290–2.

to the use of different criteria, the basic fact is that Singapore now has a relatively large amount of its territory dedicated to flora.

The amount of green cover in Singapore supposes a rise in biodiversity among not only flora but also fauna. This supposition holds for the most part, particularly when the devastation that deforestation wrought on the landscape in the first decades of colonial rule is considered. The re-establishment of new ecosystems has taken more than a century to achieve, but has also been part of an environmental trajectory begun during the colonial era; the main contribution of the independent government to these developments was an acceleration of the larger trend. While forests and nature reserves recovered from their 19th-century devastation and the mentality of preserving the environment crept into official policies, it occurred following human intervention, which has created a "modified kind of nature" under the watchful eye of scientists, government officials and capitalistic investors since the 1880s. The plants and animals that exist within these ecosystems are a mixture of native and non-native, such as the otters that capture much of the national attention, and thus reflect many of the changes that have occurred during an accelerated period within the Singaporean Anthropocene.[22]

Much of this transformation in ecosystems, and its influence on the development of Singaporean society and history, can be seen through the stories of human–animal relationships on the island, a process the governing party of Singapore regulates. Most of these relationships and how they are presented are complex, as can be seen in the plethora of institutions that deal with non-humans. On official fronts, a variety of ministries and statutory boards oversee this relationship and, as is true for much of the society, are a continuation of various policies and institutions established during the colonial era. An example of this would be the Agri-Food and Veterinary Authority of Singapore, more familiarly known as AVA in the acronym-crazy bureaucracy. This institution was the successor to Primary Production Department, which was under the Ministry of National Development, and oversaw agriculture, fisheries and veterinary issues beginning in 1959. The Primary Production Department was an

---

[22] One scientist has even estimated that 99.8% of "the original forest cover has been cleared" in Singapore. Corlett, "The Ecological Transformation of Singapore, 1819–1990," p. 415; Barnard and Heng, "A City in a Garden," pp. 281–306; Charles S. Elton, *The Ecology of Invasions by Animals and Plants* (London: Methuen, 1958), p. 145; Alex Thiam Koon Yee, et al., "Updating the Classification System for the Secondary Forests of Singapore," *Raffles Bulletin of Zoology* 32 (2016): 11.

attempt at simplifying different issues that existed within the British colonial government under the Fisheries Department, the Department of Agriculture and the Rural Board. The reconfiguration of divisions, under the rubric of administrative rationality and efficiency, continued in 2019, when the government disbanded the AVA and reconstituted various sub-agencies within the National Environmental Agency, Health Sciences Authority and Singapore Food Agency to continue the never-ending cycle. Despite their ever-changing labels, in Singapore for well over a century a variety of government institutions have overseen matters related to the environment, particularly human–animal relations, a trend that continues until today.[23]

The ability of the government—as a representative of human organization—to shape and change the landscape is manifested in numerous ways in Singapore. From organizing the replanting of forests to regulations determining where animals can live, the influence of humans on the environment and the species within it has become all encompassing. This is all representative of the Anthropocene, an era in which humans have shaped and altered the environment of an island in Southeast Asia, and can be understood in an even clearer manner through the various stories of Singaporean creatures in these histories.

Singaporean Creatures

The histories of human–animal relations in Singapore are complex and provide insight into numerous developments in the society during the Anthropocene. Many of these stories began during the period of imperial rule—which, depending on how it is parsed, ended in 1942, 1959 or even 1965—and then transitioned to independent rule carrying much of the colonial baggage, with variations and intricacies depending on individual animals, events and attitudes. In many instances programs and institutions that began in the colonial era continued, and some were intensified,

---

[23] Anonymous, "Dr. Tham is Head of New Dept. of Primary Production," *ST*, 26 Jun. 1959, p. 4. Anonymous, *AVA: A Legacy of Excellence. A Commemorative Issue* (Singapore: AVA Vision, 2019); Timothy P. Barnard and Joanna W.C. Lee, "A Spiteful Campaign: Agriculture, Forests, and Administering the Environment in Imperial Singapore and Malaya," *Environmental History* 27, 3 (2022): 467–90; Choo Ruizhi, "Fishes of Empire: Imperialism and Ichthyological Introductions in British Malaya, 1923–1942," *Journal of Southeast Asian Studies* 54, 1 (2023): 44–63.

growing in significance in how they shaped Singaporean lifestyles and landscapes. This theme can be seen in almost every contribution to this collection. Whether it is the presence of elephants in a zoo for the public to view, monkeys in parks and households, or even insects in a tropical environment, this collection reflects the changes and continuities in human–animal relationships from large to small on an island in Southeast Asia during a period of transition between imperial and independent rule.

One of the key developments in the history of Singaporean environmental history during the Anthropocene is the introduction of new species, and how they are then normalized within a changing landscape. In Chapter 1, Anthony Medrano demonstrates a clear example of such a case with his study of the tilapia, a fish that is native to Africa that came to Singapore via Java during the Japanese Occupation, thus linking a variety of issues ranging from introduced species, changing colonial rule, aquaculture and diet during a period of increased transformation of the environment. This story reflects the continuation of environmental trends on the island, which were not disrupted by a change in political control. It is a tale in which the ecosystem received a new species, that then adapted to fulfill the perceptions and needs of the humans who have gained control over the landscape, or in this case the waterscape.

Whether it is mosquitoes, songbirds or even exotic animals on display, the Anthropocene in Singapore is a period in which the arrival and integration of new species into the landscape and consciousness influenced how the society organized itself. The role of human–animal relationships, and human perceptions on how to manage them, is the focus of Chapters 2 and 3. Human reactions to insects have resulted in changes in infrastructure and living space to prevent the spread of diseases or "filth," as Nicole Taurelvicz argues in her chapter, which discusses the perceptions and reactions that Singaporeans have had towards these small pests since the late colonial period. This is linked, on a more visible scale, with efforts to control various mosquito species and the diseases they spread through programs integrating public health, monitoring and infrastructure development, which is the topic of Chapter 3. While the human ability to shape and alter the environment is a hallmark of the Anthropocene, much of it is related to how humans reacted to the various other animals in their shared space, thus providing insight into this transformational process.

The influence of domesticated spaces in a modernizing Singapore also is clearly seen in how humans have understood and interacted with wild animals, and the creation of boundaries for this interaction. In this regard, Esmond Soh, and Tim Barnard and Jennifer Yip explore the relationship between humans and crocodiles and humans and macaques in Chapters 4 and 5. During the colonial period, both animals were relatively common sights for much of the population, particularly crocodiles for those people that lived in coastal areas and in the Singapore Botanic Gardens for a specific species of monkey. Following the expansion of urban housing and the subsequent reconfiguration of space in the island after the Second World War, the place and position of these animals in society also shifted. Areas designated for animals became distinct and restricted, as human control over the landscape strengthened. This often resulted in commodification and violence against the animals as Singapore transitioned into an industrialized nation-state.

While Singapore became more of a built space in the second half of the 20th century and spaces became more clearly differentiated between domesticated and wild, an important part of this process was the advent of high-rise public housing, which further reinforced restrictions on the human–animal relationship. One of the most visible aspects of this change was limitations the government placed on pet ownership and animal husbandry. This has been the topic of studies for decades, with the work of Harvey Neo and Chan Ying-Kit being of particular interest in their consideration of pigs and cats in industrialized and urban settings.[24] In Chapter 6, Faizah Zakaria brings us into this built urban landscape with her account of a different type of pet, the songbird. These animals, usually living in cages within public housing, became a popular phenomenon in the 1960s and 1970s in Singapore, reflecting government programs promoting new lifestyles. In the process, native and non-native species became celebrated, or condemned, for their various characteristics, a metaphor for larger issues of developing a new nation, thus reflecting one aspect of how human–animal relationships transformed in the Singaporean Anthropocene as the society grew more urbanized.

The exhibition of animals is the subject of Chapters 7 and 8. Miles Powell and Choo Ruizhi explore the history of aquariums and zoos in Singapore, and how the display of animals provided a metaphor for control

---

[24] Harvey Neo, "Placing Pig Farming in Post-Independence Singapore: Community, Development and Landscapes of Rurality," in *Food, Foodways, and Foodscapes: Culture, Community and Consumption in Post-Colonial Singapore*, ed. Lily Kong and Vineeta Sinha (Singapore: World Scientific, 2016), pp. 83–102; Chan Ying-Kit, "No Room to Swing a Cat? Animal Treatment and Urban Space in Singapore," *Southeast Asian Studies* 5, 2 (2016): 305–29.

of the wild in Singapore. The perceptions of modernizing Singaporeans have of their relationship with nature also aligned with development issues within the state during this period. Just as the Singaporean environment reflects not only a continuity with the colonial past, but also an acceleration in human attempts to alter and present it to the populace for their use since the Second World War, both the aquarium and the zoo reflect the concentration of official policies related to utilization of the environment, introduction of new species, and their incorporation into an image of Singapore as a modern Garden City and a business hub. They remain among the most popular attractions for visitors—residents and non-residents alike—on the island, a place where Singaporean creatures interact and reflect basic aspects of the nation and its image.

This collection, ultimately, is an introduction to various aspects of the human–animal relationship in Singapore since the mid-20th century. This is a period of intensive development and the numerous stories revolving around the various physical and mental structures that society has erected to monitor these relationships—whether with individual animals, regulations or even institutions—help provide a clearer understanding of the history of the Anthropocene on an island in Southeast Asia. This is a preliminary investigation into a few species and their relationships with humans, all of which reflect larger historical trends in a developing nation-state. The tales of many other Singaporean creatures are waiting to be told. Enjoy the initial steps in this journey, and hopefully it will spur others to pursue the histories of other species, and humans, in Singapore.

CHAPTER ONE

Tilapia, Travel and the Making of a Singaporean Creature

Anthony D. Medrano

As fishes go, cichlids (family Cichlidae) abound.[1] They are everywhere in Singapore. They are in the drains, canals and reservoirs as well as catchments, ponds and rivers. Their presence can be seen and spotted across the estuarine zone of the island too. Brackish areas such as Sungei Buloh, Marina Channel and Pulau Ubin teem with cichlids of all colors, shapes and sizes. Cichlids are also found among the wet spaces of Nee Soon Swamp Forest.[2] Cichlids even populate the most unassuming bodies

---

[1] This chapter was made possible through the support a Social Science Research Thematic Grant (MOE2020-SSRTG-027). Additionally, I would like to thank my colleagues at the Lee Kong Chian Natural History Museum for their time, friendship, and rich biological scholarship: Darren Yeo (Director), Heok Hui Tan (Curator of Ichthyology), and Marty Low (Head of SIGNIFY, the museum's historical biodiversity archive). Finally, I would like to recognize the invaluable research assistance I received from Gemma Green, Jenelle Lee, Anastasia Kurniadi, and Felipe Waldeck—all of whom are/were student scholars at Yale-NUS College.
[2] Jonathan K.I. Ho, et al., *A Guide to the Freshwater Fauna of Nee Soon Swamp Forest* (Singapore: Tropical Marine Science Institute, 2016), pp. 57–61; J.H. Liew, et al.,

of water—often as a result of human actions. In 1961, for example, the director of the Singapore Botanic Gardens, Humphrey Morrison Burkill, expressed his acknowledgement to Charles Frederick Hickling, director of the Tropical Fish Culture Research Institute in Melaka, for supplying him with some young cichlids for Swan Lake.[3] These Melakan-born fingerlings were of the species *Coptodon zillii*, named after Charles Zill (also known as Mustapha Ben-Zill), a French naturalist who collected the type specimen from the waters of an artisan well in Touggourt, Algeria, in 1848.[4] Zill then sent the specimen to Paul Gervais, a French naturalist who named the species (originally *Acerina zillii*) and thus scripted into modern science one more cichlid. In describing this new member of the cichlid family, Gervais not only impressed upon his French readership a sense of its morphology, but also, and perhaps more importantly, its suitability for "transport" and "acclimatization." More than a century later, and nearly 11,000 kilometers away, these fish were at home in a pond at the Singapore Botanic Gardens. Cichlids are creatures that abound in ways that seem neither strange nor out of place in the Garden City.[5]

Cichlids, thus, are not native to the fresh waters of Singapore. They are diasporic fishes. Most cichlids (70–80 percent) are indigenous to Africa, "with the greatest diversity found in the Great Lakes" of Victoria, Tanzania, and Malawi.[6] Some cichlids are from the Americas too, and in

---

"Ecology and Origin of the Introduced Cichlid *Acarichthys heckelii* in Singapore's Fresh Waters—First Instance of Establishment," *Environmental Biology of Fishes* 97 (2013): 1109–18; J.H. Liew, et al., "Some Cichlid Fishes Recorded in Singapore," *Nature in Singapore* 5 (2012): 229–36.

[3] The station held stocks of several kinds of cichlids in addition to other economic fishes (*Cyprinus carpio*, *Puntius javanicus*, *Osphronemus olfax*, and *Trichogaster pectoralis*) for the study and promotion of aquaculture in Singapore and Malaya. C.F. Hickling, "The Fish Culture Research Station, Malacca," *Nature* 183, 4657 (31 January 1959): 287–9; H.M. Burkill, *Annual Report of the Botanic Gardens Department for 1961* (Singapore: Government Printing Office, 1963), p. 9.

[4] Armand Lucy, *Souvenirs de Voyage: Lettres Intimes sur la Campagne de Chine en 1860* (Marseille: Imprimerie et Lithographie Jules Barile, 1861), p. 13.

[5] Paul Gervais, "Sur les Animaux Vertebres de l'Algerie: Envisages Sous le Double Rapport, de la Geographie Zoologique et de la Domestication," *Annales de Sciences Naturalles (partie zoologie)* 3, 9 (1848): 202–3; Kelvin K.P. Lim and Peter K.L. Ng, *A Guide to Common Freshwater Fishes of Singapore* (Singapore: Singapore Science Center, 1990), p. 124. Jason Van Driesche and Roy Van Driesche, *Nature Out of Place: Biological Invasions in the Global Age* (Washington, D.C.: Island Press, 2000).

[6] J.R. Stauffer, et al., "Cichlid Fish Diversity and Speciation," in *Reconstructing the Tree of Life: Taxonomy and Systematics of Species Rich Taxa*, ed. Trevor R. Hodkinson

particular the basins and drainages of the Negro, Orinoco and Amazon rivers. Since 1944, though, approximately 30 species of this family have been introduced to Singaporean waters for anthropocentric purposes such as aquaculture, recreational angling and the aquarium trade. As a result, cichlids constitute a substantial share, nearly 20 percent, of the freshwater fish fauna of the island.[7]

Among the many cichlids found on this island in Southeast Asia there is one species that stands out for its journey to becoming a Singaporean creature: the common tilapia (*Oreochromis mossambicus*). Arriving in 1944, this fish is the earliest introduced cichlid to local waters. Wilhelm Peters, a German naturalist, first described the common tilapia in 1852, using a specimen he collected while leading a scientific expedition across Mozambique in the 1840s. While native to Africa, the common tilapia has transformed into one of the most visible creatures in Singapore's fresh waters today.[8] It is everywhere—from river to reservoir, and from urban drain to estuarine swamp. This fish's ubiquity has much to do with the fact that it can tolerate a range of water types (fresh, salt and brackish). Coupled with its adaptability, the common tilapia is wildly omnivorous, feeding on plants and animals. In turn, the most iconic Singaporean creatures feed on it, with the common tilapia forming an integral part of the diets of native predators such as smooth-coated otters (*Lutrogale perspicillata*), Malayan water monitors (*Varanus salvator*), dog-faced water snakes (*Cerberus schneiderii*), and estuarine crocodiles (*Crocodylus porosus*).[9] Yet, despite being a regular food source for the island's non-human creatures, and thus critical to the production of local biodiversity, this

---

and John A.N. Parnell (Boca Raton, Fl.: CRC Press, 2007), p. 213; Rosemary H. Lowe-McConnell, "Species of Tilapia in East African Dams, with a Key for Their Identification," *East African Agricultural Journal* 20, 4 (1955): 256–62.

[7] Heok Hee Ng and Heok Hui Tan, "An Annotated Checklist of the Non-Native Freshwater Fish Species in the Reservoirs of Singapore," *Cosmos* 6 (2010): 107–11; Tan Heok Hui, et al., "The Non-Native Freshwater Fishes of Singapore: An Annotated Compilation," *Raffles Bulletin of Zoology* 68 (2020): 150; Personal communication with Tan Heok Hui (3 Jun. 2021).

[8] Wilhelm C.H. Peters, "Diagnosen von neuen Flussfischen aus Mossambique," *Bericht über die zur Bekanntmachung geeigneten Verhandlungen der Königlichen Preussische Akademie der Wissenschaften zu Berlin* (1852): 681. Peters (1815–83) served as director of the Berlin Zoological Museum.

[9] Tan, et al., "The Non-Native Freshwater Fishes of Singapore," p. 179; Ding Li Yong, et al., "Multiple Records of Aquatic Alien and Invasive Species in Diets of Native Predators in Singapore," *BioInvasions Records* 3, 3 (2014): 201–5.

was not the plan or intention behind the introduction of the common tilapia to Singapore in 1944 nor its existence since.

This chapter uses the story of the common tilapia to explain why a history of names, fisheries and journeys provides new understandings of the fresh waters of Singapore today and the ichthyofauna that calls these natures home. In doing so, it shows how binaries such as native and non-native, displace rather than disclose not only the messiness of biodiversity change and environmental history, but also, and more importantly, the conditions under which species circulate and what happens when they do. The cichlids of Singapore, and the story of the common tilapia in particular, thus reveal and make the case for how diasporic fishes—as sources, methods and archives—can open up new pathways for knowing Singaporean creatures and the ways in which some of these local creatures came to be.[10]

Swimming through Names in the Colonial World

The story of Singapore's common tilapia begins not in Mozambique in the early 1840s but in Java in the late 1930s. It is a fish tale that starts with Hadji Moedjair (1890–1957) rather than Wilhelm Peters. Iwan Dalauk, widely known as Moedjair, was from the village of Papungan in Blitar, a coastal region in East Java. He ran a popular *satay kambing* (lamb satay) shop in the nearby town of Kanigoro. When his business became profitable, Moedjair began to gamble, eventually losing his fortune and slipping into debt; he was in a bad spot. Moedjair then traveled to the Kletak estuary for contemplation and ritual bathing, and "he saw a number of fish." Looking closer, he noticed that the "fish carried the babies in their mouths when they were in danger, and then released them in safer situations."[11]

---

[10] Eric R. Alfred, "The Fresh-Water Fishes of Singapore," *Zoologische Verhandelingen* 78 (1966): 13.
[11] Details of Hadji Moedjair's early life are drawn from interviews—conducted by Sidrotun Naim—with his surviving children, Ismoenir and Djaenuri, in Blitar in 2012. Sidrotun Naim, "Growth, Vibriosis, and Streptococcosis Management in Shrimp-Tilapia Polyculture Systems, and the Role of Quorum Sensing Gene cqsS in Vibrio harveyi Virulence" (unpublished PhD thesis, University of Arizona, 2012), pp. 32–5; Anonymous, *Perihal Ikan-Moedjair* (Djakarta: Gunseikanbu Kokumin Tosyokyoku (Balai Poestaka), 2605 [1945]), p. 3; K.F. Vaas, "Biologische Inventarisatie van de Binnenvisserij in Indonesie," *Landbouw: Landbouwkundig Tijdschrift voor*

What Moedjair observed in the shallows of the Kletak estuary was the maternal breeding behavior (known as mouthbrooding) of the common tilapia. How these African fish ended up in Java's brackish waters remains a mystery, but colonial experts at the time suspected they were fugitive fish—that is, aquarium escapees. Sensing an opportunity and a possible solution to his dire financial straits, Moedjair returned to Papungan and experimented with culturing these mouthbrooders in his backyard. After 11 attempts and several trips back to the Kletak estuary for fresh specimens, he was eventually successful in keeping four of these curious fish alive in his home pond. In so doing, Moedjair had "discovered" (*ontdekt*) and cultivated a new "economic fish" for East Java's backyard ponds, rice fields and inland waters. This achievement was recorded on 25 March 1936.[12]

Moedjair's achievement and his marketing of this new economic fish to the residents of Blitar soon caught the attention of the colonial scientists who worked at the Laboratory for Inland Fisheries in Buitenzorg (present-day Bogor). Failing to identify and determine the species of this new fish, these government experts named it *ikan moedjair* in honor of its discoverer (*ikan* means "fish" in Bahasa Indonesia).[13] Dutch and local scientists at the laboratory were amazed by this new discovery. Taxonomically, they agreed it "belonged to a species completely unknown to Indonesia" and thus began to circulate "after a short time ... under the name of *ikan moedjair*." To be sure of its species type, specimens were sent to the curator of ichthyology at the Rijksmuseum van Natuurlijke Historie in Leiden, Frederik Petrus Koumans, who identified *ikan moedjair* in 1940 as a member of the cichlid family. His analysis was correct in determining the taxonomic family; it was a cichlid, but Koumans was wrong in thinking it was the species *Tilapia zillii* (known today as *Coptodon zillii*). The identification of *ikan moedjair* as the common tilapia (at the time referred to as *Tilapia mossambica* but today known as *Oreochromis*

Nederlandsch Indie 29, 11–12 (1947): 526; M. Sachlan, "Artinja ikan Mudjair bagi Rakjat Indonesia," *Berita Perikanan* 3, 5–6 (1951): 74.
[12] Anonymous, *Perihal Ikan-Moedjair*, p. 6; Nain, "Growth, Vibriosis, and Streptococcosis," p. 33; A.E. Hofstede, *Enige Mededelingen over Ikan Moedjair* (Batavia: Departement van Landbouw en Visserij, Onderafdeling Binnenvisserij, 1941 [1948]), p. 3; Anonymous, "De Visch als Bestaansmiddel," *Indische Courant*, 12 May 1941, p. 13.
[13] This is according to oral history interviews with his descendants. Nain, "Growth, Vibriosis, and Streptococcosis," p. 34.

mossambicus) was only realized after the Second World War, in 1947. Taxonomy aside, the scientists in Buitenzorg continued to study, report, market, supply and popularize this new farmable fish under the name of its Javanese discoverer, Moedjair.[14]

By 1941, the local press on both sides of the Melaka Straits was popularizing *ikan moedjair* because it grew fast, reproduced quickly and thrived in ponds and other systems of fish culture. In Indonesia, newspaper stories championed its adaptability, saying *ikan moedjair* was one of the "most suitable species for raising in rice-fields" (*meest geschikte soort voor sawahvischkweek*).[15] The pairing of fish and rice was more than just about the economics of co-culturing "useful food" in the archipelago; it was also about food security as fish and rice constituted the daily diet of rural and urban populations alike. In Singapore, *ikan moedjair* was touted as a new "table fish" that had the potential to supply the protein needs of residents as it did in Java.[16] But just as observers were noting the role this fish could potentially play in the lives of Indonesians in 1941, *ikan moedjair* became even more important during the Japanese Occupation that followed.

In Southeast Asia, the Second World War created the conditions for *ikan moedjair* to travel out of Java as the impact of the war on food supplies mobilized Japanese imperial networks to locate new kinds of edible fish for mass cultivation in the ponds of wartime Singapore (Syōnan). In this context, authorities noted the popularity and success of growing *ikan*

---

[14] Vaas, "Biologische Inventarisatie van De Binnenvisserij in Indonesie," p. 526; Hofstede, *Enige Mededelingen over Ikan Moedjair*, 13–15 (appendixes 1–3); Raden Slamet Soeseno, *Ikan Mudjair: Ikan yang Termurah* (Djakarta: Pustaka Rakjat, 1954), p. 4; J.J. Schuurman and K.F. Vaas, "Het Rawa-Complex te Tjampoerdarat als Visscherij-Object," *Landbouw: Landbouwkundig Tijdschrift voor Nederlandsch Indie* 17, 1 (1941): 41.

[15] Anonymous, "De Visch als Bestaansmiddel," *Indische Courant*, 12 May 1941, p. 13.

[16] Similar developments in Indonesia also had occurred with *sepat siam* (*Trichopodus pectoralis*) in Celebes [Sulawesi] during this period. *Sepat siam* is commonly known as the snakeskin gourami, and it is one of the 123 non-native freshwater fishes found in Singapore. Tan, et al., "The Non-Native Freshwater Fishes of Singapore," p. 185; Anonymous, "Kediri: Een Groot Bevolkingsbelang," *Soerabiasch Handelsblad* 16 (Nov. 1940): 14; Anonymous, "De Visch als Bestaansmiddel," *Indische Courant*, 12 May 1941, p. 13; Anonymous, "De Vischvoorziening van Nederlandsch-Indie," *Sumatra Post*, 22 Jan.1941, p. 10; Anonymous, "New Variety of Table Fish," *The Straits Times* [hereafter, *ST*], 7 Feb. 1941, p. 11; Anonymous, "New Fish Found in Java Waters," *Malaya Tribune*, 11 Feb. 1941, p. 2.

Tilapia, Travel and the Making of a Singaporean Creature

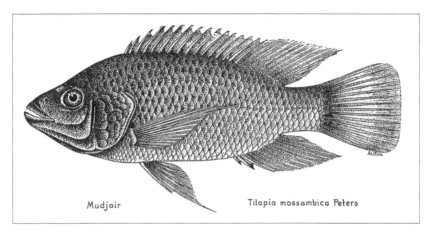

Image 1.1: "Mudjair." W.H. Schuster and R. Rustami Djajadiredja, *Mas'alah tentang Pemasukan dan Pemindahan Ikan di Indonesia* (Bandung: Balai Penjelidikan Perikanan Darat, 1950).

moedjair in Javanese waters, which had continued during the Japanese Occupation. In August 1944, the wartime government's economic affairs department, headquartered in Jakarta, even authored a small pamphlet titled *Perihal Ikan-Moedjair* (About Ikan Moedjair) that explained why this resilient food fish was so invaluable to the "world of fisheries in Djawa." Two months later, in October 1944, the wartime fisheries conglomerate *Teikoku Suisan Tōsei* (Imperial Fisheries Production) secured from Java a stock of 123 *ikan moedjair*, which was air shipped to Singapore for purposes of bolstering the local food supply.[17]

The introduction of these four-inch fingerlings marked a new chapter in the story of this diasporic fish that would include not only a new environment in Singapore but also a new name. No longer was it referred to as *ikan moedjair*, but instead simply known as *"ikan tes"*—a local Malay name born from the initials of the "enterprising Nippon firm" that secured supplies of this industrious food fish and distributed them to pond growers in Singapore.[18] The firm, of course, was the Syōnan branch of Teikoku Suisan Tōsei. After their flight to Singapore, these young *ikan tes*

---

[17] Anonymous, *Perihal Ikan-Moedjair*, p. 44; Hofstede, *Enige Mededelingen over Ikan Moedjair*, pp. 1–2.
[18] Anonymous, "Abundant Supply of Fresh Fish for People of Malai Visualized," *Syōnan Shimbun*, 11 Jan. 1945, p. 2.

were raised to maturity at Tesui Pond, a government-supervised spawning ground off of Upper Serangoon Road in Kampong Potong Pasir. At this one location, after four months of feeding, growing and reproducing, the tilapia stock multiplied immensely. By January 1945, *ikan tes* were made available to the public through a system of distribution that, in part, tapped into a network of freshwater aquaculturalists who were mainly carp farmers, but whose supply of fry from China had been disrupted and were seeking "alternative uses" for their ponds.[19]

The novel presence of "tereibia" in Syōnan created a fish buzz unlike anything before. As a "new species of freshwater fish," *ikan tes* had the potential to transform wartime diets from boosting the local food supply to supporting the "grow-more-food" campaign. Local officials now saw an opportunity to turn the tide—or at least feed a bit of public optimism—on matters of protein provision, high food prices and the colony-wide "fish problem." This optimism was based on the fecundity, taste and adaptability of the common tilapia. The local press reported that "this type of fish breed" very "easily and rapidly," noting that the stock from Java had multiplied from 123 to roughly 10,000 in just four months. Naitō Kanichi, the mayor of wartime Singapore, and his director of the food control department, Seki Yoshiko, led a group of reporters and officials on a tour of Tesui Pond, where they met with Tsukamotō Ginjiro, the supervisor who had cultivated an abundance of *ikan tes* in such a short period. Tsukamotō shared with his visitors that *ikan tes* was "quite different from any other freshwater fish" in Syōnan.[20] Officials emphasized that one important difference, which was especially relevant to the hungry island, was the way in which this cichlid differed in taste. Unlike other freshwater fish, *ikan tes* was "very tasty… and most suitably prepared by frying." In addition to learning about the promise of the common tilapia's high fecundity and remarkable edibility, these same Japanese officials emphasized that *ikan tes* was extremely adaptable; it could live and thrive in most aquatic habitats. From tin mine pools to

---

[19] D.W. Le Mare, *Report of the Fisheries Department, Malaya, 1949* (Singapore: Government Printing Office, 1950), p. 136; Ng, et al., "The Status and Impact of Introduced Freshwater Animals in Singapore," 19; Anonymous, "Abundant Supply of Fresh Fish for People of Malai Visualized."

[20] Anonymous, "Abundant Supply of Fresh Fish for People of Malai Visualized," p. 2.

coastal mangrove swamps, from carp ponds to island rivers, no body of water was beyond the possibility of tilapia cultivation.[21]

From Tesui Pond, tens of thousands of *ikan tes* were distributed across Singapore in 1945. The process of distribution was quite direct. Pond growers received coupons from the food control department. In turn, they exchanged these coupons for a supply of fingerlings, free of charge. The transaction occurred at the Teikoku Suisan Tōsei office on De Souza Road. In order to receive a coupon, however, the pond farmer needed to provide the authorities with some data such as their name and address as well as the location and size of their ponds. They were also required to secure a permit from the fisheries department. "Owing to the difficulties in obtaining these permits," explained the director of Malayan fisheries, D.W. Le Mare, in 1949, "few Chinese cultivators" were able to participate in this new food industry. In contrast, Malay communities were encouraged not only to grow food fish, but also to integrate the farming of *ikan tes*, in particular, within their new agricultural settlements. When new farms opened up in places such as Geylang Serai or when old rubber estates were converted into food-producing zones around Bedok, Ulu Bedok and Changi, the local press celebrated these wartime accomplishments because they included, in part, the cultivation of a new freshwater fish—presumably *ikan tes*.[22]

By March 1945, *ikan tes* were being raised in "42 ponds scattered all over Syōnan." One of these ponds was located in the West Coast Road area; it was stocked with 5,000 fingerlings. This well-planted pond, under the supervision of a Japanese aquaculturalist, was unfortunately built near the island's estuarine edge. As the rains came with the seasonal monsoon, flooding ensued and "a number of the fish escaped, becoming firmly established in the adjacent brackish waters."[23] From one pond in

---

[21] Anonymous, "Abundant Supply of Fresh Fish for People of Malai Visualized," p. 2; Le Mare, *Report of the Fisheries Department, Malaya, 1949*, p. 138; Gregg Huff and Gillian Huff, "The Second World War Japanese Occupation of Singapore," *JSEAS* 51, 1–2 (2020): 249–51.

[22] Le Mare, *Report of the Fisheries Department, Malaya, 1949*, p. 137; Anonymous, "Fresh-Water Fish Being Distributed in Syōnan," *Syōnan Shimbun*, 3 Mar. 1945, p. 2; Anonymous, "Geylang Serai Farm Example to Food Growers," *Syōnan Shimbun*, 5 May 1945, p. 2; Anonymous, "Malais Open Up Second Large Food-Producing Area in Syōnan," *Syōnan Shimbun*, 17 Apr. 1945, p. 2.

[23] Le Mare, *Report of the Fisheries Department, Malaya, 1949*, p. 137; Anonymous, "Fresh-Water Fish Being Distributed in Syōnan," p. 2.

Kampong Potong Pasir in 1944 to many kinds of aquatic habitats in 1945, the story of Singapore's *ikan tes* would experience yet another turn in the wake of the Second World War.

The Common Tilapia in Singapore

The end of the Japanese Occupation brought one last change in the name of *ikan tes*. Ichthyologists in Bogor, London and Amsterdam discussed and analyzed specimens that were sent before the Second World War and realized a correction was in order. With the help of the British Museum, the taxonomy of *ikan tes* was ultimately settled and clarified in 1947. This curious cichlid was not *Tilapia zillii* (now *Coptodon zillii*) as previously believed, but rather *Tilapia mossambica* (now *Oreochromis mossambicus*). Stemming from this determination, nearly all subsequent sources on the Malayan life of this diasporic fish use its scientific name or refer to it by its more popular nomenclature: the common tilapia (or tilapia for short). The first published use of the name "*Tilapia mossambica*" when describing the fish in Singapore's waters was in 1949.[24]

Even with its revised taxonomy and new name, the common tilapia quickly lost favor among the post-war public in Singapore. From Jurong to Ponggol, while ponds proliferated, there was little to no appetite for tilapia, and much of this ill-favorability was due to the return of carp from Hong Kong.[25] The reappearance of carp in Chinese-owned ponds

---

[24] The earliest newspaper account to use the name "tilapia" when referring to the fish in Malayan waters also occurs in 1949, but in Penang (Sungei Nibong) not Singapore. Anonymous, "Land to Yield Padi and Fish," *ST*, 24 Apr. 1949, p. 7. Tan, et al., "The Non-Native Freshwater Fishes of Singapore," p. 179; Soeseno, *Ikan Mudjair*, p. 4; D.W. Le Mare, *Annual Report of the Fisheries Department, Federation of Malaya and Singapore for the Year 1948* (Singapore: Government Printing Office, 1949), p. 1.

[25] The types of carp farmed in early post-war Singapore included: grass carp (*Ctenopharyngodon idellus*; *hwan yue* [Cantonese] and *chow hu* [Hokkien]); big head (*Aristichthys nobilis*; *tye tow yue* [Cantonese] and *twa thow* [Hokkien]); silver carp (*Hypophthalmichthys molitrix*; *pin yue* [Cantonese] and *peh leng* [Hokkien]); mud carp (*Cirrhina molitorella*; *tho leng yue* [Cantonese] and *leng chee* [Hokkien]); and, common carp (*Cyprinus carpio*; li yue [Cantonese] and li koh [Hokkien]). Le Mare, *Annual Report of the Fisheries Department, Federation of Malaya and Singapore for the Year 1948*, p. 15; Le Mare, *Report of the Fisheries Department, Malaya, 1949*, pp. 130–1; Anonymous, "H.K.-S'pore: Seven Hours as Fish Flies," *ST*, 24 Sep. 1947, p. 5.

Image 1.2: Carp pond in Singapore, 1949. Le Mare, *Annual Report of the Fisheries Department, Federation of Malaya and Singapore for the Year 1949*, opposite p. 120.

in Singapore signaled a resumption of inter-Asia trade as these freshwater fingerlings could once again flourish. Ponds that had been repurposed for culturing the common tilapia now teemed with another diasporic fish. Writing on the distaste for tilapia farming in 1949, D.W. Le Mare reasoned, "there is no doubt that with more choice available the strong consumers' preference and consequent demand for familiar types of fish led to the premature decline of this form of fish cultivation."[26] In addition to the carp factor, another blow to the economic life of tilapia was the recovery and resurgence of seafood in local markets and thus the public hunger for "familiar types of fish" such as *ikan bawal* (*Stromateus sp.*), *ikan kurau* (*Polynemus sp.*), *ikan merah* (*Lutianus sp.*), *ikan parang* (*Chirocentrus dorab*), and *ikan bilis* (*Stolephorus sp.*).[27]

The most telling reason for the Singaporean distaste for tilapia was its late introduction to the local protein supply. While the food control

---

[26] Le Mare, *Report of the Fisheries Department, Malaya, 1949*, p. 137.
[27] Anonymous, "Vegetables & Fish Prices," *Sunday Tribune* (Singapore), 12 Oct. 1947, p. 3; Anonymous, "Fish Prices Are Normal Again," *ST*, 1 May 1948, p. 8.

department and Teikoku Suisan Tōsei had combined efforts to distribute tilapia to pond growers across the island in 1945, these measures occurred in the waning months of the Japanese Occupation. This late introduction and the obstacles Chinese carp farmers faced in securing the necessary permits, which were required to receive free stocks of tilapia fingerlings for their ponds, meant the island's primary freshwater aquaculturalists were tilapia-less. The fish did not have an opportunity to establish itself as a market mainstay or protein staple—like it had in Indonesia, where freshwater fish culture was more diverse and widespread than in Singapore.[28] In this way, tilapia failed to live up to its economic promise during the Occupation and thus struggled to become part of the provisioning of protein in the wake of the war.

Despite its late arrival to the local food supply and the public preference for familiar marine fishes such as *ikan bawal* (*Stromateus sp.*) and *ikan kurau* (*Polynemus sp.*), the Malayan Fisheries Department saw the common tilapia as a promising economic species that could play an important role in the post-war recovery of Singapore. The capacity of this cichlid to adapt to different kinds of waters was welcomed as a timely solution to meeting society's growing food needs, particularly following a demographic surge on the "land-hungry" island. Fish, after all, were a food "acceptable to all the races of multi-racial Singapore." Under these circumstances, in late 1947, the Fisheries Department sought to increase the local fish supply by converting sections of mangrove swamp into experimental fish ponds. Economically, this move to the estuarine edge had its advantages. For one, there was an abundance of such ecozones, particularly near Pasir Panjang and along West Coast Road, that made the building of new ponds possible while also providing an opportunity to farm tilapia in brackish waters. Attuned to local sensitivities, Malayan fisheries experts observed that the "usual earthy taste typical of Tilapia reared in fresh water ponds" could be reduced or even removed if this fish was cultivated under estuarine conditions. This was traced to the presence of a higher ratio of crustaceans (particularly prawns from the Penaeidae family) to algae in brackish waters, which influenced the flavor

---

[28] W.H. Schuster and R. Rustami Djajadiredja, *Mas'alah tentang Pemasukan dan Pemindahan Ikan di Indonesia* (Bandung: Djawatan Pusat Pertanian, 1950), pp. 26–33; K.F. Vaas and J.J. Schuurman, "On the Ecology and Fisheries of Some Javanese Freshwaters," *Mededelingen van het Algemeen Proefstation voor de Landbouw* 97 (1949): 20–30, 40–54; R. Bijleveld and R.S. Martoatmodjo, "Vischstand en Visscherij in West Koetei (Oost Borneo)," *Landbouw* 16, 9 (1940): 516–50.

of the fish, making it (in theory) more palatable to post-war consumers.[29] A change in how tilapia tasted, the fisheries department hoped, would foster a change in its popularity and reception.

By 1948, officials drained the Fisheries Department test pond at Pasir Panjang and made an evaluation of culturing tilapia in brackish waters borne from mangrove swamps. The results proved that this food fish had the potential to be a productive—even "ubiquitous"—presence in the aquatic habitats of Singapore. What surprised the experts was the way in which tilapia dominated the brackish pond. As a group, they weighed exceedingly more than other food fishes, such as *ikan belanak* (*Crenimugil seheli*), *ikan selangat* (*Anodontostoma chacunda*) and Penaeid prawns, cultivated in the pond. The tilapia also excelled under estuarine conditions as compared to those grown in freshwater habitats. The scientists based this evaluation on a number of metrics, ranging from how rapidly it grew, gained weight and the fact that it reproduced at least twice in fewer than eight months. This was a case of "domination by Tilapia."

Table 1.1: Results of aquaculture experiments utilizing brackish water at Pasir Panjang Pond, 1948. Le Mare, *Annual Report of the Fisheries Department, Federation of Malaya and Singapore for the Year 1948*, p. 25.

Kind of Food Fish	Total Group Weight	Total Number of Specimens in Group
tilapia	290 kg	871
ikan belanak	52 kg	2,450
ikan selangat	44 kg	2,380
mixed fish	71.5 kg	-
Penaeid prawns	2.3 kg	-
	460 kg	

---

[29] D.W. Le Mare, "Application of the Principles of Fish Culture to Estuarine Conditions in Singapore," *Proceedings of the Indo-Pacific Fisheries Council, 2nd Meeting, Bangkok* (1951): 182; Anonymous, *Review of the Primary Production Department, 1960–1965* (Singapore: Government Printing Office, 1967), p. 33; Le Mare, *Annual Report of the Fisheries Department, Federation of Malaya and Singapore for the Year 1948*, p. 25.

Image 1.3. Brackish water pond along West Coast Road, 1949. Le Mare, *Annual Report of the Fisheries Department, Federation of Malaya and Singapore for the Year 1948*, opposite p. 121.

As D.W. Le Mare concluded, the experiment to culture "*Tilapia mossambica* in brackish water ponds in mangrove swamps" had produced "almost phenomenal results."[30]

Despite such "phenomenal results" and the perceived economic benefits of converting mangrove swamps into high-yielding tilapia farms, the brackish pond at Pasir Panjang revealed something far more impactful. This fish was able to spread with ease beyond man-made enclaves and swampy farms and enter the native aquatic systems of Singapore. Shortly after the pond was drained and its faunal population examined, this brackish farm was restocked with tilapia and other food fishes in late 1948. In a predictable manner, the Asian monsoon and extreme weather arrived soon afterward. "The whole of the South-West Coast of Singapore," as Le Mare reported, "was flooded on account of exceptionally heavy rain and high tides." This flooding served as a vector for countless tilapia not only to flow into Singapore's estuarine zone, but also to establish

---

[30] Le Mare, *Annual Report of the Fisheries Department, Federation of Malaya and Singapore for the Year 1948*, pp. 1, 24–5; Le Mare, "Application of the Principles of Fish Culture to Estuarine Conditions in Singapore," p. 183; Ng, et al., "The Status and Impact of Introduced Freshwater Animals in Singapore," p. 19.

themselves as feral communities in places such as "Kuala Jurong."[31] The results of the experiments were ecologically clear. Brackish aquaculture combined with extreme weather created a direct pathway for tilapia to make a permanent home in Singaporean waters.

The hope that the common tilapia could help meet the post-war demand for cheap protein corresponded with the fish's growing presence—to the point of ubiquity—in the natural waters of Singapore. Scientists repeated the experiments in the brackish pond at Pasir Panjang with only tilapia in 1949; the outcome was remarkable. The yield of pounds per acre per year was in the area of 1,200 pounds, which translated as 544 kilograms per 0.4 hectares. For the Malayan Fisheries Department, culturing tilapia under estuarine conditions would be the path forward. C.H. Hickling, who served as fisheries adviser to the British Colonial Office before becoming director of the Tropical Fish Culture Research Institute in Melaka, began championing tilapia as a solution to feeding Malaya's expanding population. To solidify this stance, Le Mare—in conjunction with Hickling—republished figures of global aquaculture productivity to illustrate how exceptional the results at Pasir Panjang Pond had been in 1949.[32]

Table 1.2: Comparative Edible Fish Yields, 1949. Le Mare, *Report of the Fisheries Department, Malaya, 1949*, p. 138.

Body of Water	Kind of Water	Pounds per acre per year
Lake Victoria	natural	1–4
Lake Tiberias	natural	22–25
United States	farm	200–400
Yugoslavia	farm	327
Palestine	farm	1,200
Hong Kong	farm	2,000–4,000

---

[31] The case of Kuala Jurong motivated the Fisheries Department to introduce 2,000 tilapia into Kuala Kelantan with the hope that these young cichlids would establish themselves—much as they had in Singapore—in this Malayan estuary. Le Mare, *Annual Report of the Fisheries Department, Federation of Malaya and Singapore for the Year 1948*, pp. 24, 57.

[32] Le Mare, *Report of the Fisheries Department, Malaya, 1949*, p. 138. C.F. Hickling, "Fish Farming in the Middle and Far East," *Nature* 161, 4098 (15 May 1948): 748.

Success at the Pasir Panjang Pond, however, did little to increase the public appetite for the common tilapia. Despite the efforts and results of the Malayan Fisheries Department demonstrating the high productivity of culturing tilapia in brackish ponds, and weathering as they did the floods that contributed to the spread and scale of feral populations, these diasporic fish remained out of favor—and out of flavor—in a hungry city that preferred seafood over other types of protein. To aid in popularizing the common tilapia as both a cheap protein for the everyday family and an economic opportunity for the "would-be towkay," *The Straits Times* ran a story—that originally aired on the radio—titled "The Tale of Tilly Tilapia" in 1950. Authored by Wynona "Noni" Wright, a New Zealander who worked for Radio Malaya before joining the newspaper as a feature writer and later the Cathay Organization as a film director, the tale of "Tilly"—short for *Tilapia*—retraced for the listening and reading public the journey of these "little strangers" from the lakes of East Africa to the waters of Singapore. In brief but vivid terms, it narrated how this diasporic fish "started seeing the world" and became a staple food in Indonesia, a process that could be reproduced as the conditions were ripe for Tilly to thrive in Singapore. In this way, Wright communicated the value of Tilly to the Singaporean protein supply and post-war economy. For the consumer, she noted, "they're good second-grade fish," that "could sell more cheaply than most other local fish." And, for the "careful towkay," Wright added, "there's probably a commercial future in them."[33]

It took less than a decade, from 1944 to 1953, for this traveling cichlid to become a Singaporean creature—fully naturalized, happily feral, widely common and completely at home in Malayan waters. A spokesperson for the Malayan Fisheries Department even explained that little could impact the place of tilapia on the island as it "was abundant in Singapore," while others observed that the island was "already over-populated with this fish." By 1954, Tham Ah Kow, a pioneering local scientist who worked for the Fisheries Department and later directed the fisheries biology unit at the University of Singapore, summarized the extraordinary state of tilapia on the island. While this "wonder fish" remained deeply unpopular as a post-war protein, it was massively abundant as a farmed and feral species. "There must be millions of them in the ponds at Potong Pasir and Paya Lebar to mention just two places."[34]

---

[33] Noni Wright, "The Tale of Tilly Tilapia," *ST*, 23 Feb. 1950, p. 11.
[34] Anonymous, "Tilapia Dealers Go on a Buying Spree in S'Pore," *ST*, 17 Jan. 1953,

There was indeed a commercial future in Singapore for the common tilapia, just not as a local food fish. With distaste firmly anchored in the public palate, Singaporean *towkays* began to complain as early as 1952 that there was no domestic demand for their fishery product. The economic upswing for these "wonder fish" laid not at home, but abroad. Faced with "enormous production," Singapore became a transregional supplier of common tilapia in the late 1940s and 1950s. Whether cultured in brackish ponds or freshwater farms, or netted from local estuaries, these cichlids were mobilized to "combat hunger in Asia" and beyond. Shipped to new markets and foreign waters, the common tilapia became embedded in local food cultures and protein supply chains and, in the process, established in native aquatic systems. As a result, Singapore and its "wonder fish" played an important but perhaps forgotten role in shaping the rise of the "blue revolution," referring to the massive expansion of global aquacultural production that began in the mid-20th century, and reshaped the nature of equatorial environments.[35]

The early post-war period was an especially mobile time for Singapore's tilapia, traveling as they did as part of the "blue revolution." One of Singapore's first tilapia exports was to Taiwan in 1946. Following the war, Wu Chen-hui and Kuo Chi-chang, two Taiwanese soldiers who served in the Japanese imperial army and were held in a prisoner-of-war camp in Singapore, returned to Kaohsiung with 13 tilapia that quickly grew to become "a common fish in all parts of the island."[36] In 1950, a consignment of tilapia was sent to North Borneo and introduced into

---

p. 8; Anonymous, "U.N. Offers Fish To Beat Hunger—But We've Too Much," *ST*, 12 Sep. 1952, p. 7; Anonymous, "A Wonder Fish? We've Got Millions," *Singapore Free Press*, 20 May 1954, p. 5.

[35] Wolfgang Hannig, *Towards a Blue Revolution: Socioeconomic Aspects of Brackishwater Pond Cultivation in Java* (Yogyakarta: Gadjah Mada University Press, 1988); James Coull, "Will a Blue Revolution Follow the Green Revolution? The Modern Upsurge of Aquaculture," *Area* 25, 4 (1993): 350–7; Anonymous, "U.N. Offers Fish To Beat Hunger—But We've Too Much."

[36] Kuo served in Singapore, breeding tilapia for distribution. Wu served in Sumatra and was interned in Singapore. They met in the POW camp. Anonymous, "Taiwan in Time: A Fishy Venture," *Taipei Times*, 30 Apr. 2017, p. 8; I-Chiu Liao and His-Chiang Liu, "Exotic Aquatic Species in Taiwan," in *Exotic Aquatic Organisms in Asia: Proceedings of a Workshop on Introduction of Exotic Aquatic Organisms in Asia*, ed. Sena S. de Silva (Manila: Asian Fisheries Society, 1989), p. 102; Tung-Pai Chen, *The Culture of Tilapia in Rice Paddies in Taiwan* (Taipei: Commission on Rural Reconstruction, 1953), p. 3.

local waters for the purpose of mass cultivation. In that same year, and for the same reason, Singapore sent a shipment of its tilapia to the West Indies. About 400 of these fish were then distributed to Jamaica, "where they established themselves and thrived." From Jamaica's supply of these tilapia, 103 were shipped to Haiti in 1951 and, within two months of their introduction, these fish had "multiplied by [the] hundreds." Likewise, roughly 2,500 tilapia were sent to Ceylon in 1951 and planted in the ponds of the Fisheries Research Station in Colombo. These fish "multiplied so fast that several hundred times the original number" were taken to stock ponds elsewhere on the island. One fisheries expert was astounded that this cichlid "proved equally at home in fresh and brackish waters" and observed that soon thereafter they were "readily obtainable in the principal fish markets." From Ceylon, a consignment of fingerlings was sent to Madras.[37]

Tilapia from Singapore also thrived in the Pacific. These fish excelled in Hawai'i, particularly on Oahu, where they were introduced in 1951 both as a new food fish and as a way to control the growth of plants and mosquitoes in irrigation ditches. Spanning the 1950s, these fish traveled even farther and wider. From the mid- to late 1950s, for example, they were mobilized to boost the protein production of Pacific places such as Papua, Fiji, New Guinea, the Cook Islands and "other South Pacific territories." And, like in Singapore, the common tilapia soon became feral, common and established in these various waters—from mountainous rivers and coastal swamps to urban canals and inland lakes.[38]

---

[37] T.W. Burdon, *Report of the Fisheries Department, 1950* (Singapore: Government Printing Office, 1951), p. 4; S.Y. Lin, "Fish Culture Project in Haiti," *Proceedings of the Gulf and Caribbean Fisheries Institute* 4 (1952): 114; Anonymous, *A Guide to the Fisheries of Ceylon, Bulletin No. 8* (Colombo: Fisheries Research Station, Ceylon, 1958), pp. 32–3; D.D. Peter Devadas and P.I. Chacko, "Introduction of the Exotic Cichlid, *Tilapia mossambica* Peters, in Madras," *Current Science* 22, 1 (1953): 29; P.I. Chacko and B. Krishnamurthi, "Observations on *Tilapia mossambica* Peters in Madras," *Journal of the Bombay Natural History Society* 52, 2–3 (1954): 349.

[38] John E. Randall, "Introductions of Marine Fishes to the Hawaiian Islands," *Bulletin of Marine Science* 41, 2 (1987): 492; Vernon E. Brock, "A Note on the Spawning of *Tilapia mossambica* in Sea Water," *Copeia* 1954, 1 (19 Feb. 1954): 72; A.H. Kroon, "Fish Farming," *South Pacific Commission Quarterly Bulletin* 3, 4 (1953): 16; W.J.A. Payne, "Sigatoka Agricultural Station (2)," *South Pacific Commission Quarterly Bulletin* 5, 3 (1955): 28; Anonymous, "Ikan: Dari Malaya ka-N. Guinea," *Berita Harian*, 10 Sep. 1957, p. 3; A.M. Rapson, "Fishery Investigations in Papua And New Guinea," *South Pacific Commission Quarterly Bulletin* 5, 3 (July 1955): 20;

By the end of the 1950s, these diasporic fish were popular abroad for the same reasons that inspired their initial introduction to Singapore in 1944. They matured fast, reproduced quickly and adapted easily to new types of aquatic habitats. For some, the common tilapia was not only a "table delicacy" but also a remarkable species with the critical characteristics of being able to "eat any kind of food and live in any kind of water and all sizes of ditches, canals, tanks and swamps."[39] Tasty and prolific, this diasporic fish transformed food supplies and equatorial natures in Asia and the Pacific. For the Singaporean public, however, the common tilapia remained unpalatable as a food fish. While alien to local tables and markets, this cichlid grew increasingly at home among inland and estuarine waters of the island. What is more, just as the Singaporean political and economic landscape was changing in the late 1940s and 1950s, so too was its aquatic biodiversity. In response to these changes in society and nature, new knowledge about the freshwater fishes of Singapore began to emerge.

From Common Tilapia to Singaporean Creature

In 1961, Eric Ronald Alfred, the first Malayan-born director of the Raffles Museum, published a checklist of freshwater fishes in Singapore. This checklist was a landmark in the local history of biodiversity research. By cross-referencing the collection of fish specimens at the Raffles Museum and the collections that he and other museum staff made from the field, it embodied—through its absences—the scale and scope of species loss and environmental change. While Alfred's examination of the Museum's ichthyological collection revealed "no less than 70 species of fresh-water fishes... recorded from Singapore Island," his fieldwork documented a different story as "the canalization of streams and rivers coupled

---

H. Van Pel, "Pond Culture of Tilapia," *South Pacific Commission Quarterly Bulletin* 5, 3 (1955): 30; Anonymous, "Fisheries Officer Visits Cook Group," *South Pacific Commission Quarterly Bulletin* 5, 3 (1955): 34; H. Van Pel, "Fisheries in the South Pacific," *South Pacific Commission Quarterly Bulletin* 5, 3 (1955): 4; A.M. Rapson, "Fisheries Development in Papua and New Guinea," *South Pacific Commission Quarterly Bulletin* 9, 4 (1959): 24–5.

[39] Anonymous, "Table Delicacy in the Ditch," *Singapore Free Press*, 24 Sep. 1953, p. 5.

with pollution from various sources" had "led to the extermination of many species."[40]

Alfred's checklist included 32 fishes from 15 different families—all collected from Singapore's fresh waters between 1956 and 1960. It was the fish he listed last—and the only member of the family Cichlidae—that matters most to our story. It was no. 32, the common tilapia (*Oreochomis mossambicus*). In the brief taxonomic entry, Alfred reported that these fish "occur in the feral state in some brackish and fresh-water streams and ponds."[41] As no. 32 on the checklist, the common tilapia was now officially catalogued as an established species in the natural waters of Singapore, and thus the fish had secured a biological place within the aquatic environment of the soon-to-be nation. Ichthyologically, the common tilapia had become a Singaporean creature.

Alfred's work on Singaporean freshwater fishes was significant for historical reasons too, as his short entry on the common tilapia in 1961 opened a window to a much longer, wider human story. In particular, his taxonomy recorded the Malay name of this fish as "*sepat Jepun*," a vernacular reference to its introduction from Java to Singapore during the Japanese Occupation. And, Alfred added, while it originated "in the fresh and brackish waters of Tropical Africa," this fish now found itself—in the 1960s—swimming wild in the "Seletar River and Botanic Gardens pond" as well as other "various localities" around the island.[42]

By 1966, Alfred published a second checklist that further documented the growing ubiquity of the common tilapia in Singaporean waters.[43] Widely recognized as the "first comprehensive listing of the freshwater fish fauna of Singapore," the 1966 checklist described the common tilapia as "a characteristic component of the estuarine fauna"—a real testament to its naturalization and establishment. In contrast to the widespread

---

[40] Eric R. Alfred, "Singapore Fresh-Water Fishes," *Malayan Nature Journal* 15, 1–2 (1961): 1–19.

[41] Alfred, "Singapore Fresh-Water Fishes," p. 18.

[42] Alfred, "Singapore Fresh-Water Fishes," p. 18.

[43] The 1966 checklist was largely based on the master's thesis Alfred completed at the University of Singapore in 1964. Eric R. Alfred, "Systematic Studies of the Fresh-Water Fishes of Singapore" (unpublished MA thesis, University of Singapore, 1964), pp. 1–143; Alfred, "The Fresh-Water Fishes of Singapore," pp. 3–67. Following Alfred's checklists in the early 1960s, the next comprehensive study of Singapore's freshwater fish fauna was published in 1990. Lim and Ng, *A Guide to Common Freshwater Fishes of Singapore*.

Image 1.4: *Oreochomis mossambicus*, or the common tilapia found in Singaporean waters. Photograph by Heok Hui Tan, and used with permission.

ecological life of the common tilapia in the 1960s, however, this feral fish was increasingly less significant in social or economic terms. It was "not seriously cultivated by Singapore fish culturalists" because of the poor prices it fetched in the market.[44] Taken together, the two checklists provide a post-war baseline for understanding changes in the freshwater fish fauna of Singapore that included not only the decline of native species (extirpations), but also the rise of diasporic creatures (introductions).

Today, the freshwater creatures of Singapore are far more diasporic than they are native. Recent research under Heok Hui Tan, the curator of ichthyology at the Lee Kong Chian Natural History Museum, has built on the pioneering work of Eric Alfred and catalogued 165 fish species that populate Singaporean fresh waters.[45] While 42 native fish

---

[44] Tan, et al., "The Non-Native Freshwater Fishes of Singapore: An Annotated Compilation," p. 150. Alfred, "The Fresh-Water Fishes of Singapore," p. 13; Alfred, "The Fresh-Water Fishes of Singapore," p. 47.

[45] Tan, et al., "The Non-Native Freshwater Fishes of Singapore," p. 150.

species were recorded in this most recent study, most of which collected from the "forest streams… [of] the Central Catchment and Bukit Timah Nature Reserves," the vast majority of Singaporean freshwater fishes were non-native (diasporic). These diasporic fishes were found all across the city-state: from coastline to heartland, and from river mouth to garden pond. Unsurprisingly, cichlids dominated the 2020 checklist, accounting for 24.4 percent (30 species) of the 123 non-native (diasporic) fishes established in the fresh waters of Singapore.[46]

Like our common tilapia, each one of these non-native fishes has a diasporic history. Each one has a tale about their journey from elsewhere to an island in Southeast Asia. Each one has a story about when, how, and why they got here; and, what changed when they made this island their home. The story of the common tilapia in Singapore is but one story in a growing body of literature that explores the interstices of ecological, cultural and economic life as well as the messiness of biodiversity change—from the spaces between and beside binaries such as native and non-native to the ways in which flora and fauna can serve as sources, methods and archives for writing new kinds of environmental histories. While this chapter is anchored in a history of the common tilapia in and (out of) Singaporean waters, it is a history that hopefully resonates well beyond its single-species narrative, speaking more broadly to how diasporic species become local creatures and the ways in which these local creatures, in turn, figure in the discourses and dynamics of environmental change and biodiversity research in Singapore, Southeast Asia and elsewhere.

---

[46] Tan, et al., "The Non-Native Freshwater Fishes of Singapore," pp. 150, 188.

CHAPTER TWO

One Drawback of Tropical Living

Nicole Tarulevicz

Colonial Singapore was notoriously dirty, routinely described in terms such as "incurably filthy"; in contrast, contemporary descriptions of the modern nation-state characterize the landscape as famously clean and over-sanitized. As one international newspaper article put it, the island "feels like it's been scrubbed to within an inch of its life."[1] Through institutions, infrastructure and ideology, attempts at bringing "order" to a colony in the British empire resulted in reconfigurations of physical space—constructing roads and railways, building and housing bureaucracy, piping water and digging sewers—associated with ideas of civility, modernity and morality. The post-colonial regime continues to imprint its ideology through the built environment, making the transition from dirty to sterile appear as a smooth continuation of a colonial ideology of improvement.[2] This transformation has resulted in shifting perceptions of the landscape and

---

[1] Anonymous, *Administrative Report of the Singapore Municipality, 1896*, p. 17. Oliver Milman, "The Price of Life in Singapore, City of Rules: 'It's a Faustian Deal'," *Guardian* 5 Jan. 2015, https://www.theguardian.com/cities/2015/jan/05/the-price-of-life-in-singapore-city-of-rules-its-a-faustian-deal (accessed 20 Jul. 2021).
[2] Some scholars, however, have contested this depiction. Gregory Clancey, "Hygiene in a Landlord State: Health, Cleanliness and Chewing Gum in Late Twentieth-Century Singapore," *Science, Technology and Society* 23, 2 (2018): 215.

the minute creatures that live within it, a legacy of the colonial era as well as the modern nation-state.

Insects provide an opportunity to explore the transformation from dirty to sterile. Beyond the shared characteristics of a three-part body, three pairs of legs, compound eyes and antennae, Insecta is a diverse class of animals. The cultural acceptance of its members is also varied, with some tolerated, some managed, and some that are perpetually battled. To think about insects in Singapore is to think about matter out of place. While "dirt as matter out of place"—an oft-quoted argument from Mary Douglas—is an important part of the story, Max Liboiron suggests dirt is an analytical trope about power, of order and contravention of order. It is one that can be extended to insects, especially those that are identified as pests that contravene human ideas of order. Or, as Hugh Raffles puts it, "they'll almost never do what we tell them to do. They won't keep still." When pests are literally seen—such as an unwanted fly landing on a plate of food, ants in the sugar bowl or cockroaches in the cupboards—these insects are also symbolically out of place, reflecting the ways public filth brought disease to the clean home, or the dirty home brought vermin to neighbors. Pests are out of place, but so too are the causal conditions, like unmanaged refuse or clogged drains. Such nuisances expose a non-linear narrative of dirty to clean, from colonial to independent. Pests "have defied attempts at containment" in the city, literally and conceptually, but have also reflected this transition.[3]

Pests muddy the waters of discourses of progress in multiple ways, and this is particularly true in Singapore. Colonial efforts at managing vermin often faced obstacles, despite the lack of defenders seeking to protect their habitats. This was usually due to the intersections between these pests and other activities, such as attempts to regulate street hawking, historically a potential health risk and in the public eye an attraction for these unwanted creatures. People often contested these efforts, in fear of losing access to delicious, cheap and convenient food. Singaporeans may have feared the communal nature of the satay sauce pot, but they defended the vendors against the threats from the colonial Municipal Commission because "it

---

[3] Mary Douglas, *Purity and Danger: An Analysis of Concepts of Pollution and Taboo* (New York, NY: Routledge, 1966), p. 36; Max Liboiron, "Waste is Not 'Matter Out of Place'," *Discard Studies* (2019), https://discardstudies.com/2019/09/09/waste-is-not-matter-out-of-place/ (accessed 14 Jul. 2021); Hugh Raffles, *Insectapedia* (New York, NY: Vintage Books, 2011), p. 4; Dawn Day Biehler, *Pests in the City: Flies, Bedbugs, Cockroaches, and Rats* (Seattle, WA: University of Washington Press, 2013), p. 4.

was satay." No one wants cockroaches in their cupboards, rats in their drains, flies on their food, or mosquitoes biting their skin. They do not want to get sick, have their comestibles spoiled, or deal with the waste of insects and rodents. It is in these various intersections, however, that the management of pests in Singapore is intertwined with public health, the common good and a broader history.[4] Thinking about pests, thus, lets us think about how food safety advice became central to public health messaging around disease control, and how even the smallest of creatures have shaped our perceptions of this environment.

Modern Singapore is the Garden City. As the nation-state has increasingly been conceived as a biophilic city, in which nature is both visible and accessible, the understanding of biodiversity and conservation has also transformed. Nature is filled with insects; these animals, which go by a variety of descriptors such as pests, creepy-crawlies and vermin, however, are not the kind of nature desired to be visible and accessible. They certainly are not cherished. Again, the right kind of animals, the right kind of nature is wanted. When we think of animals we might think of pets or dinner, or, more historically of charismatic war horses, elephant transportation, exotic menageries and zoological collections.[5] We tend not to think about everyday irritants, such as the ants drawn to the sugar bowl, the cockroaches that scurry out at night, the flies that land on our plate, or the mice and rats that gnaw through packaging into food supplies. But, these too are part of the inexorably linked human–animal nexus.[6]

---

[4] Nicole Tarulevicz and Can Seng Ooi, "Food Safety and Tourism in Singapore: Between Microbial Russian Roulette and Michelin Stars," *Tourism Geographies* 23, 4 (2021): 814; Daniel E. Bender, "Dipping in the Common Sauce Pot: Satay Vending and Good Taste Politics in Colonial and Post-Colonial Singapore," *Food, Culture and Society* 24, 1 (2021): 67.

[5] Timothy P. Barnard, *Imperial Creatures: Humans and Other Animals in Colonial Singapore 1819–1920* (Singapore: NUS Press, 2019); Margo DeMello, *Animals and Society: An Introduction to Human-Animal Studies* (New York, NY: Columbia University Press, 2012), p. 4.

[6] Even some mammals are seen as pests in this regard, but tolerated for how they interact with their fellow creatures. In the case of stray cats, Ying-Kit Chan has suggested that they are largely ignored when they have a utilitarian function of catching rats and cockroaches and eating waste foods, but are perceived as carriers of pests, disease and viruses at other times. Ying-Kit Chan, "No Room to Swing a Cat? Animal Treatment and Urban Space in Singapore," *Southeast Asian Studies* 5, 2 (2016): 324; Lena Chan, "Nature in the City," in *Planning Singapore: The Experimental City*, ed. Stephen Hamnett and Belinda Yuen (London: Routledge, 2019), p. 129; DeMello, *Animals and Society*, p. 4.

Taking three insects—ants, flies and cockroaches—this chapter will explore how these creatures have been discursively globalized in a modernizing Singapore, and the reactions they have provoked from humans. Drawing on Levi-Strauss' framing that food needs to be both "good to eat" and "good to think," recent scholarship has extended ideas of "good to think" to insects.[7] That is, something good to think is not only a symbol but a very part of a structure of thinking. The most famous example being in the nature/culture pairing of raw and cooked. As Rebecca Earle reminds us, "food is both a daily necessity and a potent symbol, and it is therefore particularly effective at capturing anxieties." Things that imperil the safety of food, do more than ruin dinner, they pose a threat to life and health. Food safety is a form of food security. It should come as no surprise that the threat insects pose to food—eating it, spoiling it, and turning it from source of nutrition to source of disease—has been an ongoing source of anxiety, and one that was especially heightened in the context of post-war food shortages, and the experience of vermin-infested foods during wartime.[8]

The transformation of food from health-giving to health-taking underscores the power of pests to imperil daily pleasures and necessities. Insects could turn a dish that had been lovingly prepared and served from a symbol of domestic security to something that threatened life. That is a concern of this chapter too, as insects are both comfortable to think about (able to be fitted into recognized categories and systems of knowledge) and, more significantly, useful to think of as a metaphor. Insects help us to think about attempts at the control of space, the built environment and nature, to create a sanitary Singapore. Insects also help us think about power in Singapore, and how attempts to live with them or eliminate them have become part of the natural landscape as the authorities attempt to address a major drawback of tropical living.

---

[7] Insects are, of course, considered good to eat in a number of cuisines, and there is growing global interest in insects as a sustainable food source to replace conventional meat protein. Joshua Evans, Roberto Flore, and Michael Nom Frøst, *On Eating Insects: Essays, Stories and Recipes* (London: Phaidon, 2017); Uli Beisel, Ann H. Kelly and Noémi Tousignant, "Knowing Insects: Hosts, Vectors and Companions of Insects are Good to Think Science," *Science as Culture* 22, 1 (2013): 1–15; Claude Levi-Strauss, *Totemism*, tr. Rodney Needham (Boston, Mass: Beacon Press, 1971).

[8] Rebecca Earle, "'If You Eat Their Food…': Diets and Bodies in Early Colonial Spanish America," *American Historical Review* 115, 3 (2010): 712; Wong Hong Suen, *Wartime Kitchen: Food and Eating in Singapore, 1942–1950* (Singapore: Editions Didier Millet, 2009), p. 58.

Image 2.1: Poster reminding Singaporeans that insects make good thinking. National Environmental Agency (2005). Image courtesy of National Archives of Singapore.

The Metaphorical Creature

One of the most common creatures in Singapore is the ant. As Charlotte Sleigh notes in her cultural history of members of the family Formicidae, "ants get everywhere." This is true literally, but also metaphorically, as these insects have infiltrated "diverse and often surprising areas of cultural life."[9] Despite their ubiquitous presence, ants are difficult to find in the historical record. This has resulted in the common ant appearing as a metaphor that is used to educate and elucidate. The global allegory of the industrious ant, the worker who puts the common good above themselves, was present in Singapore, as elsewhere. The moral of the story, however,

---

[9] Charlotte Sleigh, *Six Legs Better: A Cultural History of Myrmecology* (Baltimore, MD: Johns Hopkins University Press, 2007), p. 16.

shifts to fit the political and social realties of the period, as demonstrated by a newspaper editorial published shortly after the Second World War, in which the author argued that "the social system" of ants is the "nearest thing in the non-human world to a totalitarian state. In fact, I should say that the totalitarian state is the nearest thing to the social system of the ants. Heaven forbid we should study from the ants!"[10]

The metaphorical ant is again in vogue in the 21st century as their colonies provide models for on-demand transaction processing systems; the practice of reducing sociability amongst sick ants is cited as a model for reducing disease risk; the willingness of older worker ants to take on higher risk tasks reflects their commitment to community; and, the aging of ants who perform different roles shows how aging is reflective of social context.[11] Despite their capacity to ruin food and be a domestic nuisance, as well as provide allegories for larger societal issues, humans in Singapore have historically been much more tolerant of ants than other insects. This has mainly been due to the perception that ants are not a threat as they do not pose an economic risk or destroy crops, and are (mistakenly) not understood to transmit disease.

The exception to this general tolerance of the ant in Singaporean history, and an instance where it does occasionally appear on the record, is the white ant, which is actually a termite (*Coptotermes*), not an ant. This insect was vilified not only in Singapore, but throughout the empire. Using India and white ants as his example, Rohan Deb Roy highlights how "entomo-politics was an intrinsic feature of colonial power," and this was applicable to tropical Southeast Asia. White ants were frequently written about in colonial files, which the paper-eating arthropods were wont to eat. Roy uses that rather deliciously ironic example to highlight how insects and imperialism are co-constitutive, with insects both shaping and being shaped by colonial power. White ants also ate wood, a key material of colonial infrastructure, not only of the obviously built environment but also of transportation and communication, wood was used in ships,

---

[10] S.R., "Ants and Sluggards," *Sunday Tribune*, 17 Aug. 1947, p. 6.
[11] Dharmendra Prasad Mahato and Ravi Shankar Singh, "Maximizing Availability for Task Scheduling in On-Demand Computing-Based Transaction Processing System Using Ant Colony Optimisation," *Concurrency and Computation Practice and Experience* 30, 11 (2018): e4405; Nick Bos, et al., "Sick Ants Become Unsociable," *Journal of Evolutionary Biology* 25, 2 (2012): 342–51; Yao-Hua Law, "Long Live the Queen: In Insect Societies, a Queen Can Live for Years, Whereas Workers Expire in Months. What Can Hives and Anthills Reveal about Aging?," *Science* 371, 6536 (2021): 1302–05.

docks, telegraph polls and railway sleepers. In Singapore, for example, white ants were condemned in colonial reports for the damage they caused to the libraries and archives of the Singapore Botanic Gardens. The result was the development of the perception that white ants were minute enemies, undermining colonial rule. They required "networks of strategies and everyday vigilance." Within the British empire, thus, white ants posed a particular threat and their management was connected to "ideologies of improvement—personal, moral, agrarian, and colonial." In Singapore, this extended to the presence of specialist services for their eradication, which deployed some of the same chemical approaches as in India, including nicotine.[12]

As an understanding of nature and the environment was a product of specifically British and imperial knowledge systems and "pests as they are conceived today only came to exist in the Malay states with the infusion and circulation of modern biology," Peter Triantafillou suggests this was a moment of epistemological cleaning in which reality was reordered to create the category "manageable pests." This was a taxonomy that stressed the economic, and the focus was on economic threats to colonial crops. Ants did not destroy coconut palms, which merited legislation in the late 19th century, nor did they imperil the rubber crop.[13] The colonial logic of ants as nuisance rather than threat continued in the post-war

---

[12] If white ants "ate into" the foundations of the British empire, domestic ants also provided metaphorical fodder for the activities of empire. Early entomologists used ant-raiding practices as an analogy for slavery. The ants were slave-makers, "stealing the young from an industrious race, and making slaves of them," and in this sense reflected human history. Other scholars extended this metaphor to the British empire and the ideological foundations of empire, with ants providing an archetype for British colonialism. Rohan Deb Roy, "White Ants, Empire, and Entomo-Politics in South Asia," *Historical Journal* 63, 2 (2020): 413–17, 422; Starr Douglas and Felix Driver, "Imagining the Tropical Colony: Henry Smeathman and the Termites of Sierra Leone," in *Tropical Visions in an Age of Empire*, ed. Felix Driver and Luciana Martins (Chicago: University of Chicago Press, 2005), p. 92; Anonymous, "Straits Termite Company Advertisement," *Singapore Free Press* [hereafter, *SFP*], 14 May 1948, p. 5; Timothy P. Barnard, *Nature's Colony: Empire, Nation, and Environment in the Singapore Botanic Gardens* (Singapore: NUS Press, 2016), p. 173; Pierre Huber, *The Natural History of Ants* (London: Longman, Hurst, Rees, Orme, and Brown, 1820), p. 278; Carissa Chew, "The Ant as Metaphor: Orientalism, Imperialism and Myrmecology," *Archives of Natural History* 46, 2 (2019): 348, 353.

[13] Peter Triantafillou, "Governing Agricultural Progress: A Genealogy of the Politics of Pest Control in Malaysia," *Comparative Studies in Society and History* 43, 1 (2001): 196–7; Barnard, *Nature's Colony*, pp. 125–7.

era. This particular insect was simply a part of colonial society, present albeit not cherished.

Due to this non-threatening status, ants became figures of mirth or the subject of cautionary tales. The unfortunate case of Kam Ti Kian represents this understanding of the ant in Singaporean society. A 50-year-old house cook, Kam was using a lighted cigarette to kill ants in 1946, when he accidently ignited some cordite fuses left by military personnel in a recently derequisitioned property. The fatal explosive result served as a cautionary tale about the management of the pests. Or, there is the account of the ant-eater who refused to eat ants, a terrible concern for its school-teacher owner, which the press framed as an amusing anecdote. Or, the case of the ants who ate only red stamp-pad ink and not black ink at the Imperial Chemical Industries offices in England and were therefore showing their political colors (and a preference for glycerin), was likewise a joke. It was almost as amusing as when David Niven disrupted a love scene with Ann Blyth on the set of *The King's Thief* because his hair piece was full of ants.[14] All were stories conveyed in the Singaporean press.

While ants posed a threat to food, especially sweet food, they were not vilified in the same way other insects were in Singapore. This is startling because ants can carry and transfer bacteria, and are a source of food-borne illnesses. A recent study even showed that ants had a 70 percent transference rate for *E. coli*, and could also transfer listeria and salmonella. Contemporary perceptions of ants as an irritant rather than a public health risk remain and are, thus, in-step with historical perceptions, despite the role of ants as vectors of disease.[15] The challenge of managing ants led to acceptance; they were a pest that was tolerated rather than eliminated. In this sense, ants are also a *metonymy* for post-colonial Singapore, where across a number of areas regulation has been as much a strategy as prohibition.

---

[14] Anonymous, "Killed Ants, Set Fuses, Clothes Alight," *Morning Tribune*, 16 Nov. 1946, p. 3; Anonymous, "The Ant-Eater Who Refuses to Eat Ants," *SFP*, 3 Nov. 1959, p. 13; Anonymous, "The Ants Weren't Politicians," *SFP*, 7 May 1948, p. 6; Anonymous, "Toupee Tickle," *SFP*, 8 Feb. 1955, p. 11.

[15] Leckranee Simothy, Fawzi Mahomoodally and Hudaa Neetoo, "A Study on the Potential of Ants to Act as Vectors of Foodborne Pathogens," *AIMS Microbiology* 4, 2 (2018): 333; Laurent Keller and Elisabeth Gordon, *The Lives of Ants* (New York, NY: Oxford University Press, 2009), p. 139.

Indicators of Health

While ants were part of the Singaporean faunal landscape, and for the most part an accepted presence because they were not linked to matters of public health, flies were another matter entirely. These insects of the order Diptera, which refers to their "two wings" in Greek, comprise over one million different species. In Singapore, as is true in many places around the world, this mainly referred to the housefly (*Musca domestica*). Their presence was one that moved beyond the metaphorical to one linked to societal transformation. Awareness and urbanization created pests in Singapore, resulting in investments in public health and infrastructure to manage this threat.[16] Was this a public matter or a private one? Pests posed a particular threat within the home—they contaminated food, made children sick and spread disease—but the idea that they originated outside the home, in public spaces that were ill-tended, held particular sway. Who should hold private companies to account? What about itinerant merchants?

Concern for how these pests would be managed was manifested in public lamentations over poor municipal services, especially with regard to waste collection and the management of drains in Singapore. In 1948, for example, the Singaporean Ratepayers Association wrote to the Director of Medical Services and the Municipal Health Officer, to complain that many public drains were in a "filthy state," as municipal garbage collectors did not adequately clear food waste and were careless in the collection of bins, allowing rubbish to accumulate, which, in turn, provided breeding grounds for flies. An irate letter writer in 1953 continued along these same lines with complaints directed at "moth-eaten officials," that is the City Councilors who were "kind to the maggots" due to their inattention in monitoring a hygienic food supply. With sarcasm dripping from the page, the critic wondered if, with their faith that cooked food was safe, "Singaporeans take a sadistic delight in poisoning themselves." Just because toasting could make unwrapped bread safe from maggots, beetles, mice or cockroaches, it did not mean that it created sufficient public protection, he reasoned. This concern with public health and public responsibility,

---

[16] As Fiona Williamson has noted, in relation to water management and urban-planning, crisis did not necessarily translate into sustained response as the "British were ill (or un-)prepared to manage urban water" in late 19th-century Singapore. Fiona Williamson, "Responding to Extremes: Managing Urban Water Scarcity in the late Nineteenth-Century Straits Settlements," *Water History* 12, 3 (2020): 260.

and pests, continued into the decade when another letter writer noted during a drought that "we now have around us stinking pits breeding flies, encouraging vermin capable of carrying disease to each and any of us."[17] Flies were not like ants, they were more than just a nuisance, they could not just be swotted away; their buzzing signalled the need for intervention.

Flies, however, were not always considered harbingers of disease. In 19th-century America, for example, "Children's books portrayed buzzing, flitting flies as benign domestic companions, ideal for piquing infants' curiosity." Dawn Biehler has suggested that the "flies' habit of washing their faces with their forelegs gave an impression of cleanliness; they also seemed to act as the garbage-men of the insect world as they consumed organic matter." The idea that flies played a critical role as "decomposers in the order of the natural world" had existed since the 1800s. So what changed? The investigations of typhoid fever in US army bases during the Spanish-American War of 1898, which highlighted the connection between flies and disease transmission.[18] A decade later Leland Osslan Howard published his seminal treatise on the housefly, which firmly cemented the villainous role of the fly as a vector of disease. In a review of the book, *Nature* hedged its bets, noting that:

> Whether or not it acts as a carrier of infantile diarrhea, which during the summer months frequently causes great mortality among young children, is not yet conclusively established; but that it is capable of carrying tubercle bacilli is certain, and tuberculosis and the other diseases mentioned do not exhaust the list of what are at least potential dangers connected with the house-fly.[19]

---

[17] "The disgrace of Singapore" was traced to "the cesspool known as Rochor Canal." Anonymous, "Rate Payers Complain," *Sunday Tribune*, 27 Jun. 1948, p. 3; Borgia, "Councillors Are Kind to the Maggots," *SFP*, 9 Sep. 1953, p. 12; Public Health, "The Grave Danger to Health in S'pore," *The Straits Times* [hereafter, *ST*], 3 Jun. 1963, p. 8.

[18] Biehler, *Pests in the City*, pp. 4, 222; James Samuelson, *Humble Creatures: The Earthworm and the Common Housefly: In Eight Letters* (London: Van Voorst, 1858); Vincent J. Cirillo, "'Winged Sponges': House-flies as Carriers of Typhoid Fever in 19th- and Early 20th-Century Military Camps," *Perspectives in Biology and Medicine* 49, 1 (2006): 54.

[19] L.O. Howard, *The House-fly: Disease Carrier: An Account of Its Dangerous Activities and of the Means of Destroying It* (New York, NY: Frederick Stokes, 1911); A. E.,

Attitudes towards the fly had really hardened by the start of the 20th century. The "house fly came to embody fears for the mental, moral and physical well-being of nations that were intent upon populating robust empires." Flies as vectors of disease "depleted the fight ranks of patriotic soldiers," and "depleted the ranks of future generations," by mid-century this meant as carriers of poliomyelitis.[20]

In the 19th century, poliomyelitis, or polio, which had been present for thousands of years but relatively uncommon, became regularly epidemic, intensifying in the early to mid-20th century. The most likely explanation for this shift is that the age at which children encountered polio increased as hygiene increased. Infants who were infected whilst breastfeeding had sufficient antibodies from maternal milk, but that passive immunity protection declined after the first year. Better personal hygiene and public sanitation reduced low-level exposure, meaning that when they encountered the virus young children had neither passive immunity nor sufficient antibodies.[21]

Singapore followed this international pattern and experienced regular outbreaks of polio as the city grew more sanitary, and by mid-century there were annual polio seasons until mass immunisation in the 1960s. In some years, such as 1946, 1948 and 1958, the scale of the epidemic was larger, resulting in more public attention. The fly became intertwined with public health messaging and measures during this period. In the context of poor public sanitation, while polio is transmitted through contact with bodily fluids from an infected person, it is fecal contamination, especially of water, that was the common vector in polio transmission. This understanding also led to the idea that food could be the source of the virus, and that flies were the vector of transmission. In addition, polio was associated with hot weather especially in the Northern Hemisphere. It was a summertime disease, flourishing in the same environment and conditions in which flies can be found. In equatorial Singapore the logic of seasonal association was less clear, but was discussed in reference to temperature and an absence of rain. That is, the disease was a product

---

"Book Review of 'The House-fly: Disease Carrier: An Account of its Dangerous Activities and of the Means of Destroying It,'" *Nature* 88, 2202 (1912): 345–6.
[20] J.F.M. Clark, *Bugs and the Victorians* (New Haven, CT: Yale University Press, 2009), p. 217.
[21] Neal Nathanson and Olen M. Kew, "Emergence to Eradication: The Epidemiology of Poliomyelitis Deconstructed," *American Journal of Epidemiology* 172, 11 (2010): 1214.

of the dry season as cases commonly were highest from April to July, as in the 1948 epidemic.[22]

In the midst of the 1948 epidemic, an editorial on the inconsistency of the school closing policies, grappled with the contradictions of the disease. "A mystifying factor of the polio situation is the apparent extreme vulnerability of Europeans, who so infinitesimally small a proportion of the city's population, have succumbed to the disease in surprisingly large numbers." One of the perplexing characteristics of polio epidemics was that clean well-nourished middle-class children had higher rates of infection than the less privileged. This was the "too-clean problem," which refers to the hygiene hypothesis, where excessive cleaning removes the protection of exposure to dirt, allergens, viruses and so forth. Counterintuitively, cleanliness resulted in sickness. While it was eventually understood that "good sanitation provided dangerous barriers to natural infection," realization was slow, and public health officials continued to emphasize cleanliness as essential in battling polio. The British Medical Council's advice to "keep your children scrupulously clean and see they get as much fresh air as possible," as well as "pay still stricter attention to hygiene," supplemented local advice.[23]

John Laycock pushed the government at a Legislative Council Meeting in May 1948 to do more, especially in relation to cleaning up "the filthy conditions of the town." For the lawyer this issue was simple, the municipal authorities were just not doing enough, and were too slow. "People are getting tired of what they consider to be a lack of action," Laycock explained, "when they see disease spreading, they again ask that all possible measures be taken because they are not satisfied that the Commissioners are doing all they can." The Colonial Secretary, P.A.B. McKerron, had to admit that there was an accumulation of rubbish. Flies would ultimately become an indicator of the seriousness of the problem.[24]

The importance of flies arose in the early days of the 1948 outbreak, when commentators were confident about their understanding of the disease and its vectors. The situation was "serious" but, as the *Malaya Tribune* described, it was "not a cause for alarm." The reason for this

---

[22] L.H. Lee and K.A. Lim, "Prevention of Poliomyelitis in Singapore by Live Vaccine," *British Medical Journal* 1, 5390 (1964): 1077.
[23] Anonymous, "Polio and Schools," *Sunday Tribune*, 23 May 1948, p. 6; Anonymous, "Facts about Polio," *ST*, 20 Jul. 1947, p. 6; Nancy Rogers, *Dirt and Disease Polio before FDR* (New Brunswick, NJ: Rutgers University Press, 1992), p. 166.
[24] Anonymous, "Matter of Emergency," *ST*, 19 May 1948, p. 1.

One Drawback of Tropical Living

confidence was the low levels of *Musca domestica*. Polio, while "a mystery disease," it was argued, "arises from contagion, principally spread by flies." This was a matter of little concern as there are "remarkably few flies in Singapore, even in the congested and dirty parts of the city."[25] In a letter to the editor a month later a concerned resident shared three days of their "Dustbin Diary," in which every entry contained details of matters pertaining to public hygiene. As an exemplar:

> "May 23: 7am. Shocked to see near the junction of Tembeling and Duku Roads, 20 Municipal dustbins without covers each about three feet high filled to overflowing with the filth of a thickly populated area. Rats as big as cats and all the stray dogs and cats having their breakfast on the contents. Millions of flies hovering over to collect the polio germ and bring it to any unfortunate being in the vicinity."[26]

In the midst of a public health crisis the failure of the municipal authorities was being clearly articulated. The (mistaken) connection between flies and polio was accepted as common knowledge.

In another letter to the editor on the same day, someone calling themselves "Anti-Polio" provided what can only be described as an information sheet about the disease. The list-maker referred to causes, hosts, mode of infection, site of lesion, mode of spread, seven actions for prevention, immunity, and treatment. Aside from general public health advice, "Anti-Polio" recommended social distancing, "isolation of infected cases, quarantine of direct contacts," and increased hand-washing, all approaches for handling a global pandemic with which we are again familiar in the 21st century. Beyond these recommendations for human behavior, flies were the main focus as these insects were purportedly the primary vector between infected people and fecal matter. Under these circumstances, there were several tactics, all focused on eliminating the pests: "(a) Kill all flies. (b) Destroy breeding ground and fly maggots. (c) Remove or cover rubbish dumps. (d) Cattle sheds, stables – clean maintenance."[27] Singapore had a low incidence of flies but this did not mean they should be tolerated.

---

[25] Anonymous, "Polio Danger," *Malaya Tribune*, 28 Apr. 1948, p. 4.
[26] Observer, "Singapore Dustbin Diary," *ST*, 29 May 1948, p. 9.
[27] Anti-Polio, "Polio at a Glance," *ST*, 29 May 1948, p. 9.

In 1953, J.A. Reid, in a bulletin devoted to flies in Malaya for the Institute for Medical Research in the Federation of Malaya, was cautiously optimistic about the number of the insects in Singapore. Climatic advantage, especially rain-fall, and health measures were the main factors Reid identified in their non-proliferation. Complacency and a false sense of good fortune had to be held in check. The number of these pests living in the British colony was, according to Reid, only relative to drier places with more flies. Ultimately, the impression of people who lived in the good residential areas of Malaya that house-flies are uncommon was "quite incorrect" as a breakdown in hygiene could quickly led to a fly problem. Reid fundamentally believed that information was the best weapon in the war against flies, and he provided plainly written details about their lifecycle and habits to empower officials in their eradication. Using this data about the range of the creature (half a mile from breeding grounds, unless there was insufficient food), he argued for the removal of waste that attracted flies. Reid aimed to "help Health Officers" with his "non-technical as possible" bulletin. House-flies he declared, were a problem as carriers of disease because of their feeding habits:

> The female fly must have carbohydrates and water for flight, and protein to develop the eggs. One minute the fly may be feeding on faeces or other protein-containing filth, thereby fouling its feet and mouth-parts, and the next on sweet cakes, sweet drinks, or other carbohydrate foods, up which, if these are solid, it may regurgitate part of the former meal to dissolve them.[28]

Once the full horror of flies had been detailed, Reid moved back to the mantra of prevention rather than cure as "flies are best controlled by prevention of their breeding, not by trying to cure breeding after it has occurred." Eliminating desirable breeding spots, not the use of insecticides, which were expensive and not as effective, was the solution.[29]

The identification of dirty places that harbored flies in Singapore was the first step in achieving clean spaces. Reid identified vegetable gardens and pigsties as the primary fly-breeding spaces during the 1950s. The elimination of these sites appeared a difficult task, but it was the beginning

---

[28] J.A. Reid, *Notes on House-Flies and Blow-Flies in Malaya* (Kuala Lumpur: Government Press, 1953), pp. 1, 6.
[29] Reid, *Notes on House-Flies and Blow-Flies in Malaya*, p. 17.

of their being targeted by public health programs. While vegetable gardens were not prohibited, they became increasingly uncommon in late 20th-century Singapore as they were replaced by high-rise housing and pig farming was phased out by the 1980s. Fly control, Reid concluded, was like mosquito control—it required constant vigilance.[30]

The government conveyed the importance of cleanliness to all communities with particular rigor over several decades. These efforts went beyond piggeries and vegetable gardens. This is evident in a Chinatown performance program from 1958, during which the Health Minister A. J. Braga oversaw a meeting to encourage 12 "Chinatown story-tellers" to incorporate polio precautions into their opening announcements. Their advice was to "be clean" and "to eat only cooked food."[31] By numbers Chinese children were the most common victims of polio, reflecting their larger population, rather than greater susceptibility. Indians and Eurasians were smaller communities but had proportionally higher case numbers. Cases were the highest amongst Europeans (typically 74 per 100,000), and they were lowest amongst Malays (typically 23 per 100,000). In English-language mediums there was relatively little attention paid to either issues of cleanliness or other preventive measures for the Malay community. They were, however, regularly cited as victims of disease. The story of Yusoff Bin Ali, gives a good example, as he was a polio survivor who had lost the use of his arms, and created paintings by holding a brush in his mouth.[32]

---

[30] Note the similarities with mosquito prevention detailed in Timothy P. Barnard's chapter in this collection. Cynthia Chou, "Agriculture and End of Farming in Singapore," in *Nature Contained: Environmental Histories of Singapore*, ed. Timothy P. Barnard (Singapore: NUS Press, 2014), pp. 216–40; Harvey Neo, "Placing Pig Farming in Post-Independence Singapore: Community, Development and Landscapes of Rurality," in *Food, Foodways and Foodscapes: Culture, Community and Consumption in Post-Colonial Singapore*, ed. Lily Kong and Vineeta Sinha (Singapore: World Scientific, 2015), pp. 83–102; Reid, *Notes on House-Flies and Blow-Flies in Malaya*, p. 23.

[31] Although some social spaces, such as the toddy shops that Indian workers mainly frequented, were seen as especially dirty and understood to pose a threat to the social order, they were not the focus of anti-polio campaigns. Darinee Alagirisamy, "Toddy, Race, and Urban Space in Colonial Singapore, 1900–59," *Modern Asian Studies* 53, 5 (2019): 1692; Anonymous, "Chinatown Story Men Fight Polio," *ST*, 21 Oct. 1958, p. 7.

[32] J.H. Hale, M. Doraisingham and K. Kanagaratnam, "Large-Scale Use of Sabin Type 2 Attenuated Poliovirus Vaccine in Singapore During a Type 1 Poliomyelitis Epidemic," *The British Medical Journal* 1, 5137 (1959): 1542; Mohamed Khir

Image 2.2: Anti-Polio Vaccination at Lim Ah Pin Road Clinic, 21 October 1958, MITA. Courtesy of National Archives of Singapore.

The development and distribution of the polio vaccination in Singapore began in 1958 and led to an abandonment of the fly–polio nexus. Within an 11-week period that year the number of cases on the island were almost triple of that during the 1948 epidemic, and there was a particularly high infection rate among children aged 7–12. In response the Minister of Health made live-strain vaccines available to children between three months and ten years old, although there was an apprehension that this would lead to community transmission through excreted virus. Despite these concerns, there was intense community demand. In a single day in October, for example, 2,000 parents and children packed the Lim Ah Pin Road clinic for the polio vaccination. During the year, Singapore became a test site for polio prevention, successfully vaccinating 198,965 children with minimal adverse outcomes. By 1962 the polio vaccine had been added to the regular schedule of childhood vaccinations, and 60 percent of under-fives had been vaccinated by the end of that year.[33]

While much of the initial concern over flies was linked to polio, the connection between flies, disease and food persisted after the development of a vaccine because it seemed that was where the chain of infection could be broken for a variety of ailments, and this led to a rise in food safety advice. One of the most common approaches in fighting the pest of flies became washing fruits and vegetables with the disinfectant potassium permanganate, known in Singapore as "pinki" or "pinki pani," or by the brand name Condy's (Fluid). If used, these disinfectants symbolically transformed fresh food from feared to clean. The dirt and disease carried on the feet of flies could be washed away. In advice for the supervision of amahs in the 1940s, it was suggested that children should only be given fruit that had been well washed with absolutely clean water "on in a very weak solution of Condy's Fluid." As late as 1959 the "Nurse Meg" advice column recommended uncooked fruits and vegetables be washed in the pale pink solution of Condy's crystals to prevent reinfection by threadworms. The trope of disinfecting food, making clean an impure item,

---

Johari, "He Paints—With His Mouth," *Sunday Standard*, 14 Jan. 1951, p. 12.
[33] Vincent J. Cirillo, "'I am the Baby Killer!' House Flies and the Spread of Polio," *American Entomologist* 62, 2 (2016): 85; Hale, Doraisingham, and Kanagaratnam, "Large-Scale Use of Sabin Type 2 Attenuated Poliovirus Vaccine in Singapore During a Type 1 Poliomyelitis Epidemic," pp. 1537–8; Lee and Lim, "Eradication of Poliomyelitis in Singapore," pp. 35–6; Hsu Li Yang and Vincent Pang Junxiong, *Infectious Diseases and Singapore: Past, Present, and Future* (Singapore: Society of Infectious Diseases, 2015), pp. 30–2.

sat alongside the rhetoric of protecting a pure food from contamination. The pure can become contaminated and the unclean can be washed. In both instances the comestible had to be treated before consumption in order to keep the body safe.[34]

The World Health Organization noted the Singaporean success in the management of flies by the 1980s, proclaiming the nation as "by far the most 'fly-free' country in South-Eastern Asia." The source of this successful management, some three decades after Reid's initial treatise, was a "rigorous refuse disposal system" involving bagged rubbish and tight-fitting lids, which reduced breeding grounds for flies. The nation and its rubbish had evolved, although it evoked a tried-and-tested approach. The best way of dealing with the fly problem, Howard wrote in his canonical treaties on the house-fly in 1912, is to prevent them from breeding, an approach that remained a guideline for the entire 20th century. It was even repeated in a booklet from the Primary Production Department of Singapore 70 years after Howard, echoing Reid's sentiments too.[35] Cleanliness was the cornerstone to a fly-free and healthy society.

The focus on cleanliness and public health since the 1950s, and the role of insects, can be seen in a public health poster from 1961. The messaging was clear: Flies Spread Diseases. That phrase, repeated in vernacular languages, was accompanied by familiar iconography—a massively oversized fly, enormous in comparison to the people it is making sick—bears down on a plate of food to sully it with disease. The diseases it spreads are not named, but the symptoms of headaches, stomach aches, coughs, and diarrhea are illustrated through the bodies of four unwell men. The colorful plate of food gives the impression of rice, greens and fish, and contrasts with the stark and detailed black and white image of the fly. The tiny veins that run across the wings of a fly are shown, making the fly a scientific illustration, and thereby a scientific

---

[34] Lim Kok Gek, "Prevention of Polio," *Malaya Tribune*, 21 May 1948, p. 4; Cecilia Leong-Salobir, *Food Culture in Colonial Asia: A Taste of Empire* (New York, NY: Routledge, 2011), p. 132; Anonymous, "You and Your Amah," *Morning Tribune*, 26 Sep. 1941, p. 5; Nurse Meg, "You Must Keep Their Hands Clean," *SFP*, 20 Nov. 1959, p. 9.

[35] World Health Organisation, "Dengue" Haemorrhagic Fever Control Programme in Singapore: A Case Study on the Successful Control of Aedes aegypti and Aedes albopictus Using Mainly Environmental Measures as a Part of Integrated Vector "Control," WHO/VBC/86.928. Unpublished, 1986, p. 30; Anonymous, *Control of Flies* (Singapore: Primary Production Department, Pamphlet No. E 41, 1984), p. 9.

One Drawback of Tropical Living

Image 2.3: Flies Spread Diseases poster, Ministry of Culture, 1961. Courtesy of National Archives of Singapore.

threat. Even as flies were managed, the idea of a correlation between dirt and disease persisted, and can be seen in relation to other insects, such as the cockroach, a creature that has been harder to manage than the fly. Cockroaches move between public and private spaces, tracking dirt and disease with them, and attempts at eradication—along with flies, mosquitoes and a host of other insects—would become an increasingly frequent symbol of a modernizing society and how it addresses unwanted creatures in its midst.

Eliminating a Threat

In 1940, W.L. Blakemore gave a radio address in the "Health Talk" series on the perils of the cockroach. As the Health Officer for Singapore, he found similarities between flies and cockroaches. Each insect has an "unfortunate habit," he noted, with regard to their propensity for emptying "its bowel while it is feeding." Like flies, cockroaches were disliked, but elimination was complex. Having identified favored locations (drains and septic tanks), Blakemore turned to the matter of dealing with the insects.[36] He provided detailed instructions for homemade traps, made from various materials—jam jars, tin cans, cones of paper—to be laid with stale beer or peeled banana, complete with wooden or cardboard stairways for the cockroach to get from the floor to the trap. If these elaborate contraptions did not succeed, there were commercial poisons, such as borax and liquid insecticides, but there were also homemade solutions. Boric acid, Blakemore suggested, was more effective if mixed with powered chocolate or sugar. Sodium fluoride also could be mixed with powdered pyrethrum and scattered on the floor, but should be swept up in the morning. Failing all of these, he suggested killing them with a slipper or even a bare hand, a common approach to dealing with all insects. If the hand method was used, there was no need to be worried about disease, but it was advised to wash "one's hand thoroughly afterwards to remove the 'roachy' smell."[37]

Despite such an array of suggestions, cockroaches continued to be a problem in post-war Singapore. By 1962, *The Straits Times* even proposed that the time had come for the residents of the island to eliminate as many of the pests as possible. The cockroach was a hanger-on, living rent-free, but in order to fight an enemy you had to know it, according to the article, and thus paragraphs of information were provided. From species to body length, sex difference to lifecycle and rate of reproduction (on average 70 pods per female, 30 eggs per pod, 30 days to hatching), the details of the *Periplaneta american* were provided in order to show that "the damage they do is fantastic." The information was in fact a promotion for Flit, an American insecticide marketed extensively in Singapore. In its advertisements, the insects—flies most often, but also ants and cockroaches—were depicted as oversized menaces who contaminated food and imperiled the lives of vulnerable families.[38]

Throughout the 1960s Flit advertorials transformed into a regular column in the Singaporean press. The face of the articles was Lucy Huang,

---

[36] There are three species of cockroach in Singapore: the American (*Periplaneta americana*), the German (*Blatella germanica*), and the less common Brown-banded (*Supella longipalpa*).

[37] W.L. Blakemore, *Cockroaches* (Singapore: Singapore Government Printer, 1940), pp. 1–3.

[38] Anonymous, "It's Irrelevant? Not at All!," *ST*, 29 Dec. 1961, p. 6; Nicole Tarulevicz, "Sensing Safety in Singapore," *Food, Culture and Society* 21, 2 (2018): 164–79.

One Drawback of Tropical Living

Image 2.4: Flit canister, ca. 1954–55. Courtesy of the Smithsonian Institution (https://www.si.edu/object/flit-5-ddt:nmah_1141914).

who positioned Flit as a product for Chinese consumers on the island. She claimed that it was widely used in China, explaining that the word "flit" had become both a noun and a verb "to stand for insecticide altogether in the language." She detailed qualities of the product, which mirrored the conventional advertisements while also emphasizing the ability of Chinese consumers to recognize quality when they saw it. "Back home in China," Huang asserted, "we have always used Flit." First sold in 1923, Flit was thus rendered timeless. It was also, she insisted, ubiquitous. "The little Flit sentry with his high helmet and rifle hoisted on his shoulder was a family sight in every household." Flit, however, was not just for China; Huang and her husband Bill still "believe in Flit today" and used it regularly in Singapore. Their usual practice was to close all the doors and windows once a week and "Flit the whole place." As she extolled readers, "try it and see if I am not right!"[39] This was an insecticide to clean the Singaporean household.

---

[39] Lucy Huang, "Definition of Honeymoon: Glorious Holiday Month," *ST*, 9 Mar. 1962, p. 8. Flit was widely sold in China in the 1930s. When this column was published it was at the tail end of the Four Pests Campaign (除四害) which targeted mosquitos, rodents, flies, and sparrows. Although DDT was used, it is unlikely that in 1962 it was Flit Brand. Huang's reference to "Back home in China" is read here as a reference to pre-Revolutionary China.

In another advertorial, Huang focused on the insecticide and its use in an equatorial climate. Although Malayans were blessed with many sunny days in which they could enjoy swimming, picnicking, and going on drives, they also had a more sinister outcome. As Huang argued, "hot weather, fun though it may be, brings with it one of the main drawbacks of tropical living," that is insects. The tone of the column continued to darken as it detailed the danger that pests represented. This ranged from flies who "come in swarms as soon as the wet weather stops," to cockroaches who in the warmth "prowl in the evenings, drawn out of their dark hiding places by lights and hunger." The threat insects posed was then catalogued—they bite children, make a mess around lamps and ceilings (an odd combination), "soil food and eating surfaces," and are ultimately a "menace to good health." In the logic of advertising, a solution was provided: Flit. The qualities of this insecticide—ease of use, economical price, and effectiveness, especially effectiveness—were stressed. "Flit is a combination of extremely efficient insecticidal chemicals, which, put together, make a powerful bug-killer that goes to work the minute it is sprayed out of its handy gun."[40]

The role of these insecticide promotions, and their depiction of the enemy, were a standard feature in the Singaporean press since the Second World War. As the post-war period or modernity progressed, however, they soon began endorsing a new addition to the arsenal of anti-insect measure. This began as early as 1947, when a "Special Woman Correspondent" penned a long article encouraging readers not to fear of "one of the greatest scientific discoveries of the last ten years," which even "rivals the importance of penicillin." The weapons to fight insects would include the latest technologies. Flit soon incorporated formulas containing Dichlorodiphenyltrichloroethane, or DDT, a standard ingredient in insecticides used in Singapore and throughout the world for decades.[41]

An odorless and colorless chemical compound, DDT was first synthesized in the late 19th century although its insecticidal properties were only first realized in the late 1930s. The Allies employed the compound extensively during the Second World War, and it was most famously used to counter a typhus outbreak in Naples in 1942, which

---

[40] Lucy Huang, "Sunshine Again and It's Time for Outdoor Fun," *ST*, 16 Feb. 1962, p. 6.

[41] Flit contained 5% DDT, as did other brands used in Singapore during the period. Special Woman Correspondent, "Don't Be Afraid of D.D.T.," *SFP*, 17 Mar. 1947, p. 2.

was a critical juncture in public health. Vaccination, or patient treatment, no longer managed disease; vector control now took precedent, and thus medical etymology and tropical medicine became deeply entwined disciplines. This was the medicalization of the management of disease through the elimination of insects. In the case of typhus, killing the louse that transmitted it became the primary approach in treatment.[42] DDT would become a vital weapon in the war against insects, and Singapore was one of the battlegrounds.

The benefits of DDT, and its relationship to public health, became a standard feature of advertorials promoting various insecticides throughout the island. In the piece from "Special Woman Correspondent," readers were told that in Naples "1,300,000 civilians were dusted" with DDT-laced powder and "within three weeks the outbreak was completely under control, the first time in history where a typhus epidemic has been stopped mid-winter." When applied to Singapore, it would give humans a tremendous advantage over insects. If used correctly, DDT would be "a wonderful protector of life and health."[43] The story was, of course, more complicated.

The safety of DDT was insisted upon in the Singaporean press, as it was considered "completely harmless to man and all the higher animals even including fish," if used correctly. There were limits, however, to this correct usage. Although proponents of the chemical compound claimed that "the dust is harmless to animals and human beings," and "does dissolve in oil," it was best if, "when you are spraying your walls, take care to move the baby into another room!" Housewives were also encouraged to avoid spraying DDT on surfaces that came into contact with food. It was best practice to "remove your dishes and hermetically seal any cupboard in your pantry, before having your walls sprayed."[44]

In less than a decade after residents were told not to be afraid of DDT, nonetheless, the news that some house-flies were resistant to

---

[42] Special Woman Correspondent, "Don't Be Afraid of D.D.T.," *SFP*, 17 Mar. 1947, p. 2; Clark, *Bugs and the Victorians*, p. 195; Darwin H. Stapleton, "A Lost Chapter in the Early History of DDT: The Development of Anti-Typhus Technologies by the Rockefeller Foundation's Louse Laboratory, 1942–1944," *Technology and Culture* 46, 3 (2005): 521.
[43] Special Woman Correspondent, "Don't Be Afraid of D.D.T."; Thomas R. Dunlap, *DDT, Silent Spring, and the Rise of Environmentalism* (Seattle, WA: University of Washington Press, 2008), p. 5.
[44] Anonymous, "D.D.T. Can Kill Rats, Scientists Find," *SFP*, 13 Sep. 1949, p. 3; Special Woman Correspondent, "Don't Be Afraid of D.D.T."

the insecticide appeared in the local press. In one newspaper article it was noted that "as a result of the world-wide attack on disease-carrying insects, most of the flies sensitive to DDT were wiped out, permitting the resistant, hard-shelled flies to reproduce in enormous numbers." The inadvertent selective breeding of flies led not to a questioning of DDT, but to the pursuit of stronger and alternative insecticides. Tucked between the article on resistant flies and new insecticides was a brief report on the death by mosquito of a 72-year-old Australian. The story of a man who contracted tetanus poisoning through "a mass" of infected mosquito bites, however unlikely, served as a reminded of the perils of insects in the tropics, and by logical extension, the necessity of reliance on such pesticides. In Singapore, DDT remained in use and was most strongly associated with the management of mosquitos, as their effect on flies or cockroaches seemed to be limited.[45]

By 1982, the World Health Organization declared Singapore as malaria free. While DDT had played a role in this achievement, insecticides were only part of the story. Much of the management of disease-carrying mosquitoes had occurred through programs focusing on elimination of breeding grounds, public health initiatives and fines.[46] Following this designation, the government finally addressed the growing disquiet about DDT, including residual effects in humans and the environment when it discontinued the use of the chemical in 1984.[47] In 2001, Singaporean authorities finally signed the Stockholm Convention on Persistent Organic Pollutants, which sought to control the production, use, trade, and disposal of DDT, amongst other organic pollutants. The use of an insecticide aimed at eliminating insects and aid in the creation of a modern, sanitized

---

[45] Anonymous, "Mosquito Killed Norman," *Malaya Tribune*, 29 Jan. 1949, p. 5; Anonymous, "DDT Can't Kill a Common House Fly," *Malaya Tribune*, 29 Jan. 1949, p. 5; Anonymous, "New Drug to Fight Tsetse Fly," *Malaya Tribune*, 29 Jan. 1949, p. 5.

[46] See the chapter by Timothy P. Barnard on mosquitoes in this collection for further information. K.T. Goh, "Eradication of Malaria from Singapore," *Singapore Medical Journal* 20, 5 (1983): 256.

[47] Rachel Carson's *Silent Spring* (1962) drew popular attention to DDT's avian affects, which have been extended to other specifics, including through oceans, see for example: Boris Worm, "Silent Spring in the Ocean," *Proceedings of the National Academy of Science* 112 (2015): 11752–3; X.W. Luo, S.C. Foo and H.Y. Ong, "Serum DDT and DDE levels in Singapore General Population," *The Science of the Total Environment* 208, 1 (1997): 103.

society had become another item on the list that helps us think insects, and how they reflect the human–animal relationship in Singapore.[48]

Conclusion

In his 1994 history of the meteoritic rise of the laboratory fly, Robert E. Kohler argued for treating flies in laboratories as material culture, as living instruments of science, especially for genetics. Reflecting two decades later on the legacy of his work, Kohler noted that "its productivity was not a property of the fly per se but of the fly in certain kinds of human practice."[49] Increasingly in Singapore insects are becoming productive through human practice. In 2018 Insectta, an urban insect farm in Singapore opened. They raise flies that they use to process food waste, they turn fly frass (fly poo) into organic plant food, and sell larvae for animal feed, echoing the 19th-century idea of flies as valued decomposers. Even more remarkably, Insectta is producing medical-grade chitosan. This valuable biomedical product is used in a variety of ways, from antimicrobial coatings on bandages and sutures, to a cholesterol-lowering supplement.[50] The transition from pest to valuable crop is a reminder of the economic logic that drives Singapore. Insects, which became a colonial pest when they impinged on colonial crops and eventually symbols of problems with public health, may well become heroes of the 21st century if they are profitable enough. This is one of the ways in which insects are good to think, shining a revealing light of the forces that shape Singapore.

For the period of focus in this chapter, the post-war and early independence era, insects were out of place; they were in the wrong

---

[48] Despite the Singaporean ban, levels of DDT in Singapore remained relatively high into the 1990s, most likely due to bio-concentration of the chemical residue in the food chain. Fish and meat raised on fishmeal are common sources, as algae (eaten by some fish, including fish turned into fishmeal) can contain high levels of DDT through bio-accumulation. Malaysia did not ban DDT until 1999 and was thus another (and continued) source of residual food chain DDT. Because of Singapore's reliance on the global pantry, the Singaporean ban did not result in a DDT-free island. Luo, Foo and Ong, "Serum DDT and DDE levels in Singapore General Population," p. 103.
[49] Robert E. Kohler, *Lords of the Fly: Drosophila Genetics and Experimental Life* (Chicago, IL: University of Chicago Press, 1994), p. 20; Robert Kohler, "Lords of the Fly Revisited," *Journal of the History of Biology* 55, 1 (2022): 16.
[50] Judith Tan and Vanessa Liu, "Turning Singapore's Trash to Treasure," *ST*, 27 Dec. 2018, p. 2.

place. This meant that insects were Singaporean creatures that merited a reaction from the human society on the island, which resulted in a plethora of attempts to manage the pests. These attempts reflected global networks of knowledge, and ranged from radical ones, like the elimination of conducive breeding environments, and the use of insecticides, through to homemade jam-jar traps, and public health messaging about eating cooked food and maintaining a healthy society. The literal and symbolic contamination of the pure and sustaining with the dirty and diseased was a powerful trope in Singapore.

CHAPTER THREE

Mosquitoes, Public Health and the Construction of a Modern Society

Timothy P. Barnard

Known by the sobriquet "little fly" in Spanish and Portuguese, members of the Culicidae family—which contains two subfamilies, Anophelinae and Culicinae—have been residents of Singapore for millennia. Once humans arrived on the shores of the island, the importance of these minute creatures grew exponentially, although they were noticed initially only when they buzzed past an ear canal or pierced a layer of skin for a drink. This ability to annoy humans was sufficient to merit comment from colonial figures such as James Low and Isabella Bird, who complained that these insects were "rather numerous at times" and "pests" of the first magnitude, respectively. Bird was particularly aggravated. She went on to describe these little flies, better known as mosquitoes as "the curse" of the tropics for their pursuit of "bloodthirsty work."[1]

---

[1] James Low, "Extracts from an Unpublished Journal of a Residence at Singapore during Part of 1840 & 41," *The Singapore Free Press and Mercantile Advertiser*, 16 Dec. 1841, p. 3; Isabella L. Bird, *The Golden Chersonese and the Way Thither* (New

Mosquitoes begin developing from eggs that have been laid in water, and it is the type of water body that plays an important role as different species like different aquatic environments. Once these eggs hatch, larvae remain in the water and transform into pupae and then mosquitoes over a period of about a week. The mosquito then can fly into the world and seek nutrition. This is when their lives begin to differ, depending on their sex. Male mosquitoes usually live for only 7–10 days, sustain themselves on nectar and fruit juices and then die. If they avoid predators, or even the swipe of a hand, they can live up to two months. Only rarely will a male mosquito bite a mammal. It is female mosquitoes that bite other creatures. They feed on blood, which provides protein and iron necessary for the production of their eggs, which they lay in water to start the cycle over again.[2] This life cycle, this history of the mosquito, is fairly simply, repeated millions of times a year in Singapore.[3]

By the end of the 19th century, mosquitoes transformed from mere annoyance, an insect going through its life cycle, to enemy after they were identified as a vector, or carrier, of diseases that threatened public health. Humans developed approaches to eradicate them in a transforming urban environment in Singapore. These attempts to monitor, regulate and eliminate these creatures provide a framework for a larger history of the mosquito, and provide new insights into larger developments and contexts in the Singaporean past. The history of efforts to control mosquitoes, and disrupt this repetitive life cycle, ultimately provide insight into human history, particularly the development of public health and the construction of a modern society on an island in Southeast Asia. The mosquito, and how humans reacted to it, reveals many of the transformations Singapore has undergone from colonial state to modern, technocratic nation over the past century.

York, NY: G.P. Putnam's Sons, 1883), p. 110.

[2] Timothy C. Winegard, *The Mosquito: A Human History of Our Deadliest Predator* (New York, NY: Dutton, 2019), pp. 7–29; Richard Jones, *Mosquito* (London: Reaktion Books, 2012); V.P. Sharma, "Water, Mosquitoes and Malaria," in *Water and Health*, ed. P.P. Singh and V. Sharma (New Delhi: Springer India, 2014), p. 155.

[3] A focus on the life cycle of a small insect, however, should not distract us from the larger context. As a Malay proverb states, "just because you are irritated by a mosquito, you burn the mosquito net" (*Marahkan nyamuk, habis kelambu dibakar*).

Identifying an Enemy, Developing a Strategy

There are many different genera and approximately 3,500 species in the Culicidae family. A recent survey of mosquitoes in Singapore recorded 182 different species, although these numbers shift and change occasionally due to taxonomic revisions. Among these species, 25 are of particular interest as they are known vectors of disease, with nine species being of particular concern as they may carry dengue, chikungunya, Zika virus and Japanese encephalitis, as well as malaria.[4] It is the presence of these diseases that have brought mosquitoes into the spotlight in Singapore as scientists and researchers have worked to not only identify the specific species but also how to contain and eliminate them.

As there is such a plethora of mosquito species in Singapore, it is easier to zoom out to consider a few specific genera as it is at this classification level that most people deal with the insect. The three most common genera of mosquitoes in Singapore are *Culex* (with 46 species), *Aedes* (37 species) and *Anopheles* (21 species). While some attention has been given to those in the *Culex* genera, as they have been known to carry Japanese encephalitis virus and *Wuchereria bancrofti* (which causes lymphatic filariasis), both diseases are relatively rare in Singapore. In contrast, *Aedes* and *Anopheles* are the main focus of mosquitogenic concern as these genera have been linked to dengue fever and malaria.

The recognition that there was a connection between various mosquito species and disease was the turning point in the larger history of the insect, when they transitioned from an irritation to a threat to human populations. In the 19th century, with the formulation of germ theory, there was a realization that microbes—and not "bad air" (the Latin origin of "malaria")—were the cause of disease, which were spread through a variety of vectors. The *Anopheles* mosquito was identified as one the primary vectors in malaria transmission when Ronald Ross made the connection between the insect and the deadly disease, which is caused by the parasite *Plasmodium falciparum* that manifests in fever, headaches, fatigue and—in severe cases—seizures, comas and death. By the early

---

[4] The nine malaria-carrying species are *Ae. (Stg.) aegypti, Ae. (Stg.) albopictus, An. (ano.) sinensis, An. (Cel.) epiroticus, An. (Ano.) letifer, An. (Cel.) maculatus* sensu lato, *Cx. (Cux.) gelidus, Cx. (Cux.) quinquefasciatus, Cx. (Cux.) tritaeniorhynchus*. Sai-Gek Lam-Phua, et al., "Mosquitoes (Diptera: Culicidae) of Singapore: Updated Checklist and New Records," *Journal of Medical Entomology* 56, 1 (2019): 104, 112; Jones, *Mosquito*, p. 22.

20th century, these mosquitoes—with their spotted wings and head-down, tail-up pose—had transformed into the primary focus of public health efforts in tropical colonies as scientists attempted to disrupt their life cycle in order to hinder the spread of this scourge.[5]

Diseases such as malaria had been a deterrent for European imperial expansion in the tropics.[6] To address these issues, public health and tropical medicine arose with the formation of administrative bodies—such as Institute of Tropical Medicine and the India Medical Service, where Ross worked—to further understand the relationship between disease, geography and colonial control. As historian Michael Worboys has stated, "tropical diseases and malaria in particular were invested with great importance as the major impediment to the economic and political development of the tropical empire." In Singapore and Malaya, this took on greater meaning with the clearing of lands for rubber cultivation, which created ideal breeding sites for mosquitoes and the transmission of diseases. Mosquitoes endangered the maintenance of a healthy workforce among the colonized, a key factor in the imperial export economy. If malaria "could be controlled," as Malcolm Watson—a prominent figure in public health throughout the British empire and a member of the Malayan Medical Service—clearly argued, coolies could "be much more

---

[5] The four most common malaria carriers in Singapore historically have been *An. (Ano.) sinensis*, *An. (Cel.) epiroticus*, *An. (Ano.) letifer*, *An. (Cel.) maculatus* sensu lato. Historically *Anopheles epiroticus* was *Anopheles sundaicus*, and the change reflects that taxonomic names for mosquitoes are updated constantly. This chapter will continue to use *An. sundaicus* as it is the most common form found in the historical literature. Lam-Phua, et al., "Mosquitoes (Diptera: Culicidae) of Singapore," p. 112; J.W. Scharf, D.W.G. Faris and W.A. Nicholas, *Malaria-Mosquito Control in Rural Singapore* (Singapore: Government Printing Office, 1937), pp. 1–2; Jones, *Mosquito*, pp. 22–3; Yip Ka-Che, *Disease, Colonialism, and the State: Malaria in Modern East Asian History* (Hong Kong: Hong Kong University Press, 2009); Michael Worboys, "Germs, Malaria and the Invention of Mansonian Tropical Medicine: From 'Diseases of the Tropics' to 'Tropical Diseases'," in *Warm Climates and Western Medicine: The Emergence of Tropical Disease, 1500–1900*, ed. David Arnold (Amsterdam: Rodopi, 1996), pp. 181–93; J. Dworkin and S.Y. Tan, "Ronald Ross (1857–1932): Discoverer of Malaria's Life Cycle," *Singapore Medical Journal* 52, 7 (2011): 466–7.

[6] The most famous example was Batavia, the main port on Java and the center of Dutch imperial efforts in Asia, where annual death rates for Westerners approached 50% for many periods of the 18th century, which scholars attributed to an increased presence of the malaria transmitting *An. sundaicus* following reclamation projects to develop the coastline of Java. P.H. van den Brug, "Malaria in Batavia in the 18th Century," *Tropical Medicine and International Health* 2, 9 (1997): 892–902.

efficient" and allow imperial industries to flourish.[7] Public health, under these circumstances, quickly began to focus on the *Anopheles* mosquito and the threat it represented to empire.[8]

In the late 1890s, soon after Ross discovered the link between mosquitoes and malaria, the authorities in Singapore initiated preliminary attempts to eliminate this insect from colonial society through the filling of pools and clearing of stagnant water in streams and ditches, which were known breeding sites for the creature.[9] These efforts were prioritized further after authorities recorded 2,000 deaths due to malaria annually from 1907 until 1910 in Singapore. By 1911, 30 percent of all hospital admissions in Singapore were attributed to malaria, and the mosquito-borne disease was second only to tuberculosis as the leading cause of death on the island. In light of this crisis, W.R.C. Middleton—the Municipal Health Officer—formed an "anti-malarial committee" to address the situation.[10] The first step was to perform "a systematic examination of

---

[7] Watson also won a gold medal from the Rubber Growers' Association for his work that allowed them to be more "efficient" in the use of imported labor. Malcolm Watson, "Malaria and Mosquitoes: Forty Years On," *Journal of the Royal Society of Arts* 87, 4 (1939): 488; Malcolm Watson, *The Prevention of Malaria in the Federated Malay States: A Record of Twenty Years' Progress* (New York, NY: E.P. Dutton and Company, 1921); Liew Kai Khiun, "Making Health Public: English Language Newspapers and the Medical Sciences in Colonial Malaya (1840s–1941)," *East Asian Science, Technology and Society* 3, 2 (2009): 216–19; Worboys, "Germs, Malaria and the Invention of Mansonian Tropical Medicine," pp. 194, 181–3; Philip D. Curtin, "Disease and Imperialism," in *Warm Climates and Western Medicine: The Emergence of Tropical Disease, 1500–1900*, ed. David Arnold (Amsterdam: Rodopi, 1996), pp. 99–108.

[8] An important aspect of these public health measures, not included in this chapter, is the development of quinine as a treatment and prophylactic. Colonial science, particularly in the Netherlands East Indies, played an important role in the development of this drug. Andrew Goss, "Building the World's Supply of Quinine: Dutch Colonialism and the Origins of the Global Pharmaceutical Industry," *Endeavour* 38, 1 (2014): 8–18.

[9] Italian physicians and scientists, including Giovanni Lacinsi, Giambattista Grassi, and Angelo Celli, were pioneers in the development of approaches that mainly focused on "draining the swamps," which eventually became the primary method of attacking malaria in Europe, and thus was transferred to the colonies. Eliana Ferroni, Tom Jefferson, and Gabriel Gachelin, "Angelo Celli and Research on the Prevention of Malaria in Italy a Century Ago," *Journal of the Royal Society of Medicine* 105, 1 (2012): 35–40.

[10] In addition, other members of the scientific establishment in Singapore also contributed to these anti-malarial efforts. For example, Richard Hanitsch—the

school children for signs of present and past malaria, ascertain the locality of their present abodes, and make an inspection of these localities for conditions contributing to the disease." Surveys were carried out, and Telok Blangah was identified as "the most malarious district in Singapore" with one school registering a rate of 46 percent of the students having enlarged spleens, a symptom of the disease. The Municipal Health Office sprang into action. "This area was taken in hand, subsoil pipers were put down, drains made and low lying ground was filled in," while officials distributed quinine for free and promoted "education of the people in the habits of mosquitoes." Within three years, by 1914, the total percentage of spleen enlargements in Telok Blangah was only 3.7 percent and "the amount of malaria in the district," officials crowed, had "decreased to what for all practical purposes may be called zero."[11] Humans were reacting to mosquitoes in Singapore, and a combination of public health and engineering would be the basis for reshaping the society, transforming it into a modern landscape.

This initial successful campaign against malaria in Telok Blangah provided the strategic blueprint for how mosquitoes would be confronted in Singapore for the next century. Much of the strategy was codified with the passage of Ordinance 174 (Destruction of Mosquitoes) in 1919, which allowed for general taxes to fund public health measures and sanctioned the work of "the Anti-Mosquito Committee" within the

---

Director of the Raffles Museum—conducted research on local freshwater fish and determined that they contributed to lower numbers of mosquito larvae in pools, and discouraged the importation of *Girardinus poeciloides* (currently *Poecilia reticulata*, or the common guppy) from Barbados for such a purpose as it would contribute little to alleviating the problem, which was primarily due to larvae found in small temporary pools, such as tin cans. He believed that better building and sanitation in urban areas would be of more help. Hanitsch also feared the consequences of introducing numerous non-native species to Singaporean waterways. R. Hanitsch, "Mosquito Larvae and Freshwater Fish," *Journal of the Straits Branch of the Royal Asiatic Society* 62 (1912): 26–30.

[11] Anonymous, "Municipal Commission. Valuable Anti-Malarial Work Accomplished," *The Straits Times* [hereafter, *ST*], 30 Jan. 1922, p. 10; P.S. Hunter, "Anti-Malarial Work in Singapore," in *The Prevention of Malaria in the Federated Malay States: A Record of Twenty Years' Progress*, ed. Malcom Watson (New York, NY: E.P. Dutton and Company, 1921), pp. 321–2; K.T. Goh, "Eradication of Malaria from Singapore," *Singapore Medical Journal* 24, 5 (1983): 256; Watson, "Malaria and Mosquitoes: Forty Years On," pp. 482–502, National Archives of Singapore: MOH/01/66. M.J. Colbourne, "Report of an Enquiry into the Antimalarial and Antimosquito Services in the State of Singapore" [hereafter, MOH/01/66], p. C1.

Health Department. The cornerstone of the anti-mosquito strategy was an amalgam of tactics focusing on surveillance, infrastructure development and education to counter the insect in Singaporean society. It was hoped that this legislation would help in developing an understanding that mosquitoes "can be controlled if not exterminated by systematic and controlled action."[12]

"Anti-mosquito measures" began in colonial Singapore whenever authorities noted a rise in the number of malaria cases at health clinics throughout the island. Once a potential outbreak was recognized, members of a task force would spring into action. Affected neighborhoods were surveilled and potential breeding sites for *Anopheles* mosquitoes identified, which were in "clear running water generally oozing out from springs near foothills." Coolies were then deployed to take "action as may be necessary to bring their land into a condition unfavorable to the breeding of mosquitoes," which entailed a number of measures from filling in stagnant ponds to removing "empty tins, cans or bottles, and to fill with concrete holes in trees." Eventually, the area was "piped where necessary." This entailed the replacement of earthen drains that had "eroded with cleaning," and allowed pools of stagnant water to proliferate. The laying of "cement inverts" was the common solution to eliminate these pools, which also acted as a public symbol of the link between infrastructure and imperial improvement. Once installed, these drains "converted a swamp into dry land" and made it "possible to build houses on it or to cultivate it."[13]

Beyond infrastructure improvements, Ordinance 174 (Destruction of Mosquitoes) provided for surveillance of the landscape and punitive fines against humans who assisted mosquitoes. These fines added "a new terror to the owning of land as every one from the Crown downwards

---

[12] Many of these developments corresponded with similar findings in Java, as Dutch health officials identified *An. sundaicus* in many coastal fishponds near Batavia in 1918. Van der Brug, "Malaria in Batavia in the 18th Century," p. 897; Enquirer, "The Mosquito Plague," *Singapore Free Press and Mercantile Advertiser* [hereafter, *SFP*], 10 Jun. 1921, p. 7; Scharf, Faris and Nicholas, *Malaria-Mosquito Control in Rural Singapore*, pp. 3–4; Hunter, "Anti-Malarial Work in Singapore," pp. 324–7; Anonymous, "Municipal Commission. Valuable Anti-Malarial Work Accomplished"; CO275/99: Proceedings of the Legislative Council of the Straits Settlements, Monday, 16 Jun. 1919, p. B107–8.

[13] CO275/99: Proceedings of the Legislative Council of the Straits Settlements, Monday, 16 Jun. 1919, p. B107–8; Anonymous, "Municipal Commission. Valuable Anti-Malarial Work Accomplished."

Image 3.1: Before and after photographs illustrating the role of drains and subsoil pipes in anti-mosquito measures. Malcolm Watson, et al., *The Prevention of Malaria in the Federated Malay States: A Record of Twenty Years Progress* (New York, NY: E.P. Dutton and Company, 1921), opposite pages 328 and 330.

is liable if an empty tin is found on his land with mosquito larvae in it." On private lands, this meant that the authorities could "issue orders to land-owners" to ensure their properties did not house any potential breeding sites. Anyone not complying with these orders faced fines or imprisonment. To reinforce these efforts, and to ensure mosquitoes would not return, oiling of any remaining stagnant waters occurred while quinine was made available to residents of malarial areas.[14]

Public education supplemented these infrastructure improvements and efforts at surveillance. In a discussion held in in the Legislative Council in October 1919, Lim Boon Keng emphasized the importance

---

[14] Anonymous, "Municipal Commission. Valuable Anti-Malarial Work Accomplished."

of efforts to explain these programs, as it would help the society come to a deeper understanding of their role in stopping the spread of diseases. Lim reminded the Anti-Mosquito Department that officials "will need to explain that malaria is not due to Gods or devils. We have the devil in the mosquito and we want to get rid of all mosquitoes. Much can be done with propaganda, and if we can get the people to understand the necessity for this work, then I think the work will be simple." Soon afterwards, "properly qualified Sanitary Inspectors" began to visit houses "telling the people what a menace to health any sort of mosquito is." The result of these early campaigns—involving infrastructure improvements, surveillance and public education—was a reduction in "malarial mosquitoes and also of the disease itself."[15]

Singapore was an early laboratory for these various anti-mosquito measures from the late 1910s until the Second World War, marking its importance as the center of the British imperial presence in Southeast Asia.[16] Public health had become fundamental in creating a healthier environment for the humans of an imperial, urban society with the mosquito acting as a catalyst and justification for infrastructure improvement, and providing an example of a positive government program that intervened in the lives of human residents. It was a hallmark of late colonial modernity in Singapore, work that the Municipal Commission claimed with pride "was most productive and to the benefit of the town."[17] The arrival of Japanese imperial rule in 1942, however, would suspend many of these efforts, as land and labor became directed toward providing support for the ongoing conflict and the imposition of new administrative structures. When British colonial forces returned to Singapore in 1945, they were aghast at the presence of malaria on the island. It was if they

---

[15] A growing awareness of mosquitoes being disease carriers in the tropics was also reinforced through newspapers and the press. Liew, "Making Health Public," pp. 218–21; Anonymous, "War on Malaria," *SFP*, 1 Aug. 1921, p. 3; Anonymous, "Making the Tropics Safe," *SFP*, 14 May 1921, p. 12; CO275/99: Proceedings of the Legislative Council of the Straits Settlements, Monday, 6 Oct. 1919, pp. B146–7.

[16] Much of this work occurred shortly before, and then took place alongside similar efforts to counter malaria in the American south and the expansion of anti-malarial programs globally through the International Health Board and the Rockefeller Foundation. Darwin H. Stapleton, "Lessons of History? Anti-Malaria Strategies of the International Health Board and the Rockefeller Foundation from the 1920s to the Era of DDT," *Public Health Reports* 119, 2 (2004): 206–15.

[17] Anonymous, "Municipal Commission. Valuable Anti-Malarial Work Accomplished."

had to start over from scratch. These humans, however, already had a strategy to fight mosquitoes that had proven successful.

Anti-Mosquito Work

The Japanese Occupation was a positive experience for mosquitoes in Singapore. The suspension of pre-war programs to eliminate the disease-carrying pests and their breeding grounds allowed for their proliferation.[18] When British officials returned, they faced a formidable opponent. The Deputy Health Officer, W.E. Hutchinson, reported mosquito breeding "on a scale unknown pre-war" and noted with "considerable concern" the presence of the insect in abandoned agricultural fields, particularly in urban neighborhoods such as Havelock Road and River Valley Road, which "ran wild" and contained "wells, ponds, and stagnant earth drains hidden in the undergrowth." They were perfect breeding sites for *Anopheles* mosquitoes, proven through the stark rise in number of malaria cases that led to deaths from 270 in 1941 to 2,771 in 1945.[19] Under these circumstances Hutchinson revived the "Anti-Mosquito Department," a bureaucratic entity that signaled the restoration of British control over the island through a continuation of pre-war policies to limit mosquitoes and the spread of disease in the colony. Much like its predecessor, it was tasked with "control of breeding places of the vector mosquitoes" while continuing with the rehabilitation of permanent works that had begun prior to 1942.[20]

Officials initially focused on the Sungai Whampoa, Kallang and Geylang areas—due to the presence of prawn ponds and poor drainage

---

[18] Gregg Huff and Gillian Huff, "The Second World War Japanese Occupation of Singapore," *JSEAS* 51, 1–2 (2020): 265.
[19] The number of deaths due to malaria increased every year during the Occupation. They were 680 (1943), 1,886 (1944); 2,771 (1945). MOH/01/66, p. C3; N.A. Canton, *Municipality of Singapore, Health Department, Annual Report for 1947*, pp. 16, 28, 34–8; WHO/VBC/86.928: "Dengue Haemorrhagic Fever Control Programme in Singapore," p. 29.
[20] There were three entities that handled issues related to malaria in immediate post-war Singapore. They were the City Council, the Armed Forces and the Public Health Division. All three focused on "the larval control of the vectors." While the Armed Forces were tasked with ensuring that areas under their remit and transportation hubs, such as the railway station and airport, did not harbor mosquito breeding sites, it was ultimately the Public Health Department that coordinated all of these activities. Ng See Yook, *Report of the Ministry of Health for the Year Ended 31st December, 1962* (Singapore: Government Publications Bureau, 1963), p. 39.

on previously cultivated land.[21] Once these sites were cleared, authorities deemed these early efforts from a revived program a success after malaria infection rates declined steeply and quickly, with only 416 cases of malaria reported in 1947. Attention then shifted to squatter encampments and roadside drains. These "breeding places for mosquitoes" were scattered throughout the island from rural areas to "the very heart of the town itself in the hundreds of dumps of water bearing receptacles, from the abandoned army tank to the empty tin." "Patrol gangs," a post-war designation for the coolie workers of an earlier Singapore, carried out this work under the supervision of six overseers, who monitored maintenance and construction work throughout the town. The gangs went "on regular rounds, cleared and regraded earth and concrete drains outside of our recognized anti-malarial areas" while also removing any item that potentially held stagnant water. They also maintained "closer contact with the squatter, not only with the object of curbing some of his activities, but also of educating him as to what he may and may not do."[22]

The efforts of the Anti-Mosquito Department at both engineering of the human populace and the landscape soon became a constant and persistent weapon in efforts to thwart mosquitoes in post-war Singapore. Much of this is laid out in the rote annual reports of the Department of Health throughout the 1950s, in which "anti-mosquito measures" take up to half of the bureaucratic account and document a continual sequence of oiling problematic areas, trapping mosquitoes, collecting larvae, and overseeing "permanent anti-malarial works." Significant work was directed at the construction of new waterways; in 1952 alone patrol gangs "cleared and regraded 595,947 yards of earth drains and cleaned 165,681 yards of concrete drains." The efficacy of this approach was justified in reports through the citation of the almost immediate decline in the number of *An. sundaicus* specimens collected in traps as well as the number of cases and deaths contributed to malaria during this period.[23]

---

[21] For an alternative history of how these ponds and food cultivation can be framed during this period, see Anthony Medrano's contribution to this collection.
[22] Canton, *Annual Report for 1947* (Singapore: Government Printing Office, 1949), pp. 35–7; N.A. Canton, *Annual Report of the Health Department 1951* (Singapore: Government Printing Office, 1953), p. 29; Ng See Yook, *Report of the Ministry of Health for the Year Ended 31st December, 1960* (Singapore: Government Publications Bureau, 1961), p. 25; Canton, *Annual Report for 1947*, pp. 37–8, 56.
[23] Canton, *Annual Report for 1951*, p. 30; N.A. Canton, *Annual Report of the Health Department for 1952* (Singapore: Government Printing Office, 1954), p. 26.

Beyond these infrastructure improvements, the rhetoric of a modern society being one that maintained a clean environment soon took root. Civil servants were at the forefront of admonishing their fellow Singaporeans for their perceived inability to maintain hygienic and healthy surroundings, with most criticism directed at kampong dwellers whenever recently installed concrete channel drains reverted "to their previous insanitary state." A typical comment appears in the Annual Report for 1951, when N.A. Canton—the City Health Officer—proclaimed that such efforts on behalf of the state are "uneconomic, if not very nearly impossible, to render an over-crowded unplanned kampong sanitary." Freedom from malarial mosquitoes could "only be maintained with constant vigilance." This would require societal discipline, which the authorities continually promoted through pamphlets, house visits and outreach programs.[24] Eventually, the public grew so disciplined within these programs that there was "a marked increase in the number of complaints received" about "nuisance" mosquitoes, which led to the Health Department spending a considerable amount of time investigating "building excavations, badly graded drains, neglected compounds, etc., and much of the cost of oiling is due to the control of mosquitoes which are not malaria vectors."[25] Public health, surveillance and development were becoming intertwined in the creation of a modern society.

While most of the anti-mosquito measures in Singapore had been developed before the Second World War, they were now supported with more sophisticated efforts to identify potential problem areas. Larvae collection stations were established throughout the island to monitor and identify *Anopheles* populations. Data from these stations established that the main breeding places of *An. sundaicus* were ponds used in agricultural cultivation as well as tidal pools and even lorry tracks; in contrast, *An. maculatus* were found in earth wells and near creeks or inland pools. In both instances, very few specimens were found as captured samples rarely manifested any sign of disease. In problematic areas—such as Goodman Road and Kolam Ayer Lane, for example—a total of only 14 individual mosquitoes were caught in 1952, and none were found to be infected.[26]

---

[24] Morrison, *Annual Report of the Health Department 1956* (Singapore: Government Printing Office, 1957), p. 7.

[25] Morrison, *Annual Report of the Health Department 1957* (Singapore: Government Printing Office, 1959), p. 7.

[26] This also was true for all of the 1,768 female *Anopheles* mosquitoes gathered in traps in 1952. Canton, *Annual Report of the Health Department for 1952*, p. 27.

By 1956, health officers were delighted to report "no malaria vector mosquitoes were caught in the human bait traps which were set through the year" throughout Singapore.[27]

New technologies also supported these efforts at surveillance and engineering. As much as 22,579 liters (5,965 gallons) of an "anti-malaria mixture" that contained 1 percent DDT (dichlorodiphenyltrichloroethane)—a chemical compound whose insecticidal properties Swiss scientist Paul Hermann Müller identified in 1939 and only became publicly available following the Second World War—was sprayed every month, which "choked roadside drains where 'nuisance' mosquitoes were found breeding." The Anti-Mosquito Department also introduced the "Swing-Fog Machine," with four being deployed "extensively to deal with adult mosquitoes, flies and other insects" for the application of Dieldrex 15. As part of these efforts, oiling soon became more nuanced as the authorities employed new chemical formulas—all products of the Shell Oil Company—on different landscapes throughout the island. Vegetable ponds received Malariol HS as it would not damage the plants; officials sprayed benzine with 10 percent DDT along the margins of the water reservoirs; while at construction sites, Ditrene Dip was often used because oily larvicides interfered "with the proper setting of concrete." As one advertisement promised, the latter insecticide not only "protected cattle, dogs and horses," but was also quite effective when users "spray it on manure heaps."[28]

By 1960, after more than a decade of anti-mosquito measures and public education, the Chief Health Officer reported that "Singapore may be regarded as free from malaria." The number of positive cases had been plummeting throughout the 1950s; of the 18 malaria cases diagnosed in Singapore in 1957, all were found to be imported. This was reiterated further when another officer declared, "there was no indigenous malaria case in Rural areas including the surrounding islands." This was a triumph for a modernizing, developmental late colonial state, and

---

[27] H.R. Morrison, *Annual Report of the Health Department 1956*, p. 7.
[28] N.A. Canton, *Annual Report for 1951*, pp. 30–1; Anonymous, "Ditrene Dip Advertisement," *ST*, 16 Nov. 1948, p. 5; A.S. Msangi, "The Value of Spreading Agent in Larvicidal Formulations Containing DDT," *Bulletin of the World Health Organization* 21, 6 (1959): 773–8; Canton, *Annual Report for 1947*, pp. 35, 38; H.R. Morrison, *Annual Report of the Health Department 1956*, pp. 7, 36; C.Y. Chow and E.S. Thevasagayam, "A Simple and Effective Device for Housefly Control with Insecticides," *Bulletin of the World Health Organization* 8, 4 (1953): 491–5.

Image 3.2: Public Health Services' residual spraying of DDT inside a house, 1955. Ministry of Information and the Arts Collection, courtesy of National Archives of Singapore.

which the Permanent Secretary to the Ministry of Health Ng See Yook proclaimed, was "achieved only by constant unremitting vigilance and prompt effective action."[29]

Singapore was malaria free—that is, there was no "indigenous malaria" although a few people over the years tested positive after becoming infected elsewhere—for seven years until 1964, when there were 33 cases of malaria in Fuyong Estate off Bukit Timah Road. The authorities first became aware of the outbreak after both a Malay laborer and a Chinese girl living in the kampong produced positive blood tests. Malaria-ridden mosquitoes were present in the estate due to "seepage and spring water" from five granite quarries nearby as well as "some clearing of the forest" that had occurred in early 1964 for the construction of public housing flats. Once alerted to the situation, the authorities descended on the neighborhood. "A house to house search for 'fever cases' was immediately embarked upon and blood films taken," and members of the anti-mosquito task force found "ideal breeding grounds for *A. maculatus*. Larval surveys confirmed the presence of the mosquito nearby in the Nature Reserve." The re-emergence of malaria after more than a decade allowed the authorities to enact "emergency measures," including "mass drug prophylaxis and anti-adult" spraying to "break transmission while anti-larval operations were restored."[30]

The handling of the malaria outbreak in Fuyong Estate was a climax in an era of public health public policies directed at malarial mosquitoes on an island that was transitioning from colony to independent nation-state. Although a range of other conditions—from tuberculosis to heart disease to nephritis—caused more deaths than malaria in late colonial Singapore, none could be connected directly to an animal. The anti-mosquito measures also worked alongside policies to discipline the human populace while providing visible improvements to infrastructure, all under the guidance of

---

[29] According to an estimate made in the late 1950s, "over 20 per cent of persons who die in Singapore have not been in receipt of medical attention and the causes of death have had to be surmised by Inspecting Officers without the aid of clinical examination or autopsies." Under such circumstances, "the number of deaths shown as due to the various diseases must necessarily be inaccurate." H.R. Morrison, *Annual Report of the Health Department 1957*, pp. 1, 7; Ng, *Report of the Ministry of Health for the Year Ended 31st December, 1960*, p. 25.

[30] Ng See Yook, *Report of the Ministry of Health for the Year Ended 31st December, 1964* (Singapore: Government Publications Bureau, 1965), p. 29; National Archives of Singapore: MOH/01/66. M.J. Colbourne, "Report of an Enquiry into the Antimalarial and Antimosquito Services in the State of Singapore," pp. F1–F3.

technocrats. Public health and infrastructure development, often directed at fighting mosquitoes, created a modern Singapore.

The massive reduction of malaria cases and the limitations on the proliferation of its vector, was a legacy of the late colonial state, and one that would continue as Singapore became an independent nation. In this historical context, the authorities wanted to evaluate whether these approaches developed over several decades were appropriate for a society that was experiencing changing landscapes and political realities, particularly after the creation of an independent nation-state in mid-1965. With this in mind, in late 1965, the government commissioned Michael Colbourne—the head of the Department of Social Medicine and Public Health at the University of Singapore and an adviser on malaria for the World Health Organization—to write a report assessing the state of health services and what measures could be taken to anticipate new threats from mosquito-borne diseases. Colbourne submitted his report in early 1966.

The Colbourne Report of 1966 emphasized the remarkable work of the "Antimosquito Service," and used the eradication of malaria as proof that its strategies were effective. Most of the document recounts the development of efforts in Singapore over decades to contain diseases that are spread through "arthropods"—invertebrate animals with an exoskeleton, segmented bodies and jointed appendages or, in our case, insects—and the recommendation that these strategies continue to be implemented. To update the approaches for the modernizing, independent government, Colbourne offered a few suggestions to reconfigure the bureaucratic makeup of the department, mostly involving a superficial shifting of administrative tasks and titles for supervisors and administrative bodies. He proposed, for example, that the entity be renamed the "Arthropod Borne Disease Unit," a suggestion that was never seriously considered; it ultimately became the "Vector Control Unit." One specific request, however, was immediately approved. Colbourne asked that malaria be made "notifiable," meaning that it could be reported in the official records of the Ministry of Health from clinical diagnosis without laboratory confirmation, which would allow for a more effective surveillance of the disease.[31]

---

[31] Dengue hemorrhagic fever also became a notifiable disease in 1966. Dengue fever was included in 1977. Ooi, et al., "Dengue Prevention and 35 Years of Vector Control in Singapore," p. 888; NAS: MOH/01/66.

Mosquitoes, Public Health and the Construction of a Modern Society

This document, which was written shortly after Singapore became an independent country and now can be found amid reams of paper in the National Archives of Singapore, formally approved the continuation of colonial era programs in the fight against disease in a modernizing nation-state. As Singapore moved from "third world to first," in the parlance often used to describe developments in its early decades as an independent country, there was also a continual pursuit of approval from international bodies as a symbol it was being administered in a competent and effective manner. Singapore would no longer be a tropical island beset with the ailments of the third world. It was a developing, or even developed, nation with housing projects rising hundreds of meters into the sky and an environment shaped to the will of a technocratic government. Anti-mosquito policies—engineering, surveillance and public education—would be continued as a legacy of colonial rule of the island leading to the creation of a modern nation.

A New Enemy for a Clean and Healthy Nation

While the Colbourne Report of 1966 praised government programs to limit the spread of malaria and *Anopheles* mosquitoes, it also contained a warning to officials that would seem prescient in the coming decades. Colbourne was concerned that a modernizing Singapore and its changing landscape had the potential to transform a "nuisance mosquito" into a menace. While white markings on its legs and a spot on its thorax in the shape of a lyre, according to musically oriented entomologists, distinguishes this particular species, its ability to transmit a variety of tropical diseases such as yellow fever and chikungunya has attracted the attention of humans. This dangerous creature is *Aedes aegypti*. Yellow fever, however, was not the disease this mosquito transmitted that should have elicited concern in Singapore. It was dengue.[32]

A virus—technically a flavivirus—causes dengue, which manifests in two forms in humans: dengue fever, which mainly affects adults and older children; and, dengue hemorrhagic fever, which usually affects infants

---

[32] Concern over the threat this insect posed had been raised a decade earlier, in 1956, when officials issued a warning about a new mosquito that deserved scrutiny. Morrison, *Annual Report of the Health Department 1956*, p. 8; NAS: MOH/01/66, pp. 16–18.

and children up to 13 years of age.[33] The most prominent symptoms of the disease are an elevated body temperature along with severe joint and muscle pain, leading to its nickname "break-bone fever." Although dengue has existed for centuries, and is endemic in the tropics, the disease became increasingly virulent in urban centers in South and Southeast Asia beginning in the 1950s, when the introduced mosquito *Ae. aegypti* became the primary vector for transmission. By the early 1960s, this species and the disease it transmitted gained the attention of the authorities in Singapore, and a place of prominence in the Colbourne Report.[34]

Dengue is a disease mostly associated with the modern home. This is related to the behavior of *Ae. aegypti*, the primary vector of the disease, which is "highly domesticated," meaning it "lives and breeds indoors, has a limited flight range, and feeds almost exclusively on humans."[35] This is an insect that flourishes in a built-up environment. The presence of this mosquito in Singapore would have implications for a rapidly modernizing society transitioning from the kampongs and rural gardens of the colonial era to one in which public housing and construction of industrial zones embodied development and progress in an independent nation-state.[36]

While monitoring of the genus *Anopheles* continued in Singapore, it was *Aedes* that quickly became the most important disease carrying

---

[33] While there are variants within these manifestations, "dengue" will be used to refer to the entire spectrum of the disease syndrome in this chapter. World Health Organization Archives: WHO/VBC/86.928: "Dengue Haemorrhagic Fever Control Programme in Singapore: A Case Study of on the Successful Control of *Aedes Aegypti* and *Aedes Albopicus* Using Mainly Environmental Measure as a Part of Integrated Vector Control," p. 1; J. Andrew and Ananya Bar, "Morphology and Morphometry of *Aedes aegypti* Adult Mosquito," *Annual Review and Research in Biology* 3, 1 (2013): 53.

[34] Scott B. Halstead, "Mosquito-borne Haemorrhagic Fevers of South and South-East Asia," *Bulletin of the World Health Organization* 35, 1 (1966): 3–15; WHO/VBC/86.928: "Dengue Haemorrhagic Fever Control Programme in Singapore," p. 1; MOH/01/66, pp. 16–18.

[35] The disease is transferred through the bite of female mosquitoes. If the human has the disease, the mosquito can acquire the disease and then transfer it to other humans. D.J. Gubler, "The Global Pandemic of Dengue/Dengue Hemorrhagic Fever: Current Status and Prospects for the Future," in *Dengue in Singapore*, ed. K.T. Goh (Singapore: Institute of Environmental Epidemiology/Ministry of Environment, 1998), p. 15; Eng-Eong Ooi, Kee-Tai Goh and Duane J. Gubler, "Dengue Prevention and 35 Years of Vector Control in Singapore," *Emerging Infectious Diseases* 12, 6 (2006): 888.

[36] Morrison, *Annual Report of the Health Department 1956*, p. 8.

mosquito on the island. The authorities attacked this mosquito with the tried and tested approaches that had worked so well against their *Anopheles* cousins, albeit modified for an increasingly urban environment. Previously, the main focus had been on open water sources, the main breeding sites for *Anopheles* mosquitoes, which were found primarily in lands under governmental control. Redesigning drainage systems and monitoring these ponds and pools in public view were effective strategies to limit malaria and its vector in the society. *Aedes* mosquitoes, in contrast, with their ability to breed in highly urbanized and developed spaces meant that new approaches to fight this menace would now enter the homes of Singaporeans, and intersect with new programs to create public housing. They would provide a link for larger campaigns to create a clean and green society, and shift responsibility to the public in a larger process of disciplining the nation.[37]

Concern over the presence of *Aedes* mosquitoes, thus, corresponded with rhetoric promoting the construction and development of modern housing in Singapore that had arisen after the Second World War. Officials quickly returned to the policy of identifying "slums and squatter settlements"—official parlance for kampongs, which had proliferated in the aftermath of the British return to the island—as the main havens for the menace, which was a danger to public health. Residences, "typically dark and damp," contained numerous breeding sites for the mosquito "in all sorts of containers strewn about, both inside and around slum houses." Only through a sustained transformation of society could this menace be tamed, it was thought. In place of these kampongs rose Housing & Development Board (HDB) flats, which would shelter the nation in modern facilities and prevent the breeding of deadly vectors, as they "do not have any land space for accumulating unwanted containers." The rise in public housing corresponded with Singaporeans efforts to live in a sanitary and modern society. This transformation was rapid. By 1965 a quarter of the population lived in HDB flats; the percentage rose to a third of the population by 1969.[38]

---

[37] Morrison, *Annual Report of the Health Department 1957*, p. 37.
[38] Loh Kah Seng, *Squatters into Citizens: The 1961 Bukit Ho Swee Fire and the Making of Modern Singapore* (Singapore: NUS Press, 2013); Teo Siew Eng and Victor R. Savage, "Singapore Landscape: A Historical Overview of Housing Change," *Singapore Journal of Tropical Geography* 6, 1 (1985): 57–61; WHO/VBC/86.928: "Dengue Haemorrhagic Fever Control Programme in Singapore," p. 24; Ong Sze Ying, "Hello HDB, Goodbye Kampong: Experiencing Modernity in

The effect of this shift in housing in Singapore, and the use of anti-*Aedes* measures, can be seen following initial reports documenting a rise in dengue cases. In 1966, the first year dengue was "notifiable," there were 630 reported cases and 24 deaths. Over the next two years there were 826 and 848 cases with 21 and 18 deaths from the disease. Under these conditions the government launched a pilot project under the Vector Control Unit in Geylang with the goal of reducing infections through "source reduction" and health education in an attempt to reduce the use of insecticides. While positive results were achieved—determined by a decline in dengue cases—after only three months, it was quickly realized that once measures were eased, the disease returned. This would influence future campaigns and approaches in Singapore. As one report described, "it was necessary to involve active and continuous public participation and this could only be done through public health education supported by law enforcement." In this context, new legislation was required.[39]

To ensure "continuous public participation" the "Destruction of Disease Bearing Insects Act, 1968" was drafted, which provided "teeth for tighter and more effective control over persons who intentionally or unintentionally propagated" a range of animals, although it was clearly directed at mosquitoes. It allowed for "a Medical Officer of Health" to "enter and examine any premises or vessel" that may harbor disease-bearing insects and "the spraying of such premises or vessel with insecticides" if deemed necessary. Not only were officials allowed to enter private residences to search for breeding sites, but the onus of responsibility for their presence now shifted to citizens. One of the major provisions of this new legislation was the possibility of fines and prosecution for

---

Singapore," unpublished honors thesis, Department of History, National University of Singapore, 2010.

[39] Such legislation had been proposed as early as 1956. At that time, British health officials believed that without it, "complete control" of this specific species of mosquito was "not possible." The Health Department thus advocated that the government "make it an offence to have *Aedes aegypti* breeding on premises" throughout Singapore. Morrison, *Annual Report of the Health Department 1956*, p. 8; WHO/VBC/86.928: "Dengue Haemorrhagic Fever Control Programme in Singapore," p. 3; K.L. Chan, "Control of Vectors towards a Better Singapore," in *Towards a Better Singapore: Proceedings of the 1st Singapore Professional Centre Convention, 1975*, ed. Tan It Koon (Singapore: Singapore Professional Centre, 1975), pp. 107–17; B.T. Tan and B.T. Teo, "Modus Operandi in *Aedes* Surveillance and Control," in *Dengue in Singapore*, ed. K.T. Goh (Singapore: Institute of Environmental Epidemiology/Ministry of Environment, 1998), p. 109.

homeowners, as well as contractors of major development projects, if they did not eliminate potential mosquito breeding habitats.[40]

The newly developed "vector control program" used a combination of "long-term and short-term measures," which were simply the approaches taken in colonial Singapore, although they were updated to fit a society that was promoting itself as technologically and administratively modern and fighting a new genus of mosquito. "Long-term measures" referred to an integration of "environmental control, human behavioral control through health education and law enforcement, and the use of ovitraps," a dark container with water and substrate which attracts and then traps adult mosquitoes, ultimately drowning them. The first ovitrap created for "autocidal" purposes was deployed in 1969 at Paya Lebar International Airport. Once an outbreak occurred, "short-term measures" were enacted. This entailed an amplified collection and monitoring alongside a liberal use of insecticides, mainly through "fogging operations" directed at "killing the indoor population of *Ae. aegypti*" that were carried out with "cold aerosol generators or thermal foggers."[41] These various approaches, officials argued, achieved "the most lasting and effective results." This updated program was in full force by 1973, and the "aggressive" measures in vector control soon became an everyday activity in Singapore throughout the decade.[42]

An important component of these new approaches to an old problem was a renewed emphasis on public education and a shift of responsibility from the patrol gangs of the Anti-Mosquito Department (although they continued to exist in a new iteration, and focused on breeding outside

---

[40] Singapore Statutes: No. 29/1968: "Destruction of Disease-Bearing Insects Bill"; Goh, "Eradication of Malaria from Singapore," p. 256.

[41] Authorities estimated that an outbreak would result in an increase of "about 5–10 times the number of premises fogged during non-epidemic years." When used indoor, "doors and windows should be closed for 5–10 minutes in order to ensure 100% kill of the mosquito females harboring the virus." WHO/VBC/86.928: "Dengue Haemorrhagic Fever Control Programme in Singapore," pp. 23, 29; Tan Boon Teng, "New Initiatives in Dengue Control in Singapore," *Dengue Bulletin* 25 (2001): 3.

[42] While the main focus of the vector control program was on limiting *Aedes* and their ability to spread dengue, *Anopheles* and the diseases they transmitted occasionally reappeared during this period and remained a concern. There was, for example, a malaria outbreak in Telok Blangah and offshore islands in 1974 followed by another in Whampoa and Kallang in early 1975, and then Changi in 1976. These infections were labelled as "imported," but were used to emphasize the basic parameters of the program. Goh, "Eradication of Malaria from Singapore," pp. 257–64.

the household) to the individual in ensuring that the surrounding environment—which mainly constituted the home—did not encourage mosquito breeding. Officers would "check the premises" in these areas to "make an inventory of the number and types of potential breeding habitats." On subsequent visits the "inventory would be checked again." Those responsible for breeding mosquitoes would be given "an advisory letter and education materials" initially; those who disregarded these materials were "not spared again."[43]

The results of these surveys drew a picture of a Singapore under siege, and one in the populace played a key role and bore the brunt of responsibility. While both *Aedes* vectors bred in "domestic containers," ranging from jars and bowls to tin cans and tires, the authorities emphasized that *Ae. aegypti* was more likely to be found indoors, particularly in "slum houses" and shophouses. This provided impetus for governmental campaigns promoting "health education materials" to teach "simple measures to householders in the prevention and control" of mosquitoes. The Vector Control Unit worked throughout the island and began to identify "DF/DHF-sensitive areas."[44] As one report clarified, it was "of utmost importance to have continuous information on the distribution and density of vectors," as such an approach was "sound, scientific, practical and economically feasible," making it appealing and in-line with the developmental state of the 1970s and 1980s in Singapore. Officials began "carrying out larval surveys" during which they would "inspect every house for *Aedes* breeding."[45]

These home visits were paired with a larger nationwide campaign to shape the society. This first occurred with the "Keep Singapore Clean and Mosquito Free Campaign" in 1969, when Health Minister Chua Sian Chin proclaimed that mosquitoes had transformed from a "nuisance" into

---

[43] Tan and Teo, "Modus Operandi in *Aedes* Surveillance and Control," pp. 111–14.

[44] DF was the abbreviation for dengue fever, while DHF stood for dengue hemorrhagic fever, in the acronym/abbreviation loving Singaporean bureaucracy. Thus, the VCU identified DH-DHF sensitive areas using AHI. Y.C. Chan, B.C. Ho and K.L. Chan, "*Aedes aegypti* (L.) and *Aedes Albopictus* (Skuse) in Singapore City," *Bulletin of the World Health Organization* 44, 5 (1971): 651–8; WHO/VBC/86.928: "Dengue Haemorrhagic Fever Control Programme in Singapore," p. 11.

[45] To do so, "human baits" were set "in preference to animal baits" as *Ae. aegypti* and *Ae. albopictus*—the two main vectors for dengue at the time—"are anthopophilous." The mosquitoes were "collected while biting and landing on human bait with test tubes and nets." WHO/VBC/86.928: "Dengue Haemorrhagic Fever Control Programme in Singapore," pp. 5, 11.

a "dangerous disease-bearing" menace. If they could be eradicated, the public could play a substantive role in transforming Singapore into a "green city." This linked anti-mosquito measures with larger efforts to transform Singapore into a Garden City. An amalgamation of various policies, the Garden City project reflected efforts to "design the environment" becoming a "rhetorical device that would guide national discourse for decades" in the island nation-state. While much of it focused on the planting of managed greenery, a key aspect of the program was to create a sanitary space in which clean and modern Singapore emerged from the social and physical landscape. Singapore would become an example of biophilic urbanism.[46] Through the measures to limit mosquitoes, and the emphasis on keeping a neat and tidy environment with no breeding sites for the insects, the vector control programs helped mold "a clean, healthy country," that reflected "an important component of the overall image that the Government" yearned "to project in the international forum."[47]

These larger policies were manifested in an emphasis on "environmental sanitation" in which ongoing housing projects and industrialization played a key role in national development. Within such a context, this was an "upgrading" in which Singaporeans were provided with "better housing and a cleaner environment with proper ventilation, adequate lighting and social amenities so that the littering of backyards and gardens in premises" would no longer be socially acceptable. Beginning in 1971, more than 160,000 "premises were inspected annually for mosquito breeding," and this would rise to 500,000 during an outbreak. As one report emphasized, "human behavior must also be changed. The Government must discourage the propagation of mosquitoes in premises and public places. This is best done through public health education and

---

[46] National Archives of Singapore: 1998006538 "Keep Singapore Clean and Mosquito-Free Campaign 1969: Chua Sian Chin Inaugurating National Campaign Committee and at Opening Ceremony"; Jesse O'Neill, "Clean and Disciplined: The Garden City in Singapore," in *The Culture of Nature in the History of Design*, ed. Kjetil Fallan (New York, NY: Routledge, 2019), pp. 89–101; Belinda Yuen, "Creating the Garden City: The Singapore Experience," *Urban Studies* 33, 6 (1996): 955–70; Timothy P. Barnard and Corinne Heng, "A City in a Garden," in *Nature Contained: Environmental Histories of Singapore*, ed. Timothy P. Barnard (Singapore: NUS Press, 2014), pp. 281–306; Peter Newman, "Biophilic Urbanism: A Case Study on Singapore," *Australian Planner* 51, 1 (2014): 47–65.
[47] P. Reiter, "Dengue Control in Singapore," in *Dengue in Singapore*, ed. K.T. Goh (Singapore: Institute of Environmental Epidemiology/Ministry of Environment, 1998), p. 214.

Singaporean Creatures

Image 3.3: Combat Infectious Diseases poster, 1976. Ministry of Health, courtesy of National Archives of Singapore.

law enforcement" as the city developed and modernized. Singapore was becoming a Garden City.[48]

The Vector Control Unit modified and developed approaches to align with these policies. This first began in 1973, following a dengue outbreak in which there were 1,187 cases and 27 deaths. After officials collected sufficient data, scientists realized that the "*Aedes* house index" (meaning the percentage of houses infested with larvae or pupae) needed to be kept below 5 percent. This would require even more surveillance followed by swifter action. Once the house index rose above the determined level, the area "would be immediately fogged to kill the adults, and cleared of breeding habitats." Monitoring of the population and its travel habits and testing of imported laborers soon came into vogue, with maps of "malaria receptive areas" (although it was to fight dengue) continually updated and "mass blood surveys" employed to detect reservoirs of infection. In

---

[48] National Archives of Singapore: "Keep Singapore Clean and Mosquito-Free Campaign 1969: Chua Sian Chin Inaugurating National Campaign Committee and at Opening Ceremony"; WHO/VBC/86.928: "Dengue Haemorrhagic Fever Control Programme in Singapore," pp. 3–4, 13, 22.

addition, the anti-malaria drainage system that had been installed in early decades to counter *Anopheles* mosquitoes was deemed "obsolete with the rapid pace of national development." New drains were installed and oiling became an exercise that was not done when mosquitoes were detected but as regularized practice. "More than two-thirds of the country" fell under "the weekly oiling cycle" during this period, "while the highly receptive and vulnerable areas" received treatment more frequently. These strategies were further intensified following another outbreak in 1978 in which there were 384 dengue cases and two deaths.[49] The presence of mosquitoes would not be tolerated in a modern Singapore.

The re-emergence of dengue in 1973 was a surprise to a government that had been promoting the "Keep Singapore Mosquito Free" Campaign from 1969 to 1972. Officials from the Vector Control Unit bemoaned that "complacency set in," and used it as an excuse to ramp up measures in which engineered approaches would overcome social weaknesses. "Search and destroy" operations, to emphasize the military analogies, began to focus on 400 construction sites. These areas were fogged with Reslin 10/10, a move away from the use of DDT, and such an approach then shifted to housing estates late in 1973.[50] When a dip in the number of dengue cases followed, to less than 100 cases per year, other aspects of the program were intensified. This involved "a system of routine vector surveillance, continuous year-round source reduction, health education and legislation, and fogging of premises" whenever the *Aedes* house density index went above 5 percent. Following an outbreak in early 1978, further analysis led to the development of new standards in which there was an emphasis on maintaining a level of fewer than 0.2 female *Ae. aegypti*—the actual vector for dengue—per house in any given area. Once an area exceeded this newly established data point, "fogging of all premises within a radius of 200 meters" was carried out.[51]

---

[49] The "Combat Infectious Diseases" campaign in 1976, by the way, placed malaria in the same basket as syphilis as a threat to the nation. Goh, "Eradication of Malaria from Singapore," pp. 257–64; WHO/VBC/86.928: "Dengue Haemorrhagic Fever Control Programme in Singapore," pp. 4–5.

[50] For more on the reduction in DDT usage in Singapore, see Nicole Tarulevicz's contribution to this collection. K.L. Chan, S.K. Ang and L.M. Chew, "The 1973 Dengue Haemorrhagic Fever Outbreak in Singapore and Its Control, *Singapore Medical Journal* 18, 2 (1977): 81–93; WHO/VBC/86.928: "Dengue Haemorrhagic Fever Control Programme in Singapore," p. 15.

[51] Meanwhile, between 1976 and 1981, almost 10,000 water tanks that were "breeding *Aedes* vectors were mosquito-proofed." Goh, "Eradication of Malaria from

Public health education related to the mosquito–human dynamic Singapore also reached new heights during the 1970s and 1980s. As a government report described the program, it was "aimed particularly at the semi-literate or less educated population living in socioeconomically 'lower' and 'poorer' areas of the country." Officials explained the life cycle of the mosquito and how Singaporeans could thwart the insects mainly through the distribution of pamphlets during "routine house inspections." During these visits, "through personal contact, explanation and advice, vector control officers routinely encourage and motivate community participation." Travelling exhibitions at community centers supplemented these efforts, alongside television and radio commercials as well as posters displayed throughout the island and stories placed in newspapers. "Increased and sustained law enforcement" reinforced these campaigns, which were based in the Destruction of Disease Bearing Insects Act. Enforcement revolved around fines, with first-time offenders facing a maximum fine of S$1,000 or 6 months in jail, or both. Between 1973 and 1981 officials issued 54,197 orders and 7,047 summonses to offenders, which produced revenue of approximately S$200,000 per year, which "was channeled back for the control and prevention of mosquito breeding in premises." "Health education accompanied by law enforcement," officials posited, were "particularly effective tools in the prevention of *Aedes* breeding."[52]

The results of these vector control programs within the Garden City project were "spectacular," with a drastic reduction in *Ae. aegypti* density throughout the island and ultimately the number of dengue infections. This was proven through data, such as a plunge in the *Aedes* Housing Index from more than 25 in the 1960s to less than 1 after 1985, as well as the number of dengue cases in Singapore never breaching 500 in any

---

Singapore," p. 266; WHO/VBC/86.928: "Dengue Haemorrhagic Fever Control Programme in Singapore," p. 22.

[52] In most cases, fines and enforcement were stricter for building contractors and developers. Private home owners were usually given a warning and 14 days to address any issues that the enforcement officials identified. Tan and Teo, "Modus Operandi in *Aedes* Surveillance and Control," pp. 115–16; WHO/VBC/86.928: "Dengue Haemorrhagic Fever Control Programme in Singapore," pp. 23, 28; Keri Matwick and Kelsi Matwick, "Comics and Humor as a Mode of Communication on Public Hygiene Posters in Singapore," *Discourse, Context and Media* 46, 1 (2022): 100590.

Mosquitoes, Public Health and the Construction of a Modern Society

Image 3.4: Keep Singapore Clean and Prevent Mosquito Breeding poster, in Chinese, 1979. Ministry of Health, courtesy of National Archives of Singapore.

year between 1974 and 1988.[53] The absence of mosquito-borne diseases for much of the 1980s was a high-water mark for public health in Singapore. The program, based on surveillance, house inspections and a "strong legislative framework," was a hallmark of the modern Singaporean state and its developmentalist agenda. As one foreign epidemiologist explained, "the vector control program" in Singapore "was based on a foundation of scientifically acquired knowledge," which had been transformed to fit the changing conditions on the island due to "radical changes in the urban environment" that had "totally changed the habitat and perhaps even the behavior of the vectors."[54] It was a public health success story and received accolades throughout the world. Singapore became a model in

---

[53] K.T. Goh, "Changing Epidemiology of Dengue in Singapore," *The Lancet* 346, 8982 (1995): 1098; WHO/VBC/86.928: "Dengue Haemorrhagic Fever Control Programme in Singapore," pp. 3–4.
[54] Ooi, et al., "Dengue Prevention and 35 Years of Vector Control," p. 887; Shuzhen Sim, et al., "A Greener Vision for Vector Control: The Examples of the Singapore Dengue Control Programme," *PloS Neglected Tropical Diseases* 14, 8 (2020): e0008428; Reiter, "Dengue Control in Singapore," p. 213; O'Neill, "Clean and Disciplined."

the global fight against mosquitoes and their diseases, best symbolized by the World Health Organization declaring the island malaria free in 1982 and being named as the locale of one of the three successful campaigns to counter dengue in the late 20th century.[55]

The triumph of social, scientific and administrative planning had occurred through the application of methods and approaches the colonial-era Anti-Mosquito Department had employed previously in the fight against malaria. Following independence in 1965, the Vector Control Unit in the Quarantine and Epidemiology Branch of the Ministry of Health, and then under the Ministry of the Environment after 1972, updated these approaches to reflect a clean and modern environment. The development of a clean and controlled environment, however, was laying a foundation from which the insects could bite back, as limitations in colonial-era approaches could no longer be modified further in a landscape that had transformed far beyond its original state on an imperial, tropical island.

Mosquitoes Bite Back

While malaria had been effectively eliminated and dengue seemed under control in the first few decades of Singaporean independence, the latter disease refused to go away. The first sign of its lingering presence was a surge in dengue cases in the 1990s and subsequent five to six-year epidemic cycles that followed, often fueled by the rise of new variants and the magnitude increasing with each cycle. By the 2010s, there were more than 10,000 dengue cases every year, with 2013 and 2014 being particularly harsh with 22,170 and 18,326 cases respectively. Numbers that would have been unthinkable in the 1970s had become quite normal in the 21st century.[56] After the laudatory triumphs of the 1970s and 1980s, this seemed to be an anomaly in the rhetoric of a clean, sanitized Garden City.

---

[55] Two other successful campaigns against mosquitoes that were often cited were in Cuba in 1981 and a hemispheric military effort between 1947 and 1970 under the Pan-American Sanitary Bureau. Olivia Brathwaite Dick, et al., "The History of Dengue Outbreaks in the Americas," *American Journal of Tropical Medicine and Hygiene* 87, 4 (2012): 584–93; Ooi, et al., "Dengue Prevention and 35 Years of Vector Control," pp. 887–8.

[56] Goh, "Changing Epidemiology of Dengue in Singapore," p. 1098; Ooi, et al., "Dengue Prevention and 35 Years of Vector Control in Singapore," pp. 888–9.

The reasons for the rise in frequency and magnitude of dengue cases in Singapore were multifaceted. One factor was the long-term influence of anti-mosquito measures in the 1970s and 1980s. While the number of dengue cases had gone down, there had been "a concomitant reduction in herd immunity to dengue virus." With very few people contracting the disease, antibodies were not building up. This was also related to a rise in variants. There are four types of dengue, so theoretically a human can catch the disease four different times if they are extremely unlucky. Shifts in the serotype (or strain) of the disease also led to the increased intensity of dengue in Singapore. For example, an outbreak in 2004 to 2005 was attributed to a shift from Type 2 to Type 1.[57] The disease was simply adapting to its environment and finding new ways to infect its hosts.

Beyond changes in the immunology of the disease, dengue and its vectoral mosquitoes were living an increasingly rich environment in which to feed. This was due to the massive expansion in the human population of Singapore, which doubled from 2 million in 1970 to 4 million in 2000; by 2020, the number was almost 6 million. While mosquito breeding grounds had been limited through public programs instituted over decades, the feeding grounds for the insect had effectively tripled. Increased connectivity also played a role, as humans from dengue-infested countries arrived in larger numbers as Singapore became a business and tourism hub. Combined with an increased likelihood of an infectious mosquito biting a human—known as "vectorial capacity"—as the temperature rises, and there has been a recorded rise of 2 degrees in mean temperature readings since the 1970s, a rise in dengue cases seemed inevitable.[58] Singapore

---

[57] Goh, "Changing Epidemiology of Dengue in Singapore," p. 1098; Ooi, et al., "Dengue Prevention and 35 Years of Vector Control in Singapore," pp. 888–9; Hapuarchchige Chanditha Hapuarachchi, et al., "Epidemic Resurgence of Dengue Fever in Singapore in 2013–14: A Virological and Entomological Perspective," *BMC Infectious Diseases* 16, 1 (2016): 1–13; Jayanthi Rajarethinam, et al., "Dengue in Singapore from 2004 to 2016: Cyclical Epidemic Patterns Dominated by Serotypes 1 and 2," *American Journal of Tropical Medicine* 99, 1 (2018): 204–10.

[58] To further complicate matters, scientists began to realize that most people in Singapore contracted the disease outside the home. This meant that adults were more likely to get dengue, particularly dengue fever instead of dengue hemorrhagic fever. There was also a rise in cases during the hotter months of the relative dry season in Singapore. Claudio Jose Struchiner, et al., "Increasing Dengue Incidence in Singapore over the Past 40 Years: Population Growth, Climate and Mobility," *PloS ONE* 10, 8 (2015): e0136286; Duane J. Gubler, "Dengue, Urbanization and

had inadvertently created a perfect laboratory for the spread of dengue fever as it became increasingly urbanized and globalized.

To counter this sharp rise in dengue cases over a sustained period, the government continued to rely on the trinity of colonial-era practices of surveillance, public education and monitoring, supplemented with new campaigns and slogans, house visits and fogging.[59] This was further formalized in the passage of another law, this time the 1998 Control of Vectors and Pesticide Act.[60] To support these efforts the government sought the opinions of foreign epidemiologists, who approved of these efforts to enact "changes in human behavior brought about by education, in synergy with legislation backed by active law enforcement," although they were growing increasingly ineffective, steeped in their creation to counter a threat in a colonial landscape that was long gone.[61]

Dengue was rampant in a new, modern Singaporean environment. To destroy the disease vectors, the mosquitoes, using colonial-era tactics was no longer feasible, no matter how disciplined and amplified the programs became. The Singaporean demographic, physical and immunological landscape had transformed to a point that any real attempt to eliminate the pest using out-of-date tactics would have too great an impact on

---

Globalization: The Unholy Trinity of the 21st Century," *Tropical Medicine and Health* 39, 4 (2011): 3–11; Louis Lambrechts, et al., "Impact of Daily Temperature Fluctuations on Dengue Virus Transmission by *Aedes aegypti*," *Proceedings of the National Academy of Sciences of the United States of America* 108, 18 (2011): 7460–5; Ooi, et al., "Dengue Prevention and 35 Years of Vector Control in Singapore," p. 889; Goh, "Changing Epidemiology of Dengue in Singapore," p. 1098; Hapuarachchi, et al., "Epidemic Resurgence of Dengue Fever in Singapore in 2013–14," pp. 1–13.

[59] Fogging even came to include the interior of houses, although international experts argued that this policy could not be "defended on scientific, public health, or any other grounds" as it only effects adult populations. It would be more effective if larval populations were destroyed. In such a climate, ovitraps became increasingly popular, although the burr of the fogging machine and the expansion of a white cloud of chemicals over housing estates remains a weekly experience for most Singaporeans. Ooi, et al., "Dengue Prevention and 35 Years of Vector Control in Singapore," pp. 890–2; P. Reiter, "Dengue Control in Singapore," pp. 227–30.

[60] The new act simply reiterated many of the components of the vector control program from the 1970s and 1980s with the main difference being the allowance of private entities to apply pesticides and participate in surveillance activities in a neo-liberal attempt to outsource services. The Statutes of the Republic of Singapore: Control of Vectors and Pesticides Act (Chapter 59). https://sso.agc.gov.sg/Act/CVPA1998#pr35- (accessed on 9 Aug. 2021).

[61] P. Reiter, "Dengue Control in Singapore," p. 215.

Image 3.5: Just Tip It poster, 2005. National Environmental Agency.

lifestyles and economic development.[62] Singaporeans would have to accept the reality that the virus and its vectors had become a permanent fixture, a symbol of a modernized, vibrant and globally connected city-state. Dengue had become an endemic disease in Singapore.

Mosquitoes appear to have the upper hand (appendage?) in 21st-century Singapore in this long-running conflict between a disease vector and humans. Dengue cases continue to rise and the application of old approaches has done little to address the issue—despite attempts to update and refine them further. The admission of defeat—or perhaps just an acceptance of the circumstances—in this battle also led to a shift in rhetoric. While the decades-long rise in dengue cases was "disappointing," it was now acceptable. "Eradication has never been a feasible target,"

---

[62] Warwick Neville, "The Impact of Economic Development on Land Functions in Singapore," *Geoforum* 24, 2 (1993): 143–63.

one prominent epidemiologist now argued. Instead, "the aim has been to maintain the vector population at levels that are too low to sustain epidemic transmission."[63]

In light of this, the government has recently turned to a final weapon that is not rooted in social and landscape engineering. Humans are now attempting to foil mosquitoes on a genetic level. It is a new modern update in the battle, no longer dependent on changing social behavior and spreading chemicals over the landscape. This new approach would be accomplished through the dissemination of "irradiated male *Wolbachia*-carrying *Aedes aegypti*" mosquitoes, which makes the insect unable to produce offspring. *Wolbachia*, in this instance, are common bacteria present in many insect species. In female *Aedes* mosquitoes, however, *Wolbachia* makes the larvae unviable; also, once infected with *Wolbachia*, the dengue viral load is considerably reduced. Scientists, thus, have taken *Wolbachia* from fruit flies and transferred it to mosquito eggs. Young males produced in this process of genetic engineering have been introduced to Singapore through "Project Wolbachia," which began in 2016 using housing estates—mainly in Yishun and Tampines—as test sites.[64]

Anti-mosquito measures continue in Singapore. While they have been rooted in approaches developed to control a menace in a colonial society, the tactics are finally transforming to align with a modern nation-state that embraces advances in technology and science. The results from Project Wolbachia have been promising. In July 2021, the National Environmental Agency announced that there had been an 88 percent reduction in dengue cases in test sites across Singapore, and the program would be expanding. This occurred following a year in which there were 17,249 dengue cases in Singapore, as monitoring and surveillance of mosquitoes were sacrificed in light of another public health crisis, the COVID-19 pandemic. A year later, in July

---

[63] P. Reiter, "Dengue Control in Singapore," p. 215.

[64] A considerable amount of material on the program can be found on websites from the National Environmental Agency in Singapore (https://www.nea.gov.sg/corporate-functions/resources/research/wolbachia-aedes-mosquito-suppression-strategy [accessed on 8 Aug. 2021]) as well as the World Mosquito Program (https://www.worldmosquitoprogram.org/ [accessed on 8 Aug. 2021]); C. Liew, et al., "Community Engagement for *Wolbachia*-Based *Aedes aegypti* Population Suppression for Dengue Control: The Singapore Experience," in *Area-Wide Integrated Pest Management: Development and Field Application*, ed. Jorge Heindrichs, Rui Pereira and Marc J.B. Vreysen (Boca Rotan, FL: CRC Press, 2020), pp. 747–61.

2022, the program expanded further to include 31 percent of HDB blocks in Singapore, accounting for over 300,000 households, to address the continuing rise in cases.[65] *Aedes* mosquitoes are finding it more difficult to perpetuate their species on this tropical island, thus destroying the vector for dengue. If this mosquito–human dynamic will ever be concluded, or whether the vectors and their disease will adapt further in light of these new tactics, remains to be seen. It is, however, part of a longer story of human responses and reactions to "little flies" that has shaped Singaporean society for over a century, reflecting the creation of a modern, developed nation through health initiatives and the construction of public works.

---

[65] In the first six months of 2022, there were more than 15,000 dengue cases in Singapore. Timothy Goh, "Project Wolbachia to Be Expanded to Cover a Third of HDB Blocks from July as Dengue Cases Surge," *ST*, 15 Jun. 2022; Anonymous, "National Environmental Agency Press Release: Project Wolbachia-Singapore Suppresses Aedes Aegypti Mosquito Population and Reduces Dengue Cases at Release Sites" (https://www.nea.gov.sg/media/news/news/index/project-wolbachia-singapore-suppresses-aedes-aegypti-mosquito-population-and-reduces-dengue-cases-at-release-sites [accessed 8 Aug. 2021]).

CHAPTER FOUR

A Cultural History of Fear, Fascination, Fantasy and Crocodiles in Singapore

Esmond Chuah Meng Soh

In November 2019, after a crocodile (*Crocodylus porosus*) was spotted in Lower Seletar Reservoir, government officials in Singapore "advised the public against going near the edge of the water" and suspended all water and fishing activities in the vicinity. The authorities also promised to deploy frequent surveillance measures "to ensure there are no further crocodile sightings." Such sightings, however, have not always triggered alarm in Singapore. In 1957, for example, children were found swimming in a pond in Pasir Panjang even though crocodiles were found lurking nearby. The image of the creature had transformed in the intervening years as the island became the home of a modernizing nation-state. By the 21st century, crocodiles were out of place in the Garden City, as the public perceived their place—rightfully or otherwise—to be limited to uninhabited swamps or, for estuarine species, the sea. This shift in perception reveals much about the humans of Singapore and how they have interacted with the wild over the past half century.[1]

Human perception of nature, as Susan Davis reminds us, "is not natural, but social and cultural."[2] The social and cultural history of the crocodile in Singapore in the second half of the 20th century allows for a consideration of notions of how communities (re-)contextualize transgression, presence and sightings of wild animals, particularly in an urban environment.[3] Drawing on textual and pictorial sources from Chinese and English newspapers from the National Library and National Archives of Singapore, this chapter explores how crocodile sightings have shaped an imagination of a temporary, untamed and pristine nature for Singaporeans in the midst of a thoroughly urbanized environment.[4] The cultural history of the crocodile in post-war Singapore, thus, can be understood in terms of a dialectical relationship. On the one hand,

---

[1] Tee Zhuo, "1.7m Crocodile at Lower Seletar Reservoir Caught by PUB, NParks," *The Straits Times* [hereafter, *ST*], 23 Feb. 2019, https://www.straitstimes.com/singapore/17m-crocodile-at-lower-seletar-reservoir-caught-by-pub-nparks; Ang Qing, "'Crikey!': 6 Recent Crocodile Sightings around Singapore," *ST*, 6 Oct. 2021, https://www.straitstimes.com/singapore/environment/crikey-6-recent-crocodile-sightings-around-singapore; Belinda Yuen, "Creating the Garden City: The Singapore Experience," *Urban Studies* 33, 6 (1996): 955–70.

[2] Anton Tordy, "Crocodile Country," *The Singapore Free Press* [hereafter, *SFP*], 19 Jan. 1957, p. 2; Susan G. Davis, *Spectacular Nature: Corporate Culture and the Sea World Experience* (Berkeley, CA: University of California Press, 1997), p. 30.

[3] Most studies have by and large documented the contested relationships negotiated between crocodiles and rural human communities. Melvin Bolton and Miro Laufa, "The Crocodile Project in Papua New Guinea," *Biological Conservation* 22, 3 (1982): 169–79; Simon Pooley, "Using Predator Attack Data to Save Lives, Human and Crocodilian," *Oryx* 49, 4 (2015): 581–3; Kevin M. Dunham, et al., "Human–Wildlife Conflict in Mozambique: A National Perspective, with Emphasis on Wildlife Attacks on Humans," *Oryx* 44, 2 (2010): 185–93; Sebastian Brackhane, et al., "Crocodile Management in Timor-Leste: Drawing Upon Traditional Ecological Knowledge and Cultural Beliefs," *Human Dimensions of Wildlife* 24, 4 (2019): 314–31.

[4] Several of the sources analyzed in this study have been the subject of two earlier works by Kate Pocklington and Siddharta Perez, "Revulsion and Reverence: Crocodiles in Singapore," *BiblioAsia* 14, 2 (2018): 14–19; Kate Pocklington, *Beast, Guardian, Island: The Saltwater Crocodile (Crocodylus porosus Schneider, 1801) in Singapore, 1819–2017* (Singapore: Lee Kong Chian Natural History Museum, 2021). I thank Lynn Wong Yuqing and Timothy P. Barnard for bringing these references to my attention.

crocodiles represent an underutilized, untamed and uncertain pre-modern nature, which humans need to tame, regulate and utilize in order to realize developmentalist ambitions. On the other hand, wild crocodile sightings and the media frenzy that often grew around them sheds light on how Singaporeans could briefly experience a nature that defied hegemonic state control. The value of crocodile sightings laid in the apparent disregard these creatures had for human urban expectations, intruding into humanized landscapes and therefore attracting press coverage and commentary.[5] Wild crocodiles cause a stir because they contravene the notion of a well-maintained Garden City, and such megafauna sightings imply that a natural realm exists alongside the human and remains hidden, unnoticed and forgotten until an occasional encounter occurs.

Crocodiles in Pre-war Malaya and Singapore

Crocodile sightings and encounters were neither new nor uncommon to the peoples of Southeast Asia. As several scholars have pointed out, these semi-aquatic reptiles share many etymological similarities that cut across different ethnic communities in Southeast Asia. For example, in several regions of the Philippines crocodiles are known as *buaya*, which is the same term used among many communities in the Malay world, reflecting its continuing presence in Austronesian languages until the present day. Crocodiles were commonly found in the swamps and jungles of 19th-century Malaya with one even infamously seizing the dog of William Farquhar. Newspaper reports from colonial Singapore, during which the island developed into an entrepôt under British supervision, further reinforced the ubiquity of their presence with descriptions of a Singapore River that "abounded" with crocodiles.[6]

---

[5] A similar observation about how crocodiles "raise alarm and strike fear in people's hearts" when they strayed into "public recreational areas" was made in passim by Pocklington and Perez, "Revulsion and Reverence," p. 15. Likewise, see Pocklington, *Beast, Guardian, Island*, pp. 32–5.

[6] Jan van der Ploeg, Merlijn van Weerd, and Gerard A. Persoon, "A Cultural History of Crocodiles in the Philippines: Towards a New Peace Pact?" *Environment and History* 17, 2 (2011): 234–6; Abdullah bin Abdul Kadir, "The Hikayat Abdullah, An Annotated Translation by A.H. Hill," *Journal of the Malayan Branch of the Royal Asiatic Society* 28, 3 (1955): 149; Anonymous, "The Scottish Corporation and the Sultan of Johore," *Straits Times Weekly Issue*, 2 Jan. 1886, p. 9; Anonymous, "Catching a Crocodile," *ST*, 31 May 1904, p. 5; Anonymous, "Singapore River Has Interesting History," *Sunday Tribune* (Singapore), 10 Sep. 1939, p. 2. These

When human–crocodile encounters were reported in colonial Singapore, they typically doubled as untitled obituaries, reflecting how laborers on the lower rungs of Singapore's political economy were disproportionately exposed to crocodile attacks.[7] Such concerns reflected a reliance on waterways for transporting goods and people throughout the island and in the region. A coolie, "while sitting near a creek," which extended into a coconut plantation, was "carried off" by an "alligator" in 1848. The mutilated human body was found in a mangrove jungle a few days later.[8] Another Chinese victim who went to the side of a junk to wash his feet when the vessel was docked at Johor en route to Singapore suffered the same misfortunate cause of death. The list of occupations of the various victims of attacks literally placed workers in the jaws of the crocodile throughout 19th- and early 20th-century Singapore.[9]

Searching for protein in the waters around and within Singapore was also hazardous. A Chinese fisherman who wanted to catch prawns in the Serangoon River in 1871 instead returned with an arm that was "severely lacerated from the elbow to the wrist," whereas in Tanjong Rhu, in 1901, a young crocodile became entangled in a fisherman's net. Sticking to land-based occupations did not guarantee one's safety either. A rice mill that operated near a swamp in Sungei Jurong Road was also a favorite haunt of a crocodile who had "seized two Chinamen on different occasions." In another recount dated to 1931, a "Tamil woman was tapping rubber trees early in the morning on the bank of a creek when suddenly she was

---

specimens in the late 1930s most likely fed on the waste effluent in the river.

[7] For a similar relationship between economic poverty, occupational hazards vis-à-vis tiger attacks in colonial Singapore, see Miles Alexander Powell, "People in Peril, Environments at Risk: Coolies, Tigers, and Colonial Singapore's Ecology of Poverty," *Environment and History* 22, 3 (2016): 455–82.

[8] Although alligators are not native to Singapore, we do not know if the journalists were using the terms "crocodile" and "alligator" interchangeably, or if they were describing a specimen based on physical taxonomy. In-text references to "alligators," however, will be preserved in this paper to facilitate bibliographic consultation. Given that Singapore was once a center for the wildlife trade, it would be unsurprising for non-native alligators to have been released into the wild. Fiona L.P. Tan, "The Beastly Business of Regulating the Wildlife Trade in Colonial Singapore," in *Nature Contained: Environmental Histories of Singapore*, ed. Timothy P. Barnard (Singapore: NUS Press, 2014), pp. 145–78; Anonymous, "Singapore, Thursday, 30th November," *SFP*, 30 Nov. 1848, p. 2.

[9] Anonymous, "Killed by a Crocodile," *SFP*, 27 Jul. 1905, p. 56; Anonymous, "A Monster Alligator Captured in the River," *Straits Times Weekly Issue*, 23 Jul. 1890, p. 3.

seized from behind" by a crocodile.[10] Encounters with crocodiles were thus a real risk for the many riparian denizens of Singapore who plied their trades and livelihoods along the coasts and the banks of the many waterways of the island.

Many reported trappers of crocodiles in 19th- and 20th-century Singapore were also fishermen. This relationship is not necessarily surprising, for crocodiles and sharks were spotted near fishing spots fishermen frequented, again hinting at how these apex predators clustered around potential sites of prey.[11] Nevertheless, we do not know if crocodiles were a circumstantial by-catch in nets laid out by fishermen, or if the latter—armed with nets—doubled up as crocodile hunters when the need arose. When an intruding crocodile was found in the Impounding Reservoir in 1904, a trap known as the *nibong* (made from a mangrove palm, *Oncosperma tigillarium*, often used for construction involving water) was utilized to catch the beast.

> This is a spike of hardwood sharpened at both ends to the centre of which is fastened a few feet of bark rope. The nibong is secured longitudinally to the rope by a bit of thread, and is then embedded in the body of a duck. The alligator by and by swallows the duck, and after the morsel has been properly gorged, the business of discovery and capture may be properly begun. To the aforesaid length of bark rope there is fastened about 100 feet of rattan rope, the end of which is buoyed by a coconut… (when) the alligator retires to his favourite haunt, the first thing is to discover the whereabouts of the coconut, put a drag on the rattan rope, which will have the effect of snapping the thread and throwing the nibong spike across the gullet of the reptile and making it impossible to be dragged out once fairly bolted…
> As the inside of the reptile must have been severely lacerated by the spiked ends of the nibong.[12]

---

[10] Anonymous, "Tuesday, 1st August," *Straits Times Overland Journal*, 12 Aug. 1871, p. 6; Anonymous, "Tuesday, 26th November," *ST*, 26 Nov. 1901, p. 2; Anonymous, "Alligator at the Reservoir," *SFP*, 9 Jan. 1894, p. 5; Anonymous, "Fishing Tin from the Sea at Lukut: Tales from Malaya," *SFP*, 23 Dec. 1931, p. 7. See also Pocklington, *Beast, Guardian, Island*, pp. 15–16.

[11] Anonymous, "Tuesday, 26th November," *ST*, 26 Nov. 1901, p. 2.

[12] Anonymous, "Alligator at the Reservoir"; H.H. Hipwell, "The Crocodile of the

While we cannot discount the possibility of the reporter fetishizing exotic technologies in this extract, the complexity of the trap suggested that there was a body of experience and specialized knowledge, possibly passed through word-of-mouth and refined through trial and error, devoted to the capture and destruction of dangerous crocodiles. Singaporeans were far from passive when confronted with crocodiles that threatened their well-being. Unfortunately, and reflective of colonial-era journalism, we do not know who first conceived of the trap even though the two Europeans who shot the crocodile received comprehensive coverage in the second half of the article.[13]

Bathing—a term used interchangeably with swimming during the colonial period—also exposed Singaporeans to attacks from these large reptiles. "Members of the Singapore Swimming Club, and residents at the seaside of Tanjong Rhu and Tanjong Katong" were informed that a crocodile was spotted in the vicinity of popular bathing spots in January 1903. Reports warned that "bathers should be careful," particularly after the trapped animal escaped. In other instances, the presence of a well-camouflaged crocodile could not be ascertained until a bait was set. In a collection of anecdotes compiled in 1931, Malay pleasure seekers who used old mining holes as bathing spots were known to place either a dog or a duck into these ponds to test for the presence of crocodiles that might be nesting within them.[14]

Throughout 19th- and 20th-century Singapore, notices about crocodile sightings were also circulated through word-of-mouth and updates in the press. For example, in December 1906, bathers were warned about the presence of crocodiles that stalked the Tanjong Katong, Tanjong Pagar and Pasir Panjang areas. This list concluded with an advisory which urged "bathers on each side of the island… (to) be careful to use a *pagar* (fenced bathing area) or defer their sea-bath till they have one." Earlier in the same year, a notice was published to warn visitors to the Singapore Swimming Club of "an alligator of considerable size," which "was observed off the diving stage" of the premises.[15]

Straits," *ST*, 11 May 1904, p. 9. Also quoted in Pocklington, *Beast, Guardian, Island*, p. 17.
[13] On crocodile hunting in postcolonial Malaya and Singapore, see Pocklington, *Beast, Guardian, Island*, pp. 15–23.
[14] Anonymous, "Alligator at Tanjong Rhu," *ST*, 26 Jan. 1903, p. 4; Anonymous, "Fishing Tin from the Sea at Lukut."
[15] *Pagar* is Malay for fence or enclosure. The mention of a *pagar* in the 1906 reports

Image 4.1: Bathing Pagar at Katong Park. Image courtesy of National Archives of Singapore.

In practice, we do not know how well these warnings were heeded, although judging from *The Straits Times* readership, it is unlikely that those who needed such dedicated fenced-off spaces (such as less wealthy non-European laborers) would have gained access to them. Even bathing *pagar*, while providing recreational users with a defensive buffer against crocodiles, were not failproof. Two separate incidents in 1930, for example, reported how their owners received rude shocks when crocodiles were found in, or attempting to trespass into the modified swimming pool. Still, as a rule of thumb, European bathers with better equipped (and more expensive) bathing and swimming facilities in colonial Singapore were more likely to be safe from the crocodile's jaws.[16] People in Singapore were thus in constant encounter with crocodiles in Singapore, and fatalities were not uncommon even with the advent and circulation of published advisories.

Despite the number of deaths attributed to crocodile attacks in pre-independence Singapore, riparian denizens demonstrated a willingness to tolerate, if not accommodate the presence of crocodiles. "Malays," one commentator noted in 1904, "seldom trouble to get rid of the brutes," and that "the destruction of a crocodile is only decided when all attempts to drive him from the neighbourhood of the kampong have failed." The general attitude of indifference adopted towards crocodiles also baffled European observers. H.E. Burgess, reported in 1936 in the *Journal of the Bombay Natural History Society* that he had "seen men bathing on one side of the river in full view of a monster crocodile basking on the opposite bank, while one sees boys ... manoeuvring tiny shallow boats" across crocodile infested rivers in Malaya.[17]

---

refers to an enclosed lagoon that theoretically serves as an additional obstacle to marauding crocodiles. Drawing on the experience of an "unfortunate Chinese" who was dragged away by a crocodile while bathing in Tanah Merah in 1928, *The Straits Times* noted snidely that "these pagars would not be there at all if the danger of sharks and crocs was not a very real one." To compensate for these concerns, the column suggests, readers should ask the owners of these *pagar* for permission to use these communal bathing spaces, since owners of such *pagar* "are only too willing to let people use them as long as the privilege is not abused." Anonymous, "The Week-End Column," *ST*, 22 Jun. 1928, p. 11; Anonymous, "Crocodiles About: Dangers to Bathers Round Singapore," *ST*, 14 Dec. 1906, p. 7; Anonymous, "A 'Croc' at the Swimming Club," *Eastern Daily Mail and Straits Morning Advertiser*, May 1906, p. 2; Pocklington, *Beast, Guardian, Island*, p. 32.

[16] Anonymous, "Sea View's 'Croc:' Shot by Marine Police in Pagar," *ST*, 23 May 1930, p. 14; Anonymous, "Tuesday, September 30, 1930," *SFP*, 30 Sep. 1930, p. 10.

[17] H.E. Burgess, "Early Days in Malaya," *The Journal of the Bombay Natural History*

This attitude of informed nonchalance adopted by many non-European Singaporeans continued into the post-war and the pre-independence period. Although crocodiles roamed Pasir Panjang in 1957, "scores of children" continued to swim "in the pond" where a crocodile attack had taken place previously, again reflecting the risk that locals took, knowingly or unknowingly. When stray crocodiles—as per one such case in a water hyacinth pond located off Upper Serangoon—villagers reacted ambivalently to the presence of the creature. Rather than advocating capture and destruction of the animal, the sighting was simply written-off as "no surprise."[18] The indifference Singaporeans displayed to crocodiles may seem at odds with the number of injuries and deaths crocodile attacks caused. The persistence of precolonial indigenous beliefs in which such "charismatic megafauna" shared a "special spiritual relationship" with their communities, however, partially explains the somewhat reverential outlook towards crocodiles during this period. Throughout Malaya "crocodiles were symbols of danger as well as protection, a benevolent and malevolent power at once," a belief that also persisted in the Philippines. In the Malay world crocodiles were often guardians of sacred sites, commonly graves, and were occasionally considered sacred themselves. The *keramat* of Jangal Pir, located along Havelock Road, is one example of this phenomenon in Singapore as believers have long considered it to be a site where a white crocodile would visit and sleep beside a grave on "a certain night every week" before returning to the river at daybreak.[19]

Crocodiles were not only markers of *keramat*, but also the site of reverence themselves. Malay and Chinese communities who lived or made a living along these waterways believed that rivers, lakes and streams had their own guardian spirits, which could take the form of wild crocodiles.

Society 38 (1935): 254; Hipwell, "The Crocodile of the Straits."

[18] Anonymous, "7-Foot 'Croc' Shot at Pasir Panjang," *SFP*, 11 Mar. 1948, p. 5; Pocklington and Perez, "Revulsion and Reverence," p. 17; Tordy, "Crocodile Country."

[19] Faizah Zakaria, *The Camphor Tree and the Elephant: Religion and Ecological Change in Maritime Southeast Asia* (Seattle, WA: University of Washington Press, 2023); Van Weerd and Persoon, "A Cultural History of the Crocodile in the Philippines," p. 237; Yahya, "Singapore's Keramats," *ST*, 11 Jun. 1939, p. 16; Richard Olaf Winstedt, "'Karamat': Sacred Places and Persons in Malaya," *Journal of the Malayan Branch of the Royal Asiatic Society* 2, 3 (1924): 254, 264–5, 270–3; Teren Sevea, *Miracles and Material Life: Rice, Ore, Traps and Guns in Islamic Malaysia* (Cambridge: Cambridge University Press, 2020), pp. 155, 178–9.

A Cultural History of Fear, Fascination, Fantasy and Crocodiles in Singapore

In Bukit Panjang, a crocodile was touted as a *keramat* guardian of the river Sungei Kadut in 1960. Revered as the community's *genius loci*, villagers took pains to conceal the hiding spot of the crocodile from outsiders, fearing that resident "fishermen would not be able to live along the river should any harm come to the crocodile." This reverence towards a resident crocodile, to be sure, was more of an exception than the norm, but the touted harmlessness of the creature must have had made a significant impression upon the villagers who perceived the beast as a "noble" animal *keramat* and thus differentiated from other man-eaters. Two decades later, similar sentiments in which crocodiles manifested guardian spirits were echoed at the Kallang River when fishermen who caught a glimpse of two semi-mythical white crocodiles were rewarded with large catches.[20]

Such sentiments of give-and-take towards and accommodation of crocodiles could be interpreted as an internalized familiarity with these reptiles. Until the late 1960s, communities who relied on Singaporean waterways for a living would not have considered a crocodile an anomaly, even though they kept a respectful distance from the animals. Coupled with the proliferation of mangrove forests along waterways and riparian communities, crocodile–human encounters were common occurrences that did not warrant any strict attempts at demarcating human and crocodile territories.[21] Cohabitation with these reptiles in pre-independence Singapore was also possible with the adoption of common-sense measures that minimized conflict. Water-skiers who frequented Kranji in 1957, although "used to sighting crocs" which "have not been known to attack," chose to "keep a wary eye on them, steering well clear of the bigger ones." In the same report, Malay fishermen reported that crocodiles who frequented the Jurong River never bothered them. In the latter instance, it was implied that ample food—such as fish living in the Jurong River—kept resident crocodiles satiated, and thus they did not need to prey on humans.[22] When post-war journalists occasionally commented about crocodile fatalities, they were ready to attribute them to the passive

---

[20] Pocklington, *Beast, Guardian, Island*, pp. 7–11; Brackhane, et al., "Crocodile Management in Timor-Leste," pp. 322–6; Anonymous, "They Offer a Silent Prayer to 'Sacred' Crocodile," *SFP*, 19 Apr. 1960, p. 7; Anonymous, "加冷河口有'镇海鳄?' *Jialenghe kou you 'zhen hai'e*? [Are There 'Guardian Crocodiles of the Sea' at the Mouth of the Kallang River?]," *Lianhe Wanbao*, 8 Jul. 1983, p. 24.
[21] Der Ploeg, Van Weerd and Persoon, "A Cultural History of Crocodiles in the Philippines," pp. 238–42.
[22] Tordy, "Crocodile Country."

Image 4.2: Malay boy sitting on crocodile, 1920s. Lim Kheng Chye Collection, courtesy of National Archives of Singapore.

stance of the communities in which the fatalities occurred. In July 1950, a crocodile attack on a Malay kampong dweller, for example, was disparagingly attributed "to the combined ill-luck of the whole village together than to an isolated misadventure."[23]

---

[23] Depicting the victims of this attack in a passive-aggressive manner, and blaming their ethnicity, can be seen in the report, when it was attributed to their being "simple-minded folks" who "consoled themselves in the belief that the local creatures are either *kramats* (miracle workers) or else *datoks* (old chieftains) and are, therefore, not accustomed to perpetuating wanton deeds in their own locality." Similar beliefs also existed in localized Chinese communities in the region. Cheu Hock Tong, "The Datuk Kong Spirit Cult Movement in Penang: Being and Belonging in Multi-ethnic Malaysia," *Journal of Southeast Asian Studies* 23, 2 (1992): 381–404; Li Yongqiu, 专吃华人的鳄鱼：老太平的民间故事 *Zhuanmen chiren de e'yu: Lao Taiping de minjian gushi* [Crocodiles that Eat Chinese People: Folktales and Stories from Old Taiping (Malaysia)] (Taiping: Li Yongqiu, 2019); E.C. Janardanan, "Hunting the Maneating Crocs," *SFP*, 29 Jul. 1950, p. 3.

The accommodations made by humans towards crocodiles in Singapore soon began to shift. In 1960, fishermen began avoiding fishing spots in Punggol and Pulau Ubin where crocodiles frequented, or they changed their occupations altogether. In other parts of Singapore, warnings and simply staying alert in places with crocodile sightings became *di rigueur*. Mothers urged their children to stay close to home instead of wandering into localities where crocodiles have been sighted previously.[24] Such reports as Singapore neared independence suggest that, while crocodiles were not always treated as pests, they were perceived as a feature of the riverine environment that should be tolerated and prudently managed whenever possible.

Modernizing a Nation, Reducing a Habitat

This mix of ambiguous sentiments through which pre-independence Singaporeans regarded wild crocodiles changed rapidly after 1965. Like the populace of Singapore, nature was to be tamed and disciplined to ensure the success of developmental and nation-building projects that the People's Action Party (PAP) spearheaded. The newly independent nation and geo-body, to borrow Thongchai Winachukul's concept, was mobilized to conform with national values of modernization, economic development and stability.[25] This impacted crocodiles in numerous ways. For example, the mangrove swamps of Jurong Island—once home to the creatures—was reclaimed from the late 1960s to support housing and oil refinery projects for a flourishing population. The gradual disappearance of crocodiles from everyday experience coincided with the relocation of Singaporeans from riparian settlements and kampongs to high-rise Housing & Development Board (HDB) flats.[26]

---

[24] Anonymous, "Croc Scares Fishermen," *ST*, 18 Mar. 1960, p. 16; Arthur Richards, "Villagers to Hold a Feast for Kramat to Scare Away Crocs in the Canal," *SFP*, 29 Jun. 1960, p. 9.
[25] Thongchai Winachukul, *Siam Mapped: A History of the Geo-Body of a Nation* (Honolulu, HI: University of Hawai'i Press, 1994); Timothy P. Barnard and Corrine Heng, "A City in a Garden," in *Nature Contained: Environmental Histories of Singapore*, ed. Timothy P. Barnard (Singapore: NUS Press, 2014), p. 295.
[26] Tony O' Dempsey, "Singapore's Changing Landscape since c. 1800," in *Nature Contained: Environmental Histories of Singapore*, ed. Timothy P. Barnard (Singapore: NUS Press, 2014), p. 44; Loh Kah Seng, *Squatters into Citizens: The 1961 Bukit Ho Swee Fire and the Making of Modern Singapore* (Singapore: NUS Press, 2013).

Physical transformations of inland landscape as well as the waterways that lined Singapore corresponded with changes in attitudes towards crocodiles. The creatures transformed, becoming "problems" that transgressed the now-normalized urban environment. Such conceptions were not necessarily a post-1965 phenomenon but they did draw upon postcolonial impressions of crocodiles as antithetical to the disciplinary power of the state. In 1937, policeman Isnin bin Mahdan from the Hill Street Police Station gained the moniker "*brani*" (brave) when he dragged an eight-foot (2.4-meter) crocodile out of the Singapore River under the Coleman Bridge after a two-hour-long "battle" with the reptile. Likewise, in 1947, a few preliminary shots from a police car on patrol weakened a crocodile wandering around MacRitchie Reservoir before a .303 rifle dispatched from Nee Soon Police Station finished off the beast. Similarly, in March 1960, residents in Punggol summoned the aid of a police post in Paya Lebar, where a strongly worded letter to the officer-in-charge branded a loitering crocodile as "a danger to fishermen and picnickers."[27]

After independence, the crocodile—at least in the media—became a symbol of an untamed nature that had no place in the modern Garden City. The unpredictability of crocodile sightings, in contrast to the certain elimination of tigers within Singaporean borders, likely accentuated reports of mystery and awe associated with them. In 1972, the disappearance of crocodiles from Jurong, once a swampy stronghold for these animals, was noted with the construction of the eponymous industrial town. Yet, the article continues with a hint of suspense as "some of these creatures (were still) about" before panning to a reported sighting of a five- to six-foot-long crocodile spotted in the upper courses of the Jurong River. Readers, however, were assured that the crocodiles of today were nothing compared to the "man-eaters" that were once spotted in the area during the 1950s. The association of crocodiles with pre-independence (and under-developed) Singapore was unmistakeable. As the article summarized the transition, "bulldozers started levelling Jurong hills to fill up the swamps" that were once infested with crocodiles, resulting in a reduction in the saurian population.[28]

---

[27] Anonymous, "'Baby' Croc. Caught in Singapore River," *ST*, 12 Nov. 1937, p. 12; Anonymous, "Crocodile Shot in Thomson Road," *SFP*, 8 Jan. 1947, p. 1; Anonymous, "Ponggol Croc Returns with a Mate," *ST*, 26 Mar. 1960, p. 4.
[28] William Campbell, "Shedding Tears over a Vanishing Breed," *ST*, 1 Oct. 1972, p. 10.

The association of Jurong with crocodiles continued. A year later, in 1973, the newly opened Japanese Garden was described as "crocodile territory" since the beasts occasionally basked in the sun there.[29] Notwithstanding such warnings, some Singaporeans continued with their benign acceptance of crocodiles into the post-independence era. In March 1975, despite reports and signs that warned passers-by and anglers of the presence of an "11-meter-long" and "dangerous" crocodile in Jurong Lake, journalists noted that some continued to swim there while gathering water hyacinth for pig feed. Predictably, the exaggerated length of the crocodile (eventually put down to "3.5 meters long"), while eventually corrected, should give us pause. While it may have had been a journalistic error, the outrageous difference between initial and corrected reports may point to the growing association of crocodiles with the frontier of Jurong that allowed such monsters of unprecedented size to thrive.[30]

Despite the infamy of Jurong as crocodile territory in the first few decades of Singaporean independence, the location's reputation as a haunt of crocodiles was not impervious to growing disbelief and detachment among the public, most of the latter having moved into the safety of high-rise public housing. Writing to the *New Nation* in March 1975, T.A. Mugan mused that a published photograph of a crocodile had "brought crocodile tears to my eyes in sheer amusement at the imaginary creatures" in Jurong. Mugan argued that the image was bogus, because it "has not only come too close to human habitation to be true," and the photogenic poise of the creature had struck him, a reader, as beyond belief.[31] Sentiments of denial like these indicated growing disbelief that a now-urbanized Jurong could remain home to creatures who belonged only to the undeveloped Singapore of old.

The response towards this letter was equally revealing. Possibly tinged with sarcasm, the reply from the public relations manager of the Jurong Town Corporation guaranteed readers that the photographed animal was "as alive as can be," and that it "is not imaginary or legendary like the Loch Ness Monster (whose presence has yet to be proven)." In the

---

[29] Wee Beng Huat, "Fishing for Trouble in a River…," *New Nation* [hereafter, *NN*], 15 Jun. 1973, p. 2; Sonny Yap, "Jurong," *NN*, 1 Jun. 1976, pp. 10–11.
[30] Anonymous, "Crocs Alive…," *NN*, 13 Mar. 1975, p. 1; Anonymous, "Crocodile," *NN*, 14 Mar. 1975, p. 2; Mark V. Barrow, *Nature's Ghosts: Confronting Extinction from the Age of Jefferson to the Age of Ecology* (Chicago, IL: University of Chicago Press, 2009), pp. 15–26.
[31] T.A. Mugan, "The Model Croc at Jurong," *NN*, 22 Mar. 1975, p. 6.

same vein, the manager stressed that previous attempts at rounding up crocodiles in the lake had "so far failed," again underscoring the link between the crocodiles' ability to evade control and capture and their association with an untamed and semi-magical wild. Any sentiment of natural mystique evoked in this reply, however, abruptly ended in the conclusion, where readers were assured that the government-linked company was attempting to engage an "experienced group of animal trappers to clear Jurong Lake of these crocodiles."[32] Technocratic power was to be rallied to subdue these pests and bring them in line with the national vision of creating a Garden City, lest the uninvited presence of these animals—once associated with an untamed and mystical past and waterways scattered across the island—threatened Singaporeans. Transgressions like these, when reported in a brief but dramatic manner were important historical and ecological reminders for Singaporeans who craved a "wild" Singapore that no longer existed.

By the 1980s, humans no longer encountered crocodiles every day nor expected to see one at every turn in the waterways of a modern Singapore. One of the primary reasons for this shift from pre-independence attitudes was a noticeable decline in the number of wild crocodiles, even though a reliable historical number remain elusive. Statistical estimations of mangrove forest reduction since the 1960s, however, can serve as a proxy to understand the contraction in crocodile habitats. Mangrove swamps covered only 0.5 percent of Singapore by 1999, down from an original 13 percent.[33] The destruction of this important biome, land reclamation and the concretization of waterways resulted in a loss of habitat, and prohibited the growth of a sizable crocodile population in Singapore, a trend mirrored in fewer reports of crocodile–human encounters since the late 1960s.

Commodifying and Exhibiting Crocodiles

Although there was a reduction in the wild crocodile population in modern Singapore, these animals remained in the popular memory, although the perception shifted to one of the large reptile as a natural resource, exploited to ensure the success of island-state in the international

---

[32] Wee Ban Bee, "This Croc's for Real," *NN*, 8 Apr. 1975, p. 8.
[33] Peter K.L. Ng and N. Sivasothi, ed., *A Guide to the Mangroves of Singapore* (Singapore: Singapore Science Centre, 1999), pp. 8–10; Pocklington and Perez, "Revulsion and Reverence," p. 16; Pocklington, *Beast, Guardian, Island*, pp. 31–5.

economic arena. Such notions drew as much upon colonial legacies as they were inspired by modernist ambitions of a developmental state. As early as 1924, D.G. Stead, the Fisheries Enquiry Commissioner in British Malaya had observed how the ubiquity of crocodiles, coupled with their habit of "penetrating into all secret of places" and exhibiting a "toll of human life" could be transformed from the "greatest scourge" to "some form of subsidiary industry as a side-line to the various fisheries that are carried on the estuary." Despite this enthusiasm, the commodification of crocodiles only took off after the Second World War, when Singapore gained prominence as a hub for the traffic in skins of the beast. In 1948, shops in Singapore were mentioned to have reared crocodiles, pythons and lizards at their back premises for such purposes.[34] By the 1960s, crocodile farming—mainly for their skins—made headlines again due to a crime wave of theft followed by the observation that Singaporeans oversaw a "roaring trade in croc skins."[35]

Crocodile farms in Singapore shifted from "processors to manufacturers" in August 1964, when Goh Keng Swee, the then-Minister of Finance, announced that the Economic Development Board of Singapore had established a leather tannery as it would "advance the position" of where Singapore would progress up the supply chain by trading "from raw hides and skin processing to leather manufacturing." Crocodiles were now a building block for national and economic development. This was further solidified the next year after "United Nations' leather expert" Ernest Gergeley observed that reptile leather was elusive to replication by synthetic means and thus would remain in consistently high demand. Singapore, with an export industry with a worth estimated "to more than three million dollars" of "locally produced" crocodile and snake leather appeared well poised to take advantage of these changing commercial headwinds.[36]

---

[34] These animals were also sold as pets, as the article explains how these creatures were easy to feed and maintain. Anonymous, "Choose Your Own Crocodile," *ST*, 2 May 1948, p. 5; Anonymous, "Crocodile Leather," *Malayan Saturday Post*, 19 Apr. 1924, p. 8.

[35] Anonymous, "Singapore Doing Roaring Trade in Croc Skins," *ST*, 4 Jul. 1961, p. 14.

[36] Anonymous, "New Tannery 'a Govt Idea'," *ST*, 27 Aug. 1964, p. 9; Anonymous, "Fashion Trends in Fancy Leather, Reptile Skins," *ST*, 21 Oct. 1965, p. 12; Linda Low, et al., *Challenge and Response: Thirty Years of the Economic Development Board* (Singapore: Times Academic Press, 1993).

The role that the reptile skin industry played in shaping some economic activities in early independent Singapore was significant. By June 1971, crocodile farms were found across the island, from the "outskirts of the city in Punggol, Yio Chu Kang and the Chua Chu Kang areas" to "backyards in residential areas." Complementary and intermediary industries, such as marketing and tannery companies, were also beneficiaries of this boom. In the shadow of this profitable trade was the burgeoning number of crimes reported over the theft of crocodiles and their skins from different establishments throughout Singapore. In 1970, a shop was robbed of "$14,000 worth of crocodile skin," and 11 baby crocodiles were heisted from the bungalow of a crocodile breeder in Joo Koon two years later. Occasionally, related crimes became cross-border affairs, such as when 26 baby crocodiles stolen from Johor Baru were recovered in Singapore in 1971.[37]

The significance of crocodiles (and their leather by-products) in Singapore throughout the late 1960s until the mid-1970s should not be underestimated. As Singapore rebranded itself as a destination for tourists, crocodiles were gradually assimilated into this vision. Likely reflective of the self-Orientalism that underpinned tourism initiatives in post-independence Singapore, handbags and clothing made out of crocodile leather became one of the featured items sold to tourists in the Raffles Place Garden in 1965.[38] When Commonwealth delegates met in Singapore in 1971, their wives were shown a crocodile farm and tanning facility, which was touted as the "most exciting part [of the tour] for most." Elsewhere, a crocodile farm in Serangoon became a recommended site for prospective tourists who were interested in the "trades of the Orient." Indeed, demand for viewing live crocodiles and the purchase of crocodile products—a reflection of continued Singaporean reliance upon international capital and demand for goods to fuel export oriented

---

[37] Wee Beng Huat, "No Business Like Crocodile Business," *NN*, 3 Jun. 1971, p. 16; Anonymous, "Reptile-Skin Goods for Trendy World of Fashion," *NN*, 1 Apr. 1972, p. 11; Anonymous, "Robbers and Thieves Take $19,000 in 4 Raids," *ST*, 14 Dec. 1970, p. 18; Anonymous, "Three Held after 26 Stolen Baby Crocs Are Found," *ST*, 22 May 1971, p. 17; Anonymous, "Eleven Baby Crocodiles Stolen from Bungalow," *ST*, 6 Jan. 1972, p. 2; Anonymous, "Another Boost for S'pore Tourist Industry," *ST*, 27 Nov. 1965, p. 14; Anonymous, "Three Held After 26 Stolen Baby Crocs Are Found," *ST*, 22 May 1971, p. 17.

[38] Ooi Con-Seng, "The Orient Responds: Tourism, Orientalism and the National Museums of Singapore," *Tourism* 53, 4 (2005): 285–99.

A Cultural History of Fear, Fascination, Fantasy and Crocodiles in Singapore

Image 4.3: Wives of Commonwealth heads visiting a crocodile farm, 1971. Ministry of Information and the Arts Collection, courtesy of National Archives of Singapore.

industrialization—was primarily foreign, as it appealed mostly to "tourists, [in] particular Japanese, Australians and Europeans."[39]

Debates about the role crocodiles would play as a tourist attraction, or even part of the Singapore Zoo, corresponded with attempts to transform these animals into a natural resource that would spur national development. This reflected a growing disconnect with the idea that crocodiles were from the wild. They had become a tamed beast. While

---

[39] Nellie Har, "VIP Wives at Crocodile Farm," *ST*, 22 Jan. 1971, p. 9; Anonymous, "On Your Left Bak Kut Teh… Over Here Ghim Moh," *NN*, 14 Jan. 1979, p. 2; Richard Stubbs, "War and Economic Development: Export-Oriented Industrialization in East and Southeast Asia," *Comparative Politics* 31, 3 (1999): 337–55; Norman Owen, "Economic and Social Change," in *The Cambridge History of Southeast Asia*, ed. Nicholas Tarling (Cambridge: Cambridge University Press, 1993), pp. 474, 483–8; Anonymous, "Fashion Items From Fearsome Reptiles…," *NN*, 5 Jul. 1975, p. 12; Hitoshi Hirakawa and Hiroshi Shimizu, *Japan and Singapore in the World Economy: Japan's Economic Advance into Singapore 1870–1965* (London and New York, NY: Routledge, 1999), pp. 147–206; Anonymous, "Exports of Croc and Snake Skin Items Rising," *Business Times*, 2 Sep. 1977, p. 12; Pocklington, *Beast, Guardian, Island*, pp. 24–9.

crocodiles should feature as a part of the humid tropics' wealth of reptilian species and varieties, appreciation of these animals was only conceived of in terms of zoos and displays.[40]

As wild crocodile sightings became rare amidst the urban landscape of post-independence Singapore, the animal appeared in the heartlands of the public imagination as a form of popular entertainment and recreation. This is best seen in East Coast Park where, in the mid-1970s, a "crocodile aquarium" developed alongside many other amenities to entertain Singaporeans. Time spent at these recreational sites, as the journalist Nancy Koh suggested, became a romanticized encounter with a distant, controlled Singaporean past. "It's like being wafted from the prosaic rattle and hassle of modern living to an instant idyllic," she claimed, "where time belongs not to the present, nor to the future, not even to the past, but to a period of time that's as changeless as the sea, the sky and the trees."[41] While Koh was quick to associate these newly developed amenities with a timeless nostalgia, state institutions were also keen on capitalizing on these attractions to facilitate "passive and active recreation" among Singaporeans. By 1977, the state actively facilitated the transportation and display of captive crocodiles into such locations, all in the name of recreation and leisure for Singaporeans who had relocated from their kampongs into high-rise urban housing.[42]

Recreation was only one aspect of the grandiose project to transform the landscape of the nation. The obverse, a crass environmentalism manifesting in a vaguely imagined "green lung" in a Garden City, offered insight into how captive crocodiles were juxtaposed against this wider place in the nation-state. In their newest incarnation, the animals would

---

[40] See Choo Ruizhi's contribution to this collection. Garden Ecologist, "Reptile Squad—What a Pull It Can Be at Zoo," *ST*, 4 Oct. 1973, p. 12. For comparison, see Takashi Ito, "Locating the Transformation of Sensibilities in Nineteenth-Century London," in *Animal Cities: Beastly Urban Histories*, ed. Peter Atkins (Farnham, Surrey; Burlington: Ashgate, 2012), pp. 189–204; Davis, *Spectacular Nature*, pp. 48–76; David Grazian, "Where the Wild Things Aren't: Exhibiting Nature in American Zoos," *The Sociological Quarterly* 53, 4 (2012): 546–65; Adam Keul, "Embodied Encounters between Humans and Gators," *Social and Cultural Geography* 14, 8 (2013): 930–53; Pocklington and Perez, "Revulsion and Reverence," pp. 16, 19.
[41] Nancy Koh, "The Green, Green Lung of Home," *NN*, 31 Oct. 1975, pp. 10–11.
[42] National Archives of Singapore: KC.JUL.33/76: "Speech by Tan Eng Liang, Senior Minister of State for National Development at the Launching of the Singapore Scout Association's Community Project at East Coast Park"; Anonymous, "Plans For a Croc Tank in East Coast Park," *NN*, 13 Apr. 1977, p. 4; Anonymous, "Croc Tank for East Coast Park Resort," *ST*, 14 Apr. 1977, p. 9.

be featured in the Singapore Crocodilarium. They were now "powerful creatures" that "never fail to evoke a sense of danger and fear," even when they were viewed in a "man-made concrete pool." The Singapore Crocodilarium, however, remained a misnomer at best as it did not even attempt to present the creatures in their natural habitat. Visitors, at the end of their tour of the premises, would be given "insight into the way crocodiles are skinned" before being ushered into a factory-esque "showroom for crocodile skin goods like handbags, belts and wallets for souvenir hunters."[43] Crocodiles had been modernized, part of the economy and development of the nation-state.

The puzzling implications of such "aquariums" inspired fear and reverence.[44] Live crocodiles were displayed in an imagined habitat, yet they were also hard cash for the nascent Republic after slaughter. Such encounters contributed to detachment and alienation. Encounters with captive crocodiles now were juxtaposed against dispassionate economic incentives and irrational consumerism, unlike the unintended, albeit worrisome, sightings of wild crocodiles in pre-independence Singapore. Yet, elements from pre-independence Singapore persisted and were tacitly imbued into the exhibits, where crocodiles lived in a temporally suspended environment that was incommensurably different with an audience who viewed them from behind a glass screen.

Singaporeans now viewed crocodiles from the safety of viewing galleries. Writing in the *New Nation*, Gloria Chandy mused whether her readers knew any children who were, "for no rhyme and reason, afraid of cats and dogs?" While she conceded that children may gain an adverse fear of certain animals after "bad experiences with one," she ultimately placed the blame upon a lack of exposure, where children are "scared stiff simply because they have had no experiences with animals whatsoever." Unlike an earlier generation of Singaporeans who treated crocodile sightings with a mix of respect and fear, a younger generation of Singaporeans—which had no exposure to either the waterways or its fauna and flora that their elders had encountered previously—were confronted with a mix of emotions when confronted with the exact same creatures. Rather than prescribing a measure of safe exposure to animals in the wild, perhaps in the nature reserves on the island—to this recurring problem, Chandy

---

[43] Sit Meng Chue, "800 More Reptiles to Join Latest Tourist Attraction," *ST*, 20 Jan. 1980, p. 9; Anonymous, "East Coast Park Will Be Biggest 'Green Lung,'" *ST*, 15 Aug. 1977, p. 10; Koh, "The Green, Green Lung of Home."

[44] See Miles Powell's contribution to this collection.

Image 4.4: Man carrying a crocodile, late 1980s. Singapore Tourism Board Collection, courtesy of National Archives of Singapore.

proposed that each school was to "maintain two or three domestic animals for the children to keep as pets." Exposure to animals was necessary, but this was to be enforced through the use of domestic animals, a mentality reflective of urban-raised Singaporeans who by the late 1970s had already embraced the divide between a "wild" nature and a "nature contained."[45]

White Crocodiles and Unseen Nature

A diminished exposure to the waterways that had once supported Singapore socio-economic life, accompanied by an utilitarian assessment of the crocodile's worth to national development had, by the late 1970s,

---

[45] At the other extreme, six young live crocodiles were donated to the CHIJ St. Nicholas School, according to a report by Pan Xinghua, "迷你鳄鱼进校园引来欢乐与忧愁 *Mini e'yu jin xiaoyuan yinlai huanle yu youchou* [Mini crocodiles in school spark joy and worry]," *Lianhe Wanbao*, 28 Aug. 1989, p. 8; Gloria Chandy, "Teach Kids to be Kind to Animals," *NN*, 3 Sep. 1979, p. 8; Timothy P. Barnard (ed.), *Nature Contained: Environmental Histories of Singapore* (Singapore: NUS Press, 2014); Pocklington, *Beast, Guardian, Island*, pp. 28–9.

refracted into public consciousness whenever the creature was sighted. Although this tone was common among the mentality of an increasingly urbanized world that assimilated the rural into the urban, reports of crocodiles were also infused with supernatural allusions and symbols.[46] This was certainly true in 1977 when the Singapore Sea Scouts attempted to capture a white crocodile (*buaya putih*) through four (failed) expeditions around the island's waterways, reflecting a psychological hunger for an animalistic and primitive nature among residents of the nation-state. Such a mythical creature occupies an important place in Malay history and literature. In *Hikayat Hang Tuah* (The story of Hang Tuah), a classic text from the region, for example, a white crocodile surprises the eponymous hero and snatches away his powerful dagger, or *kris*. Since only those with a "pure heart" may capture such a powerful animal, which even had the ability to snatch a powerful object from the esteemed Hang Tuah, the Sea Scouts Expedition, which covered "400 kilometres of water on canoes," would take on equally legendary overtones, particularly in a modern, urbanized society.[47]

Peter Dendle has argued elsewhere that a world which is "over-explored, over-tamed and over-understood" has sparked a contemporaneous renaissance in cryptozoology. The pseudoscience's insistent belief in, and search for, unidentified animals concurrently mirrored a popular "undercurrent of resistance to beliefs" imposed by an institutionalized scientific elite. The Sea Scouts Expedition was premised upon similar anxieties. The Sea Scouts and interested public, however, were not negotiating against the hegemony of science, but interpretations of a Garden City the newly independent developmentalist state curated.[48] As the mangrove swamps and waterways in Singapore shrank and were

---

[46] This was not an entirely post-independence phenomenon. In 1936, a *Straits Times* article reported on a "rogue" crocodile living in the Katong area and compared the animal's elusiveness to that of the Loch Ness Monster. Anonymous, "'Nice Big Snake at Katong,' Python Killed," *ST*, 26 Nov. 1936, p. 12.
[47] Muhammad Haji Salleh (tr.), *The Epic of Hang Tuah* (Kuala Lumpur: Institut Terjemahan Negara Malaysia, 2010), p. 469; Pocklington, *Beast, Guardian, Island*, p. 5; Anonymous, "Scouts Hunt for White Crocodile," *NN*, 30 Apr. 1977, p. 2; Beng Tan, "A Fourth Bid to Catch White Croc," *ST*, 25 Jun. 1977, p. 12.
[48] Peter Dendle, "Cryptozoology in the Medieval and Modern Worlds," *Folklore* 117, 2 (2006): 193, 200; Han Heejin, "Singapore, A Garden City: Authoritarian Environmentalism in a Developmental State," *The Journal of Environment and Development* 26, 1 (2017): 8–18.

developed into either drainage canals or reservoirs, the crocodile became a part of a not-so-distant past.

Whether it was a product of confirmation bias or a genuine sighting of the mythical animal, the first expedition concluded in May 1977 with a single (suspected) sighting of the animal "between Seletar and Coney Island." Though these expeditions were fruitless, the taboos the Sea Scouts observed were symptomatic of a worldview that had trouble accepting the demise of a pristine, mystical and primitive nature in Singapore. The participants' abstinence from pork before their expedition testified to how folk-Islamic connotations of *keramat* worship informed their present-day search for the *buaya putih*. Likewise, the first expedition's failure in April 1977 was pinned squarely upon "the sound of the escort motor boat," which "'scared away'" the creature. The eventual substitution of motor boats with hand-paddled canoes in the pursuit of the creature reflected the prevailing mentality of the time. A pristine nature would only be accessible after one returns to the techniques and attitudes of the past.[49]

This worldview also fed into the fourth attempt at capturing the white crocodile in June 1977. When journalists reported that the beast was no fantasy, for not only had an earlier expedition sighted it in the Straits of Johor, it "was also confirmed by sea gypsies [Orang Laut] who pray to the spirit of the crocodile during traditional ceremonies." The suggestion that the Orang Laut existed in the same category as the white crocodile affirmed each other's existence and that they belonged to a Singapore untouched by the march of modernity and progress. Nevertheless, while the expedition was a psychological attempt at defying the statist narrative of control and domination over nature, the Sea Scouts paradoxically affirmed statist beliefs in taming and regulating the wild. Once the *buaya putih* had been "caught," the Sea Scouts announced, the animal would "be donated to the zoo."[50] Resistance against the state's hegemonic

---

[49] Anonymous, "Another Hunt by Scouts for White Croc," *ST*, 13 Jun. 1977, p. 8; Anonymous, "Scouts Fail in Hunt for Legendary White Croc," *ST*, 3 May 1977, p. 9; Cheu, "The Datuk Kong Spirit Cult Movement in Penang," p. 395.

[50] Anonymous, "Another Hunt by Scouts for White Croc"; "Beng Tan, "A Fourth Bid to Catch White Croc"; Anonymous, "A Fourth Bid to Catch the White Croc," *ST*, 2 May 1977, p. 5; Timothy P. Barnard, "Celates, Rayat-Laut, Pirates: The Orang Laut and Their Decline in History," *Journal of the Malaysian Branch of the Royal Asiatic Society* 80, 2 (2007): 33–49; Koh Keng We, "Familiar Strangers and Stranger-kings: Mobility, Diasporas, and the Foreign in the Eighteenth-century Malay World," *Journal of Southeast Asian Studies* 48, 3 (2017): 393, 400–1; Zakaria, *The Camphor Tree and the Elephant*.

conception of nature had its limits. Although the Sea Scouts and readers harbored hopes of a wild and untamed nature remaining in Singaporean waterways, this nature was to be subjugated and disciplined within the captivity of a zoological garden.

In October 1983, another white crocodile was sighted in Singapore. In this incarnation, it was not the Sea Scouts who were featured. Rather, it was a Chinese crocodile catcher known as Lee Ah Tee, who went by the moniker "*buaya* king" (crocodile king). Lee had established his reputation three months earlier after successfully capturing a 1.8 meter crocodile that lurked in the Kallang River and a second specimen in the Singapore River. A media circus ensued that grew around crocodile sightings. In July 1983 alone, over 10 articles in the English and Chinese press referenced Lee's career as a crocodile hunter, as well as his success in handling crocodiles. Likely capitalizing on similar eye-catching stories of crocodile capture, *Lianhe Wanbao* ran a concurrent account of "Top Ten Crocodile Incidents in Singapore" on 7 July 1983.[51] The repetitiveness, suspense and tropes of danger foregrounded by these reports point to a Singaporean desire for such sightings, and the press gladly obliged.

In spite of his reputation, Lee refused to pursue the mythical creature. His opposition to this task, despite having captured "more than 100 crocodiles from the swamps and estuaries" in Singapore, was rooted in his belief that bad luck would follow him if he led such an expedition, as white crocodiles were "tame and will not hurt anybody." The authorities were unconvinced. In a move reminiscent of the Sea Scouts' attempt at capturing the animal and presenting it to the zoo, readers were informed that "the police will probably have no choice but to turn to the Singapore Zoological Gardens for help."[52] Lee's "mystical" portrayal of the white crocodile appearance was portrayed consistently across different reading habits. A contemporaneous report in the *Lianhe Wanbao*, for example,

---

[51] Sit Yin Fong, "'Buaya King' Has Caught 100 Crocs," *Singapore Monitor*, 6 Jul. 1983, p. 2; Anonymous, "Friends Catch Crocodile from River," *ST*, 6 Jul. 1983, p. 9; Lin Dexiang and Wang Guinan, "四人合力擒鳄鱼 *Si ren he li qin e'yu* [Four cooperate to capture a crocodile]," *Lianhe Zaobao*, 6 Jul. 1983, p. 30; Qinyu, "本地'十大鳄踪'! *Bendi 'shi da e'zong'*! [Ten Local Cases of Crocodile Sightings]," *Lianhe Wanbao*, 7 Jul. 1983, p. 14.

[52] K.K. Fong, "Legend of White Crocodile Puts Off Local Catcher," *Singapore Monitor*, 5 Oct. 1983, p. 4; Yang Deshun, "白鳄不抓 *Bai'e bu zhua* [The white crocodile will not be caught]," *Lianhe Wanbao*, 4 Oct. 1983, p. 1; Suresh Nair, "Croc No. 2," *Singapore Monitor*, 10 Jul. 1983, p. 7; Pocklington, *Beast, Guardian, Island*, p. 9.

established that white crocodiles were associated with divine powers, and that disaster was sure to befall any riparian community that witnessed fights between white and black (normal colored) crocodiles. Slightly less than a month later, a team of Singaporeans, "natural sciences experts" hailing "from the Malayan Nature Society [and] the Singapore Institute of Biologists," announced that they would journey up the Endau River in Malaysia to search for white crocodiles and flesh-eating fish, with a cursory comment that "white crocodiles are rare, and many a legend has been associated with them." Similar claims about the luck-bestowing powers of these creatures were also echoed in the Chinese press.[53]

Fantastical creatures as remnants of a Singapore untouched by development could now only be found outside of the borders of the nation-state. For the bulk of pre-war and the first few decades of post-war Singapore, crocodiles and humans in Singapore had lived in an uneasy co-existence, where humans exercised care and common sense to prevent encounters with the crocodiles. In post-independence Singapore, moderately benign attitudes towards crocodiles gave way to exploitation, subjugation and apathy, be it in the form of the reptile skin trade or in the form of exhibits where the crocodiles had to suffer the cruelty of unsympathetic spectators. Stripped of their mystique and danger after they were consigned to pits and aquariums, captive crocodiles lost their awe. Wild crocodiles, in contrast, became the subject of short-lived media circuses, where contributors speculated at length about the symbolism and "motivations" posed by their subject matter. Such sensationalist responses reveal how contemporaneous Singaporeans longed for an animalistic, untamed and pristine nature. This mentality, however, was carefully curated and adapted to present-day realities and the strictures of urban life, where short bursts of intense excitement, fascination and panic dominated the discourse that surround wild crocodile sightings.

Singaporeans, as Miles Powell has argued, have lost a "cultural connection" to the sea and coast as a result of relocation into inland housing estates and careers. The short-lived media circuses that developed

---

[53] Anonymous, "鳄鱼分两种 *E'yu fen liang zhong* [Two types of crocodiles]," *Lianhe Wanbao*, 3 Oct. 1983, p. 1; Foo Mey Kien, "S'poreans in Search of the White Crocodile," *Singapore Monitor*, 25 Nov. 1983, p. 9; Anonymous, "15人探险团明年初赴彭柔两州进行搜寻白鳄探险 *15 ren tanxiantuan mingnian chu fu Peng Rou liang zhou jinxing shouxun bai'e tanxian* [A 15-person expedition will be despatched to Pahang and Johor to search for white crocodiles and adventure]," *Lianhe Wanbao*, 27 Nov. 1983, p. 4.

around sightings of wild crocodiles suggest that an imagined connection with nature has re-aligned with the constraints of urban life, creating new, urbanized connections. Untamed (or white) crocodile sightings are perfect avenues for these imaginative fantasies of an "animalistic" and "dangerous" world to precipitate in an urban environment. Wild crocodiles stray into waterways on their own whim, and they do not observe the strictures of a well-manicured Garden City, to the chagrin of state agencies.[54]

---

[54] Miles Alexander Powell, "Singapore's Lost Coast: Land Reclamation, National Development and the Erasure of Human and Ecological Communities, 1822–Present," *Environment and History* 27, 4 (2021): 635–63.

CHAPTER FIVE

Too Much Monkey Business

Timothy P. Barnard and Jennifer Yip

John Thomson, an engineer who created much of the infrastructure of early colonial Singapore, often sailed on the government vessel *Diana* in the 1840s and early 1850s as he charted the Singapore Straits and built lighthouses and other beacons that would aid ship navigation. His journeys on the ship were idyllic. Often floating in the surrounding seas for weeks, Thomson took soundings, created maps and relaxed. During these expeditions he quickly became enchanted with the reefs that often lurked under the bottom of the ship. These underwater ecosystems of coral polyps were "of all descriptions, forms and sizes, enough to fill twenty museums," and the fish that swam among them would "rival the birds of the adjacent coasts in brightness and variety." Beyond the wonder Thomson felt over the teeming sea life around him, there was another group of animals that he found equally fascinating on these journeys. These creatures lived on the ship and, among them, Thomson was particularly delighted with a "pet ape" that Captain Samuel Congalton kept on board.[1]

Monkeys are a common sight in Singapore. Among the native monkey species found on the island are the banded leaf monkey (*Presbytis*

---

[1] J.T. Thomson, *Some Glimpses into Life in the Far East* (London: Richardson and Company, 1864), pp. 211–24.

femoralis) and the Sunda slow loris (*Nycticebus coucang*), although both are extremely rare. More common is the long-tailed, or crab-eating, macaque (*Macaca fascicularis*), which lives in forested areas. Each of these primates has been present in Singapore for millennia, while other non-native species—ranging from gibbons, orangutans and other subspecies of macaques—began to arrive during the colonial period. These other monkeys were purchased from ships in the port or animal stores and incorporated into households throughout the island and even Captain Congalton's ship.

Monkeys may have been part of colonial society, but they were not domesticated animals. This basic fact became more apparent in Singapore following the Second World War, when the society went through an extended period of decolonization, integration with Malaysia and ultimately national independence. As Singapore emerged as an independent nation-state there was also a reconfiguration of societal relations on all levels. While this included the relationship between neighbors, ethnic groups and even different classes of humans, it also meant that human–animal relations transformed, as the rapidly modernizing society reconstituted how its various resident species intermingled and where they lived. Interactions between humans and monkeys—and particularly the common macaque that inhabits the forests of Singapore—were complex and multifaceted, leading to a confusion of approaches and emotions. It was a period in which there was too much monkey business, and it reflected shifting understandings of acceptable behavior and territory for all Singaporean creatures as a colonized island in Southeast Asia transformed into a Garden City.

From Attraction to Pest

Macaques are monkeys from the family Cercophithecidae and are found in Eurasia and Africa. The species found throughout Southeast Asia are known as long-tailed macaques. While there are numerous subspecies throughout the region, they only exhibit slightly different characteristics: for example, the long-tailed macaque of Singapore is "darker, smaller, and has a longer tail than others."[2] Archaeologists have confirmed that these

---

[2] Michael D. Gumert, "The Common Monkey of Southeast Asia: Long-tailed Macaque Populations, Ethnophoresy, and Their Occurrence in Human Environments," in *Monkeys on the Edge: Ecology and Management of Long-Tailed Macaques and their Interface with Humans*, ed. Michael D. Gumert, Agustín Fuentes and Lisa Jones-

monkeys have been present in Singapore for many thousands of years, as their remains have been found in excavations of pre-colonial sites.[3] As Singapore fell under British imperialism, so did macaques. Thomas Stamford Raffles first mentioned their presence "in the forests of Sumatra and the Malay islands" in 1821, with his description of the "Kra of the Malays," thus establishing their status as not only an inhabitant of the island but also part of the larger colonial construction of the landscape of the region, which continued for the next two centuries. The extent of this colonial claim upon the simian population of Singapore even extended to another inhabitant of the forest, the banded-leaf monkey, over which the East India Company official created a metaphorical ownership with attempts to rename it the Raffles' banded langur. All of these monkeys, including the long-tailed macaque, remain part of the native biodiversity of Singapore.[4]

Macaques thrive in edge environments, areas in which human settlements overlap with forest reserves due to their instinctive "patterns of [habitat] use and foraging."[5] Their impressive adaptability to changing landscapes has meant that the urbanization and ecological transformation that Singapore has undergone since the advent of imperial rule has had minimal effect on their numbers. These monkeys were certainly not victims of the "concrete jungle" and they lived in forested areas throughout an island that was becoming a Garden City. If anything, their adaptability

---

Engel (Cambridge: Cambridge University Press, 2011), pp. 11–15.
[3] John N. Miksic, "Recent Archaeological Excavations in Singapore: A Comparison of Three Fourteenth-Century Sites," *Bulletin of the Indo-Pacific Prehistory Association* 20, 4 (2000): 60; Lisa Jones-Engel, Gregory Engel, Michael D. Gumert, et al., "Developing Sustainable Human-Macaque Communities," in *Monkeys on the Edge: Ecology and Management of Long-Tailed Macaques and their Interface with Humans*, ed. Michael D. Gumert, Agustín Fuentes and Lisa Jones-Engel (Cambridge: Cambridge University Press, 2011), p. 307.
[4] Thomas Stamford Raffles, "Descriptive Catalogue of a Zoological Collection Made on Account of the Honourable East India Company, in the Island of Sumatra and Its Vicinity," *The Transactions of the Linnean Society of London* 13, 1 (1821): 246–7; Timothy P. Barnard, "The Rafflesia in the Natural and Imperial Imagination of the East India Company in Southeast Asia," in *The East India Company and the Natural World*, ed. Vinita Damoradaran, Anna Winterbottom and Alan Lester (London: Palgrave Macmillan, 2015), pp. 147–66.
[5] Agustín Fuentes, "Pets, Property and Partners: Macaques as Commodities in the Human-Other Primate Interface," in *The Macaque Connection: Cooperation and Conflict between Humans and Macaques*, ed. Sindhu Radhakrishna, Michael A. Huffman and Anindya Sinha (New York, NY: Springer, 2013), p. 108.

has allowed macaques to thrive, in stark contrast to many other species of native animals, such as the slow loris and pangolin, which by the 1960s were being described pitifully as a "fast-shrinking band of pint-sized wildlife living in terror."[6]

The population of monkeys in Singapore during the colonial era is unknown. As the amount of forest cover plummeted due to colonial policies related to the proliferation of plantation agriculture, which transformed the landscape in the 19th century, the macaque population was most likely quite small. A known edge environment in which they thrived during this era, however, was the Singapore Botanic Gardens. A managed horticultural space used for scientific research and recreation, it contained stretches of forest and food resources sufficient to sustain two troops of macaques, with one group residing in the Gardens Jungle and the other in the Economic Garden. Most observers from the time estimated that their total population was around 100 within the grounds.[7]

The macaques in the Singapore Botanic Gardens remained wild, but were constantly interacting with humans who sought the chance to feed them bananas and peanuts, which vendors sold near the entrance gate. As described in *Willis' Singapore Guide*, the joy of interacting with "a number of tame monkeys" was one of the highlights of a visit to the island as they were "usually found in the neighborhood of the jungle" and "will take food from your hand." They were considered to be "quite harmless." Popular media in colonial society reinforced this depiction of the human–animal relationship as ideal. As one newspaper article described, "the monkeys are one of the biggest attractions in the Botanic Gardens. Most of them are tame and will receive titbits from visitors' hands."[8] This conditioning of behavior, based on interaction through feeding, was a relationship that existed for decades.

---

[6] Nancy Byramji, "Last Stand by the Survivors," *The Straits Times* [hereafter, *ST*], 29 Oct. 1978, p. 16; Royal Botanic Gardens, Kew: Henry Nicholas Ridley Papers, HNR3/2/6: Notebook, Vol. 6 (1908–09), p. 43.

[7] Timothy P. Barnard, *Imperial Creatures: Humans and Other Animals in Colonial Singapore, 1819–1942* (Singapore: NUS Press, 2019), pp. 236–41; Timothy P. Barnard, *Nature's Colony: Empire, Nation and Environment in the Singapore Botanic Gardens* (Singapore: NUS Press, 2016), p. 16.

[8] This also parallels colonial era interaction with crocodiles, which is mentioned in Esmond Soh's contribution to this collection. Anonymous, "Monkeys Can Kill: Visitors Warned," *SFP*, 13 Oct. 1958, p. 5; A.C. Willis, *Willis's Singapore Guide* (Singapore: Advertising and Policy Bureau, 1936), pp. 115–17; Humphrey Morrison Burkill, Oral History Archive, Reel 6, p. 64.

The feeding of macaques took place daily in the Singapore Botanic Gardens and with few negative incidents. The decorum required was considered easy enough for a child to accomplish, which the *Singapore Free Press* satirized in an article depicting a toddler successfully providing nuts to the macaques.[9] The ease and joy of this experience was reinforced in the travel account of Edward Wassermann, who visited the gardens in the late 1930s. Although he found "nothing of tremendous interest for the tourist" in Singapore, Wassermann was fascinated with macaques. The troop in the Singapore Botanic Gardens was "the first I saw in the East. They were very friendly and came to eat from one's hand the fruits vendors sell for that purpose." Members of the local press even argued that the feeding of monkeys was a positive example of public support for larger policies and expenditures as it allowed the authorities to forgo a "food provision" although the beasts were "under the protection of the Government."[10]

The conditioning of acceptable behavior from monkeys in the Singapore Botanic Gardens extended into the household. In colonial Singapore, monkeys were popular pets, being the second most common after dogs. Almost all of these pets could be purchased from shops located along Rochor Road and North Bridge Road, with guides on proper selection of a "very delightful" simian occasionally featured in local newspapers. Once adopted, the various species of monkey were often seen in public, scurrying within household compounds or even accompanying their owners on visits to cafes or the Ponggol Zoo, where they would meet with other members "of the monkey community." Their presence was so ubiquitous in the modern, urban landscape one even attended a performance of *La*

---

[9] The rarity of a negative encounter when visiting the Gardens is reflected in the paucity of reports in the papers. For example, in 1934 a monkey bit a child twice. Beyond that, such experiences did not elicit enough scandal to appear in the press until the 1960s, despite the occasional sensational headline. Anonymous, "Monkeys in the Gardens," *ST,* 4 Jan. 1934, p. 5; Anonymous, "How to Feed a Monkey," *The Singapore Free Press* [hereafter, *SFP*], 24 Mar. 1953, p. 5; Humphrey Morrison Burkill, Oral History Archive, Reel 6, p. 64.

[10] A similar tone of fascination and positivity also was recounted in the visit of the crew of a Dutch steamer to Singapore during the same period. Anonymous, "Dutch Sailors Taken Round Singapore," *The Malayan Tribune* [hereafter, *MT*], 20 Jun. 1940, p. 3; Edward Wassermann, *Velvet Voyaging* (London: John Lane, 1940), pp. 35–6; Anonymous, "This Monkey Business....," *MT,* 5 Nov. 1938, p. 20.

Image 5.1: Feeding monkeys at Singapore Botanic Gardens, 1920s. Lim Kheng Chye Collection, courtesy of National Archives of Singapore.

Traviata at Victoria Theatre in 1925, which elicited concern from other patrons who found its "incessant chattering" disruptive.[11]

The domestication of monkeys, of course, was unsuccessful and often fell along the precarious boundary between tame and wild in colonial society. Although they were popular pets in Singapore, offering companionship and entertainment, monkeys could be troublesome. They were infamous for examining and tossing about "all property weighing less than a pikul" and placidly wandering the roofs of homes or even "your neighbor's fruit trees." Most owners quickly learned this fact, and kept the beasts in cages or attached to chains that limited their curiosity to the confines of a household. "From all practical points of view," as one commentator pointed out, "there is not much to be said in favor of keeping a monkey as a domestic pet, and if harmony is to be preserved in the home there has to be a good deal of give and take between the people who share it." Their behavior ultimately created chaos in the domesticated space, as "a monkey is less a respecter of persons or property than any other animal."[12]

The ability of monkeys to contribute to an atmosphere of colonial modernity in which humans could master animals and provide them food without fear, however, slowly came under scrutiny following the Second World War. During the 1950s, the status of monkeys in Singaporean society shifted from attraction to nuisance in reports, with a lack of temerity among the beasts and an inability to contribute to the development of society condemning the creatures. Much of this is exemplified in the comments of J. Sinclair, the keeper of the herbarium at the Singapore Botanic Gardens, who bemoaned the presence of "unintelligent" macaques in the gardens, as they possessed no talent or desire to gather plant specimens in a systematic manner for the botanists. Despite his three-year effort to train them, he believed this species was simply "too dull to work."[13]

---

[11] Anonymous, "Lucille's New Pet," *MT*, 2 Jul. 1940, p. 8; Anonymous, "The Care of Pets in Malaya," *MT*, 24 Sep. 1932, p. iv; Barnard, *Imperial Creatures*, pp. 67–73; Anonymous, "Singapore's Favorite Pets Are Dogs, Monkeys, Birds," *ST*, 14 Aug. 1938, p. 3; Anonymous, "Monkeys, Chickens, Ducks and Pigeons," *ST*, 25 Jun. 1939, p. 32; A Lover of Opera, "Animals at the Opera," *ST*, 25 Apr. 1925, p. 10.

[12] Maryann Mott, "The Perils of Keeping Monkeys as Pets," *National Geographic*, 17 Sep. 2003 (https://www.nationalgeographic.com/animals/article/news-monkeys-primates-pets-trade-ethics) (accessed 26 Apr. 2023); Anonymous, "Your Household Pets," *Malayan Saturday Post*, 26 Jun. 1926, p. 10; G.S. Hammonds, "Up to His Monkey Tricks!," *Sunday Tribune*, 1 May 1938, p. 16.

[13] Much of this was based on the presence of *berok* monkeys (*Macacus nemestrina*,

Too Much Monkey Business

The main problem with monkeys, beyond their lack of a work ethic, was the mischief they created in public spaces. In 1955, for example, J.W. Purseglove highlighted in his annual report for the Singapore Botanic Gardens that the monkeys damaged plants, creating "an unmitigated nuisance as far as horticulture is concerned."[14] These activities shifted from minor annoyance to menace in the Singapore Botanic Gardens after the macaque population rose to an estimated 300 by the end of the decade, which new Director H.M. Burkill believed to be a threat to serenity for visitors and workers. This tone was solidified in 1959, when he placed them under a new heading—"Pests and Diseases"—in the report.[15]

This changing attitude also reflected another problem. Pet owners were beginning to grow tired of the antics of monkeys in their modern, decolonized homes and began disposing of the animals in the Singapore Botanic Gardens which, along with the mischievous behavior of the resident troops, was reaching an inflection point. As Burkill described in two succinct paragraphs:

> Misguided people occasionally release monkeys from captivity in the Gardens. Most conspicuous are those with collars or wire attachments. Release in the Gardens not only contravenes the Gardens' by-laws, but exposes the wretched monkey to certain cruelty at the hands and

---

a different species than those found in the Singapore Botanic Gardens), which assisted botanists with the collection of specimens during the 1930s. While these monkeys were celebrated for their contributions, their fate was tragic. E.J.H. Corner, *Botanical Monkeys* (Cambridge: Pentland Press, 1992); Barnard, *Imperial Creatures*, pp. 236–41; Anonymous, "Garden Monkeys Are Too Dull to Work," *ST*, 3 May 1957, p. 3.

[14] J.W. Purseglove, *Annual Report of the Botanic Gardens Department for 1955* (Singapore: Government Printing Office, 1956), p. 6; Anonymous, "Gardens Monkeys Steal His Cinecamera," *ST*, 9 Aug. 1955, p. 7.

[15] The alarm had been raised in 1958 when a trishaw driver died of tetanus following a monkey bite, although it was not clear where he sustained the injury. Well, he sustained it on his finger. Where he was in Singapore was never determined, although it most likely arose through interaction with a pet. Anonymous, "Mystery of Monkey Bite that Killed Trishaman," *ST*, 9 Oct. 1958, p. 9; Anonymous, "Monkeys Can Kill: Visitors Warned"; H.M. Burkill, *Annual Report of the Botanic Gardens Department for 1957* (Singapore: Government Printing Office, 1958), p. 12; Anonymous, "Gardens Fight a Losing War on Monkeys," *SFP*, 29 Dec. 1961, p. 1; H.M. Burkill, *Annual Report of the Botanic Gardens Department for 1960* (Singapore: Lee Kim Heng, 1961), pp. 13–14.

teeth of its own kind for trespassers in each troop's preserve suffer a prolonged chastisement inevitably ending in some permanent disability, if not death.

No less than thirty plants were mauled by monkeys and six tree saplings killed. Cannas [or canna lillies, from the genus *Canna*] received regular uprooting. These depredations have to be combatted by enclosing the more valuable permanent plantings in wire netting cages till the plants are big enough to withstand being swung on and pulled about. Forty plants are so enclosed.[16]

Singaporean society and its relationship to creatures that were previously considered a unique and charming aspect of the natural environment was changing.

Methods of handling this growing menace fell back on practices exercised over the previous century and a half. In colonial Singapore, officials had a simple solution for dealing with bothersome animals, including monkeys. They were killed. This was the approach that H.N. Ridley, the influential first Director of the Singapore Botanic Gardens, took with such pests. In 1908, for example, when macaques from Lower Grange Road infiltrated the institution, they "became a great nuisance destroying things" and behaved aggressively toward a worker who was walking alone. Ridley ordered "as many to be killed as possible" and it was done with little fuss. Dealing with pesky creatures in such a manner continued throughout the 20th century, with culling being the common approach for a range of bothersome animals ranging from dogs to crows to monkeys.[17]

By the time Burkill became the Director of the Singapore Botanic Gardens in 1959 and deemed it necessary, he followed this established practice and "took action and shot them if it was safe to do so." Earlier, in the mid-1950s, Purseglove had also ordered a culling due to the presence of "a few vicious males." Burkill, however, represented a renewed vigor to an old approach when he had "about thirty" killed in his first year as Director. The culling took place through the cooperation "of an assistant from the Raffles Museum. Four others were caught alive in trap cages for the Department of Zoology of the University of Malaya."[18]

---

[16] H.M. Burkill, *Annual Report of the Botanic Gardens Department for 1959* (Singapore: Lee Kim Heng, 1960), p. 13.
[17] HNR3/2/6: p. 43; Barnard, *Imperial Creatures*.
[18] Humphrey Morrison Burkill, Oral History Archive, Reel 6, p. 65; J.W. Purseglove,

Image 5.2: A macaque at the Singapore Botanic Gardens. Ronni Pinsler Collection, courtesy of National Archives of Singapore.

The macaques in the Singapore Botanic Gardens adapted quickly to these culling exercises, as they soon began to evade capture and death, which frustrated officials. Burkill attributed the difficulties he was having with this situation to the intelligence and learned behavior of the apes, "as a single shot will scatter all the monkeys to the tree-top to safety where they pour vituperation on the helpless Gardens' staff." These issues were compounded when it was discovered that "the office shot gun was found to have bent barrels, and to this defect is attributed a major share of ineffective action." Despite receiving a new shot gun, officials killed only three monkeys the following year and they remained "the most troublesome pest and against which little can feasibly be done."[19]

Annual Report of the Botanic Gardens Department for 1955 (Singapore: Government Printing Office, 1956), p. 6; H.M. Burkill, *Annual Report of the Botanic Gardens Department for 1959* (Singapore: Lee Kim Heng, 1960), p. 13.

[19] H.M. Burkill, *Annual Report of the Botanic Gardens Department for 1961* (Singapore: Government Printing Office, 1963); Anonymous, "Gardens Fight a Losing War on Monkeys," *SFP*, 29 Dec. 1961, p. 1.

Table 5.1: Monkeys culled in the Singapore Botanic Gardens (based on annual reports)

1955	"a few vicious males"
1959	30
1960	4
1961	3
1962	No record
1963	No record
1964	No record
1965	1
1966	6
1967	10
1968	47
1969	27
1970	4

The game of predator and prey continued as the Garden macaques transitioned further from attraction to pest throughout the late 1950s and 1960s. Professional hunters, who usually worked in the forests of Malaya and exported captured macaques for scientific research, were spectacularly unsuccessful when tasked with the job during this period, only managing to capture seven monkeys in 1958. Burkill attributed this ineffectuality, once again, to the intelligence and urbanity of his fellow apes. Those of the forest "suffer the misfortune of a certain rustic simplicity," he argued. "On the other hand the Gardens' monkeys," Burkill reasoned, possess "a sharpness of wit, and a familiarity and contempt for human wiles which would have done credit to many a Dickens character." Burkill then focused on the reason for much of this behavior, which he attributed to the food visitors provided the creatures that increased human–animal interaction but also the opportunity for clashes and violence.[20] Despite identifying the feeding of monkeys as a problem, no real effort was made to alter human behavior at this time.

---

[20] H.M. Burkill, *Annual Report of the Botanic Gardens 1958* (Singapore: Government Printing Office, 1960), p. 10.

These attempts to limit the presence of macaques in a recreational space in Singapore where they had long been a presence, and shifts to understanding the human role in this relationship and the act of culling, took place during a period when the Singapore Botanic Gardens was being reconstituted under new ministries and departments in a government that was decolonizing. As part of this process, the institution became part of the Ministry of National Development.[21] When this occurred, Burkill no longer included the number of macaques culled in his annual report, at least from 1962 to 1965. The issue of how these monkeys in the Gardens were to be handled, however, did enter other public realms of power in the state. In 1962, David Marshall asked the Minister for National Development, Tan Kia Gan, during a debate in the Legislative Council about policies with regard to trapping the monkeys in the Gardens. The simple reply to a question of whether the monkeys were being exported from Singapore was "no, sir." Tan also clarified that these monkeys were "pests, but not for export."[22] These difficulties, questions and the methods that Marshall and Tan discussed, reflected changes to how such an approach to handling animals was becoming increasingly problematic in the young nation. Openly killing an animal that many saw as a companion and an attraction in a recreational space in Singapore was becoming an issue of discomfort, but the animals were also seen as an increasingly hostile presence in a civilized and developed city-state.

This problematic human–macaque interaction in the Singapore Botanic Gardens continued throughout the 1960s. Burkill did try to introduce less violent approaches to the issue, which would not result in killing his simian neighbors. During this period, he mainly directed efforts at capturing monkeys for relocation as this was considered the most humane approach. All attempts to control the creatures, however, ended in frustration. Changing attitudes from the public further complicated matters. For example, in 1962, a child was seen "striking a small monkey with a large stick and killing it," which "infuriated the rest of the monkeys."[23] The human–macaque relationship was becoming one of threats and violence, and attempts to regulate it were becoming comically ineffective. The macaques had "acquired ... a familiarity and contempt for human wiles." By 1967, with little success in dealing with

---

[21] Burkill, *Annual Report of the Botanic Gardens Department for 1959*, p. 1.
[22] Anonymous, "Monkey 'Pests' Not Leaving S'pore," *ST*, 17 Mar. 1962, p. 9; Barnard, *Nature's Colony*, pp. 230–40.
[23] Pamela Law, "Murder of a Monkey," *ST*, 15 Sep. 1962, p. 14.

the troublesome creatures, a new approach was attempted "to eliminate them by poison baiting with a-chlorolose," which had been used to cull bird populations near the airport. It was tried twice, and both attempts ended in failure. Efforts to capture the Gardens macaques also continued to be unsuccessful. Ultimately, "ten were shot but shooting presents many difficulties, not least the recognition by the monkeys of anyone carrying a gun."[24] The treatment of wild animals in a public space in Singapore was growing more contentious.

The practice of keeping pet monkeys also began to intrude further into the grounds of the Singapore Botanic Gardens, further complicating the human–macaque relationship and the acceptable space for interaction. As housing developed in the new nation, and many colonial pastimes were fading, the ability to maintain a simian in a household grew less attractive among the larger populace. This corresponded with a rise in the number of "vicious" monkeys encountered, which—once again—were traced back to released pets. As Burkill reported there were "several cases of monkey bite" from animals that "had been somebody's pet for it had a wire round its neck, and had illegally been let loose in the Gardens." These released simians, while having gained their freedom, could not find a home in the two troops that roamed the Singapore Botanic Gardens. Burkill explained that, "animals released in this manner are not accepted by the residential troops, and if they are not mauled or driven off, they lead an outcast's existence constantly attacked and harassed by the others with whom it would wish to associate. Release of pets in the Gardens, besides violating the Gardens Rules, is plainly an act of cruelty." The populations of semi-domesticated and free-roaming monkeys in Singapore were converging, and the results reflected a clash in how creatures interacted within specified territories in a modernizing Singaporean society.[25]

---

[24] Anonymous, "Sophisticated!" *ST,* 20 May 1960, p. 5; H.M. Burkill, *Annual Report of the Botanic Gardens 1967* (Singapore: Government Printing Office, 1968), p. 41.

[25] While Burkill often mentioned 300 in the early 1960s, Director Arthur George Alphonso, who presided over the grounds between 1970 and 1976, cites 140 in early 1971. The exact number of macaques is disputed, although 300 is likelier, as *The Straits Times* mentioned, independent of *The Singapore Free Press,* that culling occurred every four to five years when macaque numbers exceeded 300. Anonymous, "Gardens Fight a Losing War on Monkeys", *SFP,* 29 Dec. 1961, p. 1; Arthur George Alphonso, Oral History Interviews Reel 6, p. 73; Anonymous, "Culling Monkeys," *ST,* 25 Feb. 1971, p. 10; H.M. Burkill, *Annual Report of the Botanic Gardens 1965* (Singapore: Government Printing Office, 1966), p. 12.

By January 1971, the Gardens macaques were seen as a "nuisance that was once such a delight for our children." This transformation from amusement to "menace," according to the writer "Johnnie," had taken place over the previous five years. Monkeys had become "an army of scraggy, unkempt, underfed and vicious animals." One report summarized the endless list of malfeasances with a succinct condemnation of their ability to "roam freely over parked cars and sometimes frighten children by snatching fruit from their hands."[26] It was supposedly when they began "harassing" humans and other creatures in Dalvey Estate along Cluny Road that the issue came to the attention of Prime Minister Lee Kuan Yew and final decisions were made. According to Burkill, one day monkeys "invaded" a bungalow "and pulled it apart," which gained the attention of the prime minister. The former director, recounting the story years later, marked this moment as the end for the Gardens macaques. "That was the death spell," and "somebody" ordered officials to "get rid of them and they jolly well did."[27]

Emptying the Gardens

On 23 and 24 February 1971, a Tuesday and a Wednesday, the Singapore Botanic Gardens was closed from 6.00 am to 2.00 pm. Twenty soldiers from the Singapore Armed Forces entered the grounds and began executing macaques, with one unnamed soldier apparently doing most of the shooting. At the end of the two days officials refused "to disclose how many monkeys" had been killed, although a later report claimed 12 simians were shot on the second day. The number wounded was also uncertain. Among the macaques that remained near the Singapore Botanic Gardens, one displayed the results of the previous day's activities. It sported

---

[26] Anonymous, "Park Monkeys to Be Shot," *New Nation*, 22 Feb. 1971, p. 1; Yeong Kum Kee, "Govt. Replies....," *ST*, 5 Feb. 1971, p. 19; Johnnie, "Monkey Menace," *ST*, 23 Jan. 1971, p. 19.
[27] This account also reflects the role of rumor and whispers, and explaining government actions in an increasingly bureaucratic and centralizing society at the time, and the belief that all actions would have required approval from the top. The mention of Lee's involvement in the decision to cull, however, is limited to this one source, recorded years later, in the oral history recordings stores at the National Archives of Singapore. Burkill, Oral History Archives, Reel 5, p. 66; Nancy Byramji, "Gardens Monkeys on the Rampage," *ST*, 18 Apr. 1970, p. 6; Zaher Allam, *Urban Governance and Smart City Planning: Lessons from Singapore* (Bingley: Emerald Publishing Limited, 2020).

a "gaping gunshot wound" that raised issues about how humanely and expeditiously the entire exercise had been carried out. When questions arose over the maimed monkey, the Primary Production Department simply responded that such media coverage "will do more harm than good."[28]

The general tenor of the public reports following this violent clash in the human–monkey matrix was one of discomfort, leading to outcries of support for the macaques and condemnation of culling as an approach for eliminating troublesome animals. Schoolgirls from Marymount Convent, for example, sent a petition to the government, while residents of a nearby neighborhood expressed shock at how the exercise had been conducted. One university student who supported the culling felt it had gone too far, stating that "perhaps there is an alternative to killing them that way."[29] The emptying of the Singapore Botanic Gardens had not gone well, and had raised awkward issues regarding human–animal interaction in the nation-state and how conflicts were being managed.

Alongside the questions local residents raised with regard to the handling of the issue, there was also a rare public protest in support of the macaques. A group of visiting Americans stood outside the closed gates of the Singapore Botanic Gardens holding signs condemning the culling on 23 February 1971. Among the protesters was "Hollywood actress" Barbara Werle, who was in town performing in a nightclub show and promoting her short-lived television drama *San Francisco International Airport* (with Lloyd Bridges). Along with three other non-citizens, Werle felt compelled to protest as "someone has to speak for the monkey, and put an end to this." Four police officers arrived and told the protesters to move along. While such a performative public protest was of little concern to the authorities, the press coverage—often citing the concerns of local residents—and the botched job of eliminating the monkeys did

---

[28] According to Arthur George Alphonso, not many monkeys were actually killed on the first day of the exercise. Although "soldiers who could shoot" had been deployed, Alphonso claimed they only successfully bagged one. The rest scattered, some with wounds, while few or none were shot on the second day. Arthur George Alphonso, Oral History Archives, Reel 6 Transcript, pp. 72–4; Anonymous, "Park Monkeys to Be Shot," *New Nation*, 22 Feb. 1971, p. 1; Anonymous, "Guns to Solve Vicious Monkey Problem," *Singapore Herald*, 23 Feb. 1971, p. 6; Anonymous, "Botanic Gardens Monkeys," *ST*, 25 Feb. 1971, p. 1.

[29] Anonymous, "Shot in the Back," *New Nation*, 23 Feb. 1971, p. 1; Anonymous, "Monkey Case Probe," *New Nation*, 24 Feb. 1971, p. 1.

Image 5.3: Protestors at the gates of the Singapore Botanic Gardens on 23 February 1971. Barbara Werle is on the far right. Photograph courtesy *The Straits Times* © SPH Media Limited. Reprinted with permission.

merit responses. As an editorial in *New Nation* proclaimed, "shooting and killing monkeys is one thing, wounding them is quite another."[30]

The next day the government, in its own words, "hit back at critics" with a front-page story in *The Straits Times* in which officials stated that "the choice is obvious. Stray dogs, cats and vicious monkeys must and will be destroyed." The statement from the Primary Production Department then proceeded to criticize the newspaper *New Nation*—which had carried much of the initial coverage—for participating in "sensationalism" through its accounts of the wounded monkey. A government spokesman even claimed that the photograph had been taken prior to the shooting, and the simian in question "had received a lacerated wound in a monkey fight. The animal was later shot and an examination showed the wound to be about two weeks old." Officials went on to emphasize that macaques were "vicious," "destroyed property" and even "attacked" dogs and children, and

---

[30] Rita Loong, "Shooting of the Monkeys," *ST*, 24 Feb. 1971, p. 18; Anonymous, "The Day They Shot the Monkeys," *New Nation*, 24 Feb. 1971, p. 8.

then added that a reward was being created for anyone who came up with a better solution for eliminating the pests. This pushback materialized 12 hours after the original article in *New Nation* had appeared, and included a calmer editorial supporting the culling.[31] The government was lashing out at those who had highlighted how poorly the exercise had been handled, which had exposed the human authorities to criticism.

Although the government tried to place a positive spin on the culling of macaques in the Singapore Botanic Gardens, public disapproval continued to flow with regard to this "difficult problem." Opposition politician Felice Leon-Soh, for example, bemoaned "the indiscriminate shooting" of the monkeys and the lack of public outrage—beyond Barbara Werle and her friends—over the events in late February, and proposed that tranquilizer guns and then resettlement to "the jungles of Malaysia or the outlying island" be employed in such matters.[32] In another vein, a 12-year-old schoolboy asked readers to empathize with the monkeys by imagining beings from another planet shooting earthlings down for "silly quarrels, wars and atomic tests." Despite government attempts to control the story, monkeys maintained their status as the favorite animal of most Singaporeans.[33]

In this atmosphere of questioning and recrimination, and in an attempt to garner support for the choice to cull, the government appealed to the chairman of the Society for the Prevention of Cruelty to Animals (SPCA), S.H. Ashcroft, to issue a statement of support for the activities in the Singapore Botanic Gardens. Ashcroft described the situation as a

---

[31] The *New Nation* was an afternoon paper, and the original article had appeared on 24 Feb. *New Nation* did carry the official statement from the Primary Production Department the next day, but only stated that "a local newspaper" had been accused of sensationalism. Anonymous, "Botanic Gardens Monkeys," *ST*, 25 Feb. 1971, p. 1; Anonymous, "Culling Monkeys," *ST*, 25 Feb. 1971, p. 10; Anonymous, "Statement by the Primary Production Department," *New Nation*, 25 Feb. 1971, p. 2.

[32] The criticism of government actions did expose ethnic differences in attitudes toward the monkeys, and how it was covered in the press. Culture Minister Jek Yeun Thong noted that the "English press had splashed the news, while the Chinese papers had just laughed it off, and thought it was 'funny'." Anonymous, "Call for Review of S'pores Culture," *ST*, 23 Mar. 1971, p. 3; Felice Leon-Soh, "Untitled," *ST*, 1 Mar. 1971, p. 12.

[33] Low Yew Cheong, "Monkeys: Do Unto Others…," *New Nation*, 1 Mar. 1971, p. 8; Anonymous, "Monkey Case Probe," *New Nation*, 24 Feb. 1971, p. 1; Loong, "Shooting of the Monkeys"; Anonymous, "Monkey Shooters Today at the Gardens," *ST*, 23 Feb. 1971, p. 4; Helen Howard, "The Animal Every Kid Loves," *New Nation*, 22 Jun. 1971, p. 11.

"difficult problem."[34] When this did little to assuage public sentiment, the acting director of the Primary Production Department, Lim Ewe Hock, met publicly with Ashcroft, who finally expressed support for the culling as long as the victims were "disposed of in a humane manner and they don't suffer." After a week of being disparaged in the press over this announcement and having to field private inquiries about it, the SPCA eventually had to issue another statement making its "position" and "views clear." In a letter from the secretary of the organization, A. Xavier, the SPCA now denied that it "condoned" the action of the government, but did express concern that there was a problem with overpopulation and a heightened potential for unpleasant human–animal interaction. "For anybody to say that the monkeys should be allowed indiscriminately to multiply is unrealistic and foolish," rounded out the final statement on the issue.[35]

The government, by following a basic precept of pre-colonial human–monkey relations, had created controversy due to its continued observance of such practices. While culling had occurred for over a century, such an approach—particularly when it involved shooting an animal with a gun—was no longer considered humane and acceptable. The creation of new boundaries for humans and animals in a modern, independent society required new approaches. The proposed solution that gained the most support, and one that had been attempted for over a decade with little success, was to create an enclosed feeding area in the Singapore Botanic Gardens that would attract the animals to consume food containing tranquilizers. Once the door of the enclosure had been secured, and the animals were unconscious, the monkeys would be "painlessly destroyed by a gun which is instantaneous and available, instead of rifles." The head of the Association of Veterinary Surgeons also publicly issued a statement in favor of such an approach.[36]

Before tranquilizing could be implemented, however, the Government returned to the standard approach. On 17 March 1971, the Singapore Botanic Gardens was closed from 6.00 am to 10.00 am as hunters entered the grounds to shoot monkeys again. To ensure that no more protests took place, the police blocked all five public entrances to the gardens while seven police dogs were used to retrieve the monkey carcasses in the

---

[34] Anonymous, "Shot in the Back," *New Nation*, 23 Feb. 1971, p. 1.
[35] A. Xavier, "Now We Know People Care for Animals...," *ST*, 4 Mar. 1971, p. 8.
[36] Giam Choo Hoo, "Shooting Is Least Cruel," *ST*, 5 Mar. 1971, p. 19; Xavier, "Now We Know People Care for Animals...."

grounds. "It was not known how many monkeys were shot."[37] This was the last, public attempt to approach the issue of pestilent simians in the Gardens, and the issue of where they were allowed to exist, with firearms.

Although rather crudely carried out, and a public relations catastrophe, the campaign to eliminate these "nuisance" macaques had been relatively successful. It resulted in an emptying of monkeys from the Singapore Botanic Gardens. The two troops that had co-existed in the space for almost a century went their separate ways. One troop took refuge across Tyersall Avenue near Istana Woodneuk, the abandoned palace of the Sultan of Johor; the other fled across Cluny Road, on the other side of the Botanic Gardens where there were numerous residences. Each troop then created new issues. Those that sought sanctuary in the forest located across Tyersall Avenue were effectively under the protection of a foreign potentate and the hunters were reluctant to pursue their prey into an area that was off limits. Eventually, after new Director Arthur George Alphonso secured permission to enter the royal property, personnel moved from Holland Road into the grounds of the estate toward the Botanic Gardens. While some monkeys were spotted, they were in the forest canopy and out of rifle range. Meanwhile, the second troop of macaques were ensconced in Dalvey Estate, a housing estate where the discharge of firearms would be problematic. By the end of March, it was reported that these "stray monkeys" had begun "rummaging through dustbins for snacks" near the homes.[38]

As the monkeys were now either in the canopy of a forest designated as foreign territory or within a housing estate, new approaches were needed. Shooting them was no longer an option. The solution now was to poison the creatures, which began several months later. By August 1971 at least ten macaques were found dead on Tyersall Avenue, near Istana Woodneuk. The press reported the deaths as "mysterious," although eyewitnesses reported that the animals "seemed to be in a drugged state, and writhed and kicked their legs occasionally," before dying. At the time Alphonso claimed "no poisoning of monkeys was being carried out" and their deaths were probably attributable to being hit by cars. Years later, however, he recalled that the Primary Production Department "gave us

---

[37] Anonymous, "Dogs Used in Culling Operation," *New Nation*, 17 Mar. 1971, p. 1; Anonymous, "Police Dogs Retrieve Shot Monkeys," *ST*, 18 Mar. 1971, p. 17.
[38] Anonymous, "Monkeys Stray Outside Gardens," *ST*, 27 Mar. 1971, p. 28; Arthur George Alphonso, Oral History Archives, Reel 6 Transcript, pp. 72–4.

another kind of poison, and we did get about five or six monkeys. They died on the road." The poison was placed in bananas.[39]

By the end of 1971 residents on either side of the Singapore Botanic Gardens began to report loud noises coming from the forests. The surviving monkeys were moving en masse, "jumping from tree to tree along Balmoral Road, the university, along Adam Road, straight to MacRitchie" Reservoir.[40] Macaques that had survived efforts to shoot and poison them were migrating to the Central Catchment Area, the massive nature reserve in the center of the island, where they could live a more "natural" existence. The human–monkey relationship and their territories had been reconfigured, and now both creatures could live in their designated space in a modern, urbanized nation-state. By early 1972, people were asking, "where have all the monkeys gone?" The Ministry of National Development issued a terse "no comment" in response to the question.[41]

The exclusion of macaques from the Singapore Botanic Gardens and the process of making the presence of monkeys less acceptable within the space, was a reconfiguration of the human–animal relationship in Singapore that had existed for over a century. It was a cognitive distancing of civilized humans from savage "Others." Macaques and other monkeys were no longer an attraction; they were now "vicious" and "aggressive." The culling was an action for which the authorities were to be "congratulated," as these beasts could not meet human social standards of acceptable behavior. Primates were now classified as non-human, ultimately lacking the "self-discipline" expected of conscientious citizens of modern Singapore. After all, "they litter the grounds with waste which they dig out of the litter bins," for which a human "would no doubt be fined $500," and their rapid increases in population over the previous decade were proof that there was "no family planning for monkeys." They were not proper residents of the urban space.[42]

---

[39] Judy Young, "Dying Monkeys Riddle," *ST*, 24 Aug. 1971, p. 3; Anonymous, "More Dead Monkeys Found in Tyersall Avenue," *ST*, 25 Aug. 1971, p. 18; Anonymous, "Probe into Deaths of Gardens Monkeys," *ST*, 26 Aug. 1971, p. 4; Alphonso, Oral History Archives, Reel 6 Transcript, p. 75.

[40] Arthur George Alphonso, Oral History Archives, Reel 6 Transcript, p. 75.

[41] J. Seow, "Untitled," *ST*, 12 Jan. 1972, p. 14; Anonymous, "Monkeys a Rare Sight Now in the Gardens," *New Nation*, 2 Feb. 1972, p. 14; Anonymous, "Hitting at Silence," *New Nation*, 10 Feb. 1972 p. 8.

[42] Johnnie, "Monkey Menace," *ST*, 23 Jan. 1971, p. 19; Jun-Han Yeo and Harvey Neo, "Monkey Business: Human-Animal Conflicts in Urban Singapore," *Social and*

Beyond the restructuring of the human–animal relationship, the emptying of the Singapore Botanic Gardens was also related to the reconfiguration of territory in a modernizing nation-state. Prior to 1971, the Singapore Botanic Gardens had been a "borderland," an ambivalent, liminal space that was "neither fully domesticated nor wild, belonging neither wholly to humans nor animals." In such spaces the domains of human and animal dominance were blurred, and the increasing transgression of macaque behavior throughout the 1960s reflected violations of acceptable behavior in the shared space.[43] The Singapore Botanic Gardens was no longer liminal. It was a space reserved for humans and symbolic of an island that was becoming a Garden City. Its grounds were a created habitat, molded to fit the needs of humans for scientific research and recreation. Despite some members of the public arguing that the macaques were "living in their natural state" within the Singapore Botanic Gardens during the culling exercise of 1971, such a claim was increasingly unacceptable on an island in which the government promoted a philosophy of a developmental state that carefully managed a range of issues. This sentiment is best summarized in a forum letter that clearly framed the issue. "Is the place supposed to be a public park for the benefit of Singaporeans and their families, or is it a game park, where the animals are king?"[44] The Singapore Botanic Gardens was to be a public park.

The emptying of the Singapore Botanic Gardens, thus, was a step in establishing new spaces for humans and wild animals in Singapore. Although it had taken place successfully—from a human point of view—it had been accomplished through violence along with clashes over the perception of how to handle the issue. This made the culling and increased regulations "lamentable but necessary," as it was not just the physical space

---

Cultural Geography 11, 7 (2010): 697; D.T.D., "Children Had Been Attacked by Monkeys," *ST*, 2 Mar. 1971, p. 10; Anonymous, "Culling Monkeys," *ST*, 25 Feb. 1971, p. 10; Anonymous, "Botanic Gardens Monkeys: Government Hits Back at Critics," *ST*, 25 Feb. 1971, p. 1.

[43] Jennifer Wolch, "Anima urbis," *Progress in Human Geography* 26, 6 (2002): 721–42; Yeo and Neo, "Monkey Business"; Chris Philo, "Animals, Geography, and the City: Notes on Inclusions and Exclusions," in *Animal Geographies, Place, Politics, and Identity in the Nature-Culture Borderlands*, ed. Jennifer Wolch and Jody Emel (London: Verso, 1998), pp. 51–71.

[44] Anonymous, "Don't Kill Those Monkeys: Give Them Food," *SFP*, 22 Jul. 1971, p. 6; Barnard, *Nature's Colony*; Johnnie, "Monkey Menace," *ST*, 23 Jan. 1971, p. 19.

of the Gardens that was at stake but also the principle of human mastery over the wild.[45] In 1971 this border was redrawn. Monkeys now would live in the Central Catchment Area, a place of wildlife in the heart of the island designated for such activities. All space beyond that was now human-dominated as the nation-state was moving from "third world to first." As long as both groups kept to their designated areas, violence—the colonial approach—would not be needed to handle conflicts.

Reconfiguring the Matrix

The creation of new boundaries between civilized and savage in a modernizing nation-state, in which the Singapore Botanic Gardens became a "no-monkey's land," extended into the home with the new orders limiting and redefining pet ownership during this same period. In September 1971, the government announced that all apes—"monkeys, orangutans, chimpanzee and gibbons"—would be subject to the Monkey (Licensing) Order 1971 to ensure that owners "keep their pets under proper control." After paying a fee of $5 at the City Veterinary Center on Kampong Java Road, the owner would receive a license along with a warning that they were "liable to be prosecuted" if the animal "causes nuisance to his neighbors or members of the public." According to a statement from the Ministry of National Development, this was necessary as monkeys tend "to stray and cause damage to property and injury to children." Occasional reminders from government officials that apes could no longer be classified as pets appeared in the press. As one official framed the issue, "these animals cannot be completely tamed, unlike dogs, cats or horses."[46]

This transition in the human–monkey relationship in the Singaporean household took several years and corresponded with larger policies related to the self-titled Garden City. An amalgamation of programs the

---

[45] Anonymous, "Botanic Gardens Monkeys: Government Hits Back at Critics," *ST*, 25 Feb. 1971, p. 1.

[46] These comments came after a pet baboon "savaged" a woman—Woon Kin Fah—on her calves and legs along Guillemard Road. Woon eventually "slapped it down" and with "blood streaming down her hands, she finally hurled it into a monsoon drain." Primates, as the reports emphasized, are "ferocious." Junid Juani, "Baboon Attack," *ST*, 10 Dec. 1974, p. 7; Anonymous, "Monkeys to Be Licensed from Today," *ST*, 3 Sep. 1971, p. 19; Anonymous, "Now It's a Life in Chains for Pet Monkeys," *New Nation*, 6 Sep. 1971, p. 3; Anonymous, "Don't Let Pets Get Up to Wild Monkey Tricks…," *ST*, 16 Dec. 1974, p. 14.

developmental state promoted, the Garden City was based in management of not only the citizens of the nation but also nature, with the goal of creating a livable environment. The culling of macaques in the Singapore Botanic Gardens was part of this larger policy as new relationships and boundaries were being established between humans and apes in an increasingly regulated nation-state. All creatures were now to be closely monitored and managed, with monkeys being distanced from human-dominated environments, reflecting the growing gap between civilized and savage. The promulgation of the Monkey Order 1971 was simply another step in the creation of a Garden City. Macaques and other apes were now classified as wild animals, not semi-domesticated inhabitants of homes. Monkeys were now to be "merely tolerated."[47]

The reconfiguration of the human–animal relationship was solidified further in 1975 when the Wild Animals (Licensing) Order came into force. Under this new regulation, ownership of any wild animal—previously limited to monkeys but now including a variety of species ranging from kangaroos and tigers to elephants and dugongs—could only legally take place under government scrutiny and approval. Any animal incapable of domestication was to be purged from the household. Policies were developed to accommodate humans who voluntarily participated in the program, as any confiscated animals were given to the zoo, the University of Singapore or the SPCA. When 22 monkeys were surrendered to the Primary Production Department in 1976 and 1977, it was a development that was celebrated in the press, as it symbolized not only compliance with the policy but also acceptance of these new boundaries.[48]

While it became increasingly rare to find monkeys in Singaporean homes in the 1970s and 1980s, they still existed in the Garden City. Macaques primarily resided in the Central Catchment Area, a region originally created to act as a buffer for water and forestry resources in the 19th century, which had been designated a Nature Reserve in 1951.[49] The authorities had largely ignored this area for over a century,

---

[47] Timothy P. Barnard and Corinne Heng, "A City in a Garden," in *Nature Contained: Environmental Histories of Singapore*, ed. Timothy P. Barnard (Singapore: NUS Press, 2014), pp. 281–306; Nancy Byramji, "Last Stand by the Survivors," *ST*, 29 Oct. 1978, p. 16.

[48] Anonymous, "Licence For All Wild Animals," *ST*, 21 Mar. 1975, p. 11; Anonymous, "Owners Gave Up 22 Monkeys to PPD," *ST*, 6 Jan. 1978, p. 15; Anonymous, "Monkeys a Rare Sight Now in the Gardens"; Anonymous, "A Wildcat Too…," *ST*, 19 Jun. 1974, p. 7.

[49] Barnard, *Nature's Colony*, pp. 50–83; Timothy P. Barnard, "Forêts Impériales et

and it slowly developed into a vibrant, forested lung for the island with limited human access, distant from the controlled, urbanized space. In this respect, macaques—including those who had fled the Singapore Botanic Gardens in 1971—were at home in a region well suited to their needs. Macaque population estimates in this zone grew over the decades; while the numbers varied, their range was up to 2,000 individuals. In one survey from 2009, scientists claimed that there were between 1,200 and 1,450 macaques in Singapore, with the core population—roughly 70 percent—concentrated in the Bukit Timah and Central Catchment Nature Reserves. The remainder were found in forest fragments across the main and offshore islands.[50]

Although these wild creatures mainly kept to the biome that dominated the center of the island, the human–macaque conflict in Singapore eventually re-emerged. Much of this was due to infrastructure development, as residential complexes began sprouting up on the edges of these forested areas in the 1980s and 1990s. Road construction—such as the Bukit Timah Expressway (BKE)—placed additional pressure on the ecosystem as it fragmented the region. Humans were now aggressively intruding into the nature reserves, violating the unofficial boundaries that had been established following the culling in the Singapore Botanic Gardens in 1971. This was a process that accelerated even further with a rise in the number of people seeking solace in parks and nature reserves, a trend that grew with each subsequent decade.[51]

Réserves Naturelles à Singapour, 1883–1959," in *Protéger et Détruire: Gouverner la Nature sous les Tropiques (XX–XXIE siècle)*, ed. Guillaume Blanc, Mathieu Guérin and Grégory Quenet (Paris: CNRS, 2022), pp. 104–5.

[50] John Chi Mun Sha, et al., "Status of the Long-Tailed Macaque *Macaca fascicularis* in Singapore and Implications for Management," *Biodiversity and Conservation* 18, 11 (2009): 2915; Feng Zengkun, "Monkey Complaints Fall by Over Half After a Third of Them Culled," *ST*, 8 Apr. 2015, p. 2.

[51] John Chih Min Sha, et al., "Macaque-Human Interactions and the Societal Perceptions of Macaques in Singapore," *American Journal of Primatology* 71, 10 (2009): 826; Kalyani Chatterjea, "Sustainability of an Urban Forest: Bukit Timah Nature Reserve, Singapore," in *Sustainable Forest Management: Case Studies*, ed. Martin Garcia and Julio Javier Diez (Rijeka, Croatia: InTech, 2012), pp. 147–8; Joan C. Henderson, "The Survival of a Forest Fragment: Bukit Timah Nature Reserve, Singapore," in *Forest Tourism and Recreation: Case Studies in Environmental Management*, ed. X. Font and J. Tribe (New York, NY: CABI Publishing, 2000), pp. 23–40; Richard T. Corlett, "Bukit Timah: The History and Significance of a Small Rain-Forest Reserve," *Environmental Conservation* 15, 1 (1988): 37–44; Yeo and Neo, "Monkey Business", p. 696.

The proximity of human dwellings to the forest, a key element in creating a notion of a Garden City as a planned and maintained space in which nature could be enjoyed but never threaten economic development, was at the center of this conflict. Human residents who moved into exclusive condominiums often had unwelcome visitors, as macaques entered the grounds in search of food. This was a low-level struggle that would persist for decades. At one neighborhood committee meeting held to placate condominium residents in 2013, following years of the clashes, complaints were heard that monkeys "had entered their homes and bedrooms, stolen food, attacked pet dogs, broken lamps and roof-top lighting conductors, ransacked balconies, and pilfered fruit."[52] Tensions simmered.

The continuation of the colonial practice of feeding monkeys for entertainment, particularly in Bukit Timah Nature Reserve, also exacerbated these issues. This led to numerous contradictions in how humans understood their role in these problems. Exemplary of the ambiguities was a complaint aired in a local newspaper that described an encounter a young woman had with a troop in MacRitchie Reservoir. As she proceeded past the macaques, one jumped on her and she flung a plastic bag containing bread and water to the side, and the troop descended on the bag. She wrote that "clearly these monkeys have picked up the habit of obtaining food from humans," and while she did not support the unnecessary culling of animals, she did "suggest" that the authorities look into taking such action.[53] The proximity of human residences and the increased presence of humans in the nature reserves were a recipe for conflict. This was not a relationship that the technocratic government could allow to continue as it countered notions of an environmentally friendly society.

With the Central Catchment Area no longer acting as a site of refuge for the macaques—as "relocating monkeys is not possible in land-scarce Singapore"—the government needed to address the issue of these shifting boundaries as encounters continued to spread into an expanding liminal zone.[54] Humans, of course, would determine the course of action. At the center of this growing tension was who would bear the brunt of responsibility for these monkey–human conflicts. Should there be an

---

[52] Barnard and Heng, "A City in a Garden"; Feng Zengkun, "Monkey Complaints Up, So Culling Rises Too," *ST*, 28 Jul. 2013, pp. 2–3.
[53] Cindy Tan, "Hungry Monkeys a Threat to Trail Users," *TODAY*, 10 Feb. 2004, p. 8.
[54] Feng Zengkun, "Monkey Complaints Up, So Culling Rises Too."

Image 5.4: No Feeding of Monkeys sign, commonly found in parks throughout Singapore. This one is from Coney Island. Photograph by Claudia Ting.

attempt to alter human behavior or should authorities resort to the violence of culling to limit the simian population? The authorities decided to pursue both options, with an emphasis on changing human conduct.

Promoting a policy that had first appeared in the 1960s in the Singapore Botanic Gardens but had failed, the authorities first attempted to discourage feeding of the wild creature. This was formalized in 1997 with the National Parks Board Act (Chapter 198A), which set fines for feeding monkeys in the nature reserves. In addition, campaigns began to promulgate information on how such practices created an interdependence between macaques and humans, and altered their behavior as it habituated the simians to supplementing their diets with food sources from refuse bins or (illegal) handouts from curious visitors.[55] Human behavior was now under scrutiny.

Operating on these principles, officials from the National Parks Board began disciplining the public, with reports of it occurring 142 and 157 times in 2006 and 2007, as they conducted "raids on monkey feeders in the parks and nature reserves." Finally, in January 2008 the government raised the composition fine for feeding monkeys further, from $250 to $500 "to help curb issues relating to nuisance monkeys in our urban

---

[55] Lee and Sharon Chan, "Lessons and Challenges," p. 308.

environment."[56] Along with the announcement came a clear public statement justifying the policy.

> Monkey feeding endangers both humans and monkeys. It adversely alters the natural behavior of monkeys as it makes them reliant on humans for food. Such monkeys become too familiar with humans and this results in their nuisance and at times aggressive behavior toward people, especially children. Monkey feeding also results in an unhealthy growth of monkey population, and monkeys straying out of the nature reserves into residential areas.[57]

Meetings between authorities and residents continued to be held to try and alleviate tensions. These meetings also acted as venues to discourage feeding, all part of the comprehensive approaches that were aligned with the Singaporean culture of campaigns and the Garden City, with the primary onus of responsibility placed on humans.

Despite these efforts, which took place over a decade, observers in 2009 estimated that at least 50 percent of the commensal groups living near human residences, parks, or roads were still habituated to food provisioning.[58] With campaigns to discourage feeding doing little to lessen the monkey–human conflict, the government attempted several other approaches. These included attempts at "monkey-herding" at condominiums near nature reserves where macaques came in search of food, and loans of "free cages for the catching of monkeys." The various

---

[56] This rise in the amount came shortly after it had been raised from $200 to $250 in May 2007. Sha, et al., "Macaque-Human Interactions"; Sha, et al., "Status of the Long-Tailed Macaque," p. 2909; Official National Parks Announcement, "Tougher Measures Against Monkey Feeding," 30 Jan. 2008, https://www.nparks.gov.sg/news/2008/1/tougher-measure-against-monkey-feeding.

[57] Feng Zengkun, "Monkey Complaints Up, So Culling Rises Too"; Feng Zengkun, "Let's Not Monkey Around with Wildlife Plan."

[58] Campaigns during this period began to emphasize that the fruits of the forest were sufficient to sustain the macaque population in Singapore, although that information was not quite accurate. While the macaque diet is quite flexible, inconsistent flowering across the year and the species of trees that were used in the reforestation of the Singaporean landscape limit the resources available. Peter W. Lucas and Richard T. Corlett, "Relationship between the Diet of *Macaca fascicularis* and Forest Phenology," *Folia Primatologica* 57, 4 (1991): 201–15; Sha, et al., "Macaque-Human Interactions"; Sha, et al., "Status of the Long-Tailed Macaque," p. 2909.

conflicts, however, continued. From the perspective of the government, this left little room for negotiation. As one government official opined, "sadly, monkeys often have to be culled for this reason," before matters got "out of hand."[59]

The culling of monkeys as policy was and had been the last-chance standard response since the colonial era. The approach had remained as policy, albeit quietly, even after the disquiet created by the macaque culling in the Singapore Botanic Gardens in 1971. In 1984, for example, the Primary Production Department shot and killed three monkeys at MacRitchie Reservoir following complaints that the apes "had been overturning and damaging bins." Culling even continued after the Agri-Food and Veterinary Authority of Singapore replaced the Primary Production Department—in the national obsession to rename all things in an attempt to masquerade change—in 2000. Monkey culls took place every year in the new millennium with particularly high body counts in 2001, 2007, 2010 and 2013, as "external contractors" targeted "aggressive and nuisance-causing monkeys for safety." The main difference in the new millennium was the argument that this was "humane euthanasia of the animals as a last resort."[60]

Throughout the 2010s the uneasy relationship between macaques and humans in Singapore had reached an impasse. Monkeys were a nuisance in condominiums that bordered their territory, while humans faced fines for interacting with the wild; and, during this period, up to a quarter of the estimated macaque population was killed every year. This situation even led to non-governmental organizations, such as Animal Concerns

---

[59] Feng Zengkun, "Monkey Complaints Up, So Culling Rises Too"; Feng Zengkun, "Let's Not Monkey Around with Wildlife Plan."

[60] For example, in 2013 there were 570 macaques culled in Singapore. Feng Zengkun, "Monkey Complaints Up, So Culling Rises Too," *ST*, 28 Jul. 2013, pp. 2–3; Anonymous, "Three Nuisance Monkeys Shot Dead," *Singapore Monitor*, 1 Dec. 1984, p. 3; Robert Conceicao, "Why Shoot the Monkeys, Ask Visitors at MacRitchie," *Singapore Monitor*, 3 Dec. 1984, p 4; Feng Zengkun, "To Cull or Not to Cull Pesky Monkeys"; Feng, "Monkey Complaints Fall by Over Half After a Third of Them Culled"; Benjamin P.Y-H. Lee and Sharon Chan, "Lessons and Challenges in the Management of Long-Tailed Macaques in Urban Singapore," in *Monkeys on the Edge: Ecology and Management of Long-Tailed Macaques and Their Interface with Humans*, ed. Micheal D. Gumert, Agustín Fuentes and Lisa Jones-Engel (Cambridge: Cambridge University Press, 2011), p. 308.

Research and Education Society (ACRES) attempting to provide "human-macaque conflict management."[61]

Much of this came to a conclusion in 2018, when wildlife management in Singapore was reconstituted, as it transferred from the Agri-Food and Veterinary Authority of Singapore to the National Parks Board, which would now provide a "one-stop service on animal management and welfare issues" and manage 'human-animal interactions'" on the island. At this time culling was suspended; it now is officially used, using the rhetoric employed for decades, as a last resort. By the early 2020s, the National Parks Board following many of these guidelines, began promoting efforts to train condominium building managers and security personnel as "monkey guards" in an attempt at "protecting biodiversity" in Singapore, and to further discourage feeding. Culling, if it is used, is only to be done after the authorities "conduct population surveys and research studies to better understand the distribution of wildlife throughout Singapore," in order to "inform management strategies."[62] The monkey business of animal conflict remains in Singapore, a reflection of how the humans and animals interact within their chosen spaces on the island.

Boundaries and behavior between creatures—human and animal—have been continually negotiated in the Garden City, and are a constant subject of discussion and reconfiguration. The expulsion of macaques from the Botanic Gardens in 1971 was an inflection point at which there was a shift in the prior practice of habituating the animals into interacting with humans through provision of food, that resulted in the shift to a more natural biome in the center of the island in a Garden City. Once these new boundaries were established, further negotiation was required as higher primates soon began living on the edges of the wild space in the center of the island. This time the solution shifted to addressing human behavior, a common solution in the managed and governed space of Singapore. It

---

[61] Much of the role of ACRES and the management of such conflicts can be found on various pages on their website. https://acres.org.sg/ (accessed 27 Aug. 2021).
[62] Ministry of National Development Official Press Statement (26 Jul. 2018): "New Singapore Food Agency to Oversee Food Safety and Security, the National Parks Board to Oversee Animal and Wildlife Management, as well as Animal and Plant Health." https://www.mfa.gov.sg/Overseas-Mission/Vienna-Mission/Mission-Updates/Speeches--Press-Statements-and-other-Highlights/press20180726 (accessed 27 Aug. 2021); Toh Ting Wei, "Moves to Curb Risk of Conflicts between Humans and Wildlife," *ST*, 22 May 2022, p. A8; Sabarna Manoharan and Soh Pei Xuan, "Feeding May Have Drawn Monkeys to Clementi, Punggol: NParks," *ST*, 24 Jul. 2022, p. A16.

eventually became "a community- and science-based approach in managing wildlife in Singapore, including long-tailed macaques."[63] The handling of this relationship on an island in Southeast Asia ultimately mirrors larger policies and approaches for all creatures in Singapore as each has had to learn to live in a multi-species environment.

---

[63] Adrian Loo, "Wildlife: Measures Taken to Manage Macaques in Residential Areas," *ST*, 15 Mar. 2023, p. B7; Ang Qing, "When Wildlife Gets Too Close for Comfort," *ST*, 5 Mar. 2023, p. A22.

CHAPTER SIX

Songbirds in a Garden City

Faizah Zakaria

Ayub bin Ismail, a 46-year-old "bird enthusiast," filed a police report in October 1986. His prized *merbuk*—zebra dove (*Geopelia striata*)—had gone missing from the balcony of his eighth-floor flat in Clementi, where it had been sunning itself in a cage. This was a serious incident as the bird had won 50 trophies at national and regional bird-singing contests; each win raised the bird's value until some participants in the community placed its worth at $50,000. Newspaper reports about the disappearance mused about the creature's ability to captivate, including an apocryphal anecdote about a man driving past the bird in a Mercedes-Benz who was so entranced by its song that he got out of his car and offered the automobile in exchange for the prized songbird. Preferring his pet to the expensive vehicle, Ayub declined the offer. The bird, apparently, was never recovered.[1]

The saga of Ayub bin Ismail and his *merbuk* was one of many in the Singaporean national press from the early 1970s to the 1990s that focused on songbirds, bird-singing contests and the growth of the bird trade in the nation-state. Despite being a long-standing pastime on the island,

---

[1] Ngiam Tong Hai, "The Price and the Passion of Keeping Songbirds," *The Straits Times* [hereafter, *ST*], 19 Oct. 1986, p. 12; Anonymous, "Thieves Steal a Songbird Worth $10,000," *ST*, 8 Jun. 1987, p. 11.

however, the history of songbirds in Singapore has not been the subject of many in-depth studies. The most important account of this phenomenon is Lesley Layton's *Songbirds of Singapore*, which appeared in 1991 at the height of the phenomenon. It remains the only monograph on the subject to date and provides a nuanced picture of the hobby. Writing at the time, Layton was cautiously optimistic about the future of the pastime. "The practice of playing birds," she wrote, "is not expected to die out," as it would likely be kept alive by intergenerational ownership of birds and their emotional investment in a custom that had the capacity to bring together people of different races and classes.[2]

The fate of songbirds in Singapore since Ayub lost his zebra dove and Layton wrote her book is mixed at best. On one hand, the popularity of neighborhood bird-singing corners has significantly declined and a few, including the well-known Tiong Bahru Bird Arena, have been demolished. The hobby has become associated with nostalgia and a declining elderly population.[3] On the other hand, as environmental consciousness has grown, the efforts of bird-loving groups, such as the Singapore Cage-Bird Society and the Singapore Bird Study Group, as well as individual bird owners have pushed the pastime in new directions, continue to inspire a small but persistent public interest in sustaining a viable population of not only songbirds, but also wild birds more generally in the modern Garden City.

These developments and diversions in the fate of songbirds of Singapore over the past few decades have raised new perspectives and understandings of this unique aspect of the human–animal relationship in a modern, urbanized nation-state. One of these new areas of understanding is at the most basic, defining the animal. While Layton takes the creatures as a given category, the designation "songbird" is often place-based. Songbirds of Singapore need not be considered songbirds in other parts of the world

---

[2] Lesley Layton, *Songbirds in Singapore: The Growth of a Pastime* (Singapore: Oxford University Press, 1991), p. 84.

[3] Several blog posts evoke this sense of nostalgia for the heyday of keeping and putting songbirds in competition. See for instance, Nick Yeo, "Singapore's Bird-Singing Corners," *The Lion Raw*, 11 Jul. 2013, https://lionraw.com/2013/07/11/singapores-bird-singing-corners/ (accessed 29 May 2021); Anonymous, "Tiong Bahru Bird Singing Corner," *Remember Singapore*, 2 Jun. 2011, https://remembersingapore.org/tiong-bahru-bird-corner/ (accessed 28 May 2021); Hai Jun Ng, "The Last Bird-Singing Clubs of Singapore," *Culture Trip*, 10 Oct. 2018, https://theculturetrip.com/asia/singapore/articles/the-last-bird-singing-clubs-of-singapore/ (accessed on 21 May 2021).

and vice versa. Acknowledging "songbird" as a capacious category allows us to not only examine the histories of songbirds popularly kept as pets in Singapore but also how these histories were connected to those of passerine (perching) birds that did not achieve the same popular status in the nation-state.

This chapter will explore the history and changing fates of an already active caged bird trade in Singapore from the 1950s onwards and the many different avian species introduced to the island. Some of these birds escaped or were released, establishing viable populations that competed with indigenous birds for territorial advantage. Since the 1980s, this has resulted in ornithological designations of "migrant resident" and "indigenous" birds that have informed conservation initiatives and raised troubling questions about which birds belong in Singapore. A comparison of the experiences of two migrant resident species—the white-vented (Javan) myna (*Acridotheres javanicus*) and the white-crested laughingthrush (*Garrulax leucolophus*)—with the histories of two indigenous songbird species—the zebra dove (*Geopelia striata*) and the white-rumped shama (*Copsychus malabaricus*)—since Singapore's independence, obscures a common struggle among these birds to thrive in a city with shrinking forest cover. Migrant or indigenous, the advantage belonged to the birds whose breeding, feeding and nesting habits adapted to an urban environment, a place where they were caged. They became the modern songbirds of a Garden City.

Songbirds as Status

What is a songbird? The simplest definition is that it is a bird that produces a series of musical notes. Due to the development of muscles in the voice box, or syrinx, attached to bronchial semi-rings, songbirds are able to voice longer, rhythmic notes, produce two unrelated pitches at one time and in some cases, "sweep through more notes than on a piano keyboard in less than a tenth of second."[4] The length, range and purpose of the vocalization distinguishes a bird call from a bird song, although these differences might not always be discernible to the casual listener. Bird calls are shorter, less rhythmic and convey a sense of an impending threat, while bird songs are more structured, melodious and function

---

[4] Cornell Lab of Ornithology, "Bird Song: All About Bird Biology," *Bird Academy*, Ithaca, New York, 2014, https://academy.allaboutbirds.org/birdsong/ (accessed 1 Jun. 2021).

to attract a mate or mark a territory. Beyond these vocal characteristics, according to the Linnaean system of classification, songbirds belong to the order Passeriformes, which means that its feet were naturally adapted for perching on branches, and to the suborder Passeri.[5]

While seemingly straightforward, identifying songbirds solely through Linnaean classification has several limitations. First, such a definition excludes popular species of birds that are not perching birds but are still kept for their melodious vocalizations. The zebra dove is one such species. Also known as "peaceful dove," its Latin name is *Geopelia striata* and it belongs to the order Columbiformes, making it kin to the pigeon rather than songbirds like the robin.[6] In Linnaean classification, the zebra dove, like others in the Columbidae family are characterized by stout bodies, short necks and short slender bills. By contrast, the Southeast Asian names of the zebra dove are generally onomatopoeic. Known as *perkutut* in Indonesia, *merbuk* in Malaysia and Singapore, and *korokutuk* or *tukmo* in the Philippines, the common *-uk* sounds in these names recall the bird's soft, staccato coos.[7] From a Southeast Asian perspective, the zebra dove is unquestionably a songster, defined by the melodic sounds they produce, and it is regularly featured in bird-singing competitions in the region.

Second, using an anatomical basis for classifying songbirds neglects how bird songs change in response to the birds' environment. Ornithologists at Cornell's Bird Academy note that songbirds learn by replicating the sounds they hear around them, and some populations develop "local dialects," especially when barriers such as mountains, streams or roads isolate them from other birds. Moreover, how listeners perceive these songs contributes to their social status. After all, music is subjective to the listener. The white-vented (Javan) myna provides an illustrative example. Like other songbirds, it belongs to the order Passeriformes and is trapped and sold outside its native habitats as an exotic songbird. The songs of a Javan myna, however, often do not find a captive audience in these new environments. One such pet Javan myna in London was subject to a lawsuit in 1958 for its ability to produce "a noise like squealing brakes" and

---

[5] Frank Gill, David Donsker and Pamela Rasmussen, eds., "Orders of Birds," IOC *World Bird List*, 28 Jun. 2019, https://www.worldbirdnames.org/new/classification/orders-of-birds-draft/ (accessed 29 Mar. 2023).

[6] Clive Briffett and Sutari Bin Supari, *The Birds of Singapore* (Singapore: Oxford University Press, 1993), p. 40.

[7] Robert Kennedy, *A Guide to the Birds of the Philippines* (Kuala Lumpur: Oxford University Press, 2000), p. 149.

for singing "All the Nice Girls Love a Sailor," which disturbed neighbors at all hours of night. The bird was summarily fined £44. Related birds, such as the Indian myna (*Acridotheres tristis*), which was praised in a 1907 Australian bird guide for its cheery song that "adds considerably to the joy of living," became despised as "a kind of feathered cockroach" by 1990.[8]

A songbird, thus, is a bird that is either socially or scientifically distinguished by the sounds they vocalize and is valued for them in either the place where they originated or where they are exported. It is unclear how and when the habit of keeping songbirds began in Singapore, but traveler accounts indicate that this practice was common in the Malay Peninsula by at least the late 19th century. Isabella Bird, an Englishwoman who traveled to Perak in the 1870s, noted that local residents kept pet birds, with mynas and pigeons being the most popular. She observed that avian ability to vocalize bonded human and pet, opining "I don't know whether the mina can learn many words," but "articulated so humanly that I did not know whether a bird or a Malay spoke."[9]

A thriving bird market existed in Singapore attracting bird-sellers from all over the Malay World, as recounted by Anna Brassey in 1881. She described an entire street on the banks of Rochor River "alive with birds in baskets, cages, and coops," and "little native open boats arrive from the islands 1,500 to 3,000 miles to the southward of Singapore. Each has one little tripod mast. The whole family live on board. The sides of the boat cannot be seen for the multitudes of cockatoos, parrots, parrakeets, and birds of all sorts, fastened on little perches, with very short strings attached to them."[10] This bird market appeared to have survived in Singapore well into the 1930s although it moved from river to land.

---

[8] The transition from pet bird to pest was likewise evident in Singapore. The Javan myna arrived in Singapore's bird market in the 1920s and has since become the most common bird seen on the island, as well as the most persecuted. The target of private and state culling campaigns in response to complaints of the noise they make, the Javan myna is presently long dissociated from songbird status on a social level, if not scientifically. Cornell Lab of Ornithology, "Bird Song"; Stephen Moss, *Urban Aviary: A Modern Guide to City Birds* (London: White Lion Publishing, 2019), p. 136; Noel Luff, "A Change in Attitude: Where Did the Indian Myna Go Wrong?" *Canberra Bird Notes* 41, 2 (2016): 118–23; Anonymous, "His Singing Mynah Bird Is a £44 Nuisance," *The Singapore Free Press*, 3 Nov. 1958, p. 10.

[9] Isabella Bird, *The Golden Chersonese and the Way Thither* (New York, NY: Putnam and Sons, 1883), p. 381.

[10] Anna Brassey, *A Voyage on the Sunbeam: Our Home on the Ocean for Eleven Months*, (Chicago: Belford, Clarke and Co., 1881), pp. 411–12.

The Straits Times reported in 1927 that bird shops dominated Rochor Road and North Bridge Road. These shops "generally consist of a four-sided oblong room. Three sides of it are filled from top to bottom with cage upon cage of every conceivable denizen of the forest the average collector can want, while the fourth side opens to the street front." The types of birds, however, changed to cater to a Chinese market, with songbirds that included "Chinese robins, finches, canaries, bulbuls," in addition to the pigeons and mynas that Malays traditionally tamed. Besides Malay animal traders, Chinese pet shops had a significant presence, as did European middlemen buying exotic birds for the Western market.[11]

Despite the popularity of songbirds as pets, evidence of bird-singing competitions is difficult to find in the colonial era. While there are accounts of humans encouraging their captive pet birds to vocalize, which Bird mentioned, there is an absence in the records of cross-cultural competitions that sought to judge the quality of a bird's song that were to become hugely popular in Singapore in the second half of the 20th century. When small pet birds were put in competition, the limited available evidence points to their physique and conduct being the focus of evaluation, not their song. For example, members of the British armed forces and their families established the Singapore Cage-Bird Society and held bird shows, which were also open to non-European residents. These shows in the late 1940s included bird displays where the pets were judged on their appearance, health and behavior.[12]

The evolving fashions of bird cages further suggests that sound became a more valued commodity in the birds from the 1960s onwards. In the 1870s, traditional Malay cages for the zebra dove was formed from "strips of bamboo arranged in a circle and bent over to a point, tied and furnished with a hook on the top."[13] In the 1960s, however, a new style of cage made in China called the "Ben Hur" became popular to house the zebra dove as the cage's acoustics did not artificially amplify the sound of bird coos, unlike the traditional cages in Malaysia and

---

[11] Anonymous, "Bird and Beasts: The Animal Mart of Singapore," *ST*, 7 Nov. 1927, p. 12; Roland Braddell, *The Lights of Singapore*, (London: Methuen and Co., 1934), pp. 123–36; Layton, *Songbirds in Singapore*, p. 12; Fiona L.P. Tan, "The Beastly Business of Regulating the Wildlife Trade in Colonial Singapore," in *Nature Contained: Environmental Histories of Singapore*, ed. Timothy Barnard (Singapore: NUS Press, 2014), pp. 148–9.
[12] Layton, *Songbirds in Singapore*, p. 13.
[13] J.F. McNair, *Perak and the Malays: Sarong and Keris* (Kuala Lumpur: Oxford University Press, 1972), p. 105.

Indonesia.[14] While such fashions in cages could be due to popularity of the movie *Ben Hur*—released in 1959, as the cage was so named due to the similarity of the rattan band at the cage's top to the crossbar of a chariot—it also indicated a new concern for the quality of sound that the bird produced. The appearance of these cages, and a pre-existing, active bird trade, laid the groundwork for the unprecedented prominence of bird-singing competitions in Singapore during an important period in its formation as a nation-state.

Songbirds in a Modernizing Nation

The first, formal bird-singing contest in Singapore was staged in 1964. It took place a year after the formation of the Kelab Burung Singapura (Singapore Bird Club), which was essentially an updated version of the colonial Singapore Cage-Bird Society. The founding of this organization occurred alongside government efforts to outlaw bird fights, which not only encompassed cockfighting but also bets on fights between songbirds like the Chinese thrushes and magpie robins.[15] Such gambling had been popular in Singapore and more bird owners, deprived of that entertainment, now were willing to turn towards less violent singing contests as an alternative. While elderly bird owners Layton interviewed fondly remembered the event, there was little public information about this inaugural contest. It did not draw the attention of the national press. After the bird-fight ban in 1965, however, the profile of such contests grew, becoming ubiquitous in the young nation-state.[16]

In 1966, the Minister for Culture and Social Affairs Othman Wok opened a bird-singing contest at Pasir Panjang Park. He was not the last government official to do so. Photographic evidence in the Singapore National Archives, consisting of photographs taken of government ministers gracing public events throughout the 1970s up to the early 1990s, documents officials routinely opening such proceedings, awarding prizes, being photographed with the winners and even patronizing neighborhood

---

[14] Layton, *Songbirds in Singapore*, pp. 66–8.
[15] Cockfights had been banned in Singapore for decades. The 1960s, however, appears to be a period in which the law was actively enforced. Timothy P. Barnard, *Imperial Creatures: Humans and Other Animals in Singapore, 1819–1942* (Singapore: NUS Press, 2019), pp. 121–2; James A. Eaton, Boyd Leupen and Kanitha Krishnasamy, *Songsters of Singapore* (Petaling Jaya: TRAFFIC, 2017), p. 12.
[16] Layton, *Songbirds in Singapore*, p. 64.

Image 6.1: Minister for the Interior and Defence Lim Kim San attending at a bird-singing contest at Cairnhill Community Centre, 17 Dec. 1967. Ministry of Information and Arts Collection, courtesy of National Archives of Singapore.

bird-singing corners.[17] Their presence suggests a level of state-support for such contests during this period, and raises questions about how and why political interests intersected with bird singing. While such public displays of community support were not unusual, it was also linked to a form of political patronage in newly independent Singapore, the development of new public housing estates to replace urban kampongs.

In 1958, the Singapore Improvement Trust introduced the colonial city's first urban renewal master plan, which aimed to dismantle the kampongs that were regarded as "slums" and to reduce the demographic density at the city center by resettling the population into satellite towns in what were then rural areas such as Jurong, Woodlands and Yio Chu Kang. The post-independence government, dominated by the People's Action Party (PAP) and then-leader Lee Kuan Yew, continued with this plan. They refashioned the Singapore Improvement Trust into a government

---

[17] There are at least 15 photographs of high-level ministers attending bird-singing competitions from 1966 to 1990 in the National Archives of Singapore in addition to the one featured in this collection.

statutory body, the Housing & Development Board (HDB), which was entrusted with this mission.[18] Lee reflected in his memoirs that moving the population involved a transformation in the human–animal relationship, as the move was estranging kampong-dwellers from other creatures in a kampong. When communities were resettled, subsistence activities such as pig farming, chicken rearing and fish harvesting in communal ponds were phased out. As Lee explained:

> Resettling farmers was toughest. We paid compensation based on sized of farm structures… but even the most generous payment was not enough. Older farmers did not know what to do with themselves and their compensation money. Living in flats, they missed their pigs, ducks, chickens, fruit trees and vegetable plots which had provided them with free food. Fifteen to twenty years after being resettled in HDB new towns, many still voted against the PAP. They felt the government had destroyed their way of life.[19]

Perhaps wishing to mitigate this sense of dislocation, from early on, the housing authorities exempted pets from the general rule that animals did not belong in human homes. The types of creatures that surrounded humans in Singapore would transform.[20]

The government allowed new owners to keep small pets in their households and explicitly planned to build infrastructure that facilitated pet ownership in the new estates. Starting with Tiong Bahru estate, where new "matchbox" style utilitarian flats rose amidst the preceding art deco shophouses in the mid-1960s, space was allocated for a coffee shop, a pet shop and bird stands, all three in close proximity. Located at the foot of a block of flats, bird owners could gather at the coffee shop, hook their bird cages on a grid-like structure above their heads, and enjoy the

---

[18] Loh Kah Seng, *Squatters into Citizens: The 1961 Bukit Ho Swee Fire and the Making of Modern Singapore* (Singapore: NUS Press, 2013), pp. 26–46; Tilak Abeysinghe and Jiaying Gu, "Lifetime Income and Housing Affordability in Singapore," *Urban Studies* 48, 9 (2011): 1875–91; Chua Beng Huat, "Navigating between Limits: The Future of Public Housing in Singapore," *Housing Studies* 28, 4 (2014): 520–33.
[19] Lee Kuan Yew, *From Third World to First: The Singapore Story* (Singapore: Singapore Press Holdings, 2000), p. 207.
[20] See also Barnard and Yip's chapter in this collection regarding monkeys being included in this reconfiguration of the human–animal relationship in the home.

birdsong while chatting about the birds. In some estates, such as Kebun Baru, the bird stands were placed in an open field and were as high as a flagpole to replicate the experience of perching on tree branches, inducing the best songs from the birds. Enthusiasts hoisted their birds up with the use of pulleys, usually with a cloth covering the cage in order not to disconcert their pets. These tall stands were also used as competition arenas and could accommodate up to 1,000 cages.[21]

To some extent, these bird-singing corners helped to create intercultural community common ground. Prior to resettlement, Chinese, Malay and Indian kampong dwellers had divergent preferences for bird species. Chinese residents preferred magpie robins and Chinese thrushes, while Malay hobbyists had a marked affection for the zebra dove and other varieties of pigeons, while their Indian counterparts were inclined to keep speaking birds (rather than songbirds) such as parrots, parakeets and cockatoos. Among the reasons for these divergences were folk beliefs concerning which species brought good luck. These beliefs were fluid and sometimes changed in the course of intercultural contact; some Chinese bird keepers, for instance, grew to share the Malay belief that certain characteristics of zebra doves, such as the number of scales on their feet, were auspicious. After resettlement in housing estates, such preferences intermingled. Layton's informants described Chinese and Malay bird owners sitting together at coffee shops listening to the dawn chorus and the shifting variety of songs as the birds began to replicate each other. By the early 1970s, five species of bird emerged as clear favorites of the bird-keeping community: the white-rumped shama, zebra dove, oriental white-eye, straw headed bulbul and *hwa mei* (Chinese laughingthrush). This convergence of bird preferences indexed a simplification of the captive bird landscape in the city encouraged through the infrastructural development and intercultural organization in which pets were part of an effort to promote racial harmony in new communities.[22]

---

[21] The Kebun Baru Birdsinging Club is one of few associations dedicated to the practice that is still active today. For a description of their premises, although it has not been updated recently, see their official website at https://kebunbarubirdsingingclub. weebly.com (accessed 31 May 2021); Anonymous, "Bird Notes," *ST*, 23 Sep. 1981, p. 8; Anonymous, "Singapore Idol—For the Birds," *ST*, 5 Nov. 2012, p. 2.

[22] The Malay-language daily *Berita Harian*, however, reported bird-singing contests in Malay areas such as Geylang Serai did not feature the zebra dove at times, but the oriental white-eye and straw-headed bulbul. Anonymous, "Peraduan Suara Burung," *Berita Harian*, 29 Nov. 1973, p. 5; Anonymous, "Piala2 Pemenang Peraduan Suara Burung," *Berita Harian*, 3 Sep. 1973, p. 5; Anonymous, "250 Ekor

Besides building infrastructure conducive to the development of keeping various bird species as pets, the Singapore government actively encouraged the hobby through its affiliates such as the People's Association and HDB estate community clubs, which joined groups like the Singapore Cage-Bird Society and Kelab Burung Singapura in organizing mass competitions. These events often featured up to 200 human contestants presenting a handful of avian species. Contrary to the recollections that Layton documented of bird owners who remembered the 1964 Kelab Burung Singapura contest as the pioneering national venture, *The Straits Times* credited the Cairnhill Community Club for organizing the first formal bird-singing competition in 1966, and lauded state efforts in this direction. While reporting in 1977 on a new government exemption of bird and pet fish dealers from competing for tender to run shops at HDB housing estates—a move aimed to encourage acceptable pet keeping among residents—the daily quoted a government official taking credit for the growth of the pastime. "A green and clean city and competitions in which a large number and variety of birds sing against each other do not just happen. It took years of planning and consistent hard work to achieve," Minister for National Development and Communications Lim Kim San stated.[23]

Songbirds soon became ubiquitous in Singapore and were closely associated with the state. The Jurong Bird Park, a state-supported aviary that was the largest in Southeast Asia at the time of its opening in 1971, also hosted an annual bird-singing competition, offering relatively lucrative prizes. The Singapore Tourism Board heavily promoted the park, along with neighborhood bird singing to attract potential visitors, especially after a task force was convened to refresh national tourism initiatives in the mid-1980s. The Board also supported independent tour guides who brought tourists for walking tours of neighborhoods such as Tiong Bahru and included bird-singing corners in their itineraries. These efforts brought local bird-singing competitions some global attention; flautist

---

Burung Sertai Peraduan Suara Anjuran B. Rakyat Geylang Serai," *Berita Harian*, 11 Dec. 1973, p. 2; Anonymous, "Save These Birds from Extinction," *ST*, 16 Oct. 1977, p. 12; A.S Bucknill and F.N. Chasen, *Birds of Singapore and Southeast Asia* (Kuala Lumpur: Oxford University Press, 1988), p. 58; Anonymous, "Save These Birds from Extinction," *ST*, 16 Oct. 1977, p. 12; Layton, *Songbirds in Singapore*, p. 24; A.S. Bucknill and F.N. Chasen, *Birds of Singapore and Southeast Asia* (Kuala Lumpur: Oxford University Press, 1988), p. 58.

[23] Anonymous, "HDB to Promote Love of Nature," *ST*, 11 Jul. 1977, p. 8; Layton, *Songbirds in Singapore*, p. 24.

Herbert Mann visited the Tiong Bahru coffee shop for their birds in 1984, and a 2014 Hollywood film titled *Cages* used a bird-singing competition in Singapore as one of its set-pieces. Finally, the white-rumped shama appeared on the 50-dollar note in Singapore currency released from 1976 to 1984, circulating the image of this popular Singapore songbird.[24]

The economic advantages of encouraging songbird-rearing among local communities also became evident. While there were an estimated 25,000 songbird owners in Singapore by 1985, constituting a relatively small market, they provided a central core for the expansion of the bird business into the export market.[25] Selling birds became a multi-million-dollar business that grew to approximately S$70 million as the number of bird dealers jumped from 10 in 1977 to more than 80 in 1986. By the mid-1980s, 70 to 80 percent of the captive birds in Singapore were re-exported. According to the Chairman of the Singapore Bird Dealers Association, which was formed in 1984, the birds were caught in Thailand, Indonesia, Malaysia and, later, China, and then passed through Singapore before transferring to the United States and Europe as these countries "prefer to import from Singapore [rather than the rest of the region] because they know we take good care of the birds and keep them healthy during the quarantine period." Singapore's regulatory framework enabled trade that facilitated a global circulation of Asian songbird species; a practice that was internationally criticized as early as 1975 when Royal Society for the Protection of Birds in Britain charged that Singapore dealers were intermediaries in smuggling of protected birds from Southeast Asia.[26] Globally connected with excellent transportation infrastructure, Singapore was particularly well positioned to take advantage of both the licit and illicit trade in wildlife.

While a hard-nosed economic pragmatism is a simple explanation for state keenness to maintain the songbird trade, such an explanation

---

[24] Singapore Ministry of Trade and Industry, *Report of the Tourism Task Force* (Singapore: Ministry of Trade and Industry, 1984), p. 5; Magdalene Lum, "Tiong Bahru Tour," *ST*, 11 Apr. 1985, p. 38; D.L. Yong and Lim K.C., *A Naturalist's Guide to the Birds of Singapore* (Oxford: John Beaufoy Publishing, 2016), p. 139; David Tan, "The Pied Piper Plays On," *ST*, 23 Jun. 1984, p. 24; Anonymous, "Singapore-US Film to Be Made Here," *Today*, 28 Jul. 2004, p. 24; Christopher Hails and Frank Jarvis, *Birds of Singapore* (Singapore: Marshall Cavendish, 2018), p. 129.

[25] Layton, *Songbirds in Singapore*, p. 25.

[26] Anonymous, "A Business Worth Singing About," *ST*, 14 Jan. 1987, p. 4; Anonymous, "Wildlife Suppliers to the World," *ST*, 26 May 1975, p. 5.

is also incomplete as the cultivation of such a pastime and its attendant bird trade was not simply a pragmatic measure. The development of a domestic songbird-keeping community was consistent with the attempts to create a Garden City, a plan attributed to Lee Kuan Yew in 1967 when he spoke about a two-stage plan to build such a city, "beautiful with flowers and trees, and as tidy and litter-less as can be." A garden is the epitome of blurred boundaries between nature and culture; a space for desired species to flourish, created by human hands curating nature's gifts to what he deemed as the best advantage. The government plan involved tree planting, river clean-ups and the protection of selected species. Certain types of birds, including pet birds, fit nicely into this schema.[27] The expansion of the caged-songbird sector should be placed in the context of this vision for a curated landscape. Some birds were part of the "beautiful" nature in a modernizing nation-state, closely intertwined with the image Singaporean leaders wanted to project in the 1970s and 1980s.

In 1977, however, Ng Soon Chye, Chairman of the Singapore Conservation Board, sounded a note of alarm about the curated Garden City. He was concerned about the diminishing population of popular songbirds in the wild and argued "you can't cultivate nature by bringing it into your home. You have to go to nature." He proposed that more songbird owners contribute to the conservation movement by breeding endangered species of birds and then making them available in the market to provide an alternative to trapping wild songbirds. Ng, in his proposal, reflected the concurrent desire for broad-based conservationism through protection of wild bird habitats and curated sustainability through human intervention.[28] As environmental scholars Marco Armiero and Lisa Sedrez

---

[27] British ornithologist Christopher Hails recalls being hired in the late 1970s to "bring back the birds to the city, thanks to the personal interest of Prime Minister Lee Kuan Yew" and that his recommendations to create a statutory board in charge of parks and monitor bird populations in the city were adopted and implemented, "thanks to the support of then Minister of National Development S. Dhanabalan." Hails and Jarvis, *Birds of Singapore*, p. 6; Anonymous, "Singapore to Become Beautiful, Clean City within Three Years," *ST*, 12 May 1967, p. 4; Stephen H.K. Yeh, "The Idea of the Garden City," in *Management of Success: The Moulding of Modern Singapore*, ed. K.S. Sandhu and P. Wheatley (Singapore: Institute of Southeast Asian Studies, 1989), pp. 810–19; S.K. Lee and S.E. Chua, *More than a Garden City* (Singapore: Parks and Recreation Department, Ministry of National Development, 1992).

[28] Ng was also the chairperson of the Malaya Nature Society Singapore Branch's Bird Study Group and later worked on bird ringing to track populations of water birds

have argued, however, a synergy between wilderness-centered approaches and sustainability-centered approaches to conservation, which Ng raised, is not often possible, especially when scales of action oscillate between global and local. Put differently, environmental action requires either a change of values or an innovation of tools; doing both might not be feasible. Wilderness and sustainability represent two distinct threads in environmentalist movements that could generate tension between different groups with similar affection for the same creatures.[29] This tension further complicated the story of songbirds in a modern Garden City, which was soon manifested in the discourse of differing Singaporean communities invested in the survival of songbirds, either as pets or as a subset of endangered birds.

Environmentalism in Two Keys

Reflecting on the development of pets and prevailing assumptions of the benign or benevolent relationship between master and pet in the 1980s, Yi-Fu Tuan posited that "dominance may be cruel and exploitative with no hint of affection in it. What it produces is the victim. One the other hand, dominance may be combined with affection, and what it produces is the pet."[30] He went on to argue that power asymmetries mark our relationship with all non-human animals, especially towards the creatures that we love most. If dominance and affection are two sides of the same coin, what did affectionate dominance look like in the case of pet songbirds in Singapore? What kind of actions for the welfare of the songbird population did the human–pet bird relationship inspire? It would be instructive to look into individual acts of care for the birds and activities of groups like the Singapore Cage-Bird Society and Kelab Burung Singapura to better understand these issues.

The act of feeding birds required direct touch and careful knowledge of the bird's preferences. In general, shamas and thrushes are insectivores,

---

at the Serangoon Sewage Works. Anonymous, "Save these Birds from Extinction," *ST*, 16 Oct. 1977, p. 12; Lim Kim Seng, *The Avifauna of Singapore* (Singapore: Singapore Nature Society, 2009), p. 42.

[29] Marco Armiero and Lise Sedrez, *A History of Environmentalism: Local Struggles, Global Histories* (London: Bloomsbury, 2014), pp. 3–22.

[30] Yi-Fu Tuan, *Dominance and Affection: The Making of Pets* (New Haven, CT: Yale University Press, 1984), p. 2.

bulbuls prefer fruit, while zebra doves eat seeds.[31] Each bird also exhibits their own idiosyncrasies. Muhammad Aidil, owner of two red-whiskered bulbuls, catches live grasshoppers for his birds. At 35 years of age in 2021, he is among the younger generation of bird owners in Singapore and grew up when the pastime was declining in popularity, having learned the art of rearing the birds from his father. Aidil feeds his bulbuls insects, which are considered a "hot" food, and the birds only consume them in small amounts, following a concept similar to the schema of hot and cold practiced in traditional Malay medicine.[32] Grasshoppers also feature in memories of bird-keeping among older generations. Amnah Sirat, an 82-year-old former Javanese resident of then-newly built Tanglin Halt estate recalled how her son regularly gathered grasshoppers to sell to a Chinese-owned pet shop in their neighborhood in early 1970s. Armed with a homemade net constructed from wire mesh and a pair of socks, he would venture into secondary forests in the area with a group of friends to gather the insects, learning how to keep the creatures living with splashes of water, as they had to be alive in order to be marketable.[33]

This preference for grasshoppers as a treat for captive birds correlates with data from the 1980s when grasshoppers, crickets and mealworms provided protein to the birds who consumed them in different ways. Shamas ate the grasshoppers whole, while white-eyes required them to be served slit open so that they could peck at the soft parts. Bird owners, who did not outsource their feed preparation to ready-made packages in pet shops that became more readily available in the 1980s, engage in a "materiality of intimacy." This notion, which Juno Salazar Parreñas conceptualized, argues that affective bonds between human and non-human are built through mundane care-giving such as feeding, bathing and cleaning waste and that, moreover, wildlife rehabilitation centers depended on the need for inter-species touch, and sold such experiences to their volunteers.[34]

---

[31] Allen Jeyarajasingam and Allan Pearson, *A Field Guide to the Birds of Peninsular Malaysia and Singapore* (Oxford: Oxford University Press, 2012), pp. 189, 321, 343.
[32] Muhammad Aidil, interview with author, 6 Jun. 2021.
[33] Amnah Sirat, interview with author, 9 May 2021.
[34] In addition, bathing was also crucial as a former president of the Singapore bird club posited that "cleanliness is of paramount importance to keep the bird in tip-top condition." Layton, *Songbirds in Singapore*, p. 49; Anonymous, "Bird Disappoints Ming Ming," *New Nation*, 26 Jun. 1972, p. 3; Juno Salazar Parreñas, "The Materiality of Intimacy in Wildlife Rehabilitation: Rethinking Ethical Capitalism through

Memories of bird ownership in Singapore indicate the quality of the affective relationship changed when the landscape changed. A former resident of the Javanese Kampung Tempe from 1964 to 1969, for example, recalls how some neighbors set their zebra doves free when they moved out of the kampong.[35] Despite being allowed to bring pet birds to the newly constructed HDB estates, the bird-keeping experience in villages cultivated a different quality of affective relationships. In a more rural setting, villagers constructed bird feeders to attract zebra doves and tame zebra doves were kept in coops, much like poultry, but elevated above ground. The owners let the birds out in the afternoon but again, similar to chickens, they returned in the evenings.[36] The body of the bird connected individual, community, and spirituality. When such materiality of intimacy was rendered difficult in an urbanized setting following HDB resettlement, some chose to let the birds go rather than enact a simulacrum of the relationship in a high-rise apartment.[37]

While bird owners cultivated complex relationships of affectionate dominance through the materiality of intimacy, their feelings for the birds did not appear to be translatable to a broader public as environmental consciousness. Rather, they were mobilized to produce public spectacles that sparked awareness about birds among an urban population that rarely encountered them. Groups such as the Singapore Cage-Bird Society and the Kelab Burung Singapura conducted outreach in the form of bird shows, some of which helped them raise funds while increasing awareness of the diversity of birds. For instance, the Singapore Cage-Bird Society held bird exhibitions at Happy World Amusement Park that introduced penguins

---

Embodied Encounters with Animals in Southeast Asia," *positions: asia critique* 24, 1 (2016): 97–110; Anonymous, "The Early Birds Now Catch Fewer Worms in Singapore," *ST*, 4 Sep. 1984, p. 14.

[35] This respondent lived in Kampung Tempe from 1964–69 and then Kampung Ghim Moh up to 1974 before moving to new HDB flats in Holland Avenue. Rodiah Jirkaseh, interview with author, 1 May 2021; Yahaya Sanusi and Hidayah Amin, *Kampung Tempe: Voices from a Malay Village* (Singapore: Helang Books, 2016).

[36] The contribution that such birds made to the community went beyond song. An acidic cheap alternative to tannin, zebra dove excrement was used to *samak* (tan) the hide of cows slaughtered for village celebrations. The leather produced was used as a membrane for the *bedok*, a Malay drum that was sounded during each call to prayer, five times a day. Rodiah Jirkaseh, interview with author, 1 May 2021.

[37] It is interesting to note that a religious angle was also highlighted in Layton's oral histories. Layton, *Songbirds in Singapore*, p. 63 shows that part of the reason for zebra dove being so attractive to the Malay community was its ability to imitate sounds from the Quran.

Image 6.2: Exotic non-native birds showcased at an exhibition organized by the Singapore Cage-Bird Society at Happy World Amusement Park, 1950s. Image courtesy of the Tong Seng Mun Collection, courtesy of National Archives of Singapore.

and other non-tropical birds to Singapore residents in the mid-1950s, while Kelab Burung Singapura partnered with the Jurong Bird Park to utilize bird-singing competitions as a means of introducing enthusiasts to diverse species of birds that populated the park in the 1970s.[38]

Although these shows attracted visitors, they ultimately failed to inspire broad support among cage-bird owners for alleviating the plight of endangered bird species in the wild. A growing community of wildlife activists became ambivalent, if not skeptical about pet bird owners as allies. In 1986, for example, the advisory director of the World Society for the Protection of Animals, Marjorie Doggett, commented to *The Straits Times* that it would be hopeless to try to stop bird-singing contests but saw it as "a lesser evil, because if people spend a large sum of money to keep birds for competition, they must have some knowledge on how to take better care of them." Others saw the hobby as an outright threat

---

[38] Anonymous, "Cage Bird Show," *Singapore Standard,* 7 Nov. 1958, p. 7; Anonymous, "Bird Society to Hold Show," *ST,* 18 May 1955, p. 5; Anonymous, "Jurong Park Birdsong Contest," *ST,* 19 Aug. 1971, p. 15.

to birds in the wild. A letter writer to *The Straits Times* Forum page in 1981, railed about men being able to walk around freely in a residential estate with about 20 traps and decoy birds despite the Wild Animals and Birds Act of 1965 that protected all wild vertebrate animals apart from six species of birds.[39]

Pet bird owners and wildlife enthusiasts in Singapore, thus, were not natural allies despite their shared fondness for the animal. While affectionate care for birds among the former was directed mainly towards their pets, the latter channeled their energy towards data collection and habitat protection. From the 1970s to the 2010s, this was manifested in the publication of a significant number of bird guides, field guides and compendiums of avifauna information, often under the auspices of the Bird Study Group of the Singapore Nature Society.[40] First convened in the mid-1950s, British ornithologists from the Royal Air Force Ornithological Society and the Army Bird-Watching Club led the Bird Study Group in various projects to ring migratory birds and collect data about their movements. Their work was qualitatively different from pet bird owners as the data concerned the local bird ecosystem and it was integrated with global counterparts. Bird study groups in Singapore and the Malay Peninsula continue to maintain committees that publish sightings of birds regularly in their reports *Singapore Avifauna* and *Suara Enggang* (Voice of the Hornbill) respectively. Over time, this data has become the basis for state-of-the-bird-species summations in field guides that were published later to encourage bird watching and appreciation among the public. Christopher Hails, who led the "Bring Back the Birds" project in the 1980s, co-authored one of the first modern guides, which included

---

[39] The six species are the rock pigeon, house crow, Asian glossy starling, purple backed starling, common and Javan myna. D. Ferris, "Help Nab These Bird Trappers," *ST*, 1 Aug. 1981, p. 19; Anonymous, "When the Songbird Craze Took Off," *ST*, 19 Oct. 1986, p. 12; Lillian Chew, "Divorced from Nature," *Business Times,* 15 Nov. 1980, p. 13.

[40] A.G. Glenister, *The Birds of the Malay Peninsula, Singapore and Penang* (Kuala Lumpur: Oxford University Press, 1971); Hails and Jarvis, *Birds of Singapore*; Briffett and Sutari, *The Birds of Singapore*; G.W.H. Davison and Chew Yen Fook, *A Photographic Guides to Birds of Peninsular Malaysia and Singapore* (London: New Holland Publishers, 1995); Jeyarajasingam and Pearson, *A Field Guide to the Birds of Peninsular Malaysia and Singapore*; Lim, *The Avifauna of Singapore*; Yong Ding Li, Lim Kim Chuah and Lee Tiah Khee, *A Naturalist's Guide to Birds of Singapore* (Oxford: John Beaufoy Publishing, 2017); Lim Kim Seng, Yong Ding Li and Lim Kim Chuah, *Birds of Malaysia and Singapore* (Princeton: Princeton University Press, 2020).

practical tips on where, when and how to catch a glimpse of wild birds. Bird-watching expeditions gained popularity, transitioning from being "a rather lonely affair," in the 1970s to twice-monthly feature in the activity schedule of the Nature Society, according to naturalist Lim Kim Seng, who began birding in 1975 and has authored six guides to the hobby.[41]

The two groups—pet bird owners and wildlife advocates—became increasingly estranged in their approaches towards public engagement and consultation from the late 1980s onwards. Wildlife enthusiasts mobilized through groups such as the Singapore Nature Society and the Animal Concerns Research and Education Society (ACRES) and leaned into environmental advocacy for the protection of bird habitats worldwide. The role of the Nature Society in the establishment of the Sungei Buloh Wetland Reserve in 1991 exemplified this approach; in a rare campaign of dissent, the group successfully galvanized public support to counter government plans for an agro-technology park. ACRES supported UK-based wildlife trade monitoring network TRAFFIC in their efforts to survey Singapore bird dealers and check for illicit trade in regional birds. In a 2017 report, TRAFFIC found that Singapore had issued commercial import and export permits for at least 30 of species of birds the International Union for the Conservation of Nature (IUCN) classified as vulnerable, endangered or critically endangered. Such actions were geared towards public monitoring that aimed to birds safe from humans, in situ, in their own habitats over several decades.[42]

In this context of heightened wildlife activism, the cage-bird trade—and, indirectly, pet owners—came under criticism for contributing to the

---

[41] Lim joined the Nature Society in 1975 and holds the record for identifying the greatest number of bird species spotted in a year. Lim, *The Avifauna of Singapore*, pp. 42–3; Hails and Jarvis, *Birds of Singapore*; Cheang Suk Wai, et al., *Living the Singapore Story—Celebrating Our 50 Years: 1965–2015* (Singapore: Straits Times Press, 2015), p. 127; Y.C. Wee and R. Hale, "The Nature Society (Singapore) and the Struggle to Conserve Singapore's Nature Areas," *Nature in Singapore* 1 (2008): 41–9; Goh Hong Yi, "The Nature Society, Endangered Species and Conservation," in *Nature Contained: Environmental Histories of Singapore*, ed. Timothy P. Barnard (Singapore: NUS Press, 2014), pp. 248–53.

[42] Lim, *The Avifauna of Singapore*, p. 43; Wee and Hale, "The Nature Society (Singapore)," p. 43; Anonymous, "Bird Lovers Submit Proposals for 300-ha Nature Reserve," *ST,* 14 Dec. 1987, p. 14; Richard Hale, "From Backwater to Nature Reserve," *Nature Watch* 12, 5 (2004): 2–4; Charissa Yong, "Saving Sungei Buloh," *ST,* 9 Aug. 2015, p. 42; Eaton, Leupen and Krishnasamy, *Songsters of Singapore*, p. 3.

possible extinction of birds. While early guides such as Hails and Jarvis' *Birds of Singapore* had little comment on conservation, later guidebooks argued that the cage-bird trade threatened some local species, especially the popular straw-headed bulbul, magpie robin and white-rumped shama. Animal welfare was also a bone of contention. A member of the Singapore Bird Study Group wrote to *The Straits Times* that while he did not "doubt that caged bird keepers are bird lovers," there was "another ugly side of the bird trade which many do not fully know about—the cruelty and wastage of life through trappings and inhumane methods of transportation." He pitched the activities of the Bird Study Group as a humane model, as did other columns with similar criticisms. The position of Singapore as an entrepôt in the cage-bird trade essentially incentivized the trapping of birds elsewhere, though bird dealers refuted charges of being implicated in smuggling.[43] Pet bird owners were tainted by association.

The focus of groups like the Singapore Nature Society on habitat preservation was not the only conservation model emerging with respect to songbirds. Aligning more with pet owners' conduct of care through dominance and management, captive breeding that could augment dwindling songbird populations through science-based intervention offered another route. The Singaporean state was more receptive towards such an approach than it was towards public agitation to designate land for birds. For example, the National Parks Board worked with TRAFFIC to host the inaugural Asian Songbird Trade Crisis Summit in 2015. The proceedings recommended genetic research, captive breeding and husbandry, community education and better enforcement against illegal trade as key points of action to mitigate the dwindling populations of songbirds in Asia, sidelining the issue of habitat loss. Meanwhile, wildlife advocacy for the preservation of sites that sustained birdlife arguably met with much more failure than success, particularly after groups successfully blocked the construction of a golf course at Lower Peirce Reservoir in 1992. Since then, the government has generally ignored or marginalized counter proposals from the Nature Society with regard to land use. Reflecting on the advocacy work of the Nature Society in the 1990s, Wee Yeow Chin and Richard Hale, who were active in these efforts, observed that "those involved may have been a little naïve," failing to realize that "the

---

[43] Anonymous, "The Ugly Side of the Bird Trade," *ST,* 18 Oct. 1979, p. 15; Anonymous "Smuggling a Thing of the Past: Bird Dealers' Group," *ST,* 6 Jun. 1993, p. 22.

government had already made a major concession towards conservation" and was unlikely to concede more at the time.[44]

The limited success of these Nature Society campaigns called to question whether their vision of conserving birds in a Garden City was viable. Most notable among their rejected proposals were plans to conserve the estuary around Serangoon Sludge Treatment Works and Senoko, a degraded mangrove forest near a power station. Such hybrid, anthropocentric habitats were neither wild enough to capture public imagination nor did they fit into the aesthetics of a nature friendly Singapore. These sites were conducive for birdlife by accident rather than design. When ash from electricity generation was channeled into nearby water sources, ponds which were a "secure roosting place for tide dependent waterbirds" were formed, providing the latter with organic matter and insects to maintain a thriving population.[45] Saving insect-ridden sludge ponds for the sake of birds as suggested in these plans did not fit into the imagined Garden City as seamlessly as either the promotion of songbird keeping in housing estates or the careful, selective breeding of captive species.

Affectionate domination of birds in Singapore, therefore, led to the two divergent models of action for avian welfare. The first involved intimate everyday interactions that bonded humans to their pets and cultivated an ethics of care for the individual bird. This form of affection, however, was constrained in its conservation push even when bird owners organized themselves into groups like the Singapore Cage-Bird Society. Trade in songbirds pushed conservation efforts towards sustainability through captive means, setting as a goal the sustainability of species,

---

[44] Jessica G.H. Lee, Serene C.L. Chng and James A. Eaton, *Conservation Strategy for Southeast Asian Songbirds in Trade. Recommendation from the First Asian Songbird Trade Crisis Summit* (Singapore: Wildlife Reserves Singapore/TRAFFIC, 2015), pp. 6–7; Wee and Hale, "The Nature Society (Singapore)," p. 42; Harvey Neo, "Challenging the Developmental State: Nature Conservation in Singapore," *Asia-Pacific Viewpoint* 48, 2 (2007): 186–99.

[45] Jeyarajasingam and Pearson, *A Field Guide,* pp. 30–1; Lim Kim Seng, "Conservation Proposal for Senoko (with Checklist Appended)," (manuscript issued by Malayan Nature Society, Singapore Branch, National Library of Singapore Collection, 1990); Ng Soon Chye, "Serangoon Sludge Treatment Works: Bird Study Report," (manuscript issued by Malayan Nature Society, Singapore Branch, National Library of Singapore Collection, 1977). Anonymous, "25,000 Appeal for Senoko Bird Habitat to Be Saved," *ST,* 21 Oct. 1994, p. 3.

not the survival of ecosystems where these bird species thrived. Wildlife conservation groups such as the Nature Society provided a second way forward by questioning the vision of a Garden City that the government had put forward as an ideal. Their ideal of going back to nature, however, was not as coherent as the vision of the garden as a natural environment worth saving might not present itself as such in the eyes of the public or public policy beholders. Lacking wilderness in the fullest sense of the word, efforts to conserve bird habitats in Singapore raised questions about what land uses should be prioritized if national economic development was to continue apace. Moreover, such efforts troubled ideas about what landscapes and species belonged in modern Singapore.

Indigenous vs. Migrant Birds

A 2013 bird guide provides one of the most trenchant criticisms against the pet trade in Singapore. Part of its discomfort was directed towards an indirect consequence: the introduction of new bird species in Singapore that competed with local species for living space to the detriment of the latter. In it, authors Yong Ding Li, Lim Kim Chuah and Lee Tiah Khee wrote:

> The pet bird trade and an established songbird-keeping tradition among some locals set the stage for many escaped birds. This problem is further accentuated by religious practices that encourage the intentional release of captive animals, particularly small birds. While the Javan Myna and House Crow appear to have been deliberately introduced, others, such as the two cockatoo species Red Breasted Parakeet and White-crested laughingthrush, may have originated from the escaped birds and have since established breeding populations. The White-crested laughingthrush used to be confined to one or two locations in western Singapore but has since spread widely and is now found across much of the country. The Javan Myna was scarce when first documented a few decades ago but is now Singapore's most abundant bird. Their large noisy roosts, even in busy Orchard Road, have invoked disdain from residents and tourists. Whether these invasive birds pose a serious threat to native species

remains a matter of informed speculation, but case studies from elsewhere show that many native birds are eventually outcompeted and pushed towards extinction.[46]

Several other birding guidebooks shared this dim view of introduced species and even described them as "feral."[47] While an accepted term in conservation biology to describe introduced species that successfully push out native species in the host site, the linguistic connotation of the word as fierce, ferocious and savage seemed incongruous when applied to small birds such as the Javan myna and the white-crested laughingthrush. To what extent was the displacement of native birds by imported songbird species a problem? Beyond material history about ecological displacement, what did the discourse about competition between native and foreign species reveal about Singapore's socio-political landscape? The brief histories of these two introduced species with that of two indigenous songbirds—the zebra dove and the white-rumped shama—over the past 40 years reveals an uneasiness about unregulated spaces, even among environmentalists, while obscuring pressing concerns about habitat losses that exacerbated competition between different bird species in the wild in Singapore.

The Javan myna, a popular songbird in Bali and Java, has been central in discourses over species that did not belong in Singapore. As has been documented in various studies, the myna population rapidly increased after its introduction in the 1920s; there are an estimated 100,000 in Singapore today, even after being a target of culling campaigns by the state's Agricultural and Veterinary Agency in recent years, which emphasized their status as "foreign" birds.[48] The ambivalence, if not muted hostility, towards the Javan myna among the public and some environmentalists underscores a broader discomfort with a return to nature. Wilderness is often not a physical space. As environmental historian Miles Powell has cogently argued, wilderness is a "historically contingent vision of nature that emerged within (and shaped) specific environmental, cultural, and political circumstances, and became broadly shared among many members

---

[46] Yong and Lim, *A Naturalist's Guide*, p. 10.
[47] Note that the category of "feral" birds came from assessments of threat developed by IUCN and Birdlife International. Jeyarajasingam and Pearson, *A Field Guide*, pp. 35, 321; Lim, *Vanishing Birds of Singapore*, p. 3.
[48] Lee, "Javan Mynahs," p. 140; Rachel Au Yong, "Major Intervention to Tackle Mynah Issue," *ST*, 29 Dec. 2018, p. 21; Cynthia Choo, "Cacophony of Mynah Birds a Headache for Some Potong Pasir Residents," *Today*, 9 Aug. 2018, p. 7.

of the dominant culture."[49] Envisioning natural wilderness then, is an exercise in reflecting on which creatures—humans and non-humans—belonged where, with history as a guide.

In separate works, Powell and Peter Coates demonstrate that, in American history, prevailing attitudes over which species belong where often became entangled with question of which people belong where.[50] In Singapore too, a parallel conversation about which migrant groups of people belonged to Singapore and why, especially amidst the implementation a liberal immigration policy in the 2000s where skilled migrants were especially welcome, complicated the position of the Javan myna. Commenting in a bird ecology forum, volunteer conservationist Lee Chiu San noted that the Javan myna had outcompeted the indigenous common myna, adding, "I wonder if foreign talent has displaced local talent even in beachcombing." On the flip side, Javan mynas have their advocates who also use migration to explain their approval; for instance, a recent article on popular news website *Mothership.sg* lauded the "non-native species that had made Singapore home." It applauded among other habits, their habit of waking up "way before other birds to feast on roadkill," an allusion to the trope of hard-working, hungrier migrants.[51]

While the analogy between migrant species and migrant people is problematic, both discourses signify approval and disapproval of foreign species that hinge on categorizations of native, non-native and invasive, and rely on a baseline determined by the past that cannot be objective. Wildlife advocate Lee Jin Hee highlighted this issue when she argued that whether the Javan myna belonged was dependent on which version of past Singapore was the space of belonging. Their populations would remain susceptible to periodic targeted culling from the government, unless as Lee puts it, "we develop a culture of care for all life, including

---

[49] Miles A. Powell, *Vanishing America: Species Extinction, Racial Peril and the Origins of Conservation* (Cambridge, MA: Harvard University Press, 2016), p. 9.

[50] Powell, *Vanishing America*, pp. 82–119; Peter Coates, *Strangers on the Land: American Perceptions of Immigrant and Invasive Species* (Berkeley, CA: University of California Press, 2006).

[51] He Ruiming, "8 Non-Native Species That Have Made Singapore Home," Mothership, 11 May 2015, https://mothership.sg/2015/05/8-non-native-animal-species-that-have-made-spore-home/ (accessed 12 Jun. 2021). Bird Ecology Study Group, "Where Have All the Common Mynas Gone?" Lee Kong Chian Natural History Museum Bird Ecology Study Group, 17 May 2015, https://besgroup.org/2015/05/17/where-have-our-common-mynas-gone/ (accessed 12 Jun. 2021).

those that are newcomers to a particular place."[52] This argument reflected a nascent, radical position to rethink the position of non-human creatures through Singapore as global place, rather than bounded nation. Going further, this position requires accepting that even urbanized nature can be an unregulated space. It requires holding space for the specters of unregulated influxes of peoples and birds perceived as foreign, which detractors raised regularly. At present, that view of inclusive nature is broadly unpopular.

Migrants who know their place encounter less animosity. In avian Singapore, for example, white-crested laughingthrushes—insect-eating birds with loud, incessant songs and distinguished by a white head and erect crest as well as a broad black eyeline—were better received migrants than Javan mynas. The first recorded sighting of a white-crested laughingthrush was in 1987 when three of the species were spotted at Gillman Park; one was a "juvenile begging for food." Since they were native to South Asia and mainland Southeast Asia but not to the archipelago, bird observers speculated that they were likely escapees or released birds from the caged-songbird trade. Popular songsters in Thailand, they were not well liked in Singapore unlike local babbler the Oriental white-eye. The voice of the white-crested laughingthrush has been described in unflattering terms as "a series of maniacal laughing hoots, usually uttered in chorus," and "a series of scolding cackles." After the first sighting, two lone birds were spotted separately at the eastern end of Singapore at Jalan Loyang Besar and Sime Road. The population in the east seemed to have died out and failed to reproduce, while that in the western part of the island grew; specimens were spotted on the campuses of the two major universities in Kent Ridge and Boon Lay, as well as at Bukit Batok Nature Park where 29 birds were counted in 2003.[53] While there was abundant evidence of breeding, their numbers remained fairly small and restricted to a specific locality.

The limited population and distribution of white-crested laughingthrushes compared to the Javan myna—another introduced feral species—was due to latter's greater capacity to adapt to the urban

---

[52] For a parallel to this issue involving monkeys, see the contribution from Barnard and Yip in this collection. Lee, "Javan Mynahs," p. 153.
[53] Felix Wong Soon Huat, "The Spread and Relative Abundance of the Non-Native White-Crested Laughingthrush *Garrulax leucolophus* and Lineated Barbet *Megalaima lineata* in Singapore," *Forktail* 30 (2014): 91–2; Jeyarajasingam and Pearson, *A Field Guide*, p. 321; Lim, *The Avifauna of Singapore*, p. 451.

landscape of Singapore. Being "commensals of man," Javan mynas could survive off human food scraps, while nesting in spaced out trees such as the rain tree (*Samanea saman*) and angsana (*Pterocarpus indicus*) that are common in the Garden City, enabling them to survive without forest cover and gather in the communal roosts they prefer. White-crested laughingthrushes on the other hand, need wooded areas with a density of trees as they generally keep under tree cover, moving about in groups of four to six, hopping on low branches and making short glides while descending to the ground to forage for insects and fallen fruit. Their sociality, suggested by their Latin name *Garrulux leucolophus,* gave them an aggressive advantage over shy songbirds such as the *hwamei* (Chinese laughingthrush, *Garrulux canorus*), which they outcompeted for forest territory. The limited population of white-crested laughingthrushes in Singapore, however, indicates that winning such localized territorial competitions does not imply invulnerability; without forest cover and the undergrowth secondary forests create, their chances of thriving have been slim.[54]

White-crested laughingthrushes have essentially been confined to nature reserves, where observers cautiously accepted the migrants even as they were recognized as invasive. An important factor in this calculation is that the birds contributed to the aesthetics of the wild in Singapore, where amateur bird enthusiasts affectionately captured their preening, territorial singing, foraging and feeding, and then posted these warm observations to the same forum that had labelled the similar myna as "foreign talent." Nature reserves and a Garden City were parts of the same puzzle; reserves are pockets of complex biodiversity that gardens strive to evoke, but essentially eliminate.[55]

The consistency between aspirations of the nature reserve and parks further explains why the public regarded garden birds more positively than the city-adapted myna. Zebra doves exemplify such a garden bird. Despite being vulnerable to snares set by illegal bird trappers, zebra doves maintained a thriving population and adapted well to the Garden City.

---

[54] Jeyarajasingam and Pearson, *A Field Guide,* pp. 31, 321; Charlotte Yap, Navjot S. Sodhi and Barry W. Brook, "Roost Characteristics of Invasive Mynas in Singapore," *Journal of Wildlife Management* 66, 4 (2002): 1118–27.

[55] Bird Ecology Study Group, "White-crested Laughingthrush – Serious Singing," *Lee Kong Chian Natural History Museum Bird Ecology Study Group,* 1 Aug. 2016, https://besgroup.org/2016/01/08/white-crested-laughingthrush-%e2%80%93-serious-singing/ (accessed 12 Jun. 2021).

While they avoid the built-up city center, they are frequently spotted in parks and gardens in Singapore, which "provide very few suitable niches for native birds to exploit and are therefore very poor in terms of birdlife" not least because "weeds and other vegetation fringing ponds are periodically cleared together with aquatic vegetation," making them an unstable food source. Zebra doves, however, are an "opportunistic bird" that seeks feeding opportunities in grass seeds of open country and plantation undergrowth, as well as fruits, seeds and buds found in gardens. Their nests are "flimsy platforms of loosely placed sticks, usually constructed in trees." Despite a brief decline in the 1970s, the local population rebounded after the city tree-planting campaigns from the 1980s onwards, and the sight of the bird's grey head and brown hindcrown in open green spaces around the island, as well as on outlying islands, has become quite common.[56]

Relatively harmonious human co-existence with zebra doves and white-crested laughingthrushes suggests that perhaps the most attractive alternative to the Garden City is a space akin to it but with more autonomy in species proliferation and sustainability in its use, a Singaporean version of "the middle ground." Conceptualized by William Cronon as a rejection of the dualism inherent in the notion of wilderness, the middle ground is a space where "responsible use and non-use might attain some kind of balanced, sustainable relationship." The value in such places, he argues, is not just their wildness but that "they remind us of the wildness in our own backyards, of the nature around us ... if wildness can stop being (just) out there and start being (also) in here, if it can start being as humane as it is natural, then perhaps we can get on with the unending task of struggling to live rightly in the world."[57] The middle ground elevates ethics over the aesthetics that the Garden City valorizes, but retains its commitment to centralize human lived spaces.

If a middle ground approach is embraced in Singapore, however, it has been reflected poorly in the fate of the white-rumped shama, once a national songbird that was emblazoned prominently on 50-dollar currency notes. The male, considered the better singer, has a glossy blue-black head, upperparts, and breast with a long, black wedge-shaped tail with white outer feathers and white rump. Like the introduced white-crested laughingthrush, it thrived under forest cover, although it was also spotted,

---

[56] Jeyarajasingam and Pearson, *A Field Guide,* pp. 32, 189; Lim, *The Avifauna of Singapore,* p. 125.
[57] Brackets in the original. William Cronon, "The Trouble with Wilderness: Or, Getting Back to the Wrong Nature," *Environmental History* 1, 1 (1996): 25.

albeit rarely, in plantations and scrublands. It frequented the lower levels of the rainforest as well, keeping to thick vegetation for its diet of insects. Unlike the social laughingthrush though, the white-rumped shama moves alone or in pairs, conferring less territorial advantage to the birds. After a century of clearing forests for plantations and eventually urban dwellings, only about 3 percent of the land area in Singapore was forested. In correlation with forest decline, the population of wild white-rumped shama fell precipitously. Ubiquitous in the 1920s and still common in 1950, it retreated to the Central Catchment Area in the 1970s as its popularity as a captive songbird rose due to its beautiful voice: "a loud distinct and rich, fluty melodious song with many variations." Whether the decline was mainly due to poaching or largely attributable to a lack of suitable habitats, both factors in concert resulted in dismal numbers. Only two were counted in the mainland in 2008, seven in Pulau Ubin in 2004 and 23 on Pulau Tekong Besar in 2000.[58]

Placed in juxtaposition, the brief population trajectories of these four species of birds index multiple alternative visions to a curated Garden City that might not be possible to reconcile. They include a city that welcomes all forms of non-human life, including the Javan myna; a city that conserves wild spaces but in selective pockets that could save the white-rumped shama; and a city that creates a middle ground for the songs of the zebra dove and the white-crested laughingthrush. Competition between indigenous and migrant songbirds was perhaps less a factor in their survival than the availability and types of habitats created. Shorn of the discourses of invasion and feral-ness, the trend points towards birds maintaining a viable population only if their habits are adaptable to their Garden City surroundings, while songbirds that are vulnerable are wedded to a shrinking forest. This pattern is consistent with a biological study that found that 65 bird species became locally extinct in Singapore over the past 75 years and of these, 61 species or a whopping 91 percent were forest bird species that were dependent on primary or secondary forests.[59] This does not imply that the discourse over invasive

---

[58] Davison and Chew, *Birds of Peninsular Malaysia and Singapore*, p. 94; Lim, *Vanishing Birds of Singapore*, p. 47; Lim, *The Avifauna of Singapore*, pp. 324–5; Richard T. Corlett, "The Ecological Transformation of Singapore, 1819–1990," *Journal of Biogeography* 19, 4 (1992): 411–20.

[59] Marjorie Castelletta, Navjot S. Sodhi and R. Subaraj, "Heavy Extinctions of Forest Avifauna in Singapore: Lessons for Biodiversity Conservation in Southeast Asia," *Conservation Biology* 14, 6 (2000): 1870–80.

species is unconstructive; it raises many questions about whether national conservation initiatives should include introduced and migratory species and, if so, how. Nonetheless, these wider questions should not undercut the imperative need to ensure that rainforest ecosystems survive locally and to trouble the prevailing Garden City paradigm that Singapore preferred to manage welcomed species while keeping down undesired ones.

Conclusion

It is hard to imagine a songbird in modern Singapore so entrancing that one would offer a Mercedes to possess it, as occurred to Ayub bin Ismail in 1986. Thirty years later, an owner of 15 pet birds only known as Hadi described more modest pleasures in a short feature on Singapore's bird-singing contests from the British Broadcasting Corporation. "When I went to competitions and got a big trophy, I am going to be very happy for that day. They perform well, they make me proud…. My favourite thing [about the bird competitions]? I got to know more friends," he told the reporters.[60] Those joys, personal and social, remain cornerstones of the songbird keeping experience, with practitioners still active in sites such as Kebun Baru, where birds are still displayed on a daily basis.

As a lens into the post-war Singapore Story, such experiences reveal larger narratives of commerce inducing mass migration; of changing qualitative, inter-species relationships between diverse creatures as the city modernized; of adaptation to a changing local environment; of creating new ways to thrive in hybrid landscapes; of ambiguities over the rights of migrants and individual, asymmetric relationships; and of care that grew at the interstices of a hegemonic political vision. Bird keeping and bird singing had their heyday in the city from the 1960s to the early 1990s, spurred by the possibilities of a city-as-garden and state-driven initiatives to include forms of nature alongside Singapore's rapid modernization. The unforeseen consequences of such moves were not only environmental but also socio-political. The rapid expansion of rejected songbirds, such as the Javan myna, as a result of the cage-bird trade was likely as unexpected by the authorities as the sporadic resistance of members of the Bird Study Group in the Singapore Nature Society to accept the Garden City as an

---

[60] Anonymous, "Singapore's Bird Lovers and Their Bird-Singing Competitions," *BBC Real Time*, 23 Sep. 2014, https://www.bbc.com/news/av/world-asia-28810578 (accessed 30 Aug. 2021).

ideal and the considerable public support that their pushback received in the early 1990s.

In such a context, what do we do about the myna who is now perched where last the shama sang? The concept of the Garden City continues to be questioned in academic literature; most recently by young environmental scholar-activist Bertrand Seah who envisioned a post-carbon Singapore as "another Garden City."[61] These doubts about the continued relevance of such a vision in the age of climate change indicate a nascent desire among Singaporeans for relationships with non-human others to develop beyond a dominating affection that erects clear boundaries between human and other creations. At present, voices raising alternatives to the Garden City have yet to articulate themselves in a coherent and powerful way, even though the present situation of songbird vulnerability calls for a new environmental ethics that go beyond investment in technology that can aid captive sustainability. As songbird keeping retreats and becomes a niche pastime enjoyed by some older Singaporeans, many of the practices of localized care that the hobby engendered are no longer the primary channel for expressing affection towards birds. Rather, a step removed from dominance, songbird enthusiasts might come to question not whether another type of Garden City is possible, but where the city itself is placed within a global ecosystem in which indigenous, migrant, vagrant and migratory species are all entangled.

---

[61] Bertrand Seah, "A Plan for a Post-Carbon Singapore," 5 Sep. 2019, https://medium.com/@bertrandseah/a-plan-for-a-post-carbon-singapore-57b016bae70f (accessed 6 Oct. 2021).

CHAPTER SEVEN

Marine Life in Service of the State at Public Aquariums and Oceanariums in Singapore

Miles Alexander Powell

In 2014, staff at Underwater World Singapore discovered that one of their Indo-Pacific humpbacked dolphins (*Sousa chinensis*, also known as pink dolphins) had developed skin cancer after spending years in a shallow pool under the tropical sun. This diagnosis—and the accompanying photos of an animal that appeared to be rotting alive—further intensified protests dating back to at least 2003 against the oceanarium keeping dolphins in captivity. Local conservation and animal welfare organizations asserted that, in contrast to official claims that the dolphins were born in captivity, harvesters had captured the cetaceans at sea, reducing an already limited wild population. They further alleged that trainers used food deprivation and other inhumane methods to motivate the dolphins to perform. The controversy surrounding these dolphins, which may have contributed to Underwater World Singapore closing ahead of schedule

Marine Life in Service of the State at Public Aquariums and Oceanariums

Image 7.1: Pink dolphin with skin cancer at Underwater World, Singapore. Reproduced with permission of Sea Shepherd Singapore.

in 2016, was the culmination of the complicated relationship between humans and marine animals, and the seas more broadly, in Singapore since the Second World War.

In multiple studies, scholars have elucidated the key tensions underlying the display of marine animals in public aquariums and oceanariums. To remain financially solvent, these enterprises have had to attract and entertain crowds. Yet, onlookers have come to question whether human amusement justifies keeping wild animals in captivity. Critics have especially condemned the training of cetaceans—and other marine life recognized as intelligent—to engage in stunts and tricks that deviate from their behaviors in the wild. To offset such concerns, aquariums and oceanariums have increasingly stressed their roles in educating visitors on issues of marine ecology as well as promoting and sponsoring environmental causes.[1]

---

[1] The author would like to thank his research assistant, Tejala Rao, for her contributions to this project. Susan G. Davis, *Spectacular Nature: Corporate Culture and the Sea World Experience* (Berkeley, CA: University of California Press, 1997), pp. 68–70, 84, 119; Vernon N. Kisling, Jr., ed., *Zoo and Aquarium History: Ancient Animal*

Similar themes emerge in the histories of the country's first public aquarium, the Van Kleef Aquarium, and its first oceanarium, Underwater World Singapore. But in this island nation, officials also carefully incorporated these organizations into plans for national development that reflected the larger economic policies of an assertive modernizing government. This began with the Van Kleef Aquarium, which the Primary Production Department administered to promote a growing national aquarium fish industry. As Singapore became a world leader in this multi-million dollar trade, tropical fish grew into a major revenue earner for the young nation. Meanwhile, Underwater World formed an integral part of national efforts to fashion Sentosa Island as a global tourism hotspot through the Sentosa Development Corporation, a statutory board under the Ministry of Trade and Industry.

Both enterprises closed, in part, because of key transitions in Singapore's relationship to marine life and the oceans. Van Kleef ultimately shut its doors in 1991 because, while it was useful to the promotion of the aquarium industry, its managers could not find a way to keep it interesting to visitors—especially when the flashier Underwater World, with its popular pink dolphin shows, opened its gates that same year. The staid design and emphasis on practical fisheries research (such as the identification of local marine parasites) at the Van Kleef Aquarium also seemed less relevant to a public that no longer viewed surrounding waters as a critical source of livelihood for fishers or other vocations centering on marine life. The animal acts at Underwater World, however, also wore out their welcome over the coming decades. Singaporeans began expressing an increasing concern for animal welfare, making these performances a focal point for intense public backlash against the perceived mistreatment of charismatic marine life.[2]

Collections to Zoological Gardens (London: CRC Press, 2001), p. iv; Bernd Brunner, *The Ocean at Home: An Illustrated History of the Aquarium* (London: Reaktion Books, 2011), pp. 133–4. Dolly Jørgensen, "Mixing Oil and Water: Naturalizing Offshore Oil Platforms in Gulf Coast Aquariums," *Journal of American Studies* 46, 2 (2012): 461–80; Samantha Muka, "Conservation Constellations: Aquariums in Aquatic Conservation Networks" in *The Ark and Beyond: The Evolution of Zoo and Aquarium Conservation*, ed. Ben A. Minteer, Jane Maienschein, and James P. Collins (London: University of Chicago Press, 2018), pp. 90–104; Stefan Linquist, "Today's Awe-Inspiring Design, Tomorrow's Plexiglas Dinosaur: How Public Aquariums Contradict Their Conservation Mandate in Pursuit of Immersive Underwater Displays," in *The Ark and Beyond*, pp. 329–43.

[2] Kim Lee, ed., *Singapore Waters: Unveiling Our Seas* (Singapore: Nature Society

Marine Life in Service of the State at Public Aquariums and Oceanariums

This chapter traces the history of public aquariums and oceanariums in Singapore following the Second World War. Proceeding chronologically, it begins with the controversies over opening the Van Kleef Aquarium during a period of post-war austerity, with some considering the expense an unnecessary luxury. It then examines the debates that emerged when nearly all the aquarium's initial piscine inhabitants perished, pitting local and international expertise against each other in explanations for the losses. Next, it analyzes how the Primary Production Department successfully used Van Kleef to promote the tropical fish industry in Singapore, and considers why this ultimately proved an unsustainable basis for a public attraction. It concludes with a discussion of Underwater World Singapore, considering the controversies that emerged surrounding the pink dolphins and other captive marine life, and the environmental impacts that have resulted from oceanariums pursuing evermore awe-inspiring immersive experiences.

Van Kleef Aquarium

Finally opened in 1955, the origins of the Van Kleef Aquarium dated back much earlier. It took its name from Karl Willem Benjamin van Kleef, a Dutch businessman who made his fortune in Singapore. Upon his passing in 1930, Van Kleef bequeathed a significant sum to the municipal government for the improvement of the city. A debate emerged over how best to use these funds, with suggestions ranging from a Japanese garden, to a wireless broadcasting antenna, to a circus. Following input from William Birtwistle, the Director of Fisheries, the Van Kleef Bequest Committee determined that an aquarium would most benefit the city. Planners considered multiple locations before opting for a site on River Valley Road. Geopolitical uncertainties and the outbreak of the Second World War delayed construction, but the bequest continued to earn interest and policymakers remained committed to the idea of an aquarium.[3]

Singapore, 2003), pp. 5–6; Loke Ming Chou, "Nature and Sustainability of the Marine Environment" in *Spatial Planning for a Sustainable Singapore*, ed. Tai-Chee Wong, Belinda Yuen and Charles Goldblum (New York, NY: Springer, 2008), p. 174.
[3] Anonymous, "… And Now Aquarium Plan for Next Year," *The Straits Times* [hereafter, *ST*], 17 Sep. 1951, p. 4; Anonymous, "Luxury Building for Fish," *ST*, 13 Nov. 1951, p. 6; Timothy P. Barnard, *Imperial Creatures: Humans and Other Animals in Colonial Singapore, 1819–1942* (Singapore: NUS Press, 2019), pp. 96–8; Kevin Khoo, "Remembering Karl Van Kleef and the Van Kleef Aquarium," https://www.nas.gov.sg/archivesonline/article/remembering-karl-van-kleef (accessed 23 Nov. 2020).

In opting for an aquarium, colonial officials were pursuing what had become a standard mark of culture, learning and refinement for global cities. From ancient Rome to Song Dynasty China, people had long kept fish in tanks. Public aquariums as we know them today, however, were a relatively recent invention. In the 1830s, the pathbreaking French scientist Jeanette Power de Villepreus began experimenting with containers we might recognize as aquariums to study marine life. In the 1850s, Englishman Philip Henry Gosse coined the term "aquarium" and published books promoting their maintenance as a hobby. In 1853, the world's first public aquarium opened at Regent's Park, London. Over the course of the 19th century, other nations followed England's lead, with advances in industrial glass production and water filtration systems allowing for increasingly elaborate designs. These attractions amused and delighted crowds, while also demonstrating the importance of marine science and fisheries research. For imperial powers, like Britain and France, public aquariums additionally displayed the underwater wealth of their colonial possessions.[4]

By the time officials were weighing what to do with Van Kleef's gift, Singapore already had a long history of displaying animals on land, and residents had been calling for the addition of an aquarium. In 1875, planners added a menagerie to the colony's botanical garden. Initially featuring such formidable creatures as a tiger and a Sumatran rhino, the zoo quickly phased these out on account of their high feeding costs. Shifting to primarily displaying smaller, Malayan specimens, the zoo in the garden remained open until 1904. In 1928, William Lawrence Soma Basapa opened a private zoo in the Punggol region of northern Singapore. Coming to feature hundreds of exotic animals and thousands of birds, it was a major attraction until the British forcibly seized the grounds in 1942 in preparation for an anticipated Japanese invasion.[5]

---

[4] Brunner, *The Ocean at Home*, pp. 31–6, 105–28; Lissa Wadewitz, "Are Fish Wildlife?," *Environmental History* 16, 3 (2011): 424; Muka, "Conservation Constellations," p. 93; Sofie Lachapelle and Heena Mistry, "From the Waters of the Empire to the Tanks of Paris: The Creation and Early Years of the Aquarium Tropical, Palais de la Porte Dorée," *Journal of the History of Biology* 47 (2014): 2–3.

[5] Sally Walker, "Zoological Gardens of Asia" in *Zoo and Aquarium History: Ancient Animal Collections to Zoological Gardens*, ed. Vernon L. Kisling, Jr. (London: CRC Press, 2001), p. 232; Timothy P. Barnard, *Nature's Colony: Empire, Nation and Environment in the Singapore Botanic Gardens* (Singapore: NUS Press, 2016), pp. 101–4, 110–14; Barnard, *Imperial Creatures*, pp. 86–7, 96–7.

Although Singapore lacked a public aquarium prior to the Second World War, the idea had significant support. As early as 1922, the Natural History Society of Singapore promoted such a development. In 1931, with debates over how best to use the Van Kleef endowment raging, "E.L.S." wrote to the *Malayan Tribune* giving voice to this pent-up demand. Insisting that a public aquarium was essential for a modern city, he maintained that "it is well known that long ago public aquaria were established in Europe, America, Japan, Java, Manila, etc., and that their value and importance has been fully recognized." Through numerous delays, and the disruptions of the Japanese invasion, this sense that Singapore required a public aquarium to enter the ranks of the global cities endured, but the plan had detractors.[6]

With Singapore continuing to rebuild following the destruction of the Second World War, many residents opposed using money and materials on a seemingly non-essential development like an aquarium. In 1950, the municipal commissioners came up with an estimated cost of $470,000 for the venture. By this point the endowment had grown to $360,000, so the City Council would need to provide an additional $110,000. Contributors to *The Straits Times* questioned whether this was a reasonable undertaking when the city was operating under an austerity budget. They suggested the funds could serve more pressing needs, like schools, public libraries or swimming pools. They also questioned whether the aquarium would attract sufficient attendance to offset its running costs. In 1951, City Council candidate Lee Choon Eng summed up these concerns succinctly when he called the aquarium "a waste of money."[7]

Despite sometimes heated opposition, the City Council pushed forward with construction. After a false start in 1950, when pilings were dropped at a site the city instead chose to use for a swimming pool, building commenced in 1952 at a nearby location at the base of Fort

---

[6] E.L.S., "An Aquarium in Singapore?," *Malayan Tribune*, 25 Feb. 1931, p. 10; Anonymous, "Luxury Building for Fish"; Anonymous, "… And Now Aquarium Plan for Next Year"; Sally Walker, "Zoological Gardens of Asia," in *Zoo and Aquarium History*, p. 232; Barnard, *Imperial Creatures*, pp. 96–7.

[7] Anonymous, "Edward Edwards and Katong," *ST*, 17 Jan. 1950, p. 6; Anonymous, "Municipal Fish," *ST*, 12 Apr. 1950, p. 6; Anonymous, "Luxury Building for Fish"; Anonymous, "Aquarium 'A Waste Of Money' Says Mr Lee," *Singapore Standard* [hereafter, *SS*], 16 Nov. 1951, p. 1; Anonymous, "Promenade, Aquarium for S'pore," *The Singapore Free Press* [hereafter, *SFP*], 5 Mar. 1952, p. 5.

Canning Hill. City architect W. Irving Watson encountered a series of technological challenges as he attempted to establish an underground water storage and filtration system modeled on the aquarium at the London Zoo. He constructed two subterranean tanks, one for salt water and one for fresh water. Planners determined they would need to acquire salt water at a distance of eight to ten kilometers from shore because near-shore waters were too polluted to sustain aquatic life in captivity. The aquarium would acquire fresh water in the form of rain gathered on the roof and then drained through a series of filters into the storage container. An elaborate system of pumps would force both types of water through filtration systems into aquarium tanks, maintaining a constant system of circulation.[8]

Watson had designed the building with an eye towards making it a pleasant place for the public, rather than a site of scientific education. Local officials thus decided they would wait until they had hired an expert curator to determine the layout of the displays. This stage in the aquarium's development pitted feelings of localism versus internationalism in debates over who should run the aquarium. The City Council favored bringing in an experienced expert from the Taporevala Aquarium in Bombay (Mumbai), or some other established institution. "L.K.L." wrote to *The Straits Times* questioning whether such outside help was really necessary, and suggested local residents should have an opportunity to fill key positions at the aquarium. The City Council maintained the need for an outside expert and, after an international search, brought in Frederick Arkhurst, an assistant curator at the London Aquarium, to advise on setup until a long-term replacement could be found. Arkhurst oversaw the early development of the aquarium, although local initiatives were also significant. Chinese aquarists at the Quek Kwang Hong Aquarium in Singapore provided the first aquatic denizens, making an offer of 10 species of rare tropical fish that the City Council gratefully accepted.[9]

---

[8] Anonymous, "City to Help Pay for Aquarium," *ST,* 27 Feb. 1953, p. 4; Anonymous, "$470,000 Aquarium," *SFP,* 29 Apr. 1953, p. 3; Anonymous, "Modern Water System for Aquarium" *SFP,* 17 Jun. 1953, p. 5.

[9] Anonymous, "Aquarium Gets Its First Fish," *ST,* 4 Aug. 1953, p. 8; Anonymous, "He Will Advise on Aquarium," *SS,* 13 Aug. 1953, p. 3; L.K.L., "Call for Local Experts?," *ST,* 29 Aug. 1953, p. 9; Anonymous, "Expert to Help Build Aquarium," *SFP,* 2 Sep. 1953, p. 3; Anonymous, "Aquarium to Be Top Attraction," *ST,* 7 Dec. 1953, p. 2; Anonymous, "Gift of Rare Fish to S'pore Aquarium," *ST,* 13 Jan. 1954, p. 8; "The $470,000 Question: Who Is to Run the Aquarium?" *ST,* 8 Apr. 1954, p. 7.

During his brief stay between April and September of 1954, Arkhurst made a series of critical decisions for the aquarium. His initial work involved arranging the coral (acquired locally at Pasir Panjang) in display tanks and selecting and acquiring fish. The Briton brought some American varieties of the latter with him to Singapore, and expanded the collection by acquiring local Malayan species and trading some of them for fish from other regions. Arkhurst was also involved in hiring and training local employees. In May of 1954, the aquarium advertised for six positions. Reflecting the gendered division of labor prevalent in Singapore at the time, they desired four men—to serve as a supervisor, a senior keeper and two junior keepers—and two women—to serve as ticket sellers and cashiers. By July they had approved a senior keeper named Loh Kum Soon, but the other positions remained to be filled. This period also saw the aquarium acquire its first sea water, an endeavor that proved challenging when the initial vessel commissioned to bring water from eight kilometers off the Singaporean coast sank. Subsequent vessels fared better though, and were able to deliver the freight. Promoting a hobby that would grow into a major industry for Singapore, the temporary director also recommended for local fancy fish keepers to establish an aquarium society, an aspiration administrator S.L. Chan realized. Finally, Arkhurst trained his replacement, S.A.V. Nathan, a Singaporean with 15 years of experience on the City Council, but limited knowledge of aquariums.[10]

When the aquarium's fish began dying en masse following Arkhurst's departure, heated debates arose over the cause, and who should shoulder the blame. Insisting that the losses owed neither to a design flaw nor to inexperienced staff, City Architect W.I. Watson initially suggested that crowds visiting the still-under-construction aquarium were frightening the fish, causing them to injure themselves on sharp surfaces like the coral. He added that Arkhurst had warned him to expect such deaths

---

[10] P.L. Koh, "Van Kleef Aquarium Ready Soon," *ST*, 9 Jan. 1954, p. 3; Anonymous, "Aquarium Is Ready," *SS*, 26 Mar. 1954, p. 5; Anonymous, "All Van Kleef Fish Arrive by August," *ST*, 14 May 1954, p. 4; Anonymous, "Six Jobs Going at The Aquarium," *ST*, 25 May 1954, p. 7; Anonymous, "Aquarium Gets a Keeper," *ST*, 3 Jul. 1954, p. 8; Anonymous, "The Fish Must Wait," *ST*, 14 Aug. 1954, p. 4; Anonymous, "Sea Water Will Come as Ballast," *ST*, 15 Aug. 1954, p. 13; Anonymous, "This Ship Will Take on Special Cargo at Sea," *ST*, 23 Aug. 1954, p. 2; Anonymous, "Fish Fanciers Should Unite," *ST*, 29 Aug. 1954, p. 11; Anonymous, "S'pore Fish Fanciers to Form Society," *SFP*, 7 Sep. 1954, p. 7; Anonymous, "Aquarium Expert Works on as He Packs," *SFP*, 15 Sep. 1954, p. 2; Anonymous, "New Aquarium Chief Praises London Zoo Official," *SFP*, 23 Sep. 1954, p. 5.

Image 7.2: The Van Kleef Aquarium at River Valley Road. Ministry of Information and the Arts Collection, courtesy of National Archives of Singapore.

until the fish adjusted to their new environment. The architect, therefore, issued an order barring unauthorized access to the aquarium, until the fish had calmed down.[11]

Local aquarists quickly challenged these claims. One prominent proposal suggested that there had not been sufficient time for the coral and fresh-laid cement to cure before filling the tanks, and added that it made more sense to remove sharp objects from the tanks rather than people from the grounds. Reflecting early concern for animal welfare, another local aquarist declared that, owing to employee ineptitude, the "fish were murdered." University of Malaya Zoology Professor R.D. Purchon intensified the debate when he suggested it had been a grave mistake to import rare and expensive fish before neutralizing toxins in the water, and called on the City Council to open its purse strings to hire a qualified expert to run the aquarium. Watson continued to insist that any large aquarium would experience a high level of attrition in its early stocking efforts. With the public already concerned about the

---

[11] Anonymous, "Fish May Be Scared," *SFP*, 27 Sep. 1954, p. 5; Anonymous, "These Fish Just Pine Away in New Home," *ST*, 2 Oct. 1954, p. 8.

aquarium's costs, and skeptical of imperial expertise, however, the story became a local scandal.[12]

By late 1954, eager to put the crisis behind them and concerned that it might impact the opening date for the aquarium, the City Council proposed hiring someone with greater experience to oversee its operation in this initial stage. Nathan would remain employed in an administrative capacity, while he acquired further training in the basics of aquarium management. In making this move, the Council bowed to pressure that appeared to partly reflect the frustration of British residents at their waning authority in the colony following the Second World War. A writer to *The Straits Times* complained that the council had made a colossal blunder in only bringing in an adviser from the London Zoo for six months, leaving "the local amateurs to do their inexperienced best." As their new acting curator, the council selected John A.T. Stewart. Recently the chief purser on a British freighter, Stewart had been forced to remain in Singapore on account of illness. He did, however, possess experience as a commercial aquarist in Glasgow. When he took over, nearly all of the saltwater fish in the Van Kleef Aquarium had perished. Determining that the main trouble facing the aquarium was excess alkalinity, Stewart had the concrete in the aquarium thoroughly washed, and removed the coral until they could find a way to prevent it from releasing calcium carbonate. He also proposed acquiring sea water by pumping it through pipes to Fort Canning, rather than using ships. With some of the aquarium's issues now seemingly linked to Akhurst's choices, a colleague defended imperial reputation with the avowal that local officials had pressured the Briton to stock the aquariums too early, and that this was why he had warned of impending fish deaths.[13]

---

[12] Anonymous, "But Illness Laid Them Low After," *SFP*, 1 Oct. 1954, p. 5; Anonymous, "Keep Out Order Starts a Fish War," *ST*, 4 Oct. 1954, p. 1; Anonymous, "Down Clangs Lid on a Not So Pretty Kettle of Fish," *ST*, 6 Oct. 1954, p. 8; Anonymous, "Opinion Storm in Fishpond," *SFP*, 7 Oct. 1954, p. 4; Anonymous, "Death in the Aquarium," *ST*, 7 Oct. 1954, p. 6; Chua Ah Kow, "Tank Fish Must Be Young," *ST*, 8 Oct. 1954, p. 6; Anonymous, "Those Fish Are Still Homesick," *ST*, 4 Nov. 1954, p. 7; Anonymous, "Opinion: The Poor Fish," *SFP*, 12 Nov. 1954, p. 4; Anonymous, "Now There's No Water in the Aquarium," *ST*, 12 Nov. 1954, p. 4.
[13] "Local Amateurs" from Anonymous, "Death in the Aquarium," *ST*, 13 Nov. 1954, p. 6; Anonymous, "The Big Aquarium Secret," *ST*, 11 Nov. 1954, p. 2; Anonymous, "Official Fish Story on the Ones that DIDN'T Get Away," *ST*, 13 Nov. 1954, p. 5; Anonymous, "Aquarium Fish Are Still Very Much Alive," *SS*, 13 Nov. 1954, p. 4; Anonymous, "Why Fish Died—and What to Do About It," *ST*, 14 Nov. 1954,

Stewart became the Director of the Van Kleef Aquarium in November 1954; fish continued dying. After extensive cleaning, staff progressively restocked the tanks, ensuring that new fish were quarantined to avoid any potential infections. An advisory board of scientific experts, including local fisheries officers, oversaw progress. For a time in early 1955, the City Council expected to open the aquarium in April, but then a parasite struck the fish in the saltwater tanks. Befuddled by this newest problem, Stewart opted to reduce the percentage of seawater displays from two-thirds to one-third of the tanks, and to only stock the hardiest saltwater fish.[14]

When the aquarium finally opened on 8 September 1955, under the direction of the Parks Division, marine fish were still dying at alarming rates, requiring employees to constantly restock the saltwater tanks. Nonetheless, in terms of attendance, revenues and public opinion, the aquarium was an immediate success. Upon opening, the aquarium possessed 6,500 aquatic specimens representing 180 species. Among its highlights were juvenile sharks, several rare Malayan species, and a swamp tank featuring mud skippers. Drawn by the full air conditioning (a major plus in a tropical climate), and the only attraction of its kind in Southeast Asia, visitors came in droves. The first week saw 4,000 attendees per day, and over 270,000 arrived in the first year. Paying 30 cents for adults and 20 cents for children, they entered a dimly lit room where the brightly illuminated tanks resembled windows into an underwater world. For most Singaporeans this was an opportunity to glimpse aquatic life they had never before seen. Reflecting the influence of the fisheries scientists on the advisory board, the displays also highlighted the rich abundance of local marine resources, reminding visitors of the importance of fisheries research.[15]

---

p. 3; Anonymous, "The Big Clean-Up Begins at the Aquarium," *ST*, 19 Nov. 1954, p. 4; Anonymous, "Fish Deaths: A Prediction Came True," *ST*, 22 Nov. 1954, p. 6.
[14] Anonymous, "New Tests for Aquarium Fish," *SS*, 24 Nov. 1954, p. 3; Anonymous, "A 3-Point Plan for Aquarium," *SS*, 7 Dec. 1954, p. 8; Anonymous, "Aquarium is Well Stocked," *SS*, 1 Jan. 1955, p. 3; Anonymous, "Aquarium: Big Day to Be Fixed Today," *SFP*, 6 Jan. 1955, p. 7; Anonymous, "More Fish Die," *ST*, 21 Jan. 1955, p. 5; Anonymous, "City Aquarium Opens in April," *SS*, 10 Feb. 1955, p. 2; Anonymous, "No Ceremony for the Dead Fish," *ST*, 1 Mar. 1955, p. 5; Anonymous, "Research Study at Aquarium," *SS*, 6 Apr. 1955, p. 8; Anonymous, "Wanted: A Date for Aquarium," *ST*, 28 Jun. 1955, p. 4.
[15] Anonymous, "Aquarium Fees Fixed," *SS*, 19 Aug. 1954, p. 3; Anonymous, "Life in the Undersea Kingdom," *Sunday Standard*, 19 Jun. 1955, p. 9; Anonymous,

With its tanks recessed into the walls to resemble picture frames or windows, Van Kleef represented an intermediate stage in the development of public aquariums. Following the example of the pioneering aquarist Gosse, the earliest public aquariums tended to situate both the tanks and the equipment required to maintain aquatic life out in the open. This allowed visitors to reflect not only on the wonders of life under water, but also on the underlying respiratory and nutritional cycles that sustained this system. Aquariums adopting the recessed-tank design offered a more curated experience, akin to visiting a living art gallery. Guests learned about aquatic life not by contemplating elaborate aeration or filtration apparatuses, but from guide books or the text and images accompanying the tanks. In the case of Van Kleef, such labeling was rather minimal, generally merely identifying the species on display. Over the second half of the 20th century, this form of aquarium gave way to oceanariums. Distinguished from their predecessors by their generally larger scale, amusement park-type layout, and marine animal performances, oceanariums provided a more exciting and immersive experience for visitors. But this came at the cost of reduced opportunities for quiet reflection, and a vastly expanded environmental impact.[16]

Visitors may have been willing to overlook the ongoing losses in saltwater fish, which Stewart estimated at 350 per month, but the City Council remained concerned. They took little solace in his claim that 98 percent of marine fish in local waters possessed microparasites, rendering it "impossible to run a satisfactory marine aquarium in Malaya." Coming to the defense of local oceanic products, the advisory board of the aquarium rejected Stewart's "gloomy" view, and saw no basis for his claim that nearly

---

"Aquarium Special," *SFP*, 7 Sep. 1955, p. 1; "Another Fine Landmark for Singapore," *SFP*, 8 Sep. 1955, p. 1; Anonymous, "Van Kleef Aquarium Supplement," *SFP*, 8 Sep. 1955, pp. 2–3; Anonymous, "Expert Was Brought from U.K.," *SFP*, 8 Sep. 1955, p. 6; Anonymous, "The Aquarium—Open At Last," *SS*, 9 Sep. 1955, p. 8; Anonymous, "Siege of the Aquarium," *ST*, 17 Sep. 1955, p. 6; National Archives of Singapore [hereafter, NAS]: Primary Production Department [hereafter, PPD] #886-63 (Aug. 1961–Feb. 1966): Teo Teck Hiang, "The Van Kleef Aquarium" (n.d.), "Van Kleef Aquarium—Matters Pertaining to"; Lachapelle and Mistry, "From the Waters of the Empire to the Tanks of Paris," pp. 1–27; Khoo, "Remembering Karl Van Kleef and the Van Kleef Aquarium."

[16] Davis, *Spectacular Nature*, pp. 19–21; Brunner, *The Ocean at Home*, p. 105; Linquist, "Today's Awe-Inspiring Design, Tomorrow's Plexiglas Dinosaur," pp. 329–43.

all local marine fish carried parasites.[17] In the midst of these challenges and counterchallenges, the City Council selected a new curator, British aquarist A. Fraser-Brunner, to take over operations on 1 January 1956. Upon his arrival, Fraser-Brunner insisted that it was possible to keep the saltwater fish healthy. He quarantined infected fish in a sick tank, and had the City Council build a new pipeline that directly imported sea water from farther offshore. By April, he announced that the deaths were under control.[18]

Fraser-Brunner expanded the displays and facilities at the Van Kleef Aquarium. In 1956, staff acquired their own boat, diving equipment and lorry, which allowed for greater ease in collecting and transporting specimens to the aquarium. Staff also added more tanks and expanded the laboratory to allow for research into the parasite problem and other fish diseases. Fraser-Brunner additionally oversaw the acquisition of a parcel of land at the rear of the aquarium where they could farm ingredients for fish food. Although some wanted to see the displays restricted to Malayan species to demonstrate the abundance of local waters, Fraser-Brunner insisted on keeping both native and non-native species to give visitors a fuller appreciation for global marine life. To maintain public interest, he added crowd-pleasing species like electric eels and piranhas. Staff also updated the species identification system, replacing simple typewritten identification cards with back-lit glass squares that included a color image of the fish with its name and origin.[19]

---

[17] Anonymous, "This 'Shark' in the Aquarium Kills 350 Fish a Month," *ST*, 24 Oct. 1955, p. 8; Anonymous, "Aquarium—Curator Is Challenged," *ST*, 1 Jan. 1956, p. 9.

[18] Anonymous, "Search for Aquarium Curator is Over," *SS*, 28 Sep. 1955, p. 4; Anonymous, "70,000 Called," *SS*, 1 Oct. 1955, p. 4; Anonymous, "Dead Fish or Not, Van Kleef Booms," *ST*, 28 Dec. 1955, p. 5; Anonymous, "New Curator Sees Hope for Fish," *ST*, 2 Jan. 1956, p. 5; Anonymous, "Aquarium Problem Could Be Solved," *SS*, 4 Jan. 1956, p. 2; Anonymous, "No More Fishy Headlines, Says Aquarium Chief," *SS*, 18 Apr. 1956, p. 3; Anonymous, "Van Kleef Expert is Also an Artist," *SS*, 21 Apr. 1956, p. 2.

[19] Anonymous, "Van Kleef Will Be the Best in The World," *SS*, 23 Aug. 1956, p. 5; Anonymous, "World of Beauty at Van Kleef Aquarium," *Sunday Standard*, 23 Sep. 1956, p. 4; Anonymous, "Aquarium Pays Its Way," *ST*, 21 Oct. 1956, p. 11; Anonymous, "Rare 'Ornate Angel' Fish for Aquarium," *SS*, 2 Jan. 1959, p. 5; NAS, Ministry of Culture, Accession No. 1982000306, "The People's Singapore 9:1. Tourist Year 2," Videorecording (1960–61); Anonymous, "$30,000 Face-Lift for Van Kleef Aquarium," *SFP*, 7 Jan. 1961, p. 8.

Image 7.3: Noor Aishah Mohammad Salim, the first lady of Singapore, and Norodom Thavet Norleak, the primary spouse of King Norodom Sihanouk of Cambodia, admire the displays at the Van Kleef Aquarium, 1962. Yusof Ishak Collection, courtesy of National Archives of Singapore.

By and large, Fraser-Brunner oversaw a period of sustained growth and expansion for the aquarium. He managed to avoid controversy until he attacked anglers for their purported cruelty, resulting in reciprocal claims that keeping fish in an aquarium violated animal welfare. The dispute began on 28 December 1961, when the aquarium director gave a speech at a Rotary Club luncheon in which he accused leisure fishermen of engaging in a "blood sport." Suggesting they slaughtered for entertainment rather than food, he warned that it was a "short step from killing animals to killing men." An incensed Oh Eng Swee wrote to *The Straits Times* from Kuala Lumpur stating that Fraser-Brunner had focused on a tiny minority of anglers that killed for sport, when the vast majority of fishers in Malaya ate what they caught. Also writing from Kuala Lumpur, and going on the offensive, "Tiny Fish" contended that Fraser-Brunner had overlooked "the amount of misery and suffering caused by depriving little creatures of their freedom in order that mightier ones may find pleasure staring at them." The writer stated that, given the choice, they would prefer to freely roam the ocean, even if they risked angler's hooks.[20]

Despite this minor dispute, Fraser-Bruner remained largely popular when he passed control of the aquarium to Teo Teck Siang, a local university student he had trained as his replacement, in August 1964. Besides his work expanding the aquarium, Fraser-Brunner left a significant cultural legacy to Singapore by working with an artist to design the iconic Merlion figure for a Singapore Tourism Promotion Board logo contest in 1964. Highlighting the nation's semi-mythological origins (in which a Sumatran prince spotted a lion on the island), and its connection to the sea, the Merlion has become a popular symbol of Singapore. As seems to have been typical in the early days of the Van Kleef Aquarium, a level of drama accompanied this transition in leadership when a colleague claimed that the institution began falling apart immediately upon his departure. This prompted Teo to write to the Ministry of Social Affairs (then responsible for the aquarium) insisting that he had inherited the aquarium in a state of significant disrepair, with damage to the roof, tanks, electrical system, and air conditioning.[21]

A year later, when Diane Schofield wrote an article for the San Francisco-based *Aquarium Journal* to introduce the Van Kleef Aquarium to American audiences, the situation appeared considerably rosier. Schofield found her visit especially exhilarating because many of the exotic fish that had become popular among American aquarium hobbyists originated from Singapore. Indulging in a bit of Orientalism, Schofield waxed eloquent of Singapore, "Every time I would cross one of the sepia colored muddy streams, I would wonder… does somewhere beneath its ochre surface swim pearl, blue, or kissing gouramis?" She greatly enjoyed the aquarium, especially its displays of local fishes in tanks labeled "Singapore Polluted

---

[20] Anonymous, "Living Free: Case for the Fish," *ST*, 17 Jan. 1962, p. 8; Anonymous, "'Blood Sport' Anglers Under Fire," *ST*, 28 Dec. 1961, p. 9; Oh Eng Swee "The One that Didn't Get Away…," *ST*, 3 Jan. 1962, p. 8; Anonymous, "Fishing: The Big Bait Is Sport," *ST*, 13 Jan. 1962, p. 11; Anonymous, "Angling: It's the Motive Not the Method," *ST*, 26 Jan. 1962, p. 10.

[21] Anonymous, "He Built Up Van Kleef Aquarium to Be Best in S-E Asia," *ST*, 28 Aug. 1964, p. 13; NAS: PPD: 886-63 (Aug. 1961–Feb. 1966): Teo Teck Hiang, The Curator, Van Kleef Aquarium to the Perm. Sec. Ministry of Social Affairs, "Van Kleef Aquarium—Matters Pertaining to" (2 Sep. 1964); Anonymous, "Aquarium Curator," *ST*, 6 Jan. 1965, p. 11; Gan Yung Chyan, "Merlion and Makara Symbolise Protection," *ST*, 8 April 1999, p. 45.

Stream Fishes" and "Singapore Forest Stream Fishes." She praised the aquatic scenes painted on the tank's concrete backings, which brought the displays to life. She also delighted in Teo Teck Hiang, describing him as "a very suave young man and a very erudite one too," who "spoke excellent English." Teo explained to her how the aquarium staff acquired new specimens (as well as live food) with their vessel, grew vegetal foods like "kong" (likely *kangkong*, or river spinach), and conducted experiments to identify and eliminate marine parasites.[22] The origins and early years of the Van Kleef Aquarium had seen it overcome accusations of irrelevance and managerial ineptitude to become a popular site of leisure for locals and tourists alike. In the ensuing years, under the leadership of the Primary Production Department, the aquarium further established itself as a key facilitator of the nation's burgeoning tropical fish industry.

Fish for the Nation

On 1 July 1967, the Primary Production Department took control of the Van Kleef Aquarium, marking a major turning point in its history. With the nation having achieved independence just two years earlier, the government now integrated the aquarium into broader plans for national development. In this context, the Van Kleef Aquarium began to highlight the potential of an export-oriented aquarium fish trade as a revenue earner for Singapore. Initiated by local farmers, who combined subsistence farming and guppy rearing with assistance from a tropical fish research station at Sembawang, this industry had already grown in value from $500,000 in 1961 to $2.5 million in 1966, when Singapore exported aquarium fish to 32 countries. Seeing further opportunity for growth, the Primary Production Department hosted a series of industry shows at the Van Kleef Aquarium, a practice Teo had commenced earlier. On 25 and 26 December 1966, for example, the aquarium co-sponsored a Guppy Show with the Singapore Aquarists' Society to highlight the quality of guppies reared in Singapore. Becoming one of the most popular aquarium fish globally, guppies helped put Singapore on the map as a provider of colorful, healthy, long-living ornamental fish. On 20 August 1967 the aquarium held a second Guppy Show before hosting a broader Exhibition of Aquaria, Aquarium Accessories, Fish Foods, and Medicines between 25 December 1967 and 3 January 1968. Continuing through the 1970s, these

---

[22] Diane Schofield, "Viewing Van Kleef," *Aquarium Journal* 36, 8 (1965): 394, 397, 399.

shows were part of a broader publicity campaign the government initiated to encourage Singaporeans to enter the trade. The Primary Production Department hoped that it could form a cottage industry benefiting low-income citizens. Van Kleef Aquarium also conducted research into breeding tropical aquarium fish, and began selling filtered sea water to aspiring fish breeders for 10 cents per gallon (3.7 liters). In addition to local breeding, officials hoped to establish Singapore as a regional hub for the redistribution of fish from other locations in the region, such as Indonesia, Thailand and Hong Kong.[23]

The Primary Production Department was largely successful in building up the aquarium fish trade as a significant industry in Singapore. An intensive form of farming that required little land, tropical fish rearing fit well in the geographically tiny—but globally connected—nation of Singapore. By 1970, there were several fish farms in Singapore catering to the export aquarium trade. Some of the participants had taken up the profession after visiting promotional shows at the Van Kleef Aquarium and seeing a good business opportunity. In addition to guppies, these aquarists began producing koi (*Cyprinus rubrofuscus*) after the Japanese government presented two of these colorful carp to Prime Minister Lee Kuan Yew in 1969. The Department also acquired a 40-hectare plot of land near the airport to create a tropical fish export center where fish farmers could lease space for breeding. Working with the Singapore Tropical Aquarium Fish Breeders' Association, the Singapore Aquarium Fish Exporters' Association, and the Singapore Aquarists' Association, government officials oversaw sustained growth of the industry. The export value of Singapore's aquarium fish trade rose from $12.6 million in 1974

---

[23] Anonymous, "Now High-Quality Sea Water for Fish," *ST*, 4 Aug. 1966, p. 10; NAS: PPD: PP 187-66 (May 1966–Feb. 1968): "Guide Book Van Kleef Aquarium"; Anonymous, "Govt to Help Develop Fish Hobby into a Big Earner," *ST*, 14 Jul. 1967, p. 4; Anonymous, "Fish Market," *ST*, 15 Jul. 1967, p. 10; Anonymous, "Display of Aquaria," *ST*, 8 Dec. 1967, p. 4; Ministry of National Development [hereafter, MND], *Ministry of National Development Annual Report, 1976* (1 Jul. 1977) NAS Misc. 6 of 1977, pp. 6, 19; Ling Kai Huat, "Public Aquarium Management: A Case Study of the Van Kleef Aquarium," in *Aquarama Proceedings: First International Aquarium Fish and Accessories Conference*, ed. John A. Dawes (Singapore: Academic Associates, 1991), p. 114; Tan Delfinn Sweimay, "The History of Koi Aquaculture in Singapore from 1965 to the Present: Translating Translocated Scientific Knowledge from Japan into Biosecurity" (unpublished PhD dissertation, Nanyang Technological University, 2018), p. 127.

Image 7.4: Guppy Exhibition at the Van Kleef Aquarium, 20 August 1967. Ministry of Information and the Arts Collection, courtesy of National Archives of Singapore.

to $70 million in 1991. From this point until 2003, Singapore was the world's leading exporter of aquarium fish.[24]

The Van Kleef Aquarium also remained a popular attraction for locals and tourists, at least for a time. This was a significant feat, considering the aquarium faced competition from the Jurong Bird Park, which opened in 1971, and the Singapore Zoological Gardens, which followed two years later.[25] The latter initially focused on mammals and reptiles, so as not to overlap with the existing animal attractions. Following the cinematic

---

[24] Anonymous, "Something Fishy Down on the Farm" *Singapore Herald*, 11 Sep. 1970, p. 16, MR NL6602; MND, *Ministry of National Development Annual Report, 1975* (12 Jun. 1976), NAS, Misc. 9 of 1976, p. 32; NAS: Ministry of Communications and Information (1985–90): NAS000506/3: "Speech by Dr Lee Boon Yang, Minister of State (National Development and Home Affairs) at The Opening of the Singapore (1987) International Aquarium Fish Exhibition at Van Kleef Aquarium on 4 September 1987 9.15AM"; Anonymous, "Van Kleef Showcase for Tropical Fish," *ST*, 19 Aug. 1988, p. 22; Tan, *The History of Koi Aquaculture in Singapore from 1965 to the Present*, pp. 12, 129.

[25] See Choo Ruizhi's contribution to this collection.

release of *Jaws* in 1975, many Singaporeans ventured to the aquarium to see real sharks—though not great whites—close up. Encouraging further attendance, local community centers organized group tours of the aquarium. Singaporeans were particularly fond of visiting during the daily feeding time at noon when the fish were most active. Annual attendance grew from 310,000 in 1976 to 397,000 a year later, and peaked at 429,788 visitors in 1979.[26]

Besides using Van Kleef to promote the aquarium fish industry, the Primary Production Department also touted its pedagogic value. Acknowledging its educational facilities were limited, officials still believed it could be a useful venue for "non-formal education." In 1979, staff member Robert Lee presented a paper entitled "Van Kleef Aquarium—Its Contributions to Education." Noting that school children constituted 40 percent of the visitors to Van Kleef that year, he suggested educators should not require their pupils to memorize the scientific names on the labels. Instead, they should encourage the students to draw connections between the exhibits and local environments, providing them with a basic education in aquatic ecology. To help facilitate learning, aquarium staff also gave lectures at local schools, libraries and community centers, and invited educational groups to visit the aquarium. Youth and parents' groups frequently brought kindergarten and primary students to the attraction. In 1987, Minister of State Lee Boon Yang observed that, in addition to promoting Singapore's thriving tropical fish industry, Van Kleef was a valuable "education centre."[27]

Despite the goodwill these educational initiatives created, the aquarium still faced occasional complaints concerning animal welfare. In 1978, a visitor made "a plea" for the aquarium's crocodiles, deeming it "rather

---

[26] Anonymous, "More Visiting Van Kleef Aquarium," *ST*, 31 May 1978, p. 11; MND, *Ministry of National Development Annual Report, 1978* (7 Jul. 1979) NAS Misc. 5 of 1979, 207; MND, *Ministry of National Development Annual Report, 1979* (14 Aug. 1980) NAS Misc. 7 of 1980, 205–6; Anonymous, "The Home-Grown Tour Industry," *New Nation* [hereafter, *NN*], 2 Nov. 1980, p. 14; Walker, "Zoological Gardens of Asia," p. 233.

[27] Anonymous, "CC Outings," *ST*, 19 Dec. 1977, p. 9; Anonymous, "Non-Formal Education Seminar," *ST*, 22 Oct. 1979, p. 7; Anonymous, "Let's Ignore These Names," *NN*, 3 Nov. 1979, p. 5; MND, *Ministry of National Development Annual Report, 1981* (17 Aug. 1982) NAS Misc. 4 of 1982, 26; MND, *Ministry of National Development Annual Report, 1985* (23 Jul. 1986) NAS Cmd. 13 of 1986, 38; "Speech By Dr Lee Boon Yang"; NAS, 003396, Ang Lawrence Poh Siew, "Oral History Interview."

disturbing" that three large crocodiles were "crammed into a tiny display tank" in the reception. Similarly, in 1981, an attendee was appalled to see a seven-foot-long nurse shark sharing an "unsuitably small tank" with three sizable Hawksbill turtles and numerous groupers and snappers. The onlooker claimed the shark could "hardly... turn around, let alone swim." Aquarium staff replied that such concerns were unfounded, as the shark occupied the largest tank. A photo appearing in *The Straits Times*, however, suggested the shark had outgrown its home. Aquarium representatives countered that sharks were especially flexible, a feature facilitated by their cartilaginous skeletons, allowing the nurse shark to navigate its tank. They also hinted that the aquarium might build a larger tank in the future. All told, concerns regarding cruelty to animals at Van Kleef were significant, but more muted than those that arose at Underwater World in the 2000s. The intensity of the latter likely reflected the increasing public concern with animal welfare and the greater sympathy charismatic pink dolphins elicited.[28]

The Van Kleef Aquarium progressively lost its crowds over the course of the 1980s, as visitors observed that it had come to feel drab and dated. From nearly 430,000 visitors in 1979, attendance dropped to 323,807 in 1981 and 248,078 visitors in 1985. By way of comparison, in the mid-1980s the Singapore Bird Park and Singapore Zoo were attracting millions of visitors annually. In 1984 an observer stated that he was "greatly depressed" at the state of the aquarium, which policymakers had neglected while building up the bird park and zoo. He described poor signage, corroded tanks, faded paint, and specimens kept in "disgusting" and "overcrowded" conditions.[29]

In response to such concerns the Primary Production Department closed the Van Kleef Aquarium in 1986 for major renovations, which took more than a year and cost S$750,000. Hopes were high when the institution reopened in August of 1987 with significant repairs, and additions like speakers playing pop music spliced with ocean sounds.

---

[28] Anonymous, "Straws in the Wind," *The Business Times* [hereafter, *BT*], 6 Jan. 1978, p. 7; Anonymous, "Big Fish in Small Tank," *ST*, 25 Nov. 1981, p. 17; Anonymous, "'Space' Invader That's Quite at Home," *ST*, 26 Nov. 1981, p. 13; Anonymous, "Wanted—a Shark to Take Star Role," *ST*, 20 Sep. 1982, p. 11.

[29] MND, *Ministry of National Development Annual Report*, 1981, p. 26; Anonymous, "Join Hands to Improve Aquarium," *ST*, 19 Jul. 1984, p. 17; MND, *Ministry of National Development Annual Report, 1985*, p. 38; Khoo, "Remembering Karl Van Kleef and the Van Kleef Aquarium."

Local aquarium societies had also donated 2,000 fish, including 50 species not displayed previously. But visitors remained unimpressed, complaining the exhibits lacked the impact of the oceanarium displays then gaining popularity around the world, and provided little information about the specimens, beyond their names. The Van Kleef Aquarium had done an excellent job introducing visitors to the fisheries resources of Southeast Asia and promoting the local aquarium trade. Guests, however, were becoming less interested in marine animals as a source of livelihood and more interested in their ecological importance and entertainment potential.[30]

In May of 1991, citing dwindling crowds and an inability to compete with Singapore's newly opened oceanarium, Underwater World, the Primary Production Department announced that they would be permanently closing the "outmoded" Van Kleef Aquarium at the end of the month. Singaporeans reacted to the news with an outpouring of nostalgia. On its last day, 5,000 visitors turned up for a final chance to say goodbye to an institution that for many of them constituted a cherished childhood memory. A father who brought his children stated it was "nice to be back, to share a part of our childhood with our children. But a little sad, now that it's ending." Many others expressed similar sentiments. In an editorial piece for *The Straits Times*, Tan Sai Seong noted that Singaporeans had "lost yet another reference point in their lives" and warned that "constantly shifting landscape accompanied by frequent name changes… does nothing to help anchor Singaporeans' affections here." Nostalgia, however, did not correlate to sustained demand. When private companies attempted to reopen Van Kleef, first as World of Aquarium and then as Fort Canning Aquarium between 1991 and 1996, both ventures closed due to poor attendance. Workers demolished the building in 1998.[31]

---

[30] Anonymous, "Repair Work," *ST*, 9 Mar. 1986, p. 11; Anonymous, "Restored Van Kleef Expects More Visitors," *ST*, 2 Apr. 1987, p. 13; Anonymous, "Van Kleef's Opening Delayed," *ST*, 16 Jun. 1987, p. 11; Anonymous, "Aquarium Gets Rare Gifts for Its Reopening," *ST*, 19 Aug. 1987, p. 1; Anonymous, "Van Kleef Aquarium Reopens Today After $750,000 Facelift," *ST*, 26 Aug. 1987, p. 13; Anonymous, "Van Kleef Opens to Mixed Reaction from Visitors," *ST*, 27 Aug. 1987, p. 21; NAS: Ministry of Communications and Information: PO1928/2001: "Singapore (1987) International Ornamental Fish Exposition"; MND, *Ministry of National Development Annual Report, 1986* (28 Nov. 1987) NAS Cmd. 17 of 1987, p. 36; Ling Kai Huat, "Public Aquarium Management, p. 114; Lee, *Singapore Waters*, pp. 5–6; Loke, "Nature and Sustainability of the Marine Environment," p. 174.

[31] Anonymous, "5,000 Rush to Visit Aquarium," *The New Paper*, 29 May 1991,

Underwater World Singapore

Van Kleef Aquarium had been suffering from dwindling attendance for years, and the opening of Underwater World Singapore in 1991 dealt its coup de grâce. Developers had proposed an oceanarium for Singapore since at least the late 1970s and, in 1981, the Sentosa Development Corporation made a request to the Ministry of National Development, of which the Primary Production Department was a subsidiary, to relocate Van Kleef Aquarium to Sentosa as part of a proposed oceanarium. When this proposal was rejected, the Corporation pushed forward with its plans to construct such a facility with the goal of attracting visitors to the tourism-focused southern island. After receiving proposals from private entities for this project, the Sentosa Development Corporation ultimately opted for a combined venture with the Australian-based Underwater World International and New-Zealand-based Marinescape Corporation in 1983. After several years of delays, Underwater World Singapore was opened on 13 May 1991. Promoted as Asia's biggest tropical oceanarium, with 2,500 individual animals representing 250 species of marine life, it attracted an average of 3,000 attendees on weekdays and 8,000 on weekends. By December of 1991, it had already seen 1 million visitors.[32]

In opening Underwater World, Singaporean officials were participating in a broader global trend towards oceanariums that bridged the divide between amusement parks and sites for the promotion of marine

---

p. 6; Anonymous, "Van Kleef Aquarium to Close from Saturday," *ST*, 28 May 1991, p. 2; Anonymous, "Van Kleef Aquarium to Close for Good on Friday," *BT*, 28 May 1991, p. 20; Anonymous, "Outmoded, Says Ministry," *The New Paper*, 29 May 1991, p. 6; Anonymous, "Crowds Pack Aquarium for One Last Look," *ST*, 1 June 1991, p. 24; Tan Sai Seong, "Affection? Not with All These Landmark Changes," *ST*, 2 Jun. 1991, p. 24; Anonymous, "Van Kleef Aquarium to Reopen on Friday," *ST*, 1 Oct. 1991, p. 25; Anonymous, "World of Aquarium Has a Quiet Opening," *ST*, 5 Oct. 1991, p. 26; Anonymous, "Goodbye, Piranhas," *ST*, 15 Jan. 1992, p. 3; Anonymous, "Bad Business Forces Aquarium to Close," *ST*, 9 Feb. 1993, p. 16; Anonymous, "Thank You, Van Kleef," *The New Paper*, 25 Feb. 1998, p. 21; Anonymous, "Do We Have to See Yet Another Landmark Gone?," *ST*, 16 Mar. 1999, p. 42; Khoo, "Remembering Karl Van Kleef and the Van Kleef Aquarium."
[32] Anonymous, "Sentosa Wants Van Kleef," *NN*, 26 Mar. 1981, p. 2; Anonymous, "Sentosa Home for Aquarium?," *ST*, 27 Mar. 1981, p. 10; Anonymous, "Van Kleef Will Not Move Out," *NN*, 5 Nov. 1981, p. 5; Lisa Lee, "Investment Call from a Fantasy Isle," *BT*, 15 May 1987, p. 8; Anonymous, "Underwater Fantasy," *ST*, 18 Dec. 1987, p. 1; Lim Soon Neo, "Sentosa to Get $20m Sea Life Park," *BT*, 18 Dec. 1987, p. 1.

education and conservation. In part, these venues had emerged out of the public's increasing interest in the oceanic world in the post-war era. Cold War competition for fisheries resources and advances in submarine technology further fueled public curiosity.[33] Opening in 1938 in Florida, Marineland promoted itself as the world's first oceanarium, but Sea World, which opened its gates in 1964 in San Diego, California, became more influential. Headlined by Shamu the killer whale, Sea World touted itself as an educational institute. But critics claimed it commoditized nature and more closely resembled Disneyland than a site of learning.[34]

In contrast to the understated Van Kleef Aquarium, from which it siphoned crowds, Underwater World Singapore was modern and flashy. A major attraction for the oceanarium was its underwater tunnel. Built from six-centimeter-thick acrylic panes, it allowed visitors to pass under an immense tank containing over 3 million liters of water. Guided through the 80-meter-long tunnel by a moving walkway, guests could peer up at sharks, stingrays and other aquatic specimens, feeling as though they were walking along the seafloor. An avid diver, curator Helen Newman promised visitors that they would see as much marine life in this tunnel as they could expect on 1,000 dives. Such features reflected a global trend in oceanariums towards highly choreographed, immersive experiences that were intended to convince visitors that they were somehow experiencing wild nature. Underwater World also featured an interactive pool at which visitors could handle hermit crabs, starfish and baby turtles. Over time, the oceanarium added additional attractions, including a "deadly corridor" where visitors could view piranhas and other thrilling specimens.[35]

---

[33] Popular books, such as *The Sea Around Us*, as well as films and world renowned documentaries featuring Jacques Cousteau also contributed to and revealed this rising fascination. Rachel Carson, *The Sea Around Us* (Oxford: Oxford University Press, 1951); Davis, *Spectacular Nature*, pp. 1, 152.

[34] Wadewitz, "Are Fish Wildlife?," pp. 423–5; Jason M. Colby, *Orca: How We Came to Know and Love the Ocean's Greatest Predator* (New York, NY: Oxford University Press, 2018), p. 42; Linquist, "Today's Awe-Inspiring Design, Tomorrow's Plexiglas Dinosaur," pp. 329–43.

[35] NAS: AV recording "News," 10 May 1998, accession number: 1988000431; Natasha Emmons, "Singapore's Underwater World Back on the Road to Recovery," *Amusement Business* 111, 34 (23 Aug. 1999): 14; Rajib Deysarkar, "UWS—Signs of Aging Clearly Visible" Tripadvisor Review (23 Apr. 2017 [experience May 2016]), https://www.tripadvisor.com.sg/ShowUserReviews-g294264-d324741-r598701836-Underwater_World_and_Dolphin_Lagoon-Sentosa_Island.html#REVIEWS (accessed 15 May 2021); Linquist, "Today's Awe-Inspiring Design, Tomorrow's Plexiglas Dinosaur," p. 333; Tan, "Underwater World Singapore."

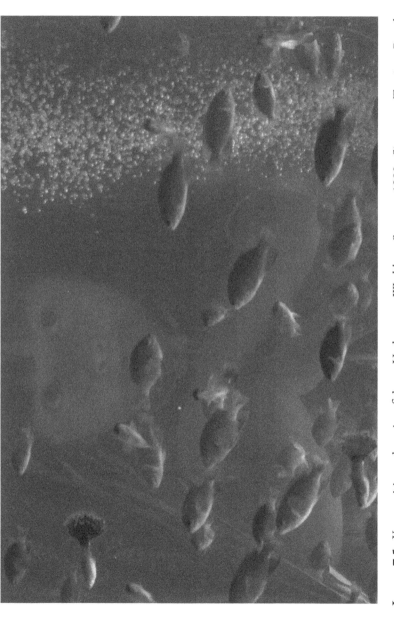

Image 7.5: Young visitor observing fish at Underwater World at Sentosa, 1990. Singapore Tourism Board Collection, courtesy of National Archives of Singapore.

The most popular attraction at this Singaporean oceanarium, if also the one that ultimately elicited the most controversy, was its Dolphin Lagoon. First opened in 1999 at an enclosed section of ocean at Central Beach, the attraction relocated to specially built outdoor pools adjacent to the oceanarium in 2010. Within its pools were six Indo-Pacific humpbacked dolphins, which Underwater World management acquired through a trade with a Thai aquarium. During shows, visitors watched dolphins perform tricks alongside a team of seals, and especially keen guests could pay an additional fee to swim with, touch, and even kiss the cetaceans.[36]

In keeping with the times, Underwater World Singapore projected itself not only as a site of recreation, but also one of education and conservation. To promote knowledge of local marine environments, the institution hosted lectures and created educational kits for teachers to use when students visited the oceanarium. There was also a "Living in the Ocean" program, which allowed children to sleep overnight in the underwater tunnel. Yet some felt the oceanarium did not provide adequate insights concerning marine ecology. Despite serving on the Education Advisory Committee for the institution, government official Ngiam Tong Tau considered Underwater World Singapore primarily a site of entertainment. He maintained that Singapore also required a modern aquarium "done more systematically [and] ecologically."[37]

Underwater World Singapore also included ecological themes in its educational messaging, and worked with partner institutions and environmental groups on several conservation programs. As typical of zoos and aquariums with animal performances, this Singaporean

---

[36] Emmons, "Singapore's Underwater World Back on the Road to Recovery," p. 14; NAS: Ministry of Trade and Industry: 20100709002: "Speech by Mr. S Iswaran, Senior Minister of State for Trade and Industry and Education, at the Official Opening of the New Dolphin Lagoon, 02 July 2010, 7:15 pm at Underwater World Singapore Sentosa"; Metcalf2015, "Pink dolphins" Tripadvisor Review (23 Apr. 2016 [experience May 2015]), https://www.tripadvisor.com.sg/ShowUserReviews-g294264-d324741-r366383984-Underwater_World_and_Dolphin_Lagoon-Sentosa_Island.html (accessed 14 May 2021); Mohammed B, "Amazing Experience and Well Worth the Money" Tripadvisor Review (26 May 2016 [experience Apr. 2016]) https://www.tripadvisor.com.sg/ShowUserReviews-g294264-d324741-r598701836-Underwater_World_and_Dolphin_Lagoon-Sentosa_Island.html#REVIEWS (accessed 14 May 2021); Tech Travel Foodie, "Dolphin Show at Sentosa, Singapore, 2013," Youtube video https://www.youtube.com/watch?v=Dw9Zy7qGeNY (accessed 15 May 2021).

[37] Anonymous, "Much to Learn on Sentosa," *ST*, 25 Dec. 1987, p. 15; NAS: Oral History Archives: 003117: Dr. Ngiam Tong Tau; "Speech by Mr. S Iswaran."

institution wove conservation lessons into its shows through displays featuring vulnerable wildlife rescued from surrounding waters, most notably an orphaned juvenile dugong discovered near Pulau Ubin in 1998. Underwater World Singapore also carried out many captive breeding programs, enjoying particular success in breeding and releasing sea horses and bamboo sharks, although from these and other such schemes the oceanarium retained some young to trade with other institutions for new specimens. Underwater World also funded external conservation projects, including efforts to rescue coral facing destruction in the face of Singapore's ongoing land reclamation.[38]

The presence of these educational and conservation initiatives, however, did not shield Underwater World Singapore from claims that it promoted the inherent cruelty of capturing and displaying wild animals. Commenters showed particular concern for the oceanarium's most iconic inhabitants, the pink dolphins. On review sites like Tripadvisor, visitors complained that trainers seemed to mistreat the dolphins and the show felt exploitative. In 2003, prominent Singaporean animal welfare group Animal Concerns Research and Education (ACRES) launched a "Suffering, not Smiling" campaign in direct response to these accusations, highlighting significant alleged animal abuse at Underwater World Singapore, including the use of starvation as a training tactic. ACRES also claimed to have uncovered proof that the dolphins were actually taken from the wild, rather than bred in captivity as previously stated. Producing a petition with 8,399 signatories, including 44 international conservation and animal welfare groups, they called on the Haw Par Corporation, owners of the oceanarium, to end the dolphin shows and rehabilitate the cetaceans for release back into the wild. Further controversy arose in 2014 when one of the dolphins, living in a shallow pool under the glaring sun, contracted skin cancer, creating gruesome images for animal welfare groups to use to demand the cetaceans' release.[39]

---

[38] NAS: Video Recording 1995000567: "News 5 At Seven," 6 Nov. 1995; 1997000324: "News 5 Tonight," 2 Sep. 1997; 2002000156: "News 5 Tonight," 6 May 2002; "Speech by Mr. S Iswaran"; Lee, *Singapore Waters*, p. 132; Miles Powell, "Singapore's Lost Coast: Land Reclamation, National Development, and the Erasure of Human and Ecological Communities, 1822–Present," *Environment and History* 27, 4 (2021): 635–63.

[39] "News 5 Tonight" (22 Oct. 2003) audiovisual recording, NAS, accession number: 2003000295; "Waste of Money and Time, Pity the Animals" Tripadvisor Review (24 May 2016 [experience May 2016]), https://www.tripadvisor.com.sg/ShowUserReviews-g294264-d324741-r598701836-Underwater_World_and_Dolphin_

Such protests reflected a growing global backlash against keeping cetaceans in captivity for entertainment purposes. Considering that within Singapore no campaigns of similar magnitude arose against Jurong Bird Park confining raptors in spaces vastly smaller than their natural ranges, while training them to perform for crowds, it is worth pondering why cetaceans have elicited such sympathy both in Singapore and throughout the world. Once perceived as monsters of the deep, in the 1970s whales emerged as icons of the environmental movement. "Save the Whales" became a rallying cry for activists inspired by recordings of whale songs and studies demonstrating the intelligence and social bonds of these creatures. By 1986, protestors had helped bring about an international moratorium on whaling. With these sea mammals now perceived as majestic, awe-inspiring and sentient, the idea of keeping them—or other cetaceans like dolphins—in captivity for the amusement of human onlookers became highly divisive. Popular films such as *Free Willy* (1993) and *Blackfish* (2013) further reinforced the idea that keeping cetaceans in captivity was inherently cruel. The physical requirements for confining the creatures might also have contributed to this backlash. Whereas birds could be kept in open-air aviaries and zoo animals could be kept in pens designed to conceal the barriers holding them in place, whales and dolphins always had to be kept in tanks with solid walls of concrete or glass. Their confinement was, for many onlookers, uncomfortably visible.[40]

Underwater World Singapore permanently closed on 31 June 2016, despite still having two years remaining on its lease. In part, like Van Kleef before it, the oceanarium was simply giving way to a flashier new rival. In 2012, Resorts World Sentosa had added the S.E.A. Aquarium, a spectacular facility that included what was then the largest aquarium

---

Lagoon-Sentosa_Island.html#REVIEWS) (accessed 14 May 2021); "In Two Minds" Tripadvisor Review (23 Jun. 2016 [experience Oct. 2015]), https://www.tripadvisor.com.sg/ShowUserReviews-g294264-d324741-r598701836-Underwater_World_and_Dolphin_Lagoon-Sentosa_Island.html#REVIEWS (accessed 14 May 2021); ACRES, "Suffering, Not Smiling," https://acres.org.sg/campaigns/current-campaigns/suffering-not-smiling/ (accessed 29 May 2021); "S'poreans Gratefully Thank Underwater World Singapore for Ensuring Pink Dolphin Only has Skin Cancer" *New Nation* (satirical news) (28 Oct. 2014), http://newnation.sg/tag/pink-dolphin/ (accessed 28 May 2021); cetacean captivity may have actually promoted conservation in some instances; Colby, *Orca*, p. 1.

[40] Kurkpatrick Dorsey, *Whales and Nations: Environmental Diplomacy on the High Seas* (Seattle: University of Washington Press, 2013), pp. 209–10, 267–92; Colby, *Orca*, pp. 245–60.

tank in the world. The significant negative publicity generated over the condition of the dolphins, however, also likely played a role in the decision to close early. As with Van Kleef at its closure, Underwater World saw a surge in crowds eager to view the oceanarium one last time, with 8,500 visitors attending its last day.[41]

The closing of Underwater World Singapore did not bring an end to the dolphin controversy, however, as plans to relocate the cetaceans to Chimelong Ocean Kingdom in Zhuhai, China, drew immediate criticism. Conservation and animal welfare groups—including ACRES, Wild Shores Singapore, and Sea Shepherds of Singapore—stated that rehabilitating the dolphins and releasing them back into the wild would be a more humane and conservation-oriented choice. If this was not possible, they argued that relocating the dolphins to local facilities would be preferable to sending them to the giant Chimelong aquarium, which had recently appeared in the international press owing to allegations of mistreating its 491 cetacean inhabitants.[42]

A year later, the fate of the dolphins remained a point of public interest. In 2017, Singaporean reporters drew on published trade data to contend that Underwater World Singapore only sent five of the seven dolphins to Chimelong. Two dolphins, including the one that had developed skin cancer, had mysteriously vanished from view. Moreover, when Sea Shepherd representatives visited Chimelong, they found that one of the five delivered dolphins was missing. Some staff stated the missing dolphin was kept in a separate tank for research, while others admitted it was gone. Animal welfare groups claimed that these discrepancies demonstrated the lack of transparency and accountability in the zoo and aquarium animal trade. Sea Shepherd Singapore representative Jaki Teo observed with contempt that "these long-living, intelligent and sensitive creatures are treated as mere commodities, and facilities are allowed to operate with appalling lack of transparency."[43]

Singaporeans and tourists now flock to S.E.A. Aquarium, one of the most spectacular oceanariums in the world. Its centerpiece is a massive 36-meter-wide by 8.3-meter-tall glass viewing panel. Standing before it, spectators can peer into the 45,000,000-liter Open Ocean tank, where

---

[41] Laura Philomin, "Underwater World Closure Plan Draws Flak from Animal Lovers," *Today*, 7 Jun. 2016, p. 6.
[42] Philomin, "Underwater World Closure Plan Draws Flak from Animal Lovers."
[43] Audrey Tan, "Not All Pink Dolphins Sent Abroad: Data," *ST*, 25 Nov. 2017, p. 1.

manta rays gently loop through the water, above passing leopard sharks, all accompanied by the sound of classical music. Like its predecessors, the S.E.A. Aquarium emphasizes its contributions to education and conservation. Also like its predecessors, the aquarium has come under fire for the perceived mistreatment of animals. Concerned activists are currently circulating a video online that appears to show a dolphin at the S.E.A. Aquarium repeatedly bashing its ahead against the tank's concrete wall. The tensions underpinning public aquariums and oceanariums appear inescapable.[44]

State-of-the-art mega-oceanariums like the S.E.A. Aquarium also face a new challenge. In their efforts to establish evermore awe-inspiring and immersive experiences, they have tremendously expanded their carbon footprint. With enormous tanks requiring continuous water circulation and filtration, their energy demands are immense. They also tend to display large, carnivorous species, meaning that staggering amounts of fish must be farmed or captured in the wild to feed the display animals. Mega-oceanariums tend to counter such concerns by suggesting that through experiencing these immersive displays, visitors will acquire a sense of biophilia, or love of nature, that will result in more environmentally friendly choices. But empirical evidence for this supposition is lacking. For these reasons, some scholars are suggesting that a return to smaller tanks, with a more regional focus, and more interactive exhibits would better serve public aquariums' claimed conservation goals. Perhaps, all things considered, Van Kleef deserved a redesign instead of demolition.[45]

---

[44] Resorts World Sentosa, "S.E.A. Aquarium" https://www.rwsentosa.com/en/attractions/sea-aquarium/explore, (accessed 15 May 2021); Empty the Tanks, "Aquarium Dolphin Bashes Head Repeatedly," https://www.facebook.com/watch/?v=273266427043222 (accessed 2 Jun. 2021).

[45] Linquist, "Today's Awe-Inspiring Design, Tomorrow's Plexiglas Dinosaur," pp. 329–43.

CHAPTER EIGHT

Nation, Nature and the Singapore Zoological Gardens, 1973–2018

Choo Ruizhi

In the early hours of 7 March 1973, three months before the official opening of the Singapore Zoological Gardens, Twiggy, a small, three-year-old panther (*Panthera pardus*) slipped through the bars of its locked enclosure in the zoo and fled into the forests of the Upper Seletar Reservoir. The startling escape of this dangerous predator triggered a massive hunt for the creature, and elicited widespread excitement from the Singaporean public. For nearly a year, until the big cat was finally cornered in an underground sewer, Twiggy periodically appeared in newspaper articles, public notices and forum letters composed by concerned citizens, government officials and local journalists. The animal had become a Singaporean creature.[1]

On 27 June 1973, while Twiggy was still roaming through the Central Catchment Area, Deputy Prime Minister Goh Keng Swee presided over the opening of the Singapore Zoological Gardens. This institution

---

[1] Unless otherwise specified, I will use "Singapore Zoological Gardens" and "Singapore Zoo" interchangeably to refer to the same institution, following the zoo's own nomenclature in this period. R. Chandran and K.S. Sidhu, "Panther: Zoo to Hold Inquiry," *The Straits Times* [hereafter, *ST*], 11 Mar. 1973, p. 1.

Singaporean Creatures

Image 8.1: Goh Keng Swee exchanging pleasantries with an orangutan at the opening of the Singapore Zoological Gardens, June 1973. Photograph courtesy *The Straits Times* © SPH Media Limited. Reprinted with permission.

was the latest addition to the "amenities available to residents" of the small nation-state. "We put in a lot of effort keeping our city clean and green," Goh emphasized in his opening speech. He hoped that this new institution would provide a recreational and educational space for "city people" increasingly disconnected from "animals and animal life."[2] Shortly afterwards, while touring the zoo, a bemused Goh shook hands with Susi the orangutan (*Pongo pygmaeus*).

Zoos are paradoxical places. As Elizabeth Hanson, a historian of American zoos, observes, "What could be more unnatural than polar bears in Miami or giraffe in New York City?" Straddling the intersections between nature and culture, the popular and the institutional, zoological gardens can tell us much about how different humans envision their relationships with the natural world. They are realms "conceived by human imagination

---

[2] Goh Keng Swee, "Speech by Dr Goh Keng Swee, Deputy Prime Minister & Minister for Defence, at the opening of the Singapore Zoological Gardens on Wednesday, 27th June 1973 at 4.45p.m." (Singapore: National Archives of Singapore, 1973); R. Chandran, "A Haven for Animal Lovers of S'pore," *ST*, 28 Jun. 1973, p. 15.

and controlled by human effort," places in which humans contemplate, express, and rework their relationships with wilderness and nature.[3]

Such contradictions and connections also emerge when we contemplate the Singapore Zoo. Despite the cherished position it holds in the memories of many residents of the island, and the historically peculiar circumstances in which it was founded, the Singapore Zoological Gardens has largely escaped scholarly notice. This oversight is not unique or anomalous. Relatively little academic attention has traditionally been directed at zoos, in part due to the way they occupy a liminal space between "science and showmanship, high culture and low ... wild animals and urban people." Nonetheless, the indifference of historians to this institution is striking, given the long record of imagining, viewing and displaying animals in the Singaporean past.[4]

This chapter expands on that animal past through an investigation of the Singapore Zoo. Rather than interpreting the institution purely as a space of power and domination over nature, however, this study further explores the institution within its historical and cultural contexts to highlight the changing relationships between Singaporeans and their national zoo. The Zoological Gardens were, after all, one of the few spaces in the young, urbanising Republic where ordinary citizens could predictably encounter and experience exotic animals. As is true with zoos throughout the world, it became "a popular destination for family excursions, a

---

[3] Elizabeth Hanson, *Animal Attractions: Nature on Display in American Zoos* (Princeton, NJ: Princeton University Press, 2002), p. 7; Bob Mullan and Garry Marvin, *Zoo Culture* (Chicago, IL: University of Illinois Press, 1999), p. xxii.

[4] The few sustained attempts at studying Singaporean zoos exist mainly as unpublished academic exercises; a chapter in a book on the Singapore Botanic Gardens zoo; and, a broader study of animals in colonial history. Lorrain Kim Hong Chong, "People-Animals Relations: The Singapore Zoo and Its Sociocultural Context," unpublished honors thesis (Department of Sociology, National University of Singapore, 1987); Michael James Graetz, "The Role of Architectural Design in Promoting the Social Objectives of Zoos: A Study of Zoo Exhibit Design with Reference to Selected Exhibits in Singapore Zoological Gardens," unpublished master's thesis (Faculty of Architecture and Building, National University of Singapore, 1995); Choo Ruizhi, "Nature Condensed: A History of the Singapore Zoological Gardens," unpublished honors thesis (Department of History, National University of Singapore, 2017); Timothy P. Barnard, *Nature's Colony: Empire, Nation and Environment in the Singapore Botanic Gardens* (Singapore: NUS Press, 2016), pp. 84–113; Timothy P. Barnard, *Imperial Creatures: Humans and Other Animals in Colonial Singapore, 1819–1942* (Singapore: NUS Press, 2019); Hanson, *Animal Attractions*, p. 7.

refuge from everyday social realities, and an ideal contact zone with the natural world". As such, it became a place where many residents (over 800,000 in 1988 alone) explored and reworked their understandings of wild animals, nature and the natural environment. As a state-supported recreational space, it was also a lens through which national aspirations and anxieties were articulated, contested and negotiated. The Singapore Zoo thus became a critical space where citizens expressed and explored their relationships with nature and their new nation.[5]

To better understand the enduring fascination of Singaporeans for animal attractions, this chapter begins by situating the Zoological Gardens within an older sequence of animal displays in the history of the island. It then examines the difficult circumstances surrounding the creation of the national zoo, which reflected the diverse ways in which Singaporeans were beginning to understand nation and nature. The metamorphosis of the zoological gardens into a globally recognised organisation in the 1980s expanded Singaporean conceptions of nature and wild animals. Finally, the life and times of Inuka, the world's first tropical polar bear, reflects how the Singaporean relationships with nature and nation have shaped and been shaped over time. When the zoo opened in June 1973, however, it did not arise spontaneously as an institution unto itself. To better understand its curious origins requires a closer look at the contexts surrounding its conception; in particular, the longstanding obsession among residents of colonial Singapore with zoos in the colony.

Zoos in the Colony

The practice of displaying and viewing wild animals in Singapore stretches as far back as the 19th century, when its port served as a significant trafficking nexus and transhipment node for the exotic animal trade in the region. Many zoos and circuses from Europe and North America, for instance, procured tropical animals from Southeast Asia via Singapore during this period. Exotic animal collections on the island also flourished

---

[5] Hanson, *Animal Attractions*, p. 8; Mullan and Marvin, *Zoo Culture*, p. 45; Cornelius Holtorf, "The Zoo as a Realm of Memory," *Anthropological Journal of European Cultures* 22, 1 (2013): 98–114; Takashi Ito, "History of the Zoo," in *Handbook of Historical Animal Studies*, ed. Mieke Roscher, André Krebber and Brett Mizelle (Berlin: De Gruyter Oldenbourg, 2021), pp. 439–45; Agnes Chen, "Sight to Soothe Savage Breast [sic]," *ST*, 22 Oct. 1989, p. 12.

as a result. In the 1870s, several prominent residents, such as Whampoa (Hoo Ah Kay), owned private menageries on their personal estates, which they opened to the public on special occasions.[6]

Public animal exhibitions, however, were still a relatively new concept in Southeast Asia at the time. As opposed to a menagerie, which refers simply to a place where live animals are kept, the "zoological garden" was a distinctly European innovation that integrated animals and plants into carefully curated, aesthetically pleasing displays. Numerous zoological gardens were built in Europe and North America during the 19th century in connection with urban public parks. Only in May 1875, however, did such an integrated space materialize in Singapore, within the Singapore Botanic Gardens. Funded by the colonial government, it was stocked with animals that local and regional dignitaries presented to the officials as gifts, such as a female two-horned Sumatran rhinoceros (*Dicerorhinus sumatrensis*) from Governor Andrew Clarke, a leopard (*Panthera pardus delacouri*) from the Court of Siam, and a sloth bear (*Melursus ursinus*) from James Birch, the first British Resident of Perak.[7]

The public zoo in the Singapore Botanic Gardens reflected the burgeoning sway of the British empire in the region through the animals it exhibited. There was, however, a subtler, subversive corollary to this thinly veiled display of imperial domination. Since admission to the zoo was free, it became a popular destination for tourists and local, non-elite visitors. This popularity resulted in the frequent abuse of the animals. While the wallabies at the Singapore Botanic Gardens, for instance, were a "source of endless admiration and amusement to the Malays and Chinese," other animals were variously taunted, maimed, poisoned and killed.[8] Visitors were hence capable of imposing their own meanings and intentions upon the space and the animals that lived there.

---

[6] Fiona L.P. Tan, "The Beastly Business of Regulating the Wildlife Trade in Colonial Singapore," in *Nature Contained: Environmental Histories of Singapore,* ed. Timothy P. Barnard (Singapore: NUS Press, 2014), pp. 145–78; John Turnbull Thomson, *Some Glimpses of Life in the Far East* (London: Richardson and Company, 1864), pp. 307–8; Frank Buck and Edward Anthony, *Bring 'em Back Alive* (New York, NY: Simon and Schuster, 1930).

[7] Hanson, *Animal Attractions,* p. 10; Mullan and Marvin, *Zoo Culture,* pp. 101–10; Barnard, *Nature's Colony,* p. 93.

[8] Barnard, *Nature's Colony,* p. 104; H.N. Ridley, "The Menagerie at the Botanic Gardens," *Journal of the Straits Branch of the Royal Asiatic Society* 46 (1906): 133–94.

Despite its popularity, the colonial state withdrew all financial support for the zoo after 1881, leaving it dependent on private contributions for operating expenses. This untenable position eventually resulted in closure of the establishment in 1904, after nearly three decades in operation. Yet, it was not indifference that led to the demise of this institution. Rather, as the historian Timothy P. Barnard scathingly concludes, "neglect" as well as "a lack of will to maintain the facilities and look after the animals" had gradually impoverished this public institution. Henry Ridley, the Director of the Botanical Gardens who had reluctantly announced the zoo's closure, hoped that "at some future time the Government might found a suitable Zoological Garden in Singapore" again.[9] It would take another 69 years before this vision of a state-supported public zoo was realized once more, and under profoundly different circumstances.

Private zoos and menageries on the island nevertheless mushroomed in the next four decades. In 1928, the animal trader William Basapa founded the Ponggol Zoo, making his animal depot for creatures he bought from hunters and sold to collectors a publicly accessible site. Over the next 13 years, the Ponggol Zoo flourished—displaying, but also selling—rare South American birds, Australian kangaroos, Bornean orangutans and Californian sea lions. The zoo, however, did not survive the Second World War. On the eve of the Japanese invasion, British authorities ordered that the dangerous animals in the zoo be "destroyed," while the "more harmless varieties" were released into the wild. Bulldozers eventually leveled the site.[10]

There were many attempts to replace the Ponggol Zoo after the Second World War, despite governmental regulations and high maintenance costs. In 1950, Aaron Eleazar, a prominent Dutch animal trader, announced plans to establish a "Singapore Zoological Park," but later abandoned the project due to prohibitive animal taxes. Another zoo was opened off Tampines Road four years later that reportedly housed cassowaries, tapirs, gibbons and snakes. Three years later, in 1957, another local animal dealer

---

[9] Queenslander, "Life at Singapore," *Straits Observer (Singapore)*, 31 May 1875, p. 3; Barnard, *Nature's Colony*, p. 110; Henry Ridley, *Annual Report on the Botanic Gardens and Forest Department for the Year 1903* (Singapore: Government Printing Office, 1904), pp. 1–2.

[10] Anonymous, "Scenes at Singapore's Zoo," *ST*, 25 Sep. 1938, p. 32; Chengko, "Singapore Zoo," *ST*, 23 Jan. 1937, p. 16; Anonymous, "S'pore Cannot Afford Zoo," *ST*, 25 Jun. 1950, p. 9; Anonymous, "S'pore Zoo Starts from Scratch," *ST*, 20 Oct. 1946, p. 5.

Nation, Nature and the Singapore Zoological Gardens, 1973–2018

Image 8.2: Entrance of the Singapore Miniature Zoo in Pasir Panjang. Courtesy of the Tong Sen Mun Collection, National Archives of Singapore.

named Tong Seng Mun opened the Singapore Miniature Zoo in Pasir Panjang, where he displayed wild animals and tropical fishes. Though it was a popular attraction amongst locals for nearly 10 years, it closed in the early 1960s due to new international wildlife regulations. In 1958, the Shaw Brothers also sought a license to run a zoo at the Great World amusement park in the city, but the application was turned down by the City Council, citing potential safety concerns to city inhabitants. In 1963, Chan Kim Suan, an exporter of rhesus monkeys, registered a private zoo near Punggol that featured tigers, crocodiles, tapirs, monkeys and kangaroos. It was closed in the early 1970s, however, due to a lack of funds, making it the last private zoo in Singapore.[11] Animal displays

---

[11] Anonymous, "Singapore Puts Up Its Elephant Tax," *The Singapore Free Press* [hereafter, *SFP*], 15 Jun. 1950, p. 5; Melody Zaccheus, "We Bought a Zoo: Singapore's Small Havens for Wild Animals," *ST*, 3 Jun. 2014, https://www.straitstimes.com/singapore/we-bought-a-zoo-singapores-small-havens-for-wild-animals (accessed 11 Aug. 2021); Anonymous, "S'pore Cannot Afford Zoo"; Anonymous, "A New Colony Zoo," *SFP*, 11 Jan. 1957, p. 2; Anonymous, "Singapore Miniature Zoo," http://www.nas.gov.sg/blogs/archivistpick/miniature-zoo/ (accessed 15 Jan. 2017);

Image 8.3: A worker feeding the penguins at the Singapore Miniature Zoo. Courtesy of the Tong Sen Mun Collection, National Archives of Singapore.

were clearly expensive to maintain in the city-state.

Despite the costs involved, zoos were an important part of the Singaporean landscape. Throughout much of the 1950s and 1960s, the idea of a state-funded zoo lingered in the public imagination, resurfacing periodically in forum letters, editorials and press statements from government officials. Echoing a link between such an institution and civic pride, Singaporean commentators insisted that the city was "ideal for… a fair-sized zoo," given its population size and prestige as a colonial city. In response, city councillors and the Singapore Municipal Commission

---

Anonymous, "Snarls in City Council over Zoo Plan," *ST*, 20 Mar. 1958, p. 4; Ilsa Sharp, *The First 21 Years: The Singapore Zoological Gardens Story* (Singapore: Singapore Zoological Gardens, 1994); Anonymous, "A Forgotten Past—A Zoo at Punggol," https://remembersingapore.org/2012/03/19/a-zoo-in-punggol/ (accessed 6 Jun. 2021); Anonymous, "Running in the Red," *New Nation* [hereafter, *NN*], 18 Dec. 1979, p. 24.

continually rebuffed such proposals, citing pressing infrastructural concerns and financial constraints. They justifiably maintained that while a "small zoo" would "benefit the people," operating this institution would be "an expensive thing." Although comprehensive plans addressing these limitations were put forward several times (in one instance by an experienced Ceylonese zoo director), the colonial administration simply lacked the financial resources and the political will needed to realize such a costly project.[12]

The long-running debates about a public zoo and the persistence of well-visited, privately run menageries, however, indicate that Singaporean residents retained their fascination with collecting and viewing wild animals. It was a fascination connected to institutions, discourses and practices stretching at least as far back as 1875. This beastly legacy perhaps also explains why even senior bureaucrats in newly independent Singapore were deliberating the possibility of a public zoo again by 1967. The time was approaching for a zoo in the nation, almost a century after a zoo in the colony first opened.

A Zoo in the Nation

In December 1967, while at lunch with A.R. Parsons, the Australian High Commissioner to Singapore, the Chairman of the Public Utilities Board, Ong Swee Law, revealed "embryonic ideas" for an "animal sanctuary or modern open-type Zoo" near the Seletar Reservoir. Having already discussed the matter with Goh Keng Swee and Toh Chin Chye—leading officials in the newly independent Singaporean government—Ong now sought help from Parsons, requesting Australian advice and expertise to enable such a project.[13] This request took place during a period of great change in Singapore, as the government wrestled with external defense

---

[12] Mullan and Marvin, *Zoo Culture*, p. 110; Anonymous, "S'pore Cannot Afford Zoo"; Anonymous, "A Zoo for Colony? Yes, But Not Now," *ST*, 3 Mar. 1955, p. 5; Anonymous, "Snarls in City Council Over Zoo Plan," *ST*, 20 Mar. 1958, p. 4; Anonymous, "Major Weinman Plans a Zoo for Singapore," *ST*, 11 Aug. 1958, p. 2; Arthur Richards, "A National Zoo for S'pore?" *SFP*, 2 Aug. 1961, p. 6; Andrew B. Robichaud, *Animal City: The Domestication of America* (Cambridge, MA: Harvard University Press, 2019), p. 233.

[13] Toh Chin Chye was the deputy prime minister, while Goh was the finance minister from 1967 to 1970. A.R. Parsons, "Singapore Zoo and Nature Reserve," Memo EA 1515, *Cultural Relations with Singapore*, C-210205-006/VO-PV/001 Series A1838-553-1-34, 16 Dec. 1967, pp. 201–2.

issues (such as a planned British military withdrawal from Singapore), and the implementation of an array of ambitious socio-economic policies.

The launch of the "Garden City" concept in May 1967 was one of the most visible of these domestic initiatives. Originating from theories championed by the English urban planner Ebenezer Howard, the creation of green spaces was a policy central to Singaporean post-war reconstruction efforts to mitigate problems with an "overgrown and congested industrial city." Singaporean leaders expanded this program further after 1967, with a very public campaign to transform the young nation into a "city beautiful with flowers and trees." An indication of how deeply this campaign permeated public policy can be found in the speech Goh Keng Swee delivered when he attended the official opening of the zoo six years later, in June 1973. This new institution was in part a response to the "troubles afflicting people living in cities", proof of the ability of the government to provide "clean and green ... parks and gardens" to citizens. The early conception of the Singapore Zoological Gardens was thus part of a broader nation-building project to reshape and reorganize the physical and mental landscapes of the island.[14]

The planning for this national zoo took six years. Several months after his lunch with Parsons, Ong assembled a team of 12 officers from the Public Utilities Board to study the feasibility of establishing such an institution; strikingly, none of the members possessed much knowledge about local fauna, let alone experience in planning a zoo. The committee thus turned immediately to international experts from San Diego, Berlin and Sydney, rather than soliciting local specialists. Lyn de Alwis, director of the Dehiwala Zoo in Colombo, was appointed as consultant-director, though he had never designed a zoo before. Similarly, Chan Kui Chuan Architects and Planners, the local company engaged to oversee construction, was "also without experience of zoo work."[15]

Given the long history of menageries and private zoos in Singapore, established local networks of animal expertise would still have existed at this time. The decision to rely heavily on overseas expertise instead suggests a

---

[14] Timothy P. Barnard and Corinne Heng, "A City in a Garden," in *Nature Contained: Environmental Histories of Singapore*, ed. Timothy P. Barnard (Singapore: NUS Press, 2014), p. 288; Anonymous, "Garden City," *ST*, 13 May 1967, p. 10; Goh, "Speech," 1973.

[15] A Public Utilities Board officer later confessed that apart from the domestic pets they owned, no one on the steering committee knew much about animals. Sharp, *21 Years*, pp. 5–13; Anonymous, "The Men Behind the Project," *ST*, 27 Jun. 1973, p. 14.

distinct, deliberate break from established local conventions of collecting, raising and displaying animals. The formal designation of the institution as a "Zoological Gardens" (as opposed to a "zoo" or a "menagerie") further reinforces this interpretation. As Hanson argues, such naming conventions represent strategies to distance modern animal displays from those of the past. Such discontinuities suggest that bureaucrats in the new nation were seeking to build a modern, dignified, national space, consciously separate from the cramped squalor of the private menageries in the colonial past.[16]

Inexperience aside, government planners were amassing a formidable trove of information about designing zoos; blueprints for the "animal sanctuary" eventually amounted to nearly 60 years of accumulated experience from international experts. The architecture borrowed from the latest "open zoo" designs, with most animals displayed in spacious, naturalistic enclosures. Extensive measures were also taken to ensure that animal waste would not contaminate Upper Seletar Reservoir, where the new Zoological Gardens would be located. Deep stormwater drains eventually ringed the entire zoo complex, and a dedicated waste treatment plant purified faunal sewage. Such measures followed "stringent standards" formulated by the Health Ministry and the Anti-Pollution Unit in the Prime Minister's Office.[17] While it might be tempting to point out that such comprehensive measures reflected the obsessive anxiety of the nascent state, such plans also arguably represented the aspirations of Singaporean planners for their new nation: one that was clean, efficient and modern.

This vision of a modern zoo resonated with the highest echelons of the Singaporean government. Goh Keng Swee, the finance minister, received the initial zoo proposal in June 1969, and was so impressed with it that he was prepared to "very favourably" underwrite its establishment. Yet, the idea of situating a zoo by a reservoir sat uneasily with some. Prime Minister Lee Kuan Yew expressed strong reservations about the presence of concentrated zoological effluent next to a key fresh-water reservoir. These concerns were well founded. When Singapore became independent in 1965, it only had three reservoirs—MacRitchie, Peirce and Seletar—that

---

[16] Hanson, *Animal Attractions*, p. 164.
[17] Sharp, *21 Years*, p. 32; Ong Swee Law, "Five Years for Idea to Come to Fruition," *ST*, 27 Jun. 1973, p. 19; Anonymous, "Keeping the Water Clean for $1.7 Million," *ST*, 29 Jan. 1973, p. 14; Anonymous, "SM: Zoo Pollution Was Main Worry," *ST*, 20 Jun. 1993, p. 3; Anonymous, "Don't Worry about Reservoir, Dhana Tells Nature Buffs," *ST*, 7 Jun. 1992, p. 3.

met less than 20 percent of national water needs. Developing more local water supplies became an overriding national imperative after Tunku Abdul Rahman, Malaysia's prime minister, coolly warned that he would sever water supplies to Singapore if the fledgling state ever crossed Malaysia. Lee hence paid exceptional attention to the island's water situation. Any domestic policy that endangered water security would be "simply vetoed." Lee eventually approved the zoo proposal, but only after assurances from Goh and cabinet ministers about the institution's extensive sanitation measures. Notably, it was also Goh, not Lee, who opened the zoo in June 1973.[18] The prime minister would continue to figure only peripherally in the development of the national zoo.

A comprehensive report was submitted to the government in September 1969, formally recommending the establishment of a Singapore Zoological Gardens. Shortly after, the state authorized the formation of a public company to design, construct and manage the new institution. Ong Swee Law was appointed as the chairman of the Gardens, while Khong Kit Soon—the chief water engineer for the Public Utilities Board—became its director.[19] Though its planners drew from diverse sources of international expertise, leading bureaucrats of the new nation would ultimately helm, plan and fund the institution.

By October 1972, three years later, the Zoological Gardens was in an advanced state of construction. The area had been extensively landscaped to create a "pleasant, garden image" for visitors. About 2,000 trees were specifically selected and planted to provide greater shade to visitors, replacing some of the "less desired" vegetation in the area. Winding pathways ensured visitors encountered a new enclosure or sight at every corner. In total, construction took only 18 months and cost the state about $9 million.[20] Serious thought had thus been given to the design and construction of the Gardens; the government had also dedicated significant human, material and financial resources to the project. Despite

---

[18] Sharp, *21 Years*, pp. 12, 61; Cecilia Tortajada, Yugal Joshi and Asit K. Biswas, *The Singapore Water Story: Sustainable Development in an Urban City-State* (Oxon: Routledge, 2013), pp. 86–8; Ong, "Five Years for Idea to Come to Fruition."

[19] The Seletar Zoological Gardens Sub-Committee, Proposal for the Development of the Seletar Zoological Gardens (Singapore, 1969), cited in Graetz, "Architectural Design," p. 3; Anonymous, "Govt's $5 Mil Firm to Set Up a Zoo," *ST*, 24 Apr. 1971, p. 11.

[20] Unless otherwise stated, all monetary figures quoted are in Singapore dollars (SGD). Sharp, *21 Years*, p. 31; P.M. Raman, "S'pore Zoological Gardens to Be Opened in Mid-June," *ST*, 30 Apr. 1973, p. 24.

these earnest, exceptional efforts, considerable gaps remained in the design, sometimes literally.

Several animals escaped from the zoo in 1973 and 1974, contributing dramatic interludes to the otherwise sedate, planned beginnings. The passionate governmental and societal responses to these episodes offer a glimpse into how Singaporeans perceived their relationships with the natural environment in the 1970s. The first of these escapes occurred on 5 March 1973, when two sun bears (*Helarctos malayanus*) were found outside their apparently locked cages. It was later ascertained that the bears had forced their way out of a gap in their enclosures. Although the animals were "tame and half-grown," one of them was shot dead 50 meters from its pen. The situation worsened two days later when Twiggy the panther slipped through the bars of a locked enclosure, which were each about 12 centimeters apart. A massive search for the escaped carnivore was launched. Along with zoo staff, policemen, and volunteer game hunters, three Reserve Units of about 150 men were deployed to comb the surrounding area. Although extensive sweeps were conducted through the secondary rainforests of Seletar, Mandai and Sembawang, it would be 11 more months before the feline fugitive was finally located again.[21]

The news that "one of the most dangerous animals in the zoo" was somewhere within the city provoked excited responses from different groups of Singaporeans. Private animal hunters personally offered their services to the zoo, while villagers in the Mandai and Seletar area—armed with shotguns, changkols, parangs and sticks—maintained 24-hour vigils and guarded their poultry. Nightlife in the nearby Sembawang Hills Estate came to a standstill, as residents and shopkeepers locked up their houses and prepared weapons to protect themselves.[22]

There were also sympathetic responses to the situation from Singaporeans. In contrast to shoot-to-kill orders issued to policemen, several letters to the press urged authorities to spare Twiggy, and to consider its "hungry, frightened and lost" plight. A "Nine-Year-Old Animal Lover" living near Mandai implored the authorities to consider tranquilizing the escaped creature rather than killing it, relating how she

---

[21] R. Chandran and K.S. Sidhu, "Panther: Zoo to Hold Inquiry," *ST*, 11 Mar. 1973, p. 1; Bharathi Mohan, "Panther Escape: Official Resigns," *NN*, 10 May 1973, p. 1; Bernard Doray, "Panther: Eight Hunters Join in Search," *ST*, 13 Mar. 1973, p. 10; Anonymous, "Pug Marks of the Missing Panther Turn Up Again," *ST*, 9 Jun. 1973, p. 12.

[22] Chandran and Sidhu, "Panther: Zoo to Hold Inquiry."

had watched television programs where animals were recaptured in this manner. "What a terrible thing that it would be," she lamented, if all escaped animals were "hunted down and shot." The zoo also received many "highly original but impractical" ideas from the public, such as using a male panther, or the employment of "sonic sounds," to recapture the beast. Likewise, *The Straits Times* was flooded with suggestions on how to trap the creature. Meanwhile, schools launched essay competitions seeking the most creative explanations for how Twiggy had escaped, and how the beast could be recaptured.[23]

The hunt for Twiggy reached its denouement on a Wednesday afternoon 11 months later. On 30 January 1974, a clerk at the Turf Club spotted the animal jumping over a fence in the area. The startled panther fled into a nearby monsoon drain, where it was soon cornered by policemen and firemen. Special cages, traps and flare guns were subsequently deployed to "smoke it out." Burning petrol was then poured into the sewer. After an inconclusive two days, police began to excavate the underground drain with a bulldozer, while policemen stood ready with submachine guns in case the beleaguered creature lashed out. As a final precaution, the drain was then flooded. Shortly afterwards, a diminutive, feline carcass floated out with noticeable burn marks on its body. After wandering Singaporean rainforests for 11 months and eluding policemen, experienced hunters and zookeepers, Twiggy had come to an ignominious end, the victim of police flares, burning petrol and columns of water. The police then carted the carcass away for an autopsy.[24]

The death of a panther in the Garden City provoked many emotional responses from the public. While Ong Swee Law expressed relief that the escape had not resulted in any human casualties, the normally restrained Singaporean press characterized the killing as a "clumsy" overreaction that "smacked of overkill." Ordinary Singaporeans joined in to express "great sadness" and widespread indignation for the "brutal killing" of a "young,

---

[23] Ecology, "Untitled," *ST*, 14 Mar. 1973, p. 18; Nine-Year-Old Animal Lover, "Don't Kill the Panther, Capture It ALIVE," *ST*, 14 Mar. 1973, p. 18; Anonymous, "Panther Probe," *ST*, 13 May 1973, p. 10; M. Ferrao, "Untitled," *ST*, 14 Mar. 1973, p. 18; Anonymous, "A Postmortem on Twiggy the Panther," *ST*, 3 Feb. 1974, p. 16.

[24] N.G. Kutty, Gerald Pereira and Jacob Daniel, "All-Night Vigil after Bid to Flush It Out Fails," *ST*, 31 Jan. 1974, p. 1; K.S. Sidhu, "Panther Found Dead in Its Hideout," *ST*, 2 Feb. 1974, p. 13; Anonymous, "Unhappy Ending," *ST*, 3 Feb. 1974, p. 8.

probably sickly panther." Some went further, blaming the animal's death on the negligence and mismanagement of zoo officials. Taken together, these highly charged responses demonstrate the breadth of responses towards wild animals amongst different segments of Singaporean society.[25]

Despite additional precautions, the new zoo continued to suffer numerous escapes. On 14 January 1974, a month before Twiggy met her untimely demise, Congo the Nile hippopotamus (*Hippopotamus amphibius*) broke through his enclosure, and plodded into the placid waters of Seletar Reservoir. Mindful of concerns about water purity, officials assured the public that the reservoir only stored untreated water. The massive creature would remain in the reservoir for 48 days, until he was finally lured back to the zoo. Other escapes included an eland (*Taurotragus oryx*), which vaulted its two-meter-high enclosure fence (but returned by itself 11 days later); and a tiger (*Panthera tigris*) that escaped from its enclosure, but was promptly enticed back with offerings of meat.[26]

While these escapes could be attributed to staff inexperience, sympathetic observers also highlighted the complexities of running an "open zoo," a concept the San Diego Zoo had popularized, to provide animals with more naturalistic surroundings. Rather than negligence, such escapes represented "teething problems" inevitably faced when operating an open zoo. International experts were nevertheless flown in to recommend tighter security measures. Higher fences, reinforced brick walls, and deeper moats were incorporated into the layout. These additional precautions paid off. There would be no further major animal escapes until December 1978, when a large ghavial (*Gavialis gangeticus*) broke out from its stockade after a torrential downpour.[27]

---

[25] See also Barnard and Yip's chapter on monkeys in this collection for a discussion of these ideas as they relate to a less dangerous creature. Gerald de Cruz, "Problems of Keeping an Open Zoo," *NN*, 12 Feb. 1974, p. 6; Anonymous, "Staying Open," *ST*, 7 Feb. 1974, p. 8; Anonymous, "Lucky Panther," *ST*, 4 Jul. 1975, p. 16; CMC, "Panther that Harmed No One," *ST*, 5 Feb. 1974, p. 12; Anonymous, "Unhappy Ending."

[26] S.M. Muthu, "Search on for Hippo Missing from Zoo," *ST*, 15 Jan. 1974, p. 1; National Archives of Singapore, Oral History Archives: Bernard Ming-Deh Harrison, accession No. 003217, Reel/Disc 4; Anonymous, "Zoo Seeks Mate for Congo," *ST*, 11 Apr. 1974, p. 6; Anonymous, "Staying Open," *ST*, 7 Feb. 1974, p. 8; Chew Lee Ching, "And Now a Tiger Almost Makes It to Freedom," *ST*, 7 Feb. 1974, p. 20.

[27] Anonymous, "The Major Flaws in Security of Zoo," *ST*, 25 Feb. 1974, p. 9; Sharp, *21 Years*, p. 32; Anonymous, "Ghavial Escapes from Mandai Zoo," *ST*, 10 Dec. 1978, p. 12; Anonymous, "Staying Open."

Singaporean Creatures

The Singapore Zoological Gardens finally opened to the public on 28 June 1973. Admission fees were $2 for adults and $1 for children. These rates appear to have been relatively affordable for most Singaporeans, given that the average monthly household income in 1973 was $318, and the fact that the zoo had welcomed its millionth visitor by November 1974, just 17 months after it had opened. Of the 11 visitors shortlisted in a contest celebrating the zoo's millionth visitor, only "a shipping manager from Hongkong" appears to have been a foreigner, suggesting that many early visitors were Singaporean. Despite the controversial escapes, which would not be resolved until March 1974, citizens appear to have taken enthusiastically to their new national zoo.[28]

The popularity of the Singapore Zoological Gardens was central to the reconceptualization of the official national landscape. As the state modernized and urbanized the economy, and its inhabitants relocated to high-rise public housing, national leaders became increasingly concerned with how citizens would cope with "the press of concrete structures and the pace of modern living."[29] Singaporeans were becoming increasingly estranged from the natural environment around them, to the extent that, as Goh Keng Swee recounted, enlisted national servicemen despatched to the countryside could mistake "young piglings" for "big rats." Alongside other recreational spaces like the Botanic Gardens, the Van Kleef Aquarium, and the Jurong Bird Park, the zoo became another scenic refuge within the Garden City in which citizens could relax. For the nation-state's leaders, "nature" had become a functional commodity that could be sequestered away into "wooded recreational reserves," or pruned into neat gardens. The development of the Singapore Zoological Gardens was thus intricately linked to how the physical and cultural landscapes of newly independent Singapore were being imagined, articulated and constructed.[30]

---

[28] Anonymous, "Zoo Expenses," *ST*, 28 Jun. 1973, p. 14; Anonymous, "Zoo Gets Set for Lucky Visitor," *ST*, 13 Nov. 1974, p. 21; Anonymous, "Big Change in Living Style…," *NN*, 12 Sep. 1973, p. 7; Anonymous, "'Magic Figure' Visitor at the Zoo," *ST*, 14 Nov. 1974, p. 11.

[29] By 1971, the Housing & Development Board had built about 133,000 public flats, housing more than 752,000 people, or about 35 percent of the Singaporean population at the time. Stephen H.K. Yeh, "Some Trends and Prospects in Singapore's Public Housing," *Ekistics* 33, 196 (1972): 182–5.

[30] In addition to considerable financial and material resources, significant technical expertise from the civil service had been devoted to this project, particularly from the Public Utilities Board. At a time when water figured so critically to national security, the continued commitment of such substantial intellectual resources also

It was not just government bureaucrats, however, who were dreaming of a new zoo, or a new Singapore. Ordinary Singaporeans themselves were also rethinking their relationships with nature and nation. Despite the potential danger an escaped panther posed, many expressed sympathy for Twiggy. The emotional outpouring in the wake of her death demonstrated how strongly Singaporeans could feel for a "plucky cat" they had only read about and imagined. Commentators castigated the authorities for perceived oversights, urging the zoo to do better. Nonetheless, it was also clear from the sheer volume of responses that Singaporeans were proud of their new national zoo. Many expressed their admiration for the Gardens' modern, "open zoo" design, applauding government attempts to provide "an educational and relaxing diversion" for citizens. At least two writers urged the state to keep admission rates affordable for less affluent residents, so as to allow the zoo to "meet the recreational, social and educational needs of an industrial society." There was a general expectation, reflected in the letters of ordinary Singaporeans and the institution's press statements, that the Zoological Gardens would be an inclusive national space, one which all citizens could experience and enjoy.[31]

With the opening of the Singapore Zoological Gardens, the Singaporean fascination with displaying and viewing animals had entered a new phase. When the zoo opened in June 1973, it was not, as Goh Keng Swee modestly suggested, just a "welcome addition to the amenities available to residents."[32] The significant resources devoted to its creation and the passionate debates it had aroused showed that Singaporeans were beginning to imagine nature and their new nation through the prism of this new establishment. Curiously, the escape of another iconic animal would similarly presage the next stage in the development of the national institution.

---

illustrates how centrally the national zoo figured in the verdant visions of leaders. See also Miles Powell's contribution to this collection. Goh Keng Swee, "Sociologists Have a Point, Says Dr Goh," *ST*, 27 Jun. 1973, p. 19; Ong, "Five Years for Idea to Come to Fruition."

[31] Anonymous, "Zoo Expenses," *ST*, 28 Jun. 1973, p. 14; Anonymous, "Mandai Zoo Meets an Urgent Need," *NN*, 28 Jun. 1973, p. 10; Anonymous, "Mandai Zoo Will Be One of World's Best: Expert," *ST*, 19 Oct. 1972, p. 3.

[32] National Archives of Singapore: "Speech by Dr Goh Keng Swee, Deputy Prime Minister and Minister for Defence, at the opening of the Singapore Zoological Gardens on Wednesday, 27th June 1973 at 4.45p.m."

Globalized Collections

At sunset on 31 March 1982, an orangutan fell from a tree in MacRitchie Reservoir, and fractured her left arm. The fall ended a three-day stand-off involving Ah Meng, the most iconic orangutan in Singaporean history, and her zookeepers. The incident had occurred after the Singapore Tourist Promotion Board commissioned a short promotional video involving the ape, which was to be filmed at the water catchment. Curious about her new environment, Ah Meng had climbed beyond the reach of her human keeper on the first day of filming, reaching the upper branches of a tall tree. Despite numerous entreaties, the ape refused to descend from her newly claimed perch. Finally, after two nights without food and water, the famished orangutan fell from the tree and injured herself. Her arboreal adventure and subsequent fall made front-page news in national newspapers. For the next few weeks, while Ah Meng convalesced, the zoo was inundated with gifts and cards wishing the creature a speedy recovery.[33]

As with Twiggy nine years earlier, the incongruous novelty of an escaped orangutan had momentarily seized the Singaporean imagination. Like the panther, Ah Meng was also an accidental icon. The zoo had groomed another orangutan, Susi, to be a zoo mascot, but she died of pregnancy complications in 1974. Ah Meng was selected to replace Susi despite being "kind of sour-faced," because she was photogenic and did not slouch. She was also comfortable with humans, having been raised as a household pet before being given to the zoo.[34] The frequent use of her likeness—in at least 28 travel promotion films and 274 published stories—would cement her status as an icon of Singapore's tourist promotion efforts by 1986.[35]

The meteoric rise of Ah Meng from household pet to national icon embodied the ways the zoo and the Singaporean nation were reinventing themselves as modernized and globalized citizens. By the late 1970s, Singapore had commenced a transition toward more technology-intensive,

---

[33] Anonymous, "Ah Meng Stages a Sit-In," *ST*, 30 Mar. 1982, p. 1; Paul Wee, "She Is Safely Back in Her Den," *ST*, 1 Apr. 1982, p. 1; Anonymous, "Get-Well Wishes and Gifts for Ah Meng," *ST*, 2 May 1982, p. 11.
[34] See Barnard and Yip's chapter in this collection for context on apes as household pets and being handed over to the government during this period.
[35] Harrison, Interview, 2008; Anonymous, *Singapore Zoological Gardens Annual Report 1982* (Singapore: Singapore Zoological Gardens, 1983), p. 5.

Image 8.4: Tourists posing with Ah Meng during "Breakfast at the Zoo," 1988. Image courtesy of the Tourist Guides Association of Singapore and National Archives of Singapore.

high-value-added industries. Its 10-year economic plan in 1981 signaled a growing emphasis on services and information technology. Attracted by the state promotion of Singapore as a regional software center, major computer firms, such as Apple, IBM, Hewlett Packard and Sperry Univac, soon set up factories, training centers and headquarters locally. After Singapore experienced its first drop in visitor arrivals in two decades in 1983, a high-level task force was convened to rejuvenate the tourist industry through determined campaigns to woo international travelers to Singapore for work and leisure. Taken together, these developments heralded the rise of an increasingly prosperous, internationally connected Singaporean middle class that was both "upwardly and outwardly mobile."[36] As the country

---

[36] Tsang Sau Yin, "Apple Embarks on $50m Expansion at Ang Mo Kio," *Business Times* [hereafter, *BT*], 8 Jan. 1982, p. 1; Wong Mai Yun, "Sperry Univac Moves South Asian Base Here," *ST*, 6 Jul. 1981, p. 4; Anonymous, "The Ten-Year Plan," *BT*, 5 Dec. 1981, p. 7; M.S. Yeow, "Task Force to Boost Tourism," *Singapore Monitor* [hereafter, *SM*], 13 Sep. 1984, p. 1; Natalie Oswin, *Global City Futures: Desire and Development in Singapore* (Athens, Georgia: University of Georgia Press,

enmeshed itself deeper into the global economy, its citizens were likewise beginning to expand their understandings of their place in the world.

In the context of such national transformations, the zoo also began to revitalize itself. In 1981, Bernard Ming-Deh Harrison became executive director of the institution. The appointment marked a turning point for the Singapore Zoological Gardens. Only 29 years old, Harrison was one of the youngest zoo directors in the world at the time. Having worked at the zoo since its inception, his leadership would shape the pace and direction of its development for the next two decades. In its 1981 annual report, officials concluded that with nearly 30 percent of the Singaporean population having already visited the zoo, it was fast approaching "saturation level." Harrison would now have to "look to the tourist segment for any substantial increase in visitor attendance." The director would be responsible for globalizing the Gardens, transforming it from a "welcome amenity" aimed simply at meeting the recreational needs of citizens to an internationally connected and recognized institution.[37]

As part of this marketing strategy, the Gardens continued leveraging the unique appeal of its animals to reach audiences. One of its more notable efforts involved guests sharing a meal with orangutans for "Breakfast at the Zoo," which was first initiated in 1982 to reverse flagging tourist interest. Priced at an "extremely expensive" $30, the package included a buffet breakfast, followed by a photography session with the primates. Just two years later, "Breakfast" was expanded to "High Tea at the Zoo" to accommodate skyrocketing demand. By 1989, a dedicated "Orang Utan Terrace" was officially opened to host the clamor of visitors wanting to sup with the great apes. It was estimated that 60,000 visitors in 1989 alone would pay for the privilege, an indication of the blistering popularity of this attraction by this time.[38]

2019), p. 28.

[37] This was also of importance as the zoo was operating at an annual deficit of about $1 million by 1981. Anonymous, "Teachers Urged to Use the Zoo as "Living Classroom," *SM*, 11 Nov. 1984, p. 3; Sam Ran, "Zoo Will Receive the SIA Ad Treatment," *ST*, 12 Dec. 1983, p. 8; Doreen Soh, "Singapore Zoo Plans to Make Children Its Prime Target," *ST*, 23 Mar. 1984, p. 21; Christina Tseng, "$500,000 Ad Blitz to Woo Malaysians," *ST*, 9 Jul. 1985, p. 48; Anonymous, *Annual Report 1982*, p. 7; Anonymous, *Annual Report 1981* (Singapore: Singapore Zoological Gardens, 1982), p. 3; Anonymous, "New Zoo Director Harrison among Youngest in the World," *ST*, 16 Feb. 1981, p. 9; Harrison, Interview, 2008; Anonymous, "Zoo Expenses."

[38] Bernard Harrison, "Breakfast at the Zoo Tour Starts in May," *ST*, 3 Apr. 1982,

Beyond the marketing strategies of sharing a meal with a great ape, during the 1980s the Singapore Zoo began to reinforce its place within an international context. This was first signaled with the admission of Bernard Harrison to the International Union of Directors of Zoological Gardens in January 1982, an honor reserved for "the top-ranking zoos in the world."[39] Membership in such organizations placed Singapore within a global web of zoological expertise, presaging a new period of co-operation and high-profile animal exchanges with other zoos, involving (amongst other animals) rare monkeys, Komodo dragons and white tigers. One of the first of these prestigious undertakings occurred soon thereafter, in March 1983, with the zoo announcing its intention to display and breed western lowland gorillas (*Gorilla gorilla*).[40] It would be the "biggest single project yet" at the institution and would, it was hoped, result in Singapore-bred gorillas.[41]

Testifying to these aspirations, the Singapore Zoological Gardens soon successfully procured four gorillas for its "Gorilla Island" exhibit. Prince Rainier of Monaco donated two "fast and aggressive" adult gorillas—Zozo and Gori—from the Monaco Zoo, while the other pair, Saul and Goliath, were juveniles obtained through long-term exchange agreements with the Bristol Zoo. The sprawling, 2,892 square meter Gorilla Island officially opened in November 1983 to great fanfare. Sponsored by the Keppel

---

p. 17; Anonymous, *Annual Report 1982*, p. 11; Nicklaus D'Cruz, "New Terrace for Zoo Breakfast," *New Paper*, 16 Oct. 1989, p. 3; Harrison, Interview, 2008.

[39] Harrison also was the president of the Southeast Asian Zoo Association (SEAZA) for two terms (six years). The SEAZA was a loose, regional grouping of Southeast Asian zoos that conducted training programs for zookeepers and shared information about their animals. Harrison, Interview, 2008; Anonymous, "New Zoo Director Harrison among Youngest in the World."

[40] Such self-assurance was not unfounded. By 1983, the Singapore Zoological Gardens had overseen eight successful orangutan births in 11 years. With 19 individuals, the institution possessed the largest captive orangutan colony in the world. This accomplishment emboldened officials to embark on more ambitious breeding projects involving other great apes; projects that would confirm its place in globalized networks of zoological collections. Angelina Choy, "No Monkey Business, This," *ST*, 9 Aug. 1984, p. 93.

[41] Since international laws banned the capture and trade of wild-caught gorillas, the price of procuring such animals from other zoos was "quite prohibitive." Singapore-bred gorillas, it was thus envisioned, could be profitably sold to other zoo collections, or traded for rarer animals to display. Anonymous, "Breeding the Big Apes," *ST*, 30 Mar. 1983, p. 40; Anonymous, *Annual Report 1981*, p. 11.

Group, the $850,000 exhibit was the first of its kind in Southeast Asia, and the zoo's most ambitious project since it opened.[42]

Gorilla Island failed swiftly and spectacularly. In December 1983, one month after its inauguration, Gori, the 23-year-old ape from Monaco, abruptly lost his appetite and developed muscular tremors. Three days later, the primate was dead. It was later ascertained that the soil bacteria *Pseudomonas pseudomallei* had killed the great ape.[43] The contagion did not subside. Twelve days later, the same pathogen felled Goliath. The two surviving gorillas were promptly quarantined in "ultra-hygienic conditions," and local vaccines were developed for them. These drastic, expensive measures, however, proved futile. In November 1984, during the local rainy season, both Saul and Zozo succumbed to the deadly bacteria.[44]

The sudden deaths of all four gorillas within a year was an extraordinary shock for the Singapore Zoological Gardens, and also attracted international ire. The International Primate Protection League called for the institution to be blacklisted and banned from exhibiting gorillas. Robert Cooper, a veterinary surgeon working in West Africa, accused the Singapore Zoo of trying to start a "gorilla cult," after rumors (later dispelled) that the zoo was procuring more apes from African trappers.[45] In contrast, the Singaporean public seems to have been remarkably unmoved by the gorilla tragedy. Unlike the passionate outcry that the death of Twiggy had evinced a decade earlier, no public recriminations or scathing editorials appeared following the primate deaths. While this may reflect

---

[42] Anonymous, "Two Male Gorillas for Zoo Due in Tomorrow," *ST*, 20 Sep. 1983, p. 7; Jeevarajah Yasotha, "Goliath and Saul Will Be First to Live in Gorilla Isle," *ST*, 7 Sep. 1983, p. 8; Anonymous, "Dr Schroeder Opens South-east Asia's First Gorilla Colony," *SM*, 27 Nov. 1983, p. 9.

[43] The microbe, endemic to Southeast Asia, is particularly infectious during rainy seasons, which in Singapore often last from December to March and June to September. Scientists in Singapore made a concerted effort in the early 2000s to develop drugs to counter it. Jason F. Kreisberg, et al., "Growth Inhibition of Pathogenic Bacteria by Sulfonylurea Herbicides," *Antimicrobial Agents and Chemotherapy* 57, 3 (2013): 1513–17; Catharine Fernando, "Gorilla which Arrived in Oct Dies," *SM-2nd Edition*, 15 Dec. 1983, p. 2; Anonymous, "Star Newcomer Gori Dies after Coma," *ST*, 16 Dec. 1983, p. 18.

[44] Jeevarajah Yasotha, "'Pseudo-Bug' Strikes at Zoo," *ST*, 29 Dec. 1983, p. 9; Jeevarajah Yasotha, "Vaccine for Gorillas Produced Here," *ST*, 28 Jul. 1984, p. 20; Anonymous, "Disease Kills Another Gorilla," *ST*, 4 Sep. 1984, p. 38; Anonymous, "Gorilla Island Banks on Health of Its Lone Survivor," *ST*, 5 Sep. 1984, p. 17.

[45] Sharp, *21 Years*, p. 94; Valerie Lee, "Zoo's 'Gorilla Cult' Comes Under Fire," *ST*, 2 Jun. 1985, p. 1.

the growing proficiency of officials with managing their public image, it also demonstrated the unpredictable, uneven ways in which Singaporeans could feel about exotic animals.

The gorilla debacle was an exception to an otherwise successful program of international animal exchanges at the Singapore Zoo. Its collections continued to expand with the procurement and display of leaf monkeys, ruffed lemurs and sea lions. In 1987, the zoo began a series of "Special Loan" exhibits, displaying rare animals from partner institutions, beginning with a pair of golden snub-nosed monkeys (*Rhinopithecus roxellana*) specially flown in from Shaanxi, China. Chinese zookeepers accompanied the primates, which were insured at a total cost of over $1.7 million, and housed in a custom-built, climate-controlled enclosure costing $650,000. Regular press coverage of the monkeys resulted in a 28 percent increase in visitor attendance after their arrival. Over 500,000 visitors, most of them local, were estimated to have seen the rare primates from May to November 1987.[46]

Further testifying to its growing presence in international animal networks, the zoo was able to despatch 34 animals in 1987 alone to counterparts in Surabaya, San Diego, Sri Lanka and Hangzhou for exchange or breeding programs. The golden monkeys were soon followed by a pair of Indian white tigers from the Cincinnati Zoo in May 1988. Approximately 370,000 visitors saw the tigers during their three-month sojourn in Singapore. Finally, Indonesian President Suharto presented a pair of rare Komodo dragons (*Varanus komodoensis*) to Singapore as a diplomatic gift in 1989, making the institution one of only seven zoos outside of Indonesia to exhibit these large lizards. The milestone concluded a decade marked by new horizons, rare animals and unexpected tragedy.[47]

---

[46] Magdalene Lum, "Very Important Primates," *ST*, 20 May 1987, p. 2; Anonymous, "Golden Monkey May Be Pregnant," *ST*, 21 Oct. 1987, p. 16; Anonymous, "A Feast of Leaves for VIP Monkeys," *ST*, 4 May 1987, p. 12; Sandra Davie, "Million-Dollar Monkeys," *ST*, 22 Apr. 1987, p. 24; Anonymous, "Golden Monkeys Arrive," *ST*, 15 May 1987, p. 13.

[47] Komodo dragons had previously been presented by President Suharto of Indonesia as diplomatic gifts to Singapore in 1975. The creatures were then housed at the Singapore Zoo. Suharto had decided to present more dragons to Singapore in 1989 in view of "Singapore's desire to have more specimens of the rare animals." Anonymous, "Komodo Dragons Gift for the Zoo from Indonesia," *ST*, 12 Aug. 1975, p. 7; Anonymous, "Komodo Dragons for S'pore," 16 Aug. 1975, p. 32; Sharon Simon, "Animal Baby Boom a Boon to Zoos Here and Abroad," *ST*, 27 Mar. 1988, p. 12; Anonymous, "White Tigers Zoo's Latest Draw," *ST*, 2 May 1988,

The remarkable internationalization of the Singapore Zoological Gardens occurred in the context of deeper shifts at a national level, as Singapore became increasingly enmeshed within the global economy and the state sought to attract more international visitors to the island for business and leisure. The zoo had cast its horizons further afield, seeking international audiences for its animals. This strategy paid off, as tourists began flocking to the institution. International visitors increased tenfold between 1980 and 1988, from 22,000 to over 250,000. Despite this rise, however, the zoo continued to cater primarily to Singaporeans. Of the 1.1 million who visited the zoo in 1988, only about "one quarter" were tourists.[48]

The enthusiasm Singaporeans displayed in zoo visits also reflected growing prosperity in the nation-state. By 1989, median and average monthly incomes in Singapore had doubled from a decade earlier, and citizens were more willing to spend on recreational activities with their families. Local companies, trade unions, community centers and residents' committees organized events at the zoo, further increasing local visitor numbers. Moreover, over 78,000 schoolchildren were brought to the Gardens every year on excursions. In response to the burgeoning appeal of the institution with younger Singaporeans, *Zoo-Ed*, the Zoo's quarterly magazine for students, increased its regular print run from 15,000 in 1979 to 35,000 copies per issue by 1989. Despite its turn to a more aggressive international marketing policy, the Singapore Zoo had also remained committed to its original aim of being "a recreational, social and educational amenity ... within easy reach of as many Singaporeans as possible."[49]

---

p. 15; Anonymous, "Popular White Tigers," *ST*, 13 Aug. 1988, p. 20; Anonymous, "Suharto's Gift to Singapore of Two Komodo Dragons Now at the Zoo," *ST*, 7 Nov. 1989, p. 16. Yang Razali Kassim, "Suharto 'Fully Satisfied' after Talks with PM on Bases Issue," *ST*, 8 Oct. 1989, p. 2.

[48] Despite a staggering 40 percent increase in admission charges, more than 825,000 citizens nonetheless visited the zoo that year. Anonymous, *Annual Report 1985*, (Singapore: Singapore Zoological Gardens, 1986), p. 16; Agnes Chen, "Sight to Soothe Savage Breast [sic]," *ST*, 22 Oct. 1989, p. 12.

[49] Bernard Harrison, "Zoo Has to Rely on Donations from the Public," *NN*, 4 Dec. 1980, p. 8; Anonymous, "Rare Leaf Monkeys Join Zoo," *ST*, 5 Feb. 1989, p. 12; Narendra Aggarwal, "Singaporeans' Average Pay Doubles in a Decade," *ST*, 12 May 1989, p. 23; Anonymous, "Teachers Urged to Use the Zoo as 'Living Classroom'," *SM*, 11 Nov. 1984, p. 3; Anonymous, "Zoo Magazine Still a Hit After 10 Years," *ST*, 5 Mar. 1989, p. 15; Anonymous, *Annual Report* 1985, p. 7; Chen, "Sight to Soothe Savage Breast [sic]."

As the Gardens globalized and diversified its collections, it also expanded the ways Singaporeans imagined, visualized and experienced "nature" and "wilderness." In the 1970s, the Zoological Gardens had offered "nature" as a means for Singaporeans to momentarily escape the stresses of modern urban life. By the late 1980s, the zoo had expanded these understandings of "nature" to encompass visions of charismatic orangutans, vulnerable gorillas and rare golden monkeys from around the world. Through its exotic animal displays, the zoo vividly reminded Singaporeans that "nature" also existed beyond Singaporean shores; citizens of the nation-state were now more closely connected to a vaster, global community of institutions, animals and ecosystems. Amidst changing socio-economic and national priorities, the Singapore Zoo had once again shaped, and in turn been reshaped by, evolving conceptions of nature and nation. As it entered the last decade of the century, the zoo and the nation would change again. A special, captive birth in 1990, one day after Christmas, would usher in this transformation.

Localized Creatures

Wednesday, 26 December 1990, was supposed to have been a routine day at the Singapore Zoological Gardens. The polar bear enclosure, which had been refurbished just two years earlier with a $620,000 government grant, housed the three resident polar bears: Sheba, Nanook and Anana. The presence of these exotic animals was symbolic of the international reach the institution had developed over the previous decade.[50] Aside from the stereotypical behavior characteristic of most polar bears confined in small spaces, there had been nothing to suggest that anything unusual was afoot. Sheba had last been seen swimming in the enclosure's pool the day before. Making their morning rounds, zookeepers were therefore astonished to discover another polar bear in the enclosure with the three full-grown adults.[51]

---

[50] The Singapore Zoological Gardens was not actually the first institution to exhibit polar bears in Singapore. Basapa's Ponggol Zoo bore that distinction, having taken delivery of a pair of polar bears in March 1937 from Germany. Specially built enclosures equipped with swimming pools were planned for the animals, although these bears were transferred to the Java Zoo two months later. Anonymous, "Polar Bears Come to Singapore," *ST*, 12 Mar. 1937, p. 12.
[51] Sharp, *21 Years*, pp. 98–101, 143; Anonymous, "Closer Encounters with Polar Bears at the Zoo," *ST*, 4 Aug. 1988, p. 21.

Sheba had given birth to a small cub weighing about half a kilogram, just one day after Christmas. Inuka, as the cub was later named, was the first polar bear born in the tropics. Although the zoo had procured and exhibited polar bears since 1978, this birth further enhanced its reputation as a world-class zoological institution. The zoo reasoned that if a polar bear, whose natural habitat differed so significantly from an equatorial tropical climate, could reproduce under its care, then it was probably "doing something right." Following a logic that had been deployed by other zoos since the 19th century, the arrival of a new resident was held up as evidence that animals in the Singapore Zoo were receiving quality care.[52]

From one perspective, the successful birth of a polar bear represented the extent of the technological and biological control the zoo exercised over its animal dependents; arguably a metaphor for state power over its citizens. Yet, institutions and administrators do not have monopolies on meaning. In subsequent years, ordinary Singaporeans would continue to articulate diverse opinions and complex emotions about Inuka through letters, newspaper articles and even scientific reports. These popular expressions would come to significantly shape the animals that the Singapore Zoological Gardens collected and displayed. Although it experienced numerous other institutional milestones after 1990—such as the 1994 opening of the award-winning Night Safari; the 1998 opening of the Fragile Forest (the organization's first fully immersive exhibit); and the incorporation of the zoo into Wildlife Reserves Singapore in 2000—it is arguably the dense corona of stories, discourses and debates surrounding the life and times of Inuka that best demonstrate how Singaporean relationships with nation and nature have changed over the years.

The zoo was quick to capitalize on the publicity potential of its charismatic cub, and its efforts were well received by the Singaporean public. A nationwide naming contest garnered 10,500 entries, with the moniker "Inuka," meaning "silent stalker" in the Inuit language, eventually selected for the new zoo resident.[53] A "guess the weight of Inuka" contest was launched the following year, to mark the cub's first birthday; by then, the young bear already weighed 110 kilograms. The contest drew a "staggering" 13,935 responses, attesting to the immense popularity of the creature with Singaporeans. Public fascination was subsequently sustained through regular press coverage of such events. A newspaper article about

---

[52] Hanson, *Animal Attractions,* p. 169.
[53] Anonymous, "Inuka Wins the Game of the Name," *ST,* 16 Jun. 1991, p. 14; Anonymous, "As Hungry as… a Bear on Its Birthday!" *ST,* 27 Dec. 1991, p. 12.

Inuka's second birthday, for instance, detailed how the bear "stood and clapped" for invited guests, while 300 people later attended his 10th birthday celebration in 2000.[54] The careful cultivation of the image of the tropical polar bear resulted in a public relations coup: years later, many visitors would continue to reminisce fondly about their visits to see an animal that bore no apparent cultural significance to Singaporeans, while plush toys of the bear remained on sale in the gift shops of the zoo even after Inuka died.

The Singapore Zoo procured its first two polar bears in April 1978 from an animal dealer in Frankfurt for $7,500 each. The male–female pair was flown in on a Singapore Airlines flight, transported to Mandai, and then housed in a specially constructed, air-conditioned enclosure. The Arctic animals were recorded as being "healthy and highly active" on the flight. Zookeepers were thus shocked to find the male bear dead in its den the next morning, less than 12 hours after its arrival, leaving the zoo with Sheba, the surviving female polar bear. One bear, however, was not enough for the administrators of the Singapore Zoo. In a telling display of its (state-funded) financial clout, self-assurance, and the lively global trade in such animals, the Singapore Zoological Gardens simply announced the day after the ursine death that it had already "placed an order for three more female polar bears." Although these three bears never materialized, the zoo's overweening ambition to exhibit these animals despite Singapore's tropical climate eventually resulted in the procurement of a male bear cub, Nanook, and another female bear, Anana.[55] The birth of Inuka in 1990 increased the zoo's polar bear population to four.[56]

---

[54] On his 10th birthday, the massive, intelligent apex predator was presented with a present of fruits, vegetables and salmon hidden inside two blocks of ice, as invited guests watched enthusiastically. Wong Kwai Chow, "The Zoo Celebrates as Inuka Turns Two," *ST*, 27 Dec. 1992, p. 25; Wong Kwai Chow, "A Very Singaporean Bear," *ST*, 27 Dec. 1995, p. 2; Alan Lin, "Born and Bread," *ST*, 14 Dec. 2000, p. 6, Anonymous, "Big Bash as Inuka Turns 10," *ST*, 14 Dec. 2000, p. 8; Ashleigh Sim, "Inuka Turns Sweet 16," *ST*, 27 Dec. 2006, p. 9.

[55] The Canadian government presented Nanook, an 11-month-old cub, to the Singapore Zoo in August 1978. The following year, the zoo procured Anana, a female polar bear. Despite two miscarriages, it was ultimately the union between Nanook and Sheba that bore fruit, producing Inuka in 1990; Ranee Govindram, "Lonesome Time for This Bear Without Her Mate," *ST*, 16 Apr. 1978, p. 6; Anonymous, "Polar Bear's Mate Arrives at Zoo," *ST*, 23 Aug. 1978, p. 8.

[56] Sharp, *21 Years*, p. 98; Anonymous, "Nanook, the Polar Bear, Dies," *ST*, 3 Jan. 1996, p. 19; Anonymous, "Tribute to Nanook," *The New Paper* [hereafter, *TNP*], 3 Jan. 1996, p. 9; Yamuna Perera, "Sad Story of the Three Bears," *TNP*, 3 Jan.

The birth of Inuka had come at an opportune moment. Three years earlier, in 1987, the first rumblings of unease about the display of animals poorly adapted for tropical environments had begun after a British animal welfare organization reported that polar bears in British zoos were turning "psychotic." Intrigued, *The Straits Times* decided to ascertain the mental and physical health of their Singaporean counterparts. Although correspondent Jill Hum observed Nanook swimming in "the same repetitive pattern," a veterinarian who accompanied her affirmed that the bears were well cared for, citing their rotundness, thick coats and lack of physical stress symptoms. Bernard Harrison, nonetheless, conceded that more could be done to allay the boredom the bears experienced, which often led to repetitive, stereotypical behavior. After her visit, Hum concluded that the Singaporean bears were "not psychotic."[57] The birth of Inuka delayed any further enquiries into the matter for several years.

Such concerns, however, eventually resurfaced. In 1996, Diana R. Lord wrote to *The Straits Times,* expressing concern for Inuka's quality of life in the tropical zoo and pointed out the fallacy of equating breeding success with well-being. The mental needs of animals, she stressed, were also important. Lord questioned if exhibiting polar bears, which were poorly adapted to an equatorial climate, was "a mere gimmick to flatter mankind's vanity." Harrison responded four days later in an uncharacteristically frank letter, published in the same newspaper. Openly admitting that the bears were a "rare exception to a sound rule," the director further conceded that even the "logic" of "finance and availability" made displaying polar bears in Singapore a questionable decision. This remarkably straightforward response hinted at an underlying unease, even within the upper echelons of the zoo administration, with keeping such "intelligent animals" in captivity.[58]

While the boredom of bears could ostensibly be addressed by "diversionary therapy" to keep them active and occupied, the sight of a green polar bear was much harder to brush off. The "greening" of captive

---

1996, p. 9; Anonymous, "Singapore Zoo's Inuka the Polar Bear Put Down at 27 on 'Humane and Welfare Grounds'," *ST,* 25 Apr. 2018, https://www.straitstimes.com/singapore/singapore-zoos-inuka-the-polar-bear-put-down-at-27-on-humane-and-welfare-grounds, (accessed 10 Aug. 2021).

[57] Jill Hum, "S'pore Zoo's Polar Bears Not Psychotic Like Some in Britain, Says Vet," *ST,* 7 Jun. 1987, p. 12.

[58] Diana R. Lord, "Keep Only Animals Native to Our Climate," *ST,* 4 Jan. 1996, p. 3; Bernard Harrison, "Zoo's Polar Bears Rare Exception to a Sound Rule," *ST,* 8 Jan. 1996, p. 12.

Image 8.5: A seemingly bored Inuka, c. 2006. Image courtesy of ACRES, taken from Amy Corrigan and Louis Ng, *What's a Polar Bear Doing in the Tropics?* (Singapore: Animal Concerns Research and Education Society, 2006), p. 32.

polar bears due to algae in their fur had been observed since 1979 in zoos worldwide. The phenomenon, however, occurred in Singapore only after 2004, when *The New Paper* reported that both Inuka and Sheba had turned a startling shade of green. While the zoo assured visitors that the algal growth "does not affect the bear's health in any way," it conceded that "warm and humid tropical conditions" had resulted in the unsightly coloration. The fur was later treated with hydrogen peroxide to remove the unsightly splotches.[59]

---

[59] Mary Rose Gasmier, "Polar Bear Nanook an Instant Hit in Debut Show," *ST*, 25 Nov. 1988, p. 22; Phillip T. Robinson and Ralph A. Lewin, "The Greening of Polar Bears in Zoos," *Nature* 278, 5703 (1979): 445–7; Hedy Khoo, "Green and Bear It, Inuka," *TNP*, 24 Feb. 2004, p. 10; Anonymous, "Seeing Red Over Green Bear," *TNP*, 4 Mar. 2004, p. 14; Anonymous, "Polar Bears Turn Green in Singapore," *BBC News*, 24 Feb. 2004, http://news.bbc.co.uk/2/hi/asia-pacific/3518631.stm, (accessed 11 Aug. 2021).

Growing public concerns for Inuka's welfare reached a crescendo in June 2006, with the publication of a sizeable report from the Animal Concerns Research and Education Society (ACRES), a local animal welfare group. The group had quietly reached out to the zoo earlier in 2004 in an attempt to improve the living conditions of Sheba and Inuka, but the extensive scope of the 105-page report now raised "serious welfare concerns" for the Zoo's two surviving bears. After a four-month-long "undercover operation," ACRES found the polar bear enclosure at the Singapore Zoo to be "undersized, barren, poorly designed," providing only about "0.0000005 percent of the polar bear's natural home range." In contrast to the reassuring depiction of bored but content bears in 1987, ACRES found the creatures exhibiting severe heat stress symptoms, along with "substantial fur loss" and loss of lean muscle mass. The bears, moreover, were housed in open-air enclosures with only limited protection from intense mid-afternoon sunlight, which even locals avoided. The report, which was produced with the support and endorsement of international polar bear specialists, biologists and zoo directors, focused intense press and public scrutiny on the Singaporean institution and its collection of exotic animals.[60]

Several months after the report's release, the Singapore Zoological Gardens announced that it would no longer procure Arctic animals for its collections, though it reiterated that its polar bears were housed in favorable conditions. This press statement drew a swift retort from Louis Ng, the President and Executive Director of ACRES. Ng called attention to how the polar bear enclosure actually failed to meet international "minimum standards of care and husbandry" needed for exhibiting the animals. Echoing earlier arguments other observers had made, Ng further underlined that animal births were not an appropriate benchmark of animal welfare, since "captive animals breed even in the most appalling conditions." Faced with a growing public outcry, zoo officials agreed to transfer Inuka to a temperate zoo after the death of his mother, as officials felt that separating the pair would cause unnecessary distress to the animals.[61] In August 2010, the Singapore Zoo further announced that it

---

[60] Adapted to freezing weather, a polar bear becomes "severely heat stressed" at 21.1°C; the average annual temperature in Singapore was 27°C in 2006. Amy Corrigan and Louis Ng, *What's a Polar Bear Doing in the Tropics?* (Singapore: Animal Concerns Research and Education Society, 2006).

[61] Sheralyn Tay, "No More Animals from the Arctic: S'pore Zoo," *TODAY*, 7 Sep. 2006, p. 6; Louis Ng, "Breeding Is No Indicator," *TODAY*, 9 Sep. 2006, p. 14;

would be building a new enclosure for the bears, with many features that ACRES had recommended in its 2006 report, such as climate-controlled quarters, and the use of natural substrates upon which the bears could forage, dig and rest. The Singapore Zoo, which had long prided itself on the meticulous care it afforded to its animals, had been swayed by the efforts of another Singaporean organization that focused on animal welfare, reflecting again the great heterogeneity of local voices and views about captive wild creatures.

Other Singaporeans also participated in this debate about Inuka during this period. *The Straits Times* reported that Inuka's 2006 birthday celebration was "clouded by a sense of sorrow." Inuka's impending move, it seemed, "saddened" many citizens. A regular visitor opined that the bear's departure would be a "difficult" experience for his family, while another wrote to the press detailing "why Inuka should stay," and hoped the zoo was not "bowing to pressure from animal rights groups." Although the zoo would later reverse its decision to send Inuka away, the varying opinions about the future of this Arctic animal from different quarters of Singaporean society reveal how differently, but strongly, Singaporeans could feel about wild animals.[62] Such feelings did not fade. In April 2018, Singapore would bear witness to one of the most shared and spontaneous outpourings of grief for a Singaporean animal.

Grief, National Icons and Singaporean Creatures

"He was as Singaporean as any of us," lamented Prime Minister Lee Hsien Loong upon hearing of the passing of Inuka. On Wednesday morning, 25 April 2018, after a significant decline in Inuka's health at the start of the month, the zoo made the "difficult but necessary decision not to revive" the bear "from anesthesia." After a lifetime spent in the confines of his enclosure, Inuka had died at the age of 27, long past the average life expectancy of his wild or captive counterparts. Prior to his death, when it was reported that his health was deteriorating rapidly, hundreds of visitors flocked to see Inuka at his enclosure. The subsequent announcement about his passing garnered over 8,700 likes, 921 comments, and over 5,000 shares on the zoo's Facebook page. Similarly, a video tribute compiled

---

Ashleigh Sim, "Inuka Turns Sweet 16," *ST*, 27 Dec. 2006, p. 9.
[62] Teo Cheng Wee, "Parting Will Be Such Sweet Sorrow," *ST*, 31 Dec. 2006, p. 2; Anonymous, "Why Inuka Should Stay," *ST*, 13 Jan. 2007, p. 96; Mak Mun San, "Inuka the Polar Bear to Stay on in Sunny S'pore," *ST*, 3 May 2007, p. 35.

for Inuka further received 20,000 unique views. For comparison, the Zoo's more mundane updates that year averaged less than 100 likes each, indicating the extent to which Inuka's death had rocked Singapore's online sphere. In addition, hundreds of zoo employees and guests attended a private memorial service for the polar bear; light blue ribbons, white roses and a memorial wall were used to commemorate the bear at the event. Many ordinary Singaporeans also expressed their anguish online. Photo filters, blogposts, articles, photographs and artworks grieving Inuka also sprang up in great profusion across numerous social media sites. Several political leaders, including Home Affairs and Law Minister K. Shanmugam and Prime Minister Lee Hsien Loong, also paid tribute to the Singaporean creature.[63]

The death of Inuka marked an end of an era, one that was memorialized through a public, collective grieving.[64] Photographs, paintings, anecdotes and opinions about the bear were shared and re-shared by thousands across a multitude of online domains. Born and raised in Singapore to parents who had come from distant lands, Inuka had been accepted as a Singaporean creature; an animal that citizens cherished and claimed as their own, an icon that represented aspects of themselves. Inuka—and by extension, the zoo that had raised him—had again become a prism through which Singaporeans contemplated and articulated their associations with nation, nature and wild animals. Though these associations were not always aligned to the objectives of education and entertainment the zoo

---

[63] Polar bears live about 15 to 18 years in the wild, and about 25 years in captivity. Wildlife Reserves Singapore, "With a Heavy Heart, We Bade Farewell to Our Beloved Senior Polar Bear Inuka This Morning." Facebook, 25 Apr. 2018, https://www.facebook.com/wrs.sg/posts/10155267621867051:0, (accessed 30 Jun. 2021); Wildlife Reserves Singapore, "Yasmin's Tribute for Inuka.mp4," Facebook, 28 Apr. 2018, https://fb.watch/6urU1W-ot1/ (accessed 2 Jul. 2021); Anonymous, "Singapore Zoo's Inuka the Polar Bear Put Down at 27"; Cheng Wen-Haus, "Inuka's Welfare is a Priority: Zoo," *ST*, 25 Apr. 2018, p. A23; Kimberley Chia, "Letting Go of Inuka," *ST*, 26 Apr. 2018, p. A10.

[64] Such public displays of grief for zoo animals had occurred in Singapore before. In 2008, when Ah Meng passed away, 4,000 well-wishers attended the memorial service at the zoo, the first time such an honor had been accorded to any animal in Singapore. Maria Almenoar, "Goodbye, Ah Meng," *ST*, 11 Feb. 2008, p. 4; Ho Lian-Yi, "Ah Meng Dies," *ST*, 9 Feb. 2008, p. 2; Nur Dianah Suhaimi, "Memorial Service for a Singapore Icon," *ST*, 10 Feb. 2008, p. 4.

promulgated, they reflected the myriad ways in which Singaporeans had come to apprehend and appreciate the natural world.[65]

Between 1973 and 2018, Singapore transformed dramatically. As it urbanized and industrialized, its agricultural farmland shrank to a fraction of its original area. Many of its rural residents were relocated to public housing, losing their traditional connections to the land. Meanwhile, nature and greenery in the city was tamed and contained, paralleling the ways in which residents were socialized into disciplined citizens of the new nation. As their economic, cultural and physical landscapes drastically transformed, the relationships between Singaporeans, animals and nature also changed. Although other recreational institutions like the Jurong Bird Park and the Van Kleef Aquarium also allowed Singaporeans to explore these relationships through their displays of avian and marine wildlife, no fish nor bird has managed to arouse the kind of emotional reactions from Singaporeans that panthers, apes and bears from the Singapore Zoological Gardens have done over the years; nor has any other animal institution on the island been so popular.[66]

The reasons for this popularity did not emerge overnight. There is a long, rich tradition of displaying and viewing animals in Singaporean history, which likely explains why the Singapore Zoo was so well received when it first opened. The significant material, technical and financial support it received from the state, however, set it apart from these older establishments. Being the first national zoo, it came to represent the aspirations and anxieties of many Singaporeans, just as zoos became symbols of civic pride in American and European cities. As the zoo increasingly presented itself as an international institution, its ambitions and animal collections correspondingly expanded. Despite mounting admission charges, ordinary Singaporeans continued to visit the national zoo in large numbers, a phenomenon that reflected their growing affluence and curiosity about the world around them. In the process, Singaporeans established new, increasingly exotic understandings of "nature" and "wild animals"; they would also begin to develop emotional attachments to some of these creatures, viewing them as "national icons" that symbolized Singapore to the world. Though neither Twiggy, Ah Meng, nor Inuka

---

[65] Hanson, *Animal Attractions*, p. 185.
[66] Although the pink dolphins at Underwater World Singapore may have also merited such a consideration. See Miles Powell's contribution to this collection for a discussion of such issues. Barnard and Heng, "A City in a Garden."

represented endemic animal species, their lives evoked passionate reactions from Singaporeans of diverse social backgrounds. These popular reactions would indirectly shape the zoo's development: from security measures, to enclosure sizes, to marketing campaigns, and to the very animals the zoo collected and displayed. The zoo had thus exposed citizens to new understandings and meanings of nature; in turn, citizens also came to shape the institution in many unexpected and indirect ways.

As "contrived meeting places for the most urban people and the most exotic animals," zoos have long been a space for humans to explore their relationships with the natural world.[67] Since it opened in 1973, the Singapore Zoological Gardens has significantly influenced the ways in which citizens envisioned and experienced nature, wilderness and wild animals. Through the Gardens, "nature" came to assume different meanings to Singaporeans: as a recreational escape; a symbol of prosperity; and even as representations of themselves. Yet, this power to make meaning and to influence policies, was not unidirectional. The perspectives of the Singaporean public also meaningfully molded and altered the institution. Popular pressure changed the ways in which the zoo collected, displayed and imagined its animals. Singaporean creatures had thus emerged as a result of the intricate entanglements between nation, nature and the Singapore Zoological Gardens.

---

[67] Hanson, *Animal Attractions*, p. 186.

List of Contributors

Timothy P. Barnard is an associate professor in the Department of History at the National University of Singapore, where he specializes in the environmental and cultural history of Singapore and the Melaka Straits. He is the author of *Nature's Colony* (2016) and *Imperial Creatures* (2019), histories of flora and fauna in Singapore, and the editor of *Nature Contained* (2014), a collection of essays on Singaporean environmental history.

Choo Ruizhi is a graduate fellow at the East-West Center and a doctoral student in the Department of History at the University of Hawaiʻi. His research interests involve environmental histories of Southeast Asia in the 19th and 20th centuries, particularly the development of agriculture and fisheries in Singapore. His writings have appeared in collections of short stories and academic journals, including the *Journal of Southeast Asian Studies*.

Anthony Medrano is an assistant professor in Environmental Studies at Yale-NUS College, and a National University of Singapore Presidential Young Professor who holds appointments at the Lee Kong Chian Natural History Museum and the Asian Research Institute. His scholarship centers on histories of economic life and biodiversity change in Southeast Asia. He is completing his first monograph, *The Edible Ocean: Science, Industry, and the Rise of Urban Southeast Asia*, which is under contract with Yale University Press.

Miles Powell is an associate professor in the School of Humanities at Nanyang Technological University. His research focuses on environmental history, particularly the development of conservation and fisheries globally. He is the author of several articles focusing on environmental change in Singapore and the monograph *Vanishing America* (2016). He is currently completing a monograph on the global history of human interactions with sharks in the 20th century.

Esmond Chuah Meng Soh is a graduate student in the history program in the School of Humanities at the Nanyang Technological University. He has published articles in *Asian Ethnology* and the *Journal of Chinese Religions*, and continues to explore his interests in the history of religion and overseas Chinese in Southeast Asia.

Nicole Tarulevicz is an associate professor and the head of History and Classics in the School of Humanities at the University of Tasmania. She has published numerous articles, book chapters and monographs on the complex history of food systems in Singapore. Her works include *Eating Curries and Kway: A Cultural History of Food in Singapore* (2013).

Jennifer Yip is an assistant professor in the Department of History at the National University of Singapore. Her research interests lie in the history of modern warfare—particularly the socio-economic effects—in Republican China. She is currently finishing a monograph on military grain procurement and transportation polices during the Second Sino-Japanese War.

Faizah Zakaria is an assistant professor in the Departments of Southeast Asian Studies and Malay Studies at the National University of Singapore, where her scholarship centers on religion and ecology in island Southeast Asia. She is the author of the monograph *The Camphor Tree and the Elephant: Religion and Ecological Change in Maritime Southeast Asia* (2023) and is currently working on histories of charismatic fauna in Southeast Asia and the long-term impacts of volcanic eruptions in the region.

Bibliography

Note on Archival Records

Archival Records are identified with their full designation the first time they are cited. In each instance, the full designation is provided before the common abbreviation is used for subsequent citations. In this sense, the India Office Records in the British Library becomes "IOR" while the Henry Nicholas Ridley collection at that Royal Botanic Gardens, Kew will be referred to as "HNR" and the "National Archives of Singapore is "NAS."

Newspapers

Berita Harian
The Business Times
The Guardian
Indische Courant
Lianhe Wanbao
The Malaya Tribune
The Mid-Day Herald
The Morning Tribune
New Nation
The New Paper
New Straits Times
Singapore Chronicle and Commercial Advertiser
The Singapore Free Press and Mercantile Advertiser
Singapore Herald
The Singapore Monitor

Singapore Standard
Soerabiasch Handelsblad
The Straits Advocate
The Straits Times
The Straits Times Overland Journal
The Straits Observer
Sunday Standard
The Sunday Tribune (Singapore)
Sumatra Post
Syonan Shimbun
Taipei Times

Print Sources

Abdullah bin Abdul Kadir. "The Hikayat Abdullah, An Annotated Translation by A.H. Hill." *Journal of the Malayan Branch of the Royal Asiatic Society* 28, 3 (1955): 1–345.

Abeysinghe, Tilak and Jiaying Gu. "Lifetime Income and Housing Affordability in Singapore." *Urban Studies* 48, 9 (2011): 1875–91.

Alagirisamy, Darinee. "Toddy, Race, and Urban Space in Colonial Singapore, 1900–59." *Modern Asian Studies* 53, 5 (2019): 1675–99.

Alfred, Eric R. "The Fresh-Water Fishes of Singapore." *Zoologische Verhandelingen* 78 (1966): 3–67.

———. "Systematic Studies of the Fresh-Water Fishes of Singapore." M.S. thesis, University of Singapore, 1964.

———. "Singapore Fresh-Water Fishes." *Malayan Nature Journal* 15, 1–2 (1961): 1–19.

Allam, Zaher. *Urban Governance and Smart City Planning: Lessons from Singapore*. Bingley: Emerald Publishing Limited, 2020.

Andrew, J. and Ananya Bar. "Morphology and Morphometry of *Aedes aegypti* Adult Mosquito." *Annual Review and Research in Biology* 3, 1 (2013): 52–69.

Anonymous. *AVA: A Legacy of Excellence. A Commemorative Issue*. Singapore: AVA Vision, 2019.

———. *Control of Flies*. Singapore: Primary Production Department, 1984.

———. "Fisheries Officer Visits Cook Group." *South Pacific Commission Quarterly Bulletin* 5, 3 (1955): 34.

———. *A Guide to the Fisheries of Ceylon, Bulletin No. 8*. Colombo: Fisheries Research Station, Ceylon, 1958.

Bibliography

———. *Perihal Ikan-Moedjair*. Djakarta: Gunseikanbu Kokumin Tosyokyoku (Balai Poestaka), 2605 [1945].

———. *Review of the Primary Production Department, 1960–1965*. Singapore: Government Printing Office, 1967.

———. *Singapore Zoological Gardens Annual Report 1981*. Singapore: Singapore Zoological Gardens, 1982.

———. *Singapore Zoological Gardens Annual Report 1982*. Singapore: Singapore Zoological Gardens, 1983.

———. *Singapore Zoological Gardens Annual Report 1985*. Singapore: Singapore Zoological Gardens, 1986.

Armiero, Marco and Lise Sedrez. *A History of Environmentalism: Local Struggles, Global Histories*. London: Bloomsbury, 2014.

Atkins, Peter (ed). *Animal Cities: Beastly Urban Histories*. Farnham, Surrey: Ashgate, 2012.

Barnard, Timothy P. "Celates, Rayat-Laut, Pirates: The Orang Laut and Their Decline in History." *Journal of the Malaysian Branch of the Royal Asiatic Society* 80, 2 (2007): 33–49.

———. "Forêts Impériales et Réserves Naturelles à Singapour, 1883–1959." In *Protéger et Détruire: Gouverner la Nature sous les Tropiques (XX-XXIE siècle)*. Ed. Guillaume Blanc, Mathieu Guérin and Grégory Quenet. Paris: CNRS, 2022. Pp. 83–108.

———. *Imperial Creatures: Humans and Other Animals in Colonial Singapore, 1819–1942*. Singapore: NUS Press, 2019.

———. *Nature's Colony: Empire, Nation, and Environment in the Singapore Botanic Gardens*. Singapore: NUS Press, 2016.

———. (ed.). *Nature Contained: Environmental Histories of Singapore*. Singapore: NUS Press, 2014.

———. "The Rafflesia in the Natural and Imperial Imagination of the East India Company in Southeast Asia." In *The East India Company and the Natural World*. Ed. Vinita Damoradaran, Anna Winterbottom and Alan Lester. London: Palgrave Macmillan, 2015. Pp. 147–66.

Barnard, Timothy P. and Mark Emmanuel. "Tigers of Colonial Singapore." In *Nature Contained: Environmental Histories of Singapore*. Ed. Timothy P. Barnard. Singapore: NUS Press, 2014. Pp. 55–80.

Barnard, Timothy P. and Corinne Heng. "A City in a Garden." In *Nature Contained: Environmental Histories of Singapore*. Ed. Timothy P. Barnard. Singapore: NUS Press, 2014. Pp. 281–306.

Barnard, Timothy P. and Joanna W.C. Lee. "A Spiteful Campaign: Agriculture, Forests, and Administering the Environment in Imperial Singapore and Malaya." *Environmental History* 27, 3 (2022): 467–90.

Bibliography

Barrow, Mark V. *Nature's Ghosts: Confronting Extinction from the Age of Jefferson to the Age of Ecology*. Chicago, IL: University of Chicago Press, 2009.

Beisel, Uli, Ann H. Kelly and Noémi Tousignant. "Knowing Insects: Hosts, Vectors and Companions of Insects are Good to Think Science." *Science as Culture* 22, 1 (2013): 1–15.

Bender, Daniel E. "Dipping in the Common Sauce Pot: Satay Vending and Good Taste Politics in Colonial and Post-Colonial Singapore." *Food, Culture and Society* 24, 1 (2021): 66–83.

Biehler, Dawn Day. *Pests in the City: Flies, Bedbugs, Cockroaches, and Rats*. Seattle, WA: University of Washington Press, 2013.

Bijleveld, R. and R.S. Martoatmodjo. "Vischstand en Visscherij in West Koetei (Oost Borneo)." *Landbouw* 16, 9 (1940): 516–50.

Bird, Isabella L. *The Golden Chersonese and the Way Thither*. New York, NY: G.P. Putnam's Sons, 1883.

Blakemore, W.L. *Cockroaches*. Singapore: Singapore Government Printer, 1940.

Bolton, Melvin and Miro Laufa. "The Crocodile Project in Papua New Guinea." *Biological Conservation* 22, 3 (1982): 169–79.

Bos, Nick, et al. "Sick Ants Become Unsociable." *Journal of Evolutionary Biology* 25, 2 (2012): 342–51.

Brackhane, Sebastian, et al. "Crocodile Management in Timor-Leste: Drawing Upon Traditional Ecological Knowledge and Cultural Beliefs." *Human Dimensions of Wildlife* 24, 4 (2019): 314–31.

Braddell, Roland. *The Lights of Singapore*. London: Methuen and Co., 1934.

Brassey, Anna. *A Voyage on the Sunbeam: Our Home on the Ocean for Eleven Months*. Chicago, IL: Belford, Clarke and Co., 1881.

Briffett, Clive and Sutari bin Supari. *The Birds of Singapore*. Singapore: Oxford University Press, 1993.

Brock, Vernon E. "A Note on the Spawning of *Tilapia mossambica* in Sea Water." *Copeia* 1954, 1 (19 February 1954): 72.

Brook, Barry W., Navjot S. Sodhi and Peter K.L. Ng. "Catastrophic Extinctions Follow Deforestation in Singapore." *Nature*, 424 (24 July 2003): 420–3.

Brug, P.H. van den. "Malaria in Batavia in the 18th Century." *Tropical Medicine and International Health* 2, 9 (1997): 892–902.

Brunner, Bernd. *The Ocean at Home: An Illustrated History of the Aquarium*. London: Reaktion Books, 2011.

Buck, Frank and Edward Anthony. *Bring 'em Back Alive*. New York, NY: Simon and Schuster, 1930.

Bibliography

Bucknill, A.S. and F.N. Chasen. *Birds of Singapore and Southeast Asia*. Kuala Lumpur: Oxford University Press, 1988.

Burdon, T.W. *Report of the Fisheries Department, 1950*. Singapore: Government Printing Office, 1951.

Burkill, H.M. *Annual Report of the Botanic Gardens Department for 1961*. Singapore: Government Printing Office, 1963.

Cantley, Nathaniel. *Report on the Forests of the Straits Settlements*. Singapore: Singapore and Straits Printing Office, 1883.

Canton, N.A. *Annual Report of the Health Department 1947*. Singapore: Government Printing Office, 1949.

―――. *Annual Report of the Health Department 1951*. Singapore: Government Printing Office, 1953.

―――. *Annual Report of the Health Department 1952*. Singapore: Government Printing Office, 1954.

Castelletta, Marjorie, Navjot S. Sodhi and R. Subaraj. "Heavy Extinctions of Forest Avifauna in Singapore: Lessons for Biodiversity Conservation in Southeast Asia." *Conservation Biology* 14, 6 (2000): 1870–80.

Chacko, P.I. and B. Krishnamurthi. "Observations on *Tilapia mossambica* Peters in Madras." *Journal of the Bombay Natural History Society* 52, 2–3 (1954): 349–53.

Chan K.L. "Control of Vectors towards a Better Singapore." In *Towards a Better Singapore: Proceedings of the 1st Singapore Professional Centre Convention, 1975*. Ed. Tan It Koon. Singapore: Singapore Professional Centre, 1975. Pp. 107–17.

Chan K.L., S.K. Ang and L.M. Chew. "The 1973 Dengue Haemorrhagic Fever Outbreak in Singapore and Its Control. *Singapore Medical Journal* 18, 2 (1977): 81–93.

Chan, Lena. "Nature in the City." In *Planning Singapore: The Experimental City*. Ed. Stephen Hamnett and Belinda Yuen. London: Routledge, 2019. Pp. 109–29.

Chan Y.C., B.C. Ho and K.L. Chan. "*Aedes aegypti* (L.) and *Aedes Albopictus* (Skuse) in Singapore City." *Bulletin of the World Health Organization* 44, 5 (1971): 651–8.

Chan Ying-Kit. "No Room to Swing a Cat? Animal Treatment and Urban Space in Singapore." *Southeast Asian Studies* 5, 2 (2016): 305–29.

Chatterjea, Kalyani. "Sustainability of an Urban Forest: Bukit Timah Nature Reserve, Singapore." In *Sustainable Forest Management: Case Studies*. Ed. Martin Garcia and Julio Javier Diez. Rijeka. Croatia: InTech, 2012. Pp. 143–60.

Bibliography

Cheang Suk Wai, et al. *Living the Singapore Story – Celebrating our 50 Years: 1965–2015*. Singapore: Straits Times Press, 2015.

Chen Tung-Pai. *The Culture of Tilapia in Rice Paddies in Taiwan*. Taipei: Commission on Rural Reconstruction, 1953.

Chew, Carissa. "The Ant as Metaphor: Orientalism, Imperialism and Myrmecology." *Archives of Natural History* 46, 2 (2019): 347–61.

Choo Ruizhi. "Fishes of Empire: Imperialism and Ichthyological Introductions in British Malaya, 1923–1942." *Journal of Southeast Asian Studies* 54, 1 (2023): 44–66.

———. "Nature Condensed: A History of the Singapore Zoological Gardens." Unpublished honors thesis, Department of History, National University of Singapore, 2017.

Chou, Cynthia. "Agriculture and End of Farming in Singapore." In *Nature Contained: Environmental Histories of Singapore*. Ed. Timothy P. Barnard. Singapore: NUS Press, 2014. Pp. 216–40.

Chou Loke Ming. "Nature and Sustainability of the Marine Environment." In *Spatial Planning for a Sustainable Singapore*. Ed. Tai-Chee Wong, Belinda Yuen and Charles Goldblum. New York, NY: Springer, 2008. Pp. 169–82.

Chow C.Y. and E.S. Thevasagayam. "A Simple and Effective Device for Housefly Control with Insecticides." *Bulletin of the World Health Organization* 8, 4 (1953): 491–5.

Chua Beng Huat. "Navigating between Limits: The Future of Public Housing in Singapore." *Housing Studies* 28, 4 (2014): 520–33.

Cirillo, Vincent J. "'I Am the Baby Killer!' House Flies and the Spread of Polio." *American Entomologist* 62, 2 (2016): 83–5.

———. "'Winged Sponges': House-flies as Carriers of Typhoid Fever in 19th- and Early 20th-Century Military Camps." *Perspectives in Biology and Medicine* 49, 1 (2006): 52–63.

Clancey, Gregory. "Hygiene in a Landlord State: Health, Cleanliness and Chewing Gum in Late Twentieth Century Singapore." *Science, Technology and Society* 23, 2 (2018): 214–33.

Clark, J.F.M. *Bugs and the Victorians*. New Haven, CT: Yale University Press, 2009.

Colby, Jason M. *Orca: How We Came to Know and Love the Ocean's Greatest Predator*. New York, NY: Oxford University Press, 2018.

Corlett, Richard T. "Bukit Timah: The History and Significance of a Small Rain-Forest Reserve." *Environmental Conservation* 15, 1 (1988): 37–44.

———. "The Ecological Transformation of Singapore, 1819–1990." *Journal of Biogeography* 19, 4 (1992): 411–20.

Bibliography

Corner, E.J.H. *Annual Report of the Director of the Gardens for the Year 1937*. Singapore: Government Printing Office, 1938.

———. *Botanical Monkeys*. Cambridge: Pentland Press, 1992.

Corrigan, Amy and Louis Ng. *What's a Polar Bear Doing in the Tropics?* Singapore: Animal Concerns Research and Education Society, 2006.

Coull, James. "Will a Blue Revolution Follow the Green Revolution? The Modern Upsurge of Aquaculture." *Area* 25, 4 (1993): 350–7.

Cronon, William. "The Trouble with Wilderness: Or, Getting Back to the Wrong Nature." *Environmental History* 1, 1 (1996): 7–28.

Curtin, Philip D. "Disease and Imperialism." In *Warm Climates and Western Medicine: The Emergence of Tropical Disease, 1500–1900*. Ed. David Arnold. Amsterdam: Rodopi, 1996. Pp. 99–108.

Davis, Susan G. *Spectacular Nature: Corporate Culture and the Sea World Experience*. Berkeley, CA: University of California Press, 1997.

Davison, G.W.H. and Chew Yen Fook. *A Photographic Guides to Birds of Peninsular Malaysia and Singapore*. London: New Holland Publishers, 1995.

DeMello, Margo. *Animals and Society: An Introduction to Human-Animal Studies*. New York, NY: Columbia University Press, 2012.

Dendle, Peter. "Cryptozoology in the Medieval and Modern Worlds." *Folklore* 117, 2 (2006): 190–206.

Devadas, D.D. Peter and P.I. Chacko. "Introduction of the Exotic Cichlid, *Tilapia mossambica* Peters, in Madras." *Current Science* 22, 1 (1953): 29.

Dick, Olivia Brathwaite, et al. "The History of Dengue Outbreaks in the Americas." *American Journal of Tropical Medicine and Hygiene* 87, 4 (2012): 584–93.

Dorsey, Kurkpatrick. *Whales and Nations: Environmental Diplomacy on the High Seas*. Seattle, WA: University of Washington Press, 2013.

Douglas, Mary. *Purity and Danger: An Analysis of Concepts of Pollution and Taboo*. New York, NY: Routledge, 1966.

Douglas, Starr and Felix Driver. "Imagining the Tropical Colony: Henry Smeathman and the Termites of Sierra Leone." In *Tropical Visions in an Age of Empire*. Ed. Felix Driver and Luciana Martins. Chicago: University of Chicago Press, 2005. Pp. 91–112.

Dunham, Kevin M., et al. "Human-Wildlife Conflict in Mozambique: A National Perspective, with Emphasis on Wildlife Attacks on Humans." *Oryx* 44, 2 (2010): 185–93.

Dunlap, Thomas R. *DDT, Silent Spring, and the Rise of Environmentalism*. Seattle, WA: University of Washington Press, 2008.

Bibliography

Dworkin, J. and S.Y. Tan. "Ronald Ross (1857–1932): Discover of Malaria's Life Cycle." *Singapore Medical Journal* 52, 7 (2011): 466–7.

E., A. "Book Review of *The House-fly: Disease Carrier: An Account of Its Dangerous Activities and of the Means of Destroying It*." *Nature* 88, 2202 (1912): 345–6.

Earle, Rebecca. "'If You Eat Their Food…': Diets and Bodies in Early Colonial Spanish America." *American Historical Review* 115, 3 (2010): 688–713.

Eaton, James A., Boyd Leupen and Kanitha Krishnasamy. *Songsters of Singapore*. Petaling Jaya: TRAFFIC, 2017.

Elton, Charles S. *The Ecology of Invasions by Animals and Plants*. London: Methuen, 1958.

Evans, Joshua, Roberto Flore and Michael Nom Frøst. *On Eating Insects: Essays, Stories and Recipes*. London: Phaidon, 2017.

Ferroni, Eliana, Tom Jefferson and Gabriel Gachelin. "Angelo Celli and Research on the Prevention of Malaria in Italy a Century Ago." *Journal of the Royal Society of Medicine* 105, 1 (2012): 35–40.

Fuentes, Agustín. "Pets, Property and Partners: Macaques as Commodities in the Human-Other Primate Interface." In *The Macaque Connection: Cooperation and Conflict between Humans and Macaques*. Ed. Sindhu Radhakrishna, Michael A. Huffman and Anindya Sinha. New York, NY: Springer, 2013. Pp. 107–23.

Gervais, Paul. "Sur les Animaux Vertebres de l'Algerie: Envisages Sous le Double Rapport, de la Geographie Zoologique et de la Domestication." *Annales de Sciences Naturalles (partie zoologie)* 3, 9 (1848): 202–8.

Glenister, A.G. *The Birds of the Malay Peninsula, Singapore and Penang*. Kuala Lumpur: Oxford University Press, 1971.

Goh Hong Yi. "The Nature Society, Endangered Species and Conservation." In *Nature Contained: Environmental Histories of Singapore*. Ed. Timothy P. Barnard. Singapore: NUS Press, 2014. Pp. 245–75.

Goh, K.T. "Changing Epidemiology of Dengue in Singapore." *The Lancet* 346, 8982 (1995): 1098.

———. "Eradication of Malaria from Singapore." *Singapore Medical Journal* 24, 5 (1983): 255–68.

———. "Social and Economic Aspects of Malaria in Singapore." *The Southeast Asian Journal of Tropical Medicine and Public Health* 17, 3 (1986): 346–52.

Graetz, Michael James. "The Role of Architectural Design in Promoting the Social Objectives of Zoos: A Study of Zoo Exhibit Design with Reference to Selected Exhibits in Singapore Zoological Gardens."

Unpublished master's thesis, Faculty of Architecture and Building, National University of Singapore, 1995.

Gubler, D.J. "The Global Pandemic of Dengue/Dengue Hemorrhagic Fever: Current Status and Prospects for the Future." In *Dengue in Singapore*. Ed. K.T. Goh. Singapore: Institute of Environmental Epidemiology/Ministry of Environment, 1998. Pp. 13–32.

Gubler, Duane J. "Dengue, Urbanization and Globalization: The Unholy Trinity of the 21st Century." *Tropical Medicine and Health* 39, 4 (2011): 3–11.

Gumert, Michael D. "The Common Monkey of Southeast Asia: Long-tailed Macaque Populations, Ethnophoresy, and Their Occurrence in Human Environments." In *Monkeys on the Edge: Ecology and Management of Long-Tailed Macaques and their Interface with Humans*. Ed. Agustín Fuentes, Michael D. Gumert and Lisa Jones-Engel. Cambridge: Cambridge University Press, 2011. Pp. 3–44.

Hails, Christopher and Frank Jarvis. *Birds of Singapore*. Singapore: Marshall Cavendish, 2018.

Hale, J.H., M. Doraisingham and K. Kanagaratnam. "Large-Scale Use of Sabin Type 2 Attenuated Poliovirus Vaccine in Singapore During a Type 1 Poliomyelitis Epidemic." *The British Medical Journal* 1, 5137 (1959): 1541–9.

Hale, Richard. "From Backwater to Nature Reserve." *Nature Watch* 12, 5 (2004): 2–4.

Halstead, Scott B. "Mosquito-borne Haemorrhagic Fevers of South and South-East Asia." *Bulletin of the World Health Organization* 35, 1 (1966): 3–15.

Han Heejin. "Singapore, A Garden City: Authoritarian Environmentalism in a Developmental State." *The Journal of Environment and Development* 26, 1 (2017): 3–24.

Hanitsch, R. "Mosquito Larvae and Freshwater Fish." *Journal of the Straits Branch of the Royal Asiatic Society* 62 (1912): 26–30.

Hannig, Wolfgang. *Towards a Blue Revolution: Socioeconomic Aspects of Brackishwater Pond Cultivation in Java*. Yogyakarta: Gadjah Mada University Press, 1988.

Hanson, Elizabeth. *Animal Attractions: Nature on Display in American Zoos*. Princeton, NJ: Princeton University Press, 2002.

Hapuarachchi, Hapuarchchige Chanditha, et al. "Epidemic Resurgence of Dengue Fever in Singapore in 2013–14: A Virological and Entomological Perspective." *BMC Infectious Diseases* 16, 1 (2016): 300.

Haraway, Donna. "Anthropocene, Capitalocene, Plantationocene, Chthulucene: Making Kin." *Environmental Humanities* 6, 1 (2015): 159–65.

Henderson, Joan C. "The Survival of a Forest Fragment: Bukit Timah Nature Reserve, Singapore." In *Forest Tourism and Recreation: Case Studies in Environmental Management*. Ed. X. Font and J. Tribe. New York, NY: CABI Publishing, 2000. Pp. 23–40.

Hickling, C.F. "The Fish Culture Research Station, Malacca." *Nature* 183, 4657 (31 January 1959): 287–9.

———. "Fish Farming in the Middle and Far East." *Nature* 161, 4098 (15 May 1948): 748–51.

Hirakawa, Hitoshi and Hiroshi Shimizu. *Japan and Singapore in the World Economy: Japan's Economic Advance into Singapore 1870–1965*. London: Routledge, 1999.

Ho, Jonathan K.I., et al. *A Guide to the Freshwater Fauna of Nee Soon Swamp Forest*. Singapore: Tropical Marine Science Institute, 2016.

Hofstede, A.E. *Enige Mededelingen over Ikan Moedjair*. Batavia: Departement van Landbouw en Visserij, Onderafdeling Binnenvisserij, 1941.

Holtorf, Cornelius. "The Zoo as a Realm of Memory." *Anthropological Journal of European Cultures* 22, 1 (2013): 98–114.

Howard, Ebenezer. *Garden Cities of To-morrow*. London: Faber and Faber, 1947.

Howard, L.O. *The House-fly: Disease Carrier: An Account of Its Dangerous Activities and of the Means of Destroying It*. New York, NY: Frederick Stokes, 1911.

Huber, Pierre. *The Natural History of Ants*. London: Longman, Hurst, Rees, Orme, and Brown, 1820.

Ito, Takashi. "History of the Zoo." In *Handbook of Historical Animal Studies*. Ed. Mieke Roscher, André Krebber and Brett Mizelle. Berlin: De Gruyter Oldenbourg, 2021. Pp. 439–45.

———. "Locating the Transformation of Sensibilities in Nineteenth-Century London." In *Animal Cities: Beastly Urban Histories*. Ed. Peter Atkins. Farnham, Surrey: Ashgate, 2012. Pp. 189–204.

Jeyarajasingam, Allen and Allan Pearson. *A Field Guide to the Birds of Peninsular Malaysia and Singapore*. Oxford: Oxford University Press, 2012.

Jones, Richard. *Mosquito*. London: Reaktion Books, 2012.

Jones-Engel, Lisa, Gregory Engel, Michael D. Gumert, et al. "Developing Sustainable Human-Macaque Communities." *Monkeys on the Edge: Ecology and Management of Long-Tailed Macaques and their Interface with Humans*. Ed. Agustín Fuentes, Michael D. Gumert and Lisa Jones-Engel. Cambridge: Cambridge University Press, 2011. Pp. 295–327.

Jørgensen, Dolly. "Mixing Oil and Water: Naturalizing Offshore Oil Platforms in Gulf Coast Aquariums." *Journal of American Studies* 46, 2 (2012): 461–80.

Keller, Laurent and Elisabeth Gordon. *The Lives of Ants*. New York, NY: Oxford University Press, 2009.

Kennedy, Robert. *A Guide to the Birds of the Philippines*. Kuala Lumpur: Oxford University Press, 2000.

Keul, Adam. "Embodied Encounters between Humans and Gators." *Social and Cultural Geography* 14, 8 (2013): 930–53.

Khoo, M.D.Y. and B.P.Y.-H. Lee. "The Urban Smooth-Coated Otters *Lutrogale perspicillata* of Singapore: A Review of the Reasons for Success." *International Zoo Yearbook* 54 (2020): 60–71.

Kim Hong Chong, Lorrain. "People-Animals Relations: The Singapore Zoo and Its Sociocultural Context." Unpublished honors thesis, Department of Sociology, National University of Singapore, 1987.

Kisling, Jr., Vernon N. (ed.). *Zoo and Aquarium History: Ancient Animal Collections to Zoological Gardens*. London: CRC Press, 2001.

Koh Keng We. "Familiar Strangers and Stranger-Kings: Mobility, Diasporas, and the Foreign in the Eighteenth-Century Malay World." *Journal of Southeast Asian Studies* 48, 3 (2017): 390–413.

Kohler, Robert. "*Lords of the Fly* Revisited." *Journal of the History of Biology* 55, 1 (2022): 15–19.

Kohler, Robert E. *Lords of the Fly: Drosophila Genetics and Experimental Life*. Chicago, IL: University of Chicago Press, 1994.

Kreisberg, Jason F., et al. "Growth Inhibition of Pathogenic Bacteria by Sulfonylurea Herbicides." *Antimicrobial Agents and Chemotherapy* 57, 3 (2013): 1513–17.

Kroon, A.H. "Fish Farming." *South Pacific Commission Quarterly Bulletin* 3, 4 (1953): 15–16.

Kwa Chong Guan and Peter Borschberg (eds.). *Studying Singapore Before 1800*. Singapore: NUS Press, 2018.

Lachapelle, Sofie and Heena Mistry. "From the Waters of the Empire to the Tanks of Paris: The Creation and Early Years of the Aquarium Tropical, Palais de la Porte Dorée." *Journal of the History of Biology* 47 (2014): 1–27.

Lam-Phua, Sai-Gek, et al., "Mosquitoes (Diptera: Culcidae) of Singapore: Updated Checklist and New Records." *Journal of Medical Entomology* 56, 1 (2019): 103–19.

Lambrechts, Louis, et al. "Impact of Daily Temperature Fluctuations on Dengue Virus Transmission by *Aedes aegypti*." *Proceedings of the National Academy of Sciences of the United States of America* 108, 18 (2011): 7460–5.

Langham-Carter, W. *Report on the Forest Reserves of the Straits Settlements during the Year 1901*. Singapore: Government Printing Office, 1902.

Law, Yao-Hua. "Long Live the Queen: In Insect Societies, a Queen Can Live for Years, Whereas Workers Expire in Months. What Can Hives and Anthills Reveal about Aging?" *Science* 371, 6536 (2021): 1201–1305.

Layton, Lesley. *Songbirds in Singapore: The Growth of a Pastime*. Singapore: Oxford University Press, 1991.

Le Mare, D.W. "Application of the Principles of Fish Culture to Estuarine Conditions in Singapore." *Proceedings of the Indo-Pacific Fisheries Council, 2nd Meeting, Bangkok* (1951): 180–3.

———. *Report of the Fisheries Department, Malaya, 1948*. Singapore: Government Printing Office, 1949.

———. *Report of the Fisheries Department, Malaya, 1949*. Singapore: Government Printing Office, 1950.

Lee, Benjamin P.Y-H. and Sharon Chan. "Lessons and Challenges in the Management of Long-Tailed Macaques in Urban Singapore." In *Monkeys on the Edge: Ecology and Management of Long-Tailed Macaques and Their Interface with Humans*. Ed. Micheal D. Gumert, Agustín Fuentes and Lisa Jones-Engel. Cambridge: Cambridge University Press, 2011. Pp. 307–12.

Lee, Jessica G.H., Serene C.L. Chng and James A. Eaton. *Conservation Strategy for Southeast Asian Songbirds in Trade. Recommendation from the First Asian Songbird Trade Crisis Summit*. Singapore: Wildlife Reserves Singapore/TRAFFIC, 2015.

Lee, Kim (ed.). *Singapore Waters: Unveiling Our Seas*. Singapore: Nature Society Singapore, 2003.

Lee Kuan Yew. *From Third World to First: The Singapore Story: 1965–2000*. Singapore: Singapore Press Holdings, 2000.

Lee L.H. and K.A. Lim. "Prevention of Poliomyelitis in Singapore by Live Vaccine." *British Medical Journal* 1, 5390 (1964): 1077–80.

Lee S.K. and S.E. Chua. *More than a Garden City*. Singapore: Parks and Recreation Department, Ministry of National Development, 1992.

Leong-Salobir, Cecilia. *Food Culture in Colonial Asia: A Taste of Empire*. New York, NY: Routledge, 2011.

Levi-Strauss, Claude. *Totemism*. Tr. Rodney Needham. Boston, MA: Beacon Press, 1971.

Lewis, Simon L. "Defining the Anthropocene." *Nature* 519 (2015): 171–80.

Li Yongqiu. 专吃华人的鳄鱼：老太平的民间故事 *Zhuanmen chiren de e'yu: Lao Taiping de minjian gushi* [Crocodiles that Eat Chinese People: Folktales and Stories from Old Taiping (Malaysia)]. Taiping: Li Yongqiu, 2019.

Liao I-Chiu and His-Chiang Liu. "Exotic Aquatic Species in Taiwan." In *Exotic Aquatic Organisms in Asia: Proceedings of a Workshop on Introduction of Exotic Aquatic Organisms in Asia*. Ed. Sena S. de Silva Manila: Asian Fisheries Society, 1989. Pp. 101–18.

Liboiron, Max. "Waste Is Not 'Matter Out of Place'," *Discard Studies* (2019), https://discardstudies.com/2019/09/09/waste-is-not-matter-out-of-place/.

Liew, C., et al. "Community Engagement for *Wolbachia*-Based *Aedes aegypti* Population Suppression for Dengue Control: The Singapore Experience." In *Area-Wide Integrated Pest Management: Development and Field Application*. Ed. Jorge Heindrichs, Rui Pereira and Marc J.B. Vreysen. Boca Rotan, FL: CRC Press, 2020. Pp. 747–61.

Liew J.H., et al. "Ecology and Origin of the Introduced Cichlid *Acarichthys heckelii* in Singapore's Fresh Waters—First Instance of Establishment." *Environmental Biology of Fishes* 97 (2013): 1109–18.

———. "Some Cichlid Fishes Recorded in Singapore." *Nature in Singapore* 5 (2012): 229–36.

Liew Kai Khiun. "Making Health Public: English Language Newspapers and the Medical Sciences in Colonial Malaya (1840s–1941)." *East Asian Science, Technology and Society* 3, 2 (2009): 209–29.

Lim, Kelvin K.P. and Peter K.L. Ng. *A Guide to Common Freshwater Fishes of Singapore*. Singapore: Singapore Science Centre, 1990.

Lim Kim Seng. *The Avifauna of Singapore*. Singapore: Singapore Nature Society, 2009.

Lim Kim Seng, Yong Ding Li and Lim Kim Chuah. *Birds of Malaysia and Singapore*. Princeton, NJ: Princeton University Press, 2020.

Lin, S.Y. "Fish Culture Project in Haiti." *Proceedings of the Gulf and Caribbean Fisheries Institute* 4 (1952): 110–18.

Ling Kai Huat. "Public Aquarium Management: A Case Study of the Van Kleef Aquarium." In *Aquarama Proceedings: First International Aquarium Fish and Accessories Conference*. Ed. John A. Dawes. Singapore: Academic Associates, 1991. Pp. 114–18.

Linquist, Stefan. "Today's Awe-Inspiring Design, Tomorrow's Plexiglas Dinosaur: How Public Aquariums Contradict Their Conservation

Mandate in Pursuit of Immersive Underwater Displays." In *The Ark and Beyond: The Evolution of Zoo and Aquarium Conservation*. Ed. Ben A. Minteer, Jane Maienschein and James P. Collins. London: University of Chicago Press, 2018. Pp. 329–43.

Loh Kah Seng. *Squatters into Citizens: The 1961 Bukit Ho Swee Fire and the Making of Modern Singapore*. Singapore: NUS Press, 2013.

Low, Linda, et al. *Challenge and Response: Thirty Years of the Economic Development Board*. Singapore: Times Academic Press, 1993.

Lowe-McConnell, Rosemary H. "Species of Tilapia in East African Dams, with a Key for Their Identification." *East African Agricultural Journal* 20, 4 (1955): 256–62.

Lucas Peter W. and Richard T. Corlett. "Relationship between the Diet of *Macaca fascicularis* and Forest Phenology." *Folia Primatologica* 57, 4 (1991): 201–15.

Lucy, Armand. *Souvenirs de Voyage: Lettres Intimes sur la Campagne de Chine en 1860*. Marseille: Imprimerie et Lithographie Jules Barile, 1861.

Luff, Noel. "A Change in Attitude: Where Did the Indian Myna Go Wrong?" *Canberra Bird Notes* 41, 2 (2016): 118–23.

Luo, X.W., S.C. Foo and H.Y. Ong. "Serum DDT and DDE levels in Singapore General Population." *The Science of the Total Environment* 208, 1 (1997): 97–104.

Mahato, Dharmendra Prasad and Ravi Shankar Singh. "Maximizing Availability for Task Scheduling in On-Demand Computing-Based Transaction Processing System Using Ant Colony Optimisation." *Concurrency and Computation Practice and Experience* 30, 11 (2018): e4405.

Malhi, Yadvinder. "The Concept of the Anthropocene." *Annual Review of Environment and Resources* 42 (2017): 77–104.

Matwick, Keri and Kelsi Matwick. "Comics and Humor as a Mode of Communication on Public Hygiene Posters in Singapore." *Discourse, Context and Media* 46, 1 (2022): 100590.

Mauzy, Diane K. and R.S. Milne. *Singapore Politics under the People's Action Party*. London: Routledge, 2002.

McNair, J.F. *Perak and the Malays: Sarong and Keris*. Kuala Lumpur: Oxford University Press, 1972.

McNeill, J.R. and Peter Engelke, *The Great Acceleration: An Environmental History of the Anthropocene since 1945*. Cambridge, MA: Harvard University Press, 2016.

Bibliography

Miksic, John N. "Recent Archaeological Excavations in Singapore: A Comparison of Three Fourteenth-Century Sites." *Bulletin of the Indo-Pacific Prehistory Association* 20, 4 (2000): 56–61.

Morrison, H.R. *Annual Report of the Health Department 1956*. Singapore: Government Printing Office, 1957.

———. *Annual Report of the Health Department 1957*. Singapore: Government Printing Office, 1959.

Moss, Stephen. *Urban Aviary: A Modern Guide to City Birds*. London: White Lion Publishing, 2019.

Msangi, A.S. "The Value of Spreading Agent in Larvicidal Formulations Containing DDT." *Bulletin of the World Health Organization* 21, 6 (1959): 773–8.

Muka, Samantha. "Conservation Constellations: Aquariums in Aquatic Conservation Networks." In *The Ark and Beyond: The Evolution of Zoo and Aquarium Conservation*. Ed. Ben A. Minteer, Jane Maienschein and James P. Collins. London: University of Chicago Press, 2018. Pp. 90–104.

Mullan, Bob and Garry Marvin. *Zoo Culture*. Chicago, IL: Illinois: University of Illinois Press, 1999.

Mumford, Lewis. *The City in History*. New York, NY: Harcourt, Brace and World, 1961.

Naim, Sidrotun. "Growth, Vibriosis, and Streptococcosis Management in Shrimp-Tilapia Polyculture Systems, and the Role of Quorum Sensing Gene cqsS in Vibrio harveyi Virulence." Unpublished PhD thesis, University of Arizona, 2012.

Nathanson, Neal and Olen M. Kew. "Emergence to Eradication: The Epidemiology of Poliomyelitis Deconstructed." *American Journal of Epidemiology* 172, 11 (2010): 1213–29.

Neo, Harvey. "Challenging the Developmental State: Nature Conservation in Singapore." *Asia-Pacific Viewpoint* 48, 2 (2007): 186–99.

———. "Placing Pig Farming in Post-Independence Singapore: Community, Development and Landscapes of Rurality." In *Food, Foodways, and Foodscapes: Culture, Community and Consumption in Post-Colonial Singapore*. Ed. Lily Kong and Vineeta Sinha. Singapore: World Scientific, 2016. Pp. 83–102.

Neville, Warwick. "The Impact of Economic Development on Land Functions in Singapore." *Geoforum* 24, 2 (1993): 143–63.

Newman, Peter. "Biophilic Urbanism: A Case Study on Singapore." *Australian Planner* 51, 1 (2014): 47–65.

Ng Heok Hee and Heok Hui Tan. "An Annotated Checklist of the Non-Native Freshwater Fish Species in the Reservoirs of Singapore." *Cosmos* 6 (2010): 107–11.

Ng, Peter K.L. and N. Sivasothi (eds.). *A Guide to the Mangroves of Singapore*. Singapore: Singapore Science Centre, 1999.

Ng, See Yook. *Report of the Ministry of Health for the Year Ended 31st December, 1962*. Singapore: Government Publications Bureau, 1963.

Nichols, Kyle and Bina Gogineni. "The Anthropocene's Dating Problem: Insights with Geosciences and the Humanities." *The Anthropocene Review* 5, 2 (2018): 107–19.

O'Dempsey, Tony. "Singapore's Changing Landscape since c. 1800." In *Nature Contained: Environmental Histories of Singapore*. Ed. Timothy P. Barnard. Singapore: NUS Press, 2014. Pp. 17–48.

O'Neill, Jesse. "Clean and Disciplined: The Garden City in Singapore." In *The Culture of Nature in the History of Design*. Ed. Kjetil Fallan. New York, NY: Routledge, 2019. Pp. 89–101

Ooi, Eng-Eong, Kee-Tai Goh and Duane J. Gubler. "Dengue Prevention and 35 Years of Vector Control in Singapore." *Emerging Infectious Diseases* 12, 6 (2006): 887–93.

Oswin, Natalie. *Global City Futures: Desire and Development in Singapore*. Athens, Georgia: University of Georgia Press, 2019.

Owen, G.P. "Shikar." In *One Hundred Years of Singapore, Being an Account of the Capital of the Straits Settlements from its Foundation by Sir Stamford Raffles on the 6th February 1819 to the 6th February 1919*, vol. II. Ed. Walter Makepeace, Gilbert E. Brooke and Roland St. J. Braddell. London: John Murray, 1921. Pp. 367–80.

Owen, Norman. "Economic and Social Change." In *The Cambridge History of Southeast Asia. Volume 2. The Nineteenth and Twentieth Centuries*. Ed. Nicholas Tarling. Cambridge: Cambridge University Press, 1993. Pp. 467–528.

Parreñas, Juno Salazar. "The Materiality of Intimacy in Wildlife Rehabilitation: Rethinking Ethical Capitalism through Embodied Encounters with Animals in Southeast Asia." *positions: asia critique* 24, 1 (2016): 97–110.

Payne, W.J.A. "Sigatoka Agricultural Station (2)." *South Pacific Commission Quarterly Bulletin* 5, 3 (1955): 27–9.

Peters, Wilhelm C.H. "Diagnosen von neuen Flussfischen aus Mossambique." *Bericht über die zur Bekanntmachung geeigneten Verhandlungen der Königlichen Preussische Akademie der Wissenschaften zu Berlin* (1852): 275–6, 681–5.

Philo, Chris. "Animals, Geography, and the City: Notes on Inclusions and Exclusions." In *Animal Geographies, Place, Politics, and Identity in the Nature-Culture Borderlands*. Ed. Jennifer Wolch and Jody Emel. London: Verso, 1998. Pp. 51–71.

Ploeg, Jan van der, Merlijn van Weerd and Gerard A. Persoon. "A Cultural History of Crocodiles in the Philippines: Towards a New Peace Pact?" *Environment and History* 17, 2 (2011): 229–64.

Pocklington, Kate. *Beast, Guardian, Island: The Saltwater Crocodile (Crocodylus porosus Schneider, 1801) in Singapore, 1819–2017*. Singapore: Lee Kong Chian Natural History Museum, 2021.

Pocklington, Kate and Siddharta Perez, "Revulsion and Reverence: Crocodiles in Singapore." *BiblioAsia* 14, 2 (2018): 14–19.

Pooley, Simon. "Using Predator Attack Data to Save Lives, Human and Crocodilian." *Oryx* 49, 4 (2015): 581–3.

Poorter, Lourens, et al. "Multidimensional Tropical Forest Recovery." *Science* 374, 6573 (2021): 1370–6.

Pöttker, Horst. "The Detached Observer: On a Necessary Change to the Self-image of Journalists in the Digital World." *Javnost-The Public* 25, 1/2 (2018): 169–73.

Powell, Miles A. *Vanishing America: Species Extinction, Racial Peril and the Origins of Conservation*. Cambridge, MA: Harvard University Press, 2016.

Powell, Miles Alexander. "Harnessing the Great Acceleration: Connecting Local and Global Environmental History at the Port of Singapore." *Environmental History* 27, 3 (2022): 441–66.

———. "People in Peril, Environments at Risk: Coolies, Tigers, and Colonial Singapore's Ecology of Poverty." *Environment and History* 22, 3 (2016): 455–82.

———. "Singapore's Lost Coast: Land Reclamation, National Development and the Erasure of Human and Ecological Communities, 1822–Present." *Environment and History* 27, 4 (2021): 635–63.

Raffles, Hugh. *Insectapedia*. New York, NY: Vintage Books, 2011.

Raffles, Thomas Stamford. "Descriptive Catalogue of a Zoological Collection Made on Account of the Honourable East India Company, in the Island of Sumatra and Its Vicinity." *The Transactions of the Linnean Society of London* 13, 1 (1821): 239–74.

Rajarethinam, Jayanthi, et al. "Dengue in Singapore from 2004 to 2016: Cyclical Epidemic Patterns Dominated by Serotypes 1 and 2." *American Journal of Tropical Medicine* 99, 1 (2018): 204–10.

Randall, John E. "Introductions of Marine Fishes to the Hawaiian Islands." *Bulletin of Marine Science* 41, 2 (1987): 490–502.

Rapson, A.M. "Fisheries Development in Papua and New Guinea." *South Pacific Commission Quarterly Bulletin* 9, 4 (1959): 24–5.

———. "Fishery Investigations in Papua And New Guinea." *South Pacific Commission Quarterly Bulletin* 5, 3 (July 1955): 20, 24.

Reid, J.A. *Notes on House-Flies and Blow-Flies in Malaya*. Kuala Lumpur: Government Press, 1953.

Reiter, P. "Dengue Control in Singapore." In *Dengue in Singapore*. Ed. K.T. Goh. Singapore: Institute of Environmental Epidemiology/Ministry of Environment, 1998. Pp. 213–42.

Ridley, H.N. *Annual Report on the Botanic Gardens and Forest Department for the Year 1903*. Singapore: Government Printing Office, 1904.

———. "The Menagerie at the Botanic Gardens." *Journal of the Straits Branch of the Royal Asiatic Society* 46 (1906): 133–94.

Robichaud, Andrew B. *Animal City: The Domestication of America*. Cambridge: Harvard University Press, 2019.

Robinson, Phillip T. and Ralph A. Lewin. "The Greening of Polar Bears in Zoos." *Nature* 278, 5703 (1979): 445–7.

Rogers, Nancy. *Dirt and Disease: Polio before FDR*. New Brunswick, NJ: Rutgers University Press, 1992.

Roy, Rohan Deb. "White Ants, Empire, and Entomo-Politics in South Asia." *Historical Journal* 63, 2 (2020): 411–36.

Sachlan, M. "Artinja Ikan Mudjair bagi Rakjat Indonesia." *Berita Perikanan* 3, 5-6 (1951): 74–6.

Salleh, Muhammad Haji (tr.). *The Epic of Hang Tuah*. Kuala Lumpur: Institut Terjemahan Negara Malaysia, 2010.

Samuelson, James. *Humble Creatures: The Earthworm and the Common Housefly: In Eight Letters*. London: Van Voorst, 1858.

Samways, Michael. "Translocating Fauna to Foreign Lands: Here Comes the Homogenocene." *Journal of Insect Conservation* 3, 2 (1999): 65–6.

Sanusi, Yahaya and Hidayah Amin. *Kampung Tempe: Voices from a Malay Village*. Singapore: Helang Books, 2016.

Saw Swee-Hock. "Population Trends in Singapore, 1819–1967." *Journal of Southeast Asian History* 10, 1 (1969): 36–49.

Scharf, J.W., D.W.G. Faris and W.A. Nicholas. *Malaria-Mosquito Control in Rural Singapore*. Singapore: Government Printing Office, 1937.

Schneider-Mayerson, Matthew. "Introduction: Seeing Singapore with New Eyes." In *Eating Chilli Crab in the Anthropocene: Environmental Perspectives on Life in Singapore*. Ed. Matthew Schneider-Mayerson. Singapore: Ethos Books, 2019. Pp. 9–17.

Schofield, Diane. "Viewing Van Kleef." *Aquarium Journal* 36, 8 (1965): 394–9.

Schuster, W.H. and R. Rustami Djajadiredja. *Mas'alah tentang Pemasukan dan Pemindahan Ikan di Indonesia*. Bandung: Djawatan Pusat Pertanian, 1950.

Schuurman, J.J. and K.F. Vaas. "Het Rawa-Complex te Tjampoerdarat als Visscherij-Object." *Landbouw: Landbouwkundig Tijdschrift voor Nederlandsch Indie* 17, 1 (1941): 13–55.

Sevea, Teren. *Miracles and Material Life: Rice, Ore, Traps and Guns in Islamic Malaysia*. Cambridge: Cambridge University Press, 2020.

Sha, John Chih Min, et al. "Macaque-Human Interactions and the Societal Perceptions of Macaques in Singapore." *American Journal of Primatology* 71, 10 (2009): 825–39.

———. "Status of the Long-Tailed Macaque *Macaca fascicularis* in Singapore and Implications for Management." *Biodiversity and Conservation* 18, 11 (2009): 2909–26.

Sharma, V.P. "Water, Mosquitoes and Malaria." In *Water and Health*. Ed. P.P. Singh and V. Sharma. New Delhi: Springer India, 2014. Pp. 155–68.

Sharp, Ilsa. *The First 21 Years: The Singapore Zoological Gardens Story*. Singapore: Singapore Zoological Gardens, 1994.

Sim Shuzhen, et al. "A Greener Vision for Vector Control: The Examples of the Singapore Dengue Control Programme." *PloS Neglected Tropical Diseases* 14, 8 (2020): e0008428.

Simothy, Leckranee, Fawzi Mahomoodally and Hudaa Neetoo. "A Study on the Potential of Ants to Act as Vectors of Foodborne Pathogens." *AIMS Microbiology* 4, 2 (2018): 319–33.

Sivosathi, N. and Burhanuddin Hj. Md. Nor. "A Review of Otters (Carnivora: Mustalidae: Lutrinae) in Malaysia and Singapore. In *Ecology and Conservation of Southeast Asian Marine and Freshwater Environments including Wetland. Developments in Hydrobiology*. Ed. A. Sasekumar, N. Marshall, and D.J. Macintosh. Dordrecht: Springer, 1994. Pp. 151–70.

Sleigh, Charlotte. *Six Legs Better: A Cultural History of Myrmecology*. Baltimore, MD: Johns Hopkins University Press, 2007.

Soeseno, Raden Slamet. *Ikan Mudjair: Ikan yang Termurah*. Djakarta: Pustaka Rakjat, 1954.

Stapleton, Darwin H. "Lessons of History? Anti-Malaria Strategies of the International Health Board and the Rockefeller Foundation from the 1920s to the Era of DDT." *Public Health Reports* 119, 2 (2004): 206–15.

———. "A Lost Chapter in the Early History of DDT: The Development of Anti-Typhus Technologies by the Rockefeller Foundation's Louse Laboratory, 1942–1944." *Technology and Culture* 46, 3 (2005): 513–40.

Stauffer. J.R., et al. "Cichlid Fish Diversity and Speciation." In *Reconstructing the Tree of Life: Taxonomy and Systematics of Species Rich Taxa*. Ed. Trevor R. Hodkinson and John A.N. Parnell. Boca Raton, Fl.: CRC Press, 2007. Pp. 213–25.

Steffen, Will, et al. "The Anthropocene: Conceptual and Historical Perspectives." *Philosophical Transactions of the Royal Society* 369, 1938 (2011): 842–67.

Struchiner, Claudio Jose, et al. "Increasing Dengue Incidence in Singapore over the Past 40 Years: Population Growth, Climate and Mobility." *PloS ONE* 10, 8 (2015): e0136286.

Stubbs, Richard. "War and Economic Development: Export-Oriented Industrialization in East and Southeast Asia." *Comparative Politics* 31, 3 (1999): 337–55.

Tan, B.T. and B.T. Teo. "Modus Operandi in *Aedes* Surveillance and Control." In *Dengue in Singapore*. Ed. K.T. Goh. Singapore: Institute of Environmental Epidemiology/Ministry of Environment, 1998. Pp. 108–23.

Tan Boon Teng, "New Initiatives in Dengue Control in Singapore." *Dengue Bulletin* 25 (2001): 1–6.

Tan Delfinn Sweimay. "The History of Koi Aquaculture in Singapore from 1965 to the Present: Translating Translocated Scientific Knowledge from Japan into Biosecurity." Unpublished PhD dissertation, Nanyang Technological University, 2018.

Tan, Fiona L.P. "The Beastly Business of Regulating the Wildlife Trade in Colonial Singapore." In *Nature Contained: Environmental Histories of Singapore*. Ed. Timothy P. Barnard. Singapore: NUS Press, 2014. Pp. 145–78.

Tan Heok Hui, et al. "The Non-Native Freshwater Fishes of Singapore: An Annotated Compilation." *Raffles Bulletin of Zoology* 68 (2020): 150–95.

Tarulevicz, Nicole. "Sensing Safety in Singapore." *Food, Culture and Society* 21, 2 (2018): 164–79.

Tarulevicz, Nicole and Can Seng Ooi. "Food Safety and Tourism in Singapore: Between Microbial Russian Roulette and Michelin Stars." *Tourism Geographies* 23, 4 (2021): 810–32.

Teo Siew Eng and Victor R. Savage. "Singapore Landscape: A Historical Overview of Housing Change." *Singapore Journal of Tropical Geography* 6, 1 (1985): 48–63.

Theng, Meryl and N. Sivasothi. "The Smooth-Coated Otter *Lutrogale perspicillata* (Mammalia: Mustelidae) in Singapore: Establishment and Expansion in Natural and Semi-Urban Environments." *IUCN Otter Specialist Group Bulletin* 33, 1 (2016): 37–49.

Thomson, J.T. *Some Glimpses into Life in the Far East.* London: Richardson and Company, 1864.

Tong Cheu Hock. "The Datuk Kong Spirit Cult Movement in Penang: Being and Belonging in Multi-ethnic Malaysia." *Journal of Southeast Asian Studies* 23, 2 (1992): 381–404.

Tortajada, Cecilia, Yugal Joshi and Asit K. Biswas. *The Singapore Water Story: Sustainable Development in an Urban City-State.* Oxon: Routledge, 2013.

Triantafillou, Peter. "Governing Agricultural Progress: A Genealogy of the Politics of Pest Control in Malaysia." *Comparative Studies in Society and History* 43, 1 (2001): 193–221.

Trocki, Carl A. *Singapore: Wealth, Power and the Culture of Control.* London: Routledge, 2006.

Tuan, Yi-Fu. *Dominance and Affection: The Making of Pets.* New Haven, CT: Yale University Press, 1984.

Tweedie, M.W.F. "The Stone Age in Malaya." *Journal of the Malayan Branch of the Royal Asiatic Society* 26, 2 (1953): 3–90.

Vaas, K.F. "Biologische Inventarisatie van de Binnenvisserij in Indonesie." *Landbouw: Landbouwkundig Tijdschrift voor Nederlandsch Indie* 29, 11–12 (1947): 522–43.

Vaas, K.F. and J.J. Schuurman. "On the Ecology and Fisheries of Some Javanese Freshwaters." *Mededelingen van het Algemeen Proefstation voor de Landbouw* 97 (1949): 20–30, 40–54.

Van Driesche, Jason and Roy Van Driesche. *Nature Out of Place: Biological Invasions in the Global Age.* Washington, D.C.: Island Press, 2000.

Van Pel, H. "Fisheries in the South Pacific." *South Pacific Commission Quarterly Bulletin* 5, 3 (1955): 2–4.

———. "Pond Culture of Tilapia." *South Pacific Commission Quarterly Bulletin* 5, 3 (1955): 30–1.

Wadewitz, Lissa. "Are Fish Wildlife?" *Environmental History* 16, 3 (2011): 424–7.

Walker, Sally. "Zoological Gardens of Asia." In *Zoo and Aquarium History: Ancient Animal Collections to Zoological Gardens.* Ed. Vernon L. Kisling, Jr. London: CRC Press, 2001. Pp. 239–74.

Wassermann, Edward. *Velvet Voyaging.* London: John Lane, 1940.

Bibliography

Watson, Malcolm. "Malaria and Mosquitoes: Forty Years On." *Journal of the Royal Society of Arts* 87, 4 (1939): 482–502.

———. *The Prevention of Malaria in the Federated Malay States: A Record of Twenty Years' Progress*. New York, NY: E.P. Dutton and Company, 1921.

Wee, Y.C. and R. Hale. "The Nature Society (Singapore) and the Struggle to Conserve Singapore's Nature Areas." *Nature in Singapore* 1 (2008): 41–9.

Williamson, Fiona. "Responding to Extremes: Managing Urban Water Scarcity in the late Nineteenth-Century Straits Settlements." *Water History* 12, 3 (2020): 251–63.

Willis, A.C. *Willis's Singapore Guide*. Singapore: Advertising and Policy Bureau, 1936.

Winachukul, Thongchai. *Siam Mapped: A History of the Geo-Body of a Nation*. Honolulu, HI: University of Hawai'i Press, 1994.

Winegard, Timothy C. *The Mosquito: A Human History of Our Deadliest Predator*. New York, NY: Dutton, 2019.

Winstedt, Richard Olaf. "'Karamat': Sacred Places and Persons in Malaya." *Journal of the Malayan Branch of the Royal Asiatic Society* 2, 3 (1924): 264–79.

Wolch, Jennifer. "Anima urbis." *Progress in Human Geography* 26, 6 (2002): 721–42.

Wolford, Wendy. "The Plantationocene: A Lusotropical Contribution to Theory." *Annals of the American Association of Geographers* 111, 6 (2021): 1622–39.

Wong Hong Suen. *Wartime Kitchen: Food and Eating in Singapore, 1942–1950*. Singapore: Editions Didier Millet, 2009.

Wong Soon Huat, Felix. "The Spread and Relative Abundance of the Non-Native White-Crested Laughingthrush *Garrulax leucolophus* and Lineated Barbet *Megalaima lineata* in Singapore." *Forktail* 30 (2014): 90–5.

Worboys, Michael. "Germs, Malaria and the Invention of Mansonian Tropical Medicine: From 'Diseases of the Tropics' to 'Tropical Diseases'." In *Warm Climates and Western Medicine: The Emergence of Tropical Disease, 1500–1900*. Ed. David Arnold. Amsterdam: Rodopi, 1996. Pp. 181–207.

Worm, Boris. "Silent Spring in the Ocean." *Proceedings of the National Academy of Science* 112 (2015): 11752–3.

Worm, Boris and Robert T. Paine. "Humans as a Hyperkeystone Species." *Trends in Ecology and Evolution* 31, 8 (2016): 600–7.

Yang, Hsu Li and Vincent Pang Junxiong. *Infectious Diseases and Singapore: Past, Present, and Future*. Singapore: Society of Infectious Diseases, 2015.

Bibliography

Yap, Charlotte, Navjot S. Sodhi and Barry W. Brook. "Roost Characteristics of Invasive Mynas in Singapore." *Journal of Wildlife Management* 66, 4 (2002): 1118–27.

Yee, Alex Thiam Koon, et al. "Updating the Classification System for the Secondary Forests of Singapore." *Raffles Bulletin of Zoology* 32 (2016): 11–21.

———. "The Vegetation of Singapore – An Updated Map." *Gardens' Bulletin Singapore* 63, 1/2 (2011): 205–12.

Yeh, Stephen H.K. "The Idea of the Garden City." In *Management of Success: The Moulding of Modern Singapore*. Ed. K.S. Sandhu and P. Wheatley. Singapore: Institute of Southeast Asian Studies, 1989. Pp. 810–19.

———. "Some Trends and Prospects in Singapore's Public Housing." *Ekistics* 33, 196 (Mar 1972): 182–5.

Yeo, Jun-Han and Harvey Neo. "Monkey Business: Human-Animal Conflicts in Urban Singapore." *Social and Cultural Geography* 11, 7 (2010): 681–99.

Yip Ka-Che. *Disease, Colonialism, and the State: Malaria in Modern East Asian History*. Hong Kong: Hong Kong University Press, 2009.

Yong, D.L. and Lim K.C. *A Naturalist's Guide to the Birds of Singapore*. Oxford: John Beaufoy Publishing, 2016.

Yong, Ding Li, et al. "Multiple Records of Aquatic Alien and Invasive Species in Diets of Native Predators in Singapore." *BioInvasions Records* 3, 3 (2014): 201–5.

Yuen, Belinda. "Creating the Garden City: The Singapore Experience." *Urban Studies* 33, 6 (1996): 955–70.

Zakaria, Faizah. *The Camphor Tree and the Elephant: Religion and Ecological Change in Maritime Southeast Asia*. Seattle, WA: University of Washington Press, 2023.

Index

Agri-Food Veterinary Authority (AVA), 13–14, 153, 154
Ah Meng (*see also* orangutan), 232–4, 246n64, 247–8
Alfred, Eric Ronald, 37–8
Animal Concerns Research and Education Society (ACRES), 153–4, 174, 211, 213, 243–5
ants, 42–50
Anthropocene, 4–11
aquariums, 16–17, 118, 186–214
    general history of, 190–2
Arkhurst, Frederick, 192–3

Balestier Road, 1
Basapa, William Lawrence Soma, 190
birds (*see also* individual species), 8, 156–85
    bird fights/contests, 162
Bird, Isabella, 67, 160
blue revolution, 35–6
Bridges, Lloyd, 140
        starring in *San Francisco International Airport*, 140

Bukit Timah Nature Reserve, 40, 81, 149–50
Burkill, Humphrey Morrison, 20, 133–9

cats, 16, 43n6, 53, 119, 141, 147
Central Catchment Area, 7, 9, 12n21, 40, 145–50, 183, 215, 232
cichlids (*see also* tilapia), 19–22, 23, 30, 34–8, 40
City Council, Singapore, 49, 76n20, 191–8, 221
cockroaches, 42, 43–4, 49, 59–62, 64, 160
Colbourne Report of 1966, 82–4
Corner, E.J.H, 10, 132n13
coral reefs, 126
COVID-19 pandemic, 1–3, 98
crocodile (*Crocodile porosus*), 16, 21, 100–25
    buaya putih (white crocodile), 121–3
    farms, 115–18
cryptozoology, 121–5

274

Index

culling, 134–8, 139–47, 148–54, 160n8, 178, 179

Dalvey Estate, 139, 144–5
DDT (dichlorodiphenyltrichloroethane), 61–4, 65n48, 79–81, 91
dengue fever, 69, 82n31, 83–99
    Specifics on the disease of, 83–5
dolphins (Indo-Pacific humpbacked, *Sousa chinensis*), 186–8, 205, 210–14

Economic Development Board, 115

Farquhar, William, 102
fish (*see also* specific species), 2, 19–40
Flit (*see also* pesticide), 60–2
fly (*see* housefly)
fogging (anti-mosquito measure), 87, 91, 96
Fraser-Brunner, A., 198–200
Fuyong Estate, 81

Garden City, 11–13, 43, 89–90, 92, 94, 100–1, 112, 114, 118, 128–9, 146–50, 151–4, 158, 168–9, 181–5, 224–6, 247
Goh Keng Swee, 115, 215–16, 223–5, 230
gorilla (*Gorilla gorilla*), 235–7

Harrison, Bernard Ming-Deh, 234–5, 242
housefly (*Musca domestica*), 42, 49–59
Housing and Development Board (HDB), 85, 99, 111–12, 163–6, 171

Impounding Reservoir (*see also* MacRitchie Reservoir), 104
industry, aquarium fish, 201–4
    crocodiles, 115–17
insects (*see also* specific species), 14–15, 41–66, 67–99
Inuka (*see also* polar bear), 218, 240–6, 247
Istana Woodneuk, 144

Japanese Occupation (*see* Second World War)
Java, 22–5, 38, 70n6, 73n12
Javan myna (*Acridotheres javanicus*), 9, 158–61, 173n39, 177–84
Johor, 2, 6, 103, 116, 122
    sultan of, 144
Jurong, 33, 103, 109, 111–14, 163,
Jurong Bird Park, 166, 172, 203, 212, 230, 247

keramat, 108–9, 122
koi fish (*Cyprinus rubrofuscus*), 2, 202
Komodo dragon (*Varanus komodiensis*), 235, 237

Laycock, John, 52
Lee Hsien Loong, 245–6
Lee Kong Chian Natural History Museum (*see also* Raffles Museum), 39
Lee Kuan Yew, 139, 163, 168, 202, 225
legislation, 47–8, 73–4, 86–7, 96, 147–8, 151–2
    anti-mosquito, 73–4, 86–7, 96
LeMare, D.W., 27, 29, 32
Lim Boon Keng, 74–5

275

Index

macaques (*Macaca fascicularis*), 127–55
MacRitchie Reservoir, 103, 112, 145, 150, 153, 225, 232
malaria, 64, 68–82
    anti-malarial committee, 71–6
Malayan Fisheries Department, 27, 30–4
Middleton, W.R.C., 71–2
Moedjair, Hadji (Iwan Dalauk), 22–5
monkeys (*see also* specific species), 15, 126–55
    culling, 134–8, 139–47, 148–54
    human interaction with, 129–32, 143–6, 149–52
mosquitoes, 15, 36, 43, 59, 64, 67–99
    Aedes aegypti, 69n4, 83–99
    Anopheles, 69, 70–8, 83–7, 91
    life cycle, 68
Municipal Commission, 42–3, 75, 191, 222

Nathan, S.A.V., 193–5
National Environmental Agency, 12, 14, 98
Natural History Society of Singapore, 191
Ng, Louis, 244

Ong Swee Law, 223–8
Orang Laut (sea peoples), 122–3
orangutan (*Pongo pygmaeus*), 127, 147, 216, 220, 232–5
Ordinance 174 (Destruction of Mosquitoes), 72–3
otters, 1–4, 13, 21
    smooth-coated (*Lutrogale perspicillata*), 1–4, 13, 21
    small-clawed (*Aonyx cinerus*), 2n3

pangolin, 129
panther (*Panthera pardus*), 215, 227–9, 231
Pasir Panjang, 30–4, 99, 100, 105, 108, 162, 193, 221
People's Action Party (PAP), 1, 11, 13–14, 111, 163–4
pesticide, 59–64, 79–81, 90–1
pets and pet ownership, 2n3, 16, 115, 120, 126–32, 138, 147–50, 160–2, 163–6
    licensing, 147–8
pigs, 16, 54, 164
polar bear (*Ursus maritimus*), 216, 218, 239–46
polio, 51–7
Ponggol Zoo, 130, 220, 239n50
Primary Production Department (*see also* Agri-Food Veterinary Authority), 13–14, 58, 140–5, 148, 153, 188, 201–6, 207
Project Wolbachia, 98–9
public health, 49–55, 58, 68–99
public housing, *see* Housing and Development Board
Public Utilities Board, 223–4, 223, 226, 230n30
Pulau Ubin, 3, 19, 111, 183, 211

Raffles Museum, 37, 71–72n10
Raffles, Thomas Stamford, 128
reservoirs (*see also* specific sites), 7, 19, 21, 79, 100, 104, 112, 122, 145, 150, 153, 175, 215, 223, 225, 229, 232
Ridley, Henry Nicholas, 134, 220
Ross, Ronald, 69–71

S.E.A. Aquarium, 212–14
Sea Shepherd Society, 187, 213

Index

Second World War (Japanese Occupation, 1942–45), 10, 24–8, 62, 75–6, 189, 191, 220
Seletar Reservoir, Lower and Upper, 100, 215, 223, 225, 227, 229
Serangoon, 103, 108, 116, 176
Serangoon River, 103
Shell Oil Company, 79
Singapore Bird Study Group, 157
Singapore Botanic Gardens, 1, 20, 38, 47, 129–46, 149, 190, 219–20
Singapore Cage-Bird Society, 157, 161–2, 166, 171–2
Singapore Miniature Zoo, 220–3
Singapore Sea Scouts, 121–4
Singapore Zoo, 4, 15–17, 117–18, 122–3, 148, 205, 215–48
  construction of, 224–6
  escapes from, 215, 226–8, 229–30
  general history of zoos in Singapore, 218–23
Society for the Prevention of Cruelty to Animals (SPCA), 142–4, 148
songbirds (*see also* specific species), 15, 16, 156–85
  definition of, 158–60
Stewart, John A.T., 195–7
Sungei Buloh Nature Reserve, 2, 19, 174
swimming (humans), 100, 105–7, 108, 113

Teikoku Suisan Tosei ([Japanese] Imperial Fisheries Production), 25, 27, 30
Telok Blangah, 72, 87n42
Teo Teck Siang, 200–1
termite (Coptotermes), 46–7
Thomson, John, 126–7
tilapia (*Oreochromis mossambicus*) (also, *ikan tes, ikan moedjair*), 15, 19–40
Tiong Bahru, 157, 164, 166–7
Twiggy (*see also* panther), 215, 227–31

Underwater World Singapore, 186–7, 188, 207–13

Van Kleef Aquarium, 189–206, 247
Vector Control Unit, 82–8, 90–4

Werle, Barbara, 140–2
white-crested laughingthrush (*Garrulax leucolophus*), 158, 165, 177–83
white-rumped shama (*Copsychus malabaricus*), 158, 165–71, 178, 182–5
World Health Organization, 58, 64, 82, 94

zebra dove (*merbuk*; [*Geopelia striata*]), 156–8, 159, 161, 165, 170–1, 181–3